FIGHTING FOR CREDIBI

US Reputation and International Politics

When Bashar al-Assad used chemical weapons against his own people in Syria, he clearly crossed President Barack Obama's "red line." At the time, many argued that the president had to bomb in order to protect America's reputation for toughness, and therefore its credibility, abroad; others countered that concerns regarding reputation were overblown, and that reputations are irrelevant for coercive diplomacy.

Whether international reputations matter is the question at the heart of *Fighting for Credibility*. For skeptics, past actions and reputations have no bearing on an adversary's assessment of credibility; power and interests alone determine whether a threat is believed. Using a nuanced and sophisticated theory of rational deterrence, Frank P. Harvey and John Mitton argue the opposite: ignoring reputations sidesteps important factors about how adversaries perceive threats. Focusing on cases of asymmetric US encounters with smaller powers since the end of the Cold War including Bosnia, Kosovo, Iraq, and Syria, Harvey and Mitton reveal that reputations matter for credibility in international politics. This dynamic and deeply documented study successfully brings reputation back to the table of foreign diplomacy.

FRANK P. HARVEY is Dean of the Faculty of Arts and Social Sciences at Dalhousie University where he also holds the Eric Dennis Chair of Government and Politics.

JOHN MITTON is a PhD candidate in the Department of Political Science at Dalhousie University and a Fulbright Visiting Researcher at the University of Southern California.

Fighting for Credibility

US Reputation and International Politics

FRANK P. HARVEY AND JOHN MITTON

UNIVERSITY OF TORONTO PRESS
Toronto Buffalo London

ISBN 978-1-4875-0075-7 (cloth)   ISBN 978-1-4875-2054-0 (paper)

Printed on acid-free, 100% post-consumer recycled paper
with vegetable-based inks.

Library and Archives Canada Cataloguing in Publication

Harvey, Frank P. (Frank Paul), 1962–, author
Fighting for credibility : US reputation and international politics /
Frank P. Harvey and John Mitton.

Includes bibliographical references and index.
ISBN 978-1-4875-0075-7 (cloth). – ISBN 978-1-4875-2054-0 (paper)

1. World politics – 1995–2005.   2. World politics – 21st century.
3. Reputation – United States.   4. United States – Foreign relations –
1993–2001.   5. United States – Foreign relations – 2001–2009.   6. United
States – Foreign relations – 2009–.   I. Mitton, John, author   II. Title.

E183.7.H34 2016   327.73   C2016-905858-1

This book has been published with the help of a grant from the Federation
for the Humanities and Social Sciences, through the Awards to Scholarly
Publications Program, using funds provided by the Social Sciences and
Humanities Research Council of Canada.

University of Toronto Press acknowledges the financial assistance to its
publishing program of the Canada Council for the Arts and the Ontario
Arts Council, an agency of the Government of Ontario.

Canada Council   Conseil des Arts
for the Arts   du Canada

ONTARIO ARTS COUNCIL
CONSEIL DES ARTS DE L'ONTARIO
an Ontario government agency
un organisme du gouvernement de l'Ontario

Funded by the   Financé par le
Government   gouvernement
of Canada   du Canada

Canadä

Contents

Acknowledgments   ix

Introduction   3
    Chemical Weapons in Syria, 2012–13   5
        Credibility and International Politics: The Case for
            Reputations   5
        Credibility and International Politics: The Case against
            Reputations   14
        Coercive Outcome in Syria   21
        Syria as a Deterrence/Compellence "Success"?   23
        Postscript   25
    Outline and Objectives   28

1 Reputations Research and Premature Closure of Inquiry   30
    The Press-Mercer-Hopf Consensus   31
        1.1 Hopf (1994) "Peripheral Visions"   38
        1.2 Press (2005) "Calculating Credibility"   41
        1.3 Mercer (1996) "Reputation and International Politics"   46
        Premature Closure of Inquiry: An Illustration   50
        1.4 Application of P-M-H Consensus Excludes Important
            Research on International Reputations   54
        The Missing Scholarship   55
    Conclusion   69

2 Reputations Matter: Rational Deterrence Theory and Credibility
  Reconsidered   71
        2.1 Four Core Prerequisites of Credible Coercive Threats   72
        RDT and Necessity and Sufficiency   76
        Reassessing Fearon   79

2.2 Reputations and Imperfect Information   82
2.3 Similarity and Transferability of Reputations and
      Credibility   88
2.4 Reputations and Miscalculations   93
2.5 General versus Specific Reputations   96
2.6 Reputations, Credibility, and Transferability Are in the Eyes
      of the Beholder   99
Conclusion   104

3 US Reputation Building in Deterrence Encounters, 1991–2003   105
Case 1 – Bosnia-Herzegovina (1992–5)   108
Case 2 – Kosovo (1998–9)   120
Case 3 – Iraq (1991–2003)   135
Conclusion   148

4 The Strategic Logic of US Coercion: Explaining Deterrence Failures
and Successes in Syria, 2011–13   149
4.1 Defining Success in Syria   150
4.2 Syria: RDT versus P-M-H   157
     US Reputations and Past Actions   162
     Escalation and Mission Creep   164
4.3 Protracted Crises, Probes, and Tipping Points   168
     Assad's Miscalculations   171
4.4 Credibility Paradox – Punishments and Promises   175
4.5 Summary and Conclusions   177
     Extremes Are Wrong   177
     Relevant Reputations (and Credibility) Are in the Eyes of the
        Beholder   178
     Similarities, Differences, and Relevant Cases   179

5 RDT, Domestic Politics, and Audience Costs   181
5.1 Domestic Politics, US Credibility, and the Eyes of the
      Beholder   185
     Domestic Politics, Past Actions, and Reputations   187

6 Reputations, Credibility, and Transferability: Reconsidering Syria's
Relevance to Iran, North Korea, and Beyond   191
6.1 Why Transferability Matters   197
6.2 Complex Credibility and Transferability   202
     Complex Credibility in Syria   202
6.3 Iran, Transferability, and the Credibility Paradox
      Revisited   210

7 Responding to Critics: Alternative Explanations and Competing
    Policy Recommendations   212
    7.1 Alternative Explanations for the Syria Disarmament
        Deal   212
    7.2 The Real Costs of Bluffing in Syria   216
        P-M-H Consensus: Reputations Are Irrelevant, so Bluffing
            Is Costless   217
    7.3 Bluffing and Bad Poker Analogies: What the Critics
        Miss   221
        Why Bluffing Matters   221
        When Bluffing Matters   224
        Why Bluffing in International Politics Is Not Like Poker   225
        Unintended Consequences of Congressionally Endorsed
            Bluffing   229
8 Expanding Theory-Policy Gaps in International Relations   232
    8.1 Theory-Policy Gap(s) and Confirmation Bias(es)   233
    8.2 Theory-Policy Gaps and Confirmation Bias: The Case of
        Post-Iraq Intelligence Reform   237
    8.3 Theory-Policy Gaps and Confirmation Bias: The Case of
        Coercive Diplomacy in Syria, 2013   240
        Richard Price on Syria   241
        Jonathan Mercer on Syria   244
        Stephen Walt on Syria   246
        Establishing Continuity in US Foreign Policy   251
    8.4 From Policy to Theory: The "MIT School" and Syria   255

References   265

Index   293

Acknowledgments

Frank Harvey would like to acknowledge the Social Sciences and Humanities Research Council (grant #435–2014–1529) for generous financial support.

John Mitton would like to acknowledge the Fulbright Program, the Social Sciences and Humanities Research Council (grant #752–2015–1381), and the Killam Trusts for their financial support. Thanks also to Ron, Susan, Charlotte, Harold, Julia, and, especially, Heather for love and support.

Both authors would also like to thank the staff in the Department of Political Science at Dalhousie University and at the Centre for the Study of Security and Development for their hard work and assistance.

FIGHTING FOR CREDIBILITY

US Reputation and International Politics

Introduction

Is fighting for credibility prudent? Does a failure to follow through on a coercive diplomatic or military threat undermine a leader's credibility? Can leaders or states acquire reputations from adversaries for being resolute or irresolute? How do these reputations emerge or change, and are they transferable from one context (administration, opponent, time frame, issue area, region, or crisis) to another? These critically important questions framed the foreign policy debate following the sarin gas attacks by the Syrian military in the late summer of 2013; they also exemplify the ongoing debates in the field of international relations regarding the connection between reputations (particularly a reputation for resolve) and credibility. This book directly challenges the emerging consensus that reputations and past actions are irrelevant to credibility, or that reputations are independent, non-transferable, and, therefore, never worth fighting for.

A focus on reputations is important for at least three reasons. First, as Dafoe, Renshon, and Huth recently noted in their review of the literature, the proportion of articles dealing with reputations in conflict settings has increased over the past four decades.[1] Arguably, research

---

1 See Dafoe, Renshon, and Huth 2014. What follows is the authors' description of the methodology they used to "estimate the interest in reputation and status in the study of international relations in four prominent journals: *International Security*, *Journal of Conflict Resolution*, *American Political Science Review*, and *Foreign Affairs*. Plot is a smoothed estimate of the proportion of articles referencing 'war' that also reference one of the following keywords: 'reputation,' 'honor OR honour,' or 'prestige.' 'Status' is not included as a keyword because this term is too often used in other, unrelated contexts (e.g., 'status quo'). Interest in these topics has been prevalent

4 Fighting for Credibility

on the credibility and effectiveness of coercive diplomacy is becoming more important, because deterring (controlling) escalation of military-security crises constitutes a core feature of the foreign policies of the US and its key allies, as our case studies will illustrate.

Second, several major works over the past two decades have questioned the relevance of reputation for determining the credibility of coercive threats. Protecting and reinforcing a reputation for resolve has long been considered a cornerstone of effective coercive diplomacy,[2] but this standard assumption has been systematically challenged in qualitative research by Daryl Press, Jonathan Mercer, and Ted Hopf[3] – hereafter referred to as P-M-H. Reputations, this research concludes, are irrelevant; past behavior has no bearing on future credibility, so backing down or bluffing carries no consequences for subsequent confrontations – crisis behavior is essentially a product of comparative interests and capabilities (power). However, despite being embraced by a growing number of scholars, the findings from this particular research program have never been subjected to the kind of systematic theoretical and empirical analysis they demand. This oversight is particularly troubling in light of the propensity by many experts to issue foreign policy advice that relies heavily on findings from P-M-H, which brings us to our next point.

Heated debates about reputations resurfaced during the Syrian chemical weapons (CW) crisis in 2013. Many high-profile scholars and foreign policy analysts (bloggers, journalists, and academics) repeatedly cited evidence from P-M-H to mount what they believed was a rock solid case against the Obama administration's coercive strategy in Syria. In fact, these findings were presented as definitive "proof" that fighting to protect a credible reputation for resolve was foolish; there was no logical or military-strategic reason for Obama to reinforce his red-line threat (issued in August 2012), even if that threat failed to

---

throughout the twentieth century. In recent decades, interest in 'reputation' and possibly 'honor' seems to be increasing; interest in (or terminological preference for) 'prestige' has declined. We do not identify any notable persistent differences across journals. 95% confidence intervals provide an assessment of whether the observed proportions could have come from the same underlying distribution. Data and R code are available at http://hdl.handle.net/1902.1/22179."

2 For an excellent review of the work of Alexander George and his contributions to the study of deterrence and coercive diplomacy, see Levy 2008.

3 See Press 2005; Mercer 1996; and Hopf 1994.

prevent the Syrian regime from launching the attacks on civilians in Ghouta in 2013. In a largely unanticipated about-face, however, Bashar al-Assad agreed to dismantle his CW capability under the threat of unilateral US air strikes. This outcome, we argue, represents a major coercive diplomatic success that raises serious questions about assertions inspired by P-M-H regarding the irrelevance of reputations. The research we present in our book demonstrates the exact opposite: reputations matter.

Understanding the causes and consequences of inter-state interactions during the Syria case, buttressed in the following chapters by significant empirical evidence derived from post–Cold War crises involving the US in asymmetric conflicts, will broaden our understanding of reputations in international relations. Our goal is to extract important lessons about the theory and practice of coercive diplomacy based on evidence from over two decades of crisis behavior, drawing out the causal implications for what happened in Syria; it is impossible to explain Syria's (and Russia's) capitulation to the multilaterally endorsed UN disarmament agreement without appreciating the lessons learned by opponents (including Assad) about US resolve and credibility in previous cases. Our objective is not to assess the foreign policy legacy of the Obama administration, or the success/failure of Washington's overall Syria strategy – it is to contribute to the literature on reputations in international politics, rational deterrence theory, and the relevance of past actions when adversaries assess the credibility of US coercive threats.

Chemical Weapons in Syria, 2012–13

A brief account of the 2012–13 Syria crisis will help position the book's main thesis in relation to the policy debates that unfolded at the time.

Credibility and International Politics:
The Case for Reputations

In response to the August 2013 sarin attacks, President Obama joined senior members of his national security team in repeatedly emphasizing – in every press conference and congressional testimony – the linked imperatives to enforce global prohibitions on the use of chemical weapons by reinforcing the credibility of the president's "red-line" warning (issued a year earlier):[4] "We have communicated in no uncertain terms with every player in the region that that's a *red line* for us and that there would be *enormous consequences* if we start seeing movement on the chemical weapons front or the use of chemical weapons. That would change my calculations significantly." Almost exactly one year later, on 21 August 2013, the Syrian military launched a series of sarin gas attacks against rebel strongholds throughout the Ghouta agricultural belt east of Damascus, killing 1400 Syrians (including 400 children). Bashar al-Assad's flagrant disregard of the red-line threat represented a clear case of US deterrence failure. Punitive air strikes against the regime, Obama's team argued, were now essential to bolster Washington's credibility (particularly in light of its failure to respond to eleven previous chemical attacks by the Syrian military), provide additional military support to the insurgency, impose costs on Assad for violating a widely endorsed international norm, and strengthen the administration's reputation for enforcing red lines tied to this and other deterrent threats – a message directed, in part, at officials in Iran and North Korea.[5] The success or failure of coercive diplomacy in Syria, administration officials warned, was connected in some way to the looming nuclear crisis with Iran.[6]

Obama issued the following warning at the time in an effort to boost support for a stronger response, linking the costs of the current crisis to risks beyond Syria:[7]

> If we fail to act, the Assad regime will see no reason to stop using chemical weapons. As the ban against these weapons erodes, other tyrants will have no reason to think twice about acquiring poison gas, and using them [*sic*]. Over time, our troops would again face the prospect of chemical

---

4 See White House 2013a (emphasis added). For a complete review of the red-line threat and subsequent related statements, see Kessler 2013.

5 With respect to US–Iran relations, for example, the president had already issued a separate red-line warning in March 2013 (in an interview with Israel's Channel 2 News): "I have been crystal clear about my position on Iran possessing a nuclear weapon. That is a red line for us. It is not only something that would be dangerous for Israel. It would be dangerous for the world" (quoted in Carter 2013).

6 Mead (2013) provides a good summary of the political costs to the president if he would have decided in favor of backing away from his now-reinforced deterrent threats: "If Obama doesn't bomb Syria now, he's toast."

7 White House 2013c, emphasis added.

warfare on the battlefield. And it could be easier for terrorist organizations to obtain these weapons, and to use them to attack civilians. If fighting spills beyond Syria's borders, these weapons could threaten allies like Turkey, Jordan, and Israel. *And a failure to stand against the use of chemical weapons would weaken prohibitions against other weapons of mass destruction, and embolden Assad's ally, Iran* – which must decide whether to ignore international law by building a nuclear weapon, or to take a more peaceful path.

... After careful deliberation, I determined that it is in the national security interests of the United States to respond to the Assad regime's use of chemical weapons through a targeted military strike. The purpose of this strike would be to deter Assad from using chemical weapons, to degrade his regime's ability to use them, *and to make clear to the world that we will not tolerate their use.*[8]

The same sentiments regarding US credibility and the importance of Washington's reputation for following through on its threats were expressed by senior members of the administration in congressional testimony. Secretary of Defense Chuck Hagel, for example, issued the following warning about lost credibility in his prepared statement in early September 2013:

The Syrian regime's actions risk eroding the nearly century-old international norm against the use of chemical weapons ... *Weakening this norm could embolden other regimes to acquire or use chemical weapons.* For example, North Korea maintains a massive stockpile of chemical weapons that threatens our treaty ally, the Republic of Korea, and the 28,000 US troops stationed there. I have just returned from Asia, where I had a very serious and long conversation with South Korea's Defense Minister about the threat that North Korea's stockpile of chemical weapons presents to them. *Our allies throughout the world must be assured that the United States will fulfill its security commitments.*

... The Assad regime, under increasing pressure by the Syrian opposition, could feel empowered to carry out even more devastating chemical weapons attacks without a response ... *A refusal to act would undermine the*

---

8 For several other videos of speeches and statements by senior administration officials and congressional leaders, see White House n.d.

credibility of America's other security commitments – including the President's commitment to prevent Iran from acquiring a nuclear weapon. The word of the United States must mean something. It is vital currency in foreign relations and international and allied commitments.[9]

Perhaps the most explicit case for the importance of US credibility and resolve came from Secretary of State John Kerry when he outlined the consequences of simply backing away from the now-reinforced coercive threats issued by the president:

It matters deeply to the credibility and the future interests of the United States of America and our allies. It matters because a lot of other countries, whose policies challenges [sic] these international norms, are watching. They are watching. They want to see whether the United States and our friends mean what we say. It is directly related to our credibility and whether countries still believe the United States when it says something. They are watching to see if Syria can get away with it, because then maybe they too can put the world at greater risk. And make no mistake, in an increasingly complicated world of sectarian and religious extremist violence, what we choose to do or not do matters in real ways to our own security.

... It matters because if we choose to live in the world where a thug and a murderer like Bashar al-Assad can gas thousands of his own people with impunity, even after the United States and our allies said no, and then the world does nothing about it, *there will be no end to the test of our resolve and the dangers that will flow from those others who believe that they can do as they will. This matters also beyond the limits of Syria's borders. It is about whether Iran, which itself has been a victim of chemical weapons attacks, will now feel emboldened, in the absence of action, to obtain nuclear weapons. It is about Hezbollah, and North Korea, and every other terrorist group or dictator that might ever again contemplate the use of weapons of mass destruction.* (emphasis added)[10]

The president also received considerable support from House Speaker John Boehner, who applied the same logic to forcefully defend

---

9 Hagel 2013.
10 United States Department of State 2013a.

action against the Syrian regime in light of serious concerns about the costs of losing US credibility:

The use of these weapons has to be responded to and only the United States has the capability and the capacity to stop Assad and *to warn others around the world that this type of behavior is not going to be tolerated* ... We have enemies around the world that need to understand that we're not going to tolerate this type of behavior. We also have allies around the world and allies in the region who also need to know that America will be there and stand up whether [*sic*] it is necessary. (emphasis added)[11]

Senators John McCain and Lindsey Graham, as well as former senators Joe Lieberman and Jon Kyl, all concurred with this view. As McCain explained,

Now that a resolution is going to be before the Congress of the United States, we want to work to make that resolution something that majorities of the members of both houses could support ... A rejection of that, a vote against the resolution by Congress, I think would be catastrophic, *because it would undermine the credibility of the United States of America and of the President of the United States. None of us want that.*[12]

McCain went even further, suggesting that the administration should move beyond limited air strikes and develop a more comprehensive strategy aimed, ultimately, at regime change: "What we do want is an articulation of a goal that over time to degrade [*sic*] Bashar Assad's capabilities, increase and upgrade the capabilities of the Free Syrian Army and the Free Syrian government so they can reverse the momentum on the battlefield." This view was shared by others who similarly "fear[ed] that the limited airstrikes the White House appears inclined to pursue ... have not yet been tied to a broader strategy, even though President Obama has said that Assad must go."[13] For some, in other words, even more robust action was warranted in order to preserve and enhance American credibility by signaling that crossing

---

11 Halper 2013.
12 Miller 2013. Also, see McCain and Graham 2014. McCain and Graham criticize the president for his policy on Syria and its effects on US credibility.
13 Lieberman and Kyl 2013.

red lines would result in the gravest of consequences (for Assad, his removal from power).

Such serious concerns about US credibility went beyond policy-makers pushing for a stronger military response – the same concerns were expressed by several journalists, bloggers, and analysts. Charles Krauthammer, for example, argued that Obama has "backed himself into a corner: Be forced into a war he is firmly resolved to avoid, or *lose credibility*, which for a superpower on whose word relies the safety of a dozen allies is *not just embarrassing but dangerous.*"[14] Elliot Abrams made explicit connections between demonstrating a reputation for resolve in Syria and the looming showdown with Iran:

> The problem today is not only that this may leave Assad free to use chemical weapons again. A related issue of great consequence is what the administration has said about the use of chemical weapons: *that it would be a game changer, that it is a red line, that it is unacceptable, and that all options are on the table for a US response.* Sound familiar? The administration has used exactly such language – "unacceptable," "all options are on the table" – about the Iranian nuclear program. If such terms become synonyms for "we will not act," the regime in Tehran will soon conclude that there is no danger of an American military attack and therefore no need to negotiate seriously. They may have reached that conclusion already. *What is at stake here is not only the future of Syria, but our own government's credibility.* (emphasis added)[15]

This sentiment was echoed by several other commentators (John Bolton,[16] Max Boot,[17] Lawrence Haas,[18] John Judis,[19] Amitai Etzioni,[20] and Roger Cohen,[21] among others), who similarly underscored the dangers of eroding US credibility given crossed red lines and unenforced deterrent threats in Syria.

---

14 Krauthammer 2013.
15 Abrams 2013.
16 Bolton 2013.
17 Boot 2013.
18 Haas 2014.
19 Judis 2013.
20 Etzioni 2013.
21 Cohen 2013.

Joshua Goodman, for his part, was one of the few explicitly citing academic work (by Tingley and Walter)[22] to argue that reputations do in fact matter in the long run:

> By setting red lines and threatening military action, the United States is attempting to deter the entry of other actors into a "forbidden market" (the use of chemical weapons). By failing to invest in reputation early, the United States is signaling that it will not act as a barrier to entry into this market. Even more damaging, by clearly stating the red line and then failing to carry out threats, the US signals not only that it will not act to deter when it remains silent, but that it will not act to deter even when it says it will. This not only increases the risk of the use of chemical weapons by other regimes in the future, but also increases the risk of interstate conflict in the future by increasing the belief that the United States will not carry out its threats.[23]

This analysis is particularly important given the paucity of such references compared to the numerous invocations of social scientific research in defense of the alternative claim that reputations are irrelevant and, therefore, backing down in Syria inconsequential (see below).

Finally, Lionel Beehner offered perhaps the most clear and forceful arguments in favor of protecting US credibility:

> Broken commitments affect our future ability to credibly deter aggression and hurt our relationships with and promises made to allies … On Syria, if the United States does not either intervene or escalate its pressure on the regime, the message is clear: First, we are helpless to do anything, so dictators, go nuts. Second, if you have WMD you have a blanket of immunity from outside intervention, so be sure to rearm those chemical, biological, and nuclear stockpiles. Finally, to Iran – any red line we draw in the sand is basically just suggestive. Go on spinning those centrifuges because we really don't mean what we say.[24]

---

22 Tingley and Walter 2011.
23 Goodman 2013.
24 Beehner 2013.

In fact, Beehner's position elevated the protection of reputation and credibility above the risks associated with a crisis that worsens after US intervention:

> A US or NATO-led intervention is not some panacea that will paper over all the sectarian grievances, personal feuds, or other triggers for postwar violence in Syria. It will hasten the fall of the regime, but not guarantee a smooth aftermath. In fact, it could easily portend a messier post-Assad Syria, simply because it will leave in place several armed actors whose relative power will be left unclear, tipping the scales toward those who are best organized and most willing to use violence, which in this case are Islamist parties ...[25]

Despite the risks of escalation, however, Beehner concluded that Obama "should either a) not draw red lines or make promises he has no intention of keeping; or b) follow through on his ultimatum by gradually tightening the noose around Assad."[26] Inaction by Obama would convince Assad that Obama's threats were bluffs. If Assad was probing the administration for weaknesses in their commitments to defend the red lines (as many analysts believed to be the case with the previous chemical attacks), then the absence of any retaliation would prove to the regime that Washington had no intention of preventing the use or escalation of chemical weapons – the bluff would have been called.

Brian Haggerty did a good job summarizing the views of those convinced that reputations and credibility are crucial to US security interests:

> A US interest in maintaining credibility has been repeatedly invoked by advocates of greater involvement throughout the debate over US policy in Syria ... These [red-line] statements have led some to believe that a failure to make good on calls for al-Asad [sic] to leave power and force-fully respond to the use of chemical weapons would result in a substantial loss of US credibility with grave consequences for its ability to exercise coercion in general, especially in relation to the US dispute with Iran over its nuclear program. Were al-Asad [sic] to go unpunished, the logic goes, Iran would believe the US has been bluffing in its vows to prevent Iran

---

25 Ibid.
26 Ibid.

from acquiring nuclear weapons and therefore discount future US threats. A fear of lost credibility has even been embraced by the Obama administration in its attempts to mobilize public and congressional support for its plans to launch a limited strike. Finally, those concerned with the defense of US credibility point not only to its effect on US adversaries, but to its potential effect on US allies who depend on US assistance for their own defense. Should the US "back down" in Syria, they argue, US allies may be convinced the US "cannot be trusted" and take matters into their own hands. Should they do so, it is implied this would be contrary to US interests.[27]

The president needed to strike the Assad regime in order to demonstrate Washington's resolve to follow through on its deterrent threats. This would send a strong signal to Assad and Putin that the use of chemical weapons was unacceptable and risked US military retaliation. A credible threat was also expected to convey an important message to other states regarding Washington's commitment to sustaining the credibility of its coercive threats. Administration officials (as well as the commentators cited above) appeared to believe that US actions in one crisis would have a direct impact on adversaries' calculation of Washington's resolve and likely behavior in future crises, because these aspects of credibility are transferable across cases. Repeated failures to follow through on the president's red-line threat seriously damaged US credibility and required a clear act to re-establish Washington's resolve. Failure to do so would increase the probability that other adversaries would pick up important signals about US weaknesses – weaknesses that had become more apparent in the aftermath of two costly wars in Afghanistan and Iraq.

As we shall see, strict views as to the *perfect* transferability of reputations across potentially diverse and substantively different cases are as flawed as the "emerging consensus" regarding zero transferability and the irrelevance of reputation discussed below. To say that US behavior *anywhere* matters to allies and adversaries *everywhere* (no matter the real and important differences between cases and situations) is to oversimplify and exaggerate the role of reputation as a component in calculating credibility. Reputation helps determine resolve, which is itself merely one of several variables used to assess an adversary's credibility;

---

27 Haggerty 2013.

reputation is important but not definitive, and its *relative* importance is determined, in part, by the similarities and differences between the present situation and the past cases that states (that is to say, state leaders) invoke for lessons and analogies. The transfer of lessons can be expected (and, indeed, is extremely important) in some cases, but not in others. In the Syria case, the arguments raised by the administration and others were generally sound; these same or similar arguments, however, do not hold for other international crises – for example, putative lessons from Syria did not (and do not) have major implications for US credibility in Ukraine, given the fundamental and important differences between the two cases.[28] These important points will be discussed in greater detail in chapter 2 – for now it is sufficient to emphasize the *gradation* of the relevance of reputation (and attendant implications for its transferability between cases), particularly as we turn to a discussion of the other, more prominent (at least in academic and journalistic circles) position in this debate: the total irrelevance of past behavior, called bluffs, and reputations for resolve in international politics.

Credibility and International Politics: The Case against Reputations

Almost immediately after administration officials began extolling the virtues of protecting US credibility and resolve, scores of widely cited (and retweeted) articles, op-eds, and blog posts were published by policymakers, prominent international relations scholars, and foreign policy experts directly challenging the strategic logic underpinning Obama's response to the Syrian attacks.[29] This position greatly outweighed the view of those cited above (Krauthammer, Goodman, Beehner, Cohen, Abrams, etc.), and in fact often belittled and ridiculed the "outdated" belief in the importance of reputation that the latter position espoused.[30] Citing an "emerging consensus" in the academic literature, connected

---

28 For an example of the argument that such lessons *did* (and do) transfer, see Slaughter 2014.

29 For a sample of the stronger criticisms directed against Obama's preoccupation with US credibility, reputations, and the application of coercive diplomacy (deterrence) in Syria, see Zakaria 2013; Walt 2013b; Drezner 2013a; Larison 2013b; Matthews 2013; Fallows 2013; Biddle 2013; Friedersdorf 2013a; and Manzi 2013.

30 Outweighed not merely in volume but, more importantly, in terms of the *authority* that was invoked to defend and legitimate its arguments. Most arguments emphasizing the importance of maintaining credibility were framed using simple

primarily to the findings from historical case studies of reputation building in international politics by Daryl Press, Jonathan Mercer, and Ted Hopf, critics dismissed as foolish the threat to strike Syria to reinforce the president's mistakenly issued red line.[31] "What is most striking about this affair," Stephen Walt argued, "is how Obama seems to have been dragged, reluctantly, into doing something that he clearly didn't want to do ... He foolishly drew a 'red line' a few months back, so now he's getting taunted with the old canard about the need to 'restore US credibility.'"[32] Walt joined many other foreign policy analysts to summarily reject the notion that threatening to fight for credibility in Syria made any sense. The president's strategy, they insisted, would have no bearing on impressions of Washington's resolve to protect the country's core interests in other regions and is completely unrelated to strengthening the credibility of red lines issued against other adversaries.

The main problem, as Mercer explains in his work, is that reputations are in the *eye of the beholder* – the same actions can generate as many reputations as there are adversaries. Reputations are not properties we can retain or strategically manipulate, nor are they easily transferable across cases or adversaries.[33] Among the more important lessons

---

logic or long-held "common sense" principles of international diplomacy. By contrast, those arguing against the importance of fighting to maintain credibility invoked cutting-edge, evidence-based (and supposedly value-free) social science research. This is a key distinction. By framing their arguments in this manner, the latter camp was able to claim an authority not available to the former. Obviously, a position that claims legitimacy through evidence and research is more rhetorically powerful than one that does not, underscoring the importance and prominence of such arguments in the debate over Syria and the negative consequences of (in)action.

31 Press 2005; Mercer 1996; Hopf 1994. There were other references that were cited (Huth and Russett 1984; Snyder and Deising 1977), but the three most consistent references were to Press, Mercer, and Hopf. Mercer and Press also published pieces in *Foreign Affairs* (Mercer 2013) and *Foreign Policy* (Press and Lind 2013) in an effort to apply their research and policy recommendations to the Syria case.

32 See Walt's (2013b) commentary on how Obama allowed himself to be pulled into attacking Syria: "We're going to war because we just can't stop ourselves."

33 Although the "eye of the beholder" thesis is a perfectly reasonable interpretation of how and why US reputations matter (they are not something US officials own, but are assigned to the US by adversaries and are products of their perceptions and misperceptions), the logical implications of this observation are not fully understood or applied by any critics of reputation, including Press, Mercer, and Hopf. A careful examination of what the "eye of the beholder" assumption actually implies about US reputations, transferability, and reputations' connection to credibility is addressed in more detail in chapter 4.

extracted from Mercer's research is that states can acquire a reputation from adversaries for being resolute (standing firm, following through on a coercive threat), but they almost never acquire a reputation for backing down, so "decision-makers would be well served to remember one simple policy maxim: fighting to create a reputation for resolution with adversaries is unnecessary."[34]

Daryl Press also found very little empirical support for the view that political leaders (or their regimes) acquire reputations from adversaries for appearing weak or backing down in a crisis; adversaries rarely if ever consider past behavior when assessing the credibility of a coercive threat. According to the evidence extracted from the cases Press studied, the credibility of any given coercive threat is a function of rational assessments of the relative capabilities and interests of the states involved; past actions and related reputations are essentially irrelevant, so fighting now to establish credibility in future crises makes no logical sense, and this pattern applied even when leaders repeatedly bluffed or backed down in previous cases.

Finally, Ted Hopf found that Soviet assessments of American credibility during the Cold War had little or nothing to do with US victories or defeats in the Third World (the "periphery"). As such, a core tenet of US foreign policy during this period was fundamentally flawed; military interventions (such as Vietnam) were less effective than non-military (economic and political) means for communicating resolve and establishing credibility (thereby achieving deterrence), particularly regarding core US interests in Western Europe and the Middle East. The practical implication of Hopf's analysis, as Carter summarizes, is to "remind officials that intervening *here* to send a message *there* is dangerous" (emphasis in original).[35]

A more detailed engagement with each of these works can be found in chapter 2; for now, it is sufficient to recognize the influence they exerted in recent debates on American foreign policy.[36] For example,

---

34 Mercer 1996, 228. The political and social psychological theories underpinning Mercer's thesis will be critically addressed in chapter 1. For other works in political psychology that highlight cognitive and motivation biases in crisis decision making, see Lebow 1981; Jervis, Lebow, and Stein 1985; and Jervis 1979 and 1976.

35 Carter 1996, 132.

36 This influence is by no means limited to the impasse over Syrian chemical weapons usage in the summer of 2013. A year later, in August 2014, the same P-M-H

Brian Haggerty nicely summarizes the P-M-H consensus that emerged in debates surrounding the Syria crisis:

> Analysts acknowledge the importance of maintaining US credibility for effective deterrence, but suggest that leaders rarely, if ever, assume that the failure of other leaders to make good on past threats is a reliable signal they will be irresolute in the future. Credibility, they argue, is not the product of a reputation for carrying out past threats. Rather, calculations of an opponent's credibility rely on an appraisal of his capabilities and interests over the issue at stake in the here-and-now. A US capability to destroy Iran's nuclear facilities and its interests in nuclear nonproliferation will be far more relevant in Iranian calculations of US credibility, they argue, than anything the US does in Syria.[37]

But journalists, academics, and foreign policy bloggers who were critical of Obama's policy on Syria, because of its assumptions and related efforts to do too much in the interests of US credibility, did not simply refer to the P-M-H argument or evidence – they cited it as if this work collectively represented a generational shift in thinking about reputations in international politics, and a growing, powerful, and almost indisputable consensus that all but disconfirmed the relevance of reputations – i.e., definitive proof of the futility of Obama's foreign policy

---

consensus was being pushed by Benjamin Friedman of the Cato Institute in the context of broader debates about US foreign policy. For example, Friedman writes: "In US foreign policy, presidents typically drum up support for even minor actions with soaring talk about its strategic and moral importance. But most people, especially statesmen, understand that interests vary across time and circumstances ... Historical studies show [this sentence is hyperlinked to Press's book] that leaders deciding whether to defy foreign threats focus on the balance of military power and the material interests of the threatening state, not on its opponent's record of carrying out past threats. Credibility doesn't travel well." Friedman's article also contains references to Mercer's book, as well as the blog posting by Press and Lind on Syria. See Friedman 2014. Similarly, the view that credibility is perfectly transferable also remains prominent, particularly among policymakers. To wit, Friedman's article itself was largely a response to an op-ed written by Senator Bob Corker (ranking Republican on the Senate Foreign Relations Committee), who argues that a series of alleged foreign policy mistakes in the form of false promises or no follow-through (in Syria, Ukraine, Iraq, and elsewhere) have led to a systematic erosion of US credibility across the board, with allies and adversaries alike. See Corker 2014.

37 Haggerty 2013.

strategy, or any other strategy that focused so myopically on the protection of reputations for resolve. Consider the following examples.[38]

Fareed Zakaria reassured his readers that "political scientists have studied the subject of credibility *extensively*" (emphasis added) and described Mercer's research as "comprehensive."[39] John Mearsheimer's blurb on the back cover of Press's book praised the contribution as "truly important" because it *"demolishes* the widely held belief that a state that backs down in a crisis loses credibility in the next crisis. In fact, [Press] shows that a state's past behavior has *almost no effect* on how other states assess its credibility" (emphasis added). Walt went even further with his endorsement by inviting Daryl Press and a co-author, Jennifer Lind, to guest post on his *Foreign Policy* blog – not surprisingly, the two authors reconfirmed the quality of Press's original research and findings: "Every time analysts and leaders call for war, they warn that inaction will jeopardize America's credibility. *What is more surprising, however, is how little evidence there is for this view.*"[40]

Max Fisher, a prominent foreign policy blogger for the *Washington Post*, cites Press's book to support his conclusion that "there's *no historical evidence* suggesting that backing down in a crisis ... reduces a country's future credibility."[41] In his testimony before the House Committee on Homeland Security, Stephen Biddle referred to the results of *"a generation of scholarship,"* suggesting that "statesmen often overestimate the degree to which reputation shapes others' behavior in future crises."[42] Dylan Matthews refers to P-M-H research when describing what he regards as a *"severe lack of evidence"* that credibility matters in cases like Syria, or that the US has to intervene to protect a reputation for

---

38 For other examples of critics who reject the credibility arguments, see Menon 2013a and 2013b. Menon doesn't cite Press's, Mercer's, or Hopf's arguments, but does dismiss the importance of credibility vis-à-vis Syria and the logic of the credibility argument more generally.
39 Zakaria 2013. It should be noted that Zakaria cited the same scholarship when assessing criticisms of US credibility in the lead-up to the 2014 Ukraine crisis and Russia's annexation of Crimea. Although the argument about a lack of transferability regarding reputation from Syria to Ukraine is sound, the logic cannot be extended to dismiss transferability more generally. Again, transferability must be evaluated in the context of degrees, not absolutes. See Zakaria 2014.
40 Press and Lind 2013; see also Drezner 2013a.
41 Fisher 2013a, emphasis added.
42 Committee on Homeland Security 2013, 7, emphasis added.

resolve.[43] Christopher Fettweis refers to the *"mountain of research from political science* to suggest that [fighting for credibility] is an illusion, that credibility earned today does not lead to successes tomorrow and therefore is *never worth fighting for."*[44] Benjamin Friedman of the Cato Institute argued, in his dismissal of the need to reinforce red lines in Syria: "Historical studies show that foreigners do not assess US willingness to intervene based on whether we carried out past threats. They focus, instead, on the local balance of military power and US interests in their case."[45]

Daniel Larison argued that applying the "credibility" argument in the Syria case is "nonsense" as well as "ridiculous and embarrassing."[46] In a follow-up piece on the same subject, he bolstered this "consensus" by citing Press and Lind's blog post, claiming they *"dismantle* the 'credibility' argument for intervention in Syria," and subsequently that "US interests in and around Syria aren't important enough to warrant military action, and Syria hawks are indirectly acknowledging as much with this new fixation on preserving 'credibility' that isn't in danger of being lost."[47] In yet another follow-up, Larison referenced Zakaria's article (cited above) as confirmation of a growing consensus on the irrelevance of credibility: "As Zakaria pointed out yesterday, *scholarship on the subject has found* that the standard argument about the dangers of losing credibility *isn't supported by the evidence."*[48] He then cited the same P-M-H evidence to repeat one more time his contention that "the dangers of losing credibility isn't [sic] supported by the evidence," and then to argue that "warning about lost 'credibility' is just a pretext to cajole the administration into doing what Syria hawks have wanted to do all along. It would be wise to dismiss it as such."[49] Larison found it amazing "that US policymakers can convince themselves that *their credibility is so frequently in jeopardy when it isn't."* As he concluded: "Invoking the danger of lost 'credibility' is almost always a scare tactic designed to make people stop thinking about the absurdity of the proposed policy

---

43 Matthews 2013, emphasis added.
44 Fettweis 2014, emphasis added.
45 Friedman 2013b.
46 Larison 2013a.
47 Larison 2013b, emphasis added.
48 Larison 2013c, emphasis added.
49 Ibid.

and to worry about other, unrelated problems that will somehow be made worse if the bad policy isn't implemented."[50]

Although Daniel Drezner offered a more balanced take on the many complexities associated with exploring the role of reputations and credibility in international politics, he too cited the emerging consensus from P-M-H scholarship:[51] "The odd thing about all of this emphasis on "credibility" is that *the trend in international relations scholarship has moved in the opposite direction* ... The notion that a country or its leader has a single reputation for resolve or credibility has been *pretty much dismissed.*"

With all these criticisms in mind, the most reasonable option for the Obama administration – that is, the one that stood the best chance of actually protecting US interests in Syria – was to ignore the original red-line threat, acknowledge the bluff, halt any plans for punitive air strikes against the Syrian regime, and reject any suggestion that backing off would damage Washington's reputation for resolve or undermine the credibility of its deterrent threats here or elsewhere. What Washington does or does not do in Syria bears no relationship to Washington's credibility with other adversaries over other issues. Threats are independent, credibility is not transferable from one case to another, and adversaries never rely on information from past actions when calculating US resolve or credibility – every case is sufficiently different, so the only important factors on which adversaries rely when assessing US credibility are "interests" and "power."

The harshest criticisms leveled against the administration for its supposed obsessions with reputations and credibility were reserved for Secretary of State John Kerry, for issuing the following deterrent threat:

> We will be able to hold Bashar al-Assad accountable without engaging in troops on the ground or any other prolonged kind of effort in a very limited, very targeted, short-term effort that degrades his capacity to deliver chemical weapons without assuming responsibility for Syria's civil war. That is exactly what we are talking about doing – *unbelievably small*, limited kind of effort.[52]

---

50 Larison 2013d, emphasis added.
51 Drezner 2013a, emphasis added.
52 Quoted in Waldie 2013, emphasis added.

As Stephen Walt joked, "Syrian [chemical] use is a moral outrage that demands a very limited response that poses no risk of escalation or quagmire."[53] The threat of "unbelievably small" air strikes was expected to contribute nothing to US credibility and could not possibly satisfy the conditions for successful coercion. Even worse, critics argued, limited attacks would carry enormous risks of escalation (mission creep) with no reasonable guarantee of resolving the underlying issues. In sum, Obama should accept the "fact" that fighting for credibility is a waste of time, acknowledge his red-line threat was a bluff, and fold. As Jerome Slater counseled, "The United States would greatly benefit from a healthy dose of isolationism to at least partly balance what ought to be called 'mindless interventionism.'"[54]

Coercive Outcome in Syria

Despite these strong criticisms, dire warnings, and impassioned policy recommendations from both sides to do much more (McCain, Graham, Lieberman, Krauthammer, etc.) or much less (Press, Mercer, Zakaria, Walt, Larison, etc.), the Obama administration discarded the critics' advice and continued to bolster its coercive stance, openly moved forward with operational plans to mount punitive air strikes against the Assad regime, approached the US Congress for authorization, and buttressed the threat by extending the deployments of warships and aircraft carriers in the eastern Mediterranean.[55] White House officials and several senior congressional leaders from both parties used every opportunity they were given to highlight the country's (and international community's) obligation to enforce global norms against the use of chemical weapons, and consistently underscored the strategic imperative to reinforce American credibility and resolve. While the specific details of the Syria case will be discussed in chapters 4–7, a brief overview of coercive outcomes here provides context for the book as a whole, highlighting the relevance of the theoretical critiques and supplementary case evidence contained in chapters 1–3.

On 3 September 2013, the US Senate Foreign Relations Committee boosted the credibility of Washington's coercive threat by voting in favor

---

53 Walt 2013d.
54 Slater 2013.
55 Shanker and Gordon 2013.

of a draft resolution authorizing the president to "use the Armed Forces of the United States as he determines to be necessary and appropriate" in a limited and tailored manner against legitimate military targets in Syria, only to: "(1) respond to the use of weapons of mass destruction by the Syrian government in the conflict in Syria; (2) deter Syria's use of such weapons in order to protect the national security interests of the United States and to protect our allies and partners against the use of such weapons; and (3) degrade Syria's capacity to use such weapons in the future."[56] The resolution gave the president up to 60 days to complete the initial operation, and another 30 days if required – essentially two weeks longer than the successful 78-day bombing campaign launched by US/NATO forces in 1999 against Serb targets in Kosovo and Belgrade.

When Secretary of State John Kerry suggested in a press conference that Assad could avoid the air strikes if he turned over "every single bit of his chemical weapons to the international community in the next week … without delay and [with] full and total accounting," Russian President Vladimir Putin jumped at the offer, immediately accepted the conditions stipulated in Kerry's unscripted comments, persuaded Assad to take the deal, and initiated discussions leading to the UN disarmament resolution. Notwithstanding the many concerns expressed by critics, both Assad and Putin ultimately concluded that the probability, risks, and costs of a US air campaign were simply too high, regardless of the limits implicit in an "unbelievably small" strike or any qualifying conditions attached to the draft congressional resolution. As Obama pointed out, "In part because of the credible threat of US military force, we now have the opportunity to achieve our objectives through diplomacy."[57]

In fact, coercive diplomacy (both deterrence and compellence) ultimately succeeded in Syria: Assad acknowledged for the first time Syria's possession of chemical weapons, signed the Chemical Weapons Convention (CWC) prohibiting further production and deployment of proscribed weapons, provided details to UN inspectors outlining the exact location of the regime's stockpiles and production facilities (a list validated by US intelligence records), and continues to comply with requirements stipulated in UN Security Council Resolution 2118, which

---

56 United States Congress 2013.
57 White House 2013d.

demanded the full and complete dismantling of the regime's chemical weapons and related capabilities.[58] In light of the strategic role chemical weapons played in the conflict up to that point, and the deterrent value Syrian officials assigned to these weapons in relation to their rivalry with Israel, a formal agreement to destroy these weapons constitutes an impressive foreign policy success and a clear victory for the credible application of coercive diplomacy. This agreement would have been far less likely (arguably impossible) had the Obama administration accepted the critics' arguments to do much more (because reputations and credibility are everything) or much less (because reputations are nothing to worry about).

Contrary to the P-M-H consensus, then, Assad's and Putin's assessment of Washington's "reputation for resolve" – based in part on past US actions in similar asymmetric conflicts (e.g., Bosnia, Kosovo, Iraq) – provides the most compelling explanation for the outcome. Simply put, reputations *did* play an important role in establishing the credibility of the US deterrent and compellent threats, and led to the dismantling of Syria's stockpiles of chemical weapons. In fact, past actions have played an important role in adversaries' assessments of US credibility for decades, a central argument of the book that will be developed in more detail in chapters 2 and 3. The Syria case is but the latest illustration of a long series of US deterrence encounters in asymmetric crises that seriously challenge the P-M-H consensus on logical, theoretical, and empirical grounds.

Syria as a Deterrence/Compellence "Success"?

Readers may well be puzzled by the contention that Syria is here considered a "success." The brutality of the ongoing civil war certainly suggests otherwise, as do allegations of chlorine gas use by the Assad regime. To be clear, we do not define "success" in Syria in terms of resolving the broader crisis. Rather, success is here defined exclusively in terms of the stated objectives (i.e., the objectives of deterring WMD use and compelling WMD disarmament under the CWC that were expressly outlined by Obama's team at the time), the strategy implemented to achieve these objectives, and the relationship between the strategy, elements of coercive diplomacy, and the resolution of the

---

58 For the full text of the resolution, see United Nations Security Council 2013a.

WMD issue in the form of the UN agreement. We are not rendering any judgment about the successes or failures of US foreign policy in relation to the larger and ongoing civil war in Syria, nor are we making any claims about Obama's foreign policy legacy. The dismantling of Syria's chemical weapons stockpiles and production facilities is, however, a significant diplomatic achievement that should be studied in the context of deterrence theory and policy, in part because no one at the time imagined this outcome was even possible (if anyone did predict that outcome, they certainly didn't write or blog about it). Most informed observers at the time (both proponents and critics of Obama's air strike strategy) assumed that these weapons were an important element of Assad's military strategy against various elements of an expanding opposition, a key component of Syria's strategic deterrent against Israel's nuclear capability, and essential for regime survival in the face of mounting external pressures for Assad to relinquish his power. In this context, the UN disarmament deal *has* been largely a success, as has been carefully documented by the Organisation for the Prevention of Chemical Weapons (OPCW).[59] This point is elaborated in chapter 4.

---

59 The final 8% of Syria's declared stockpiles were handed over for destruction in June 2014 (Borger 2014). For additional reports, updates, and statistical analyses related to Syrian disarmament, see Organisation for the Prohibition of Chemical Weapons 2015. Also see the comments made by OPCW director general Ambassador Ahmet Üzümcü in the second annual Justice Stephen Breyer International Law Lecture hosted by the Brookings Institution on 9 April 2015; full text, audio, and video available through the Brookings Institution (2015). Nonetheless, it is important to note that a fact-finding report released by the OPCW in December of 2014 found compelling evidence that chlorine gas had been used as a chemical weapon in Syria. While the report did not assign blame, witnesses reported the use of helicopters, strongly indicating government involvement (the report can be found through the Organisation for the Prohibition of Chemical Weapons [2014]). If true, the use of chlorine as a weapon is obviously troubling, and calls into question the success of the 2013 disarmament deal. Still, because chlorine has many industrial purposes, it is not considered a chemical weapon under the Chemical Weapons Convention (though its *use* as a chemical weapon is banned by international law) and was therefore not listed as part of the government's chemical weapons stockpiles to be dismantled. While using chlorine for hostile purposes violates the spirit of the 2013 disarmament deal, the possession of chlorine gas itself is not a violation, marking out somewhat of a gray area moving forward. Ultimately, the success of the initial deal cannot be entirely dismissed, even if future negotiations are required to address Syria's use of chemical agents not covered under the CWC. If anything, this new round of probing by the Assad regime lends support to the "protracted crisis" approach to coercive diplomacy outlined in this book.

Postscript

While the focus of this book is on the policy debates occurring at the time of the chemical weapons crisis in the late summer and early fall of 2013, it is worth noting how the impasse has come to be viewed in retrospect. The conventional wisdom today is very different from the interpretation we defend in this book (see, in particular, chapters 4–7). According to proponents of the standard historical account, the Obama administration fecklessly backed away from the red line he set in Syria; indeed, the entire episode is typically cited as one of the major foreign policy blunders of the president's tenure. When asked about the red line in September 2015, Richard Haass – president of the Council on Foreign Relations – suggested that "probably the most consequential thing the president didn't do in his presidency was follow up on his pledges in Syria to attack the regime after they used chemicals … This is in a sense the biggest problem arguably with his foreign policy legacy, what he hasn't done in this part of the world."[60] For many, this interpretation has become so widespread that it requires no further explanation or justification. In the spring of 2016, for example, Bret Stephens, in a roundtable discussion with several other prominent foreign policy experts (Gideon Rose, Ian Bremmer, Jane Harman, and John Micklethwait), prefaced a comment with the following assertion: "In September of 2013 or August 2013, when the president has [*sic*] set a red line about acting in Syria in the face of chemical weapons, *all of us would agree he retreated from that red line* with visible consequences for the sense in Saudi Arabia and elsewhere that the United States was a reliable ally [and] that the president would do what he said he would do."[61] Tellingly, no objections were raised against this basic interpretation of the crisis. Jeffrey Goldberg's widely discussed article in *The Atlantic*, discussing President Obama's foreign policy legacy ("The Obama Doctrine") similarly positions this interpretation as widely accepted, noting, "Even commentators who have been broadly sympathetic to Obama's policies saw this episode as calamitous."[62] Nor has this assessment been limited to commentators and analysts: Leon Panetta and Robert Gates – former secretaries of defense under President Obama – have respectively stated that the red

---

60 Quoted in Griswold 2015.
61 Stephens et al. 2016, emphasis added.
62 Goldberg 2016, 76.

line was "damaging"[63] and a "serious mistake."[64] We respectfully reject this very popular version of history that has, in the words of John Kerry, taken on "a life of its own."[65]

Proponents of the standard narrative begin by embracing a vague and unfocused interpretation of success or failure, tying the decision not to strike to the subsequent deterioration of conditions in the wider Syrian conflict. They also endorse a somewhat questionable (and simplistic) model of foreign policy decision making that assumes Obama essentially *decided* not to follow through with air strikes, and that the red line was therefore a sham; this is buttressed by insider accounts, outlined by Goldberg and others, regarding the machinations of the decision to seek congressional approval, and the associated bureaucratic in-fighting between Obama and members of his foreign policy team.[66] According to this view, the subsequent disarmament deal was, in the words of Goldberg, a convenient and miraculous "deus ex machina" that somehow saved face for the Obama administration, salvaging compromise from the wreckage of a clear foreign policy disaster. Any explanation of a major foreign policy outcome that relies almost exclusively on dumb luck requires careful scrutiny, particularly when relevant historical evidence is ignored or overlooked.

Consider the following facts: the purpose of the red-line threat was to *deter* the use of chemical weapons in Syria, not to resolve the larger conflict. This line was crossed, quite clearly, in Ghouta. The Obama administration threatened air strikes and communicated to the Assad regime that the only way to avoid the impending strikes was to give up their chemical weapons. The regime complied, and as a result it no longer has the capacity to use any prohibited chemical weapons in Syria.[67] If the purpose of the red line was to deter the use of CW, surely the *removal* of these proscribed weapons (and therefore the impossibility of their use) constitutes a success. Again, the objective of any red-line threat is to achieve deterrence – a credible threat of punishment to prevent the unacceptable behavior from occurring. Having to follow through with

63 Panetta quoted in Miller 2014.
64 Gates quoted in Engel 2016.
65 Quoted in Goldberg 2016, 76.
66 See, for example, the interview given by former secretary of defense Chuck Hagel regarding Obama's decision to "ignore his own red line," in De Luce 2015.
67 Reported use of chlorine gas notwithstanding; see n. 59.

punishing military air strikes would constitute a failure. Critics get the history and the strategy completely backward.

Which leads to perhaps the most crucial misunderstanding on the part of purveyors of the conventional wisdom – that Obama's "decision" to stand down was known, at the time, by the *targets* of his coercive diplomacy: Syria (Assad) and Russia (Putin). As we outline in chapters 4 to 7, the threat to strike was *still credible*, even after the decision to seek congressional approval, for a variety of sound, strategic reasons, including US reputation and past behavior. Goldberg's reporting focuses on what we know now, several years after the crisis, about the backroom intrigue playing out at the time within the Obama administration. For Assad and Putin, this information was unknown in August/September 2013 and would likely have been irrelevant even if it had been known – it is only in retrospect that Obama's "decision" not to strike has (supposedly) become clear. Imagine if one had been following events in real time; as Goldberg points out, many within the administration, including the secretary of state, secretary of defense, and many key senior advisers, were actively pushing *for* strikes; Obama himself did not rule strikes out, but felt going to Congress would buy extra time and stamp greater legitimacy on any such action; given past US behavior, and the known imperatives for protecting red lines to maintain credibility, it would have been entirely reasonable for Assad and Putin to conclude strikes were still likely. It is easy now to claim Obama never intended to strike, but for those facing the wrong end of a barrage of cruise missiles, knowledge of the tense discussions occurring at the White House – in which those pushing for strikes were in the strong majority – would have provided very little comfort. In any event, both Assad and Putin believed that strikes were likely to occur, which *explains* the offer from Russia to broker (and Syria to accept) the disarmament deal. In this interpretation, therefore, Goldberg's "deus ex machina" can actually be explained quite well – Russia's intervention was less a fortunate "act of god" than a predictable outcome of strategic logic. As scholars of international relations, we should never be satisfied with explanations that rely on apparently random and fortuitous interventions; the adjudication of competing theories, after all, rests in part on their respective ability to deal with discrepant facts – and in this case, the *fact to be explained* (i.e., the outcome of the coercive encounter itself) is congruent with the theory outlined in this book, but lies decidedly outside the conventional story of the Syria crisis.

Finally, many have argued that the outcome of the Syria case has been, in fact, a dangerous diminution of American credibility – that is, the failure to strike the Assad regime has sent the message to other rogue regimes around the world that the use of CW or other WMD will go unpunished. It is difficult to say with certainty just what lessons other regimes will draw from the outcome of the Syria case for reasons we explain in chapters 5 and 6 – credibility is both complex (i.e., multifaceted) and in the eye of the beholder. Yet, given what actually occurred in Syria, surely the more reasonable lesson would not be that CW or WMD can be used with impunity, but rather that if leaders mobilize and use such capabilities, they should be prepared to lose them.[68]

Outline and Objectives

The book addresses three central questions. First, with respect to their theories, logic, evidence, and advice, what did Obama's critics get wrong in the Syria case, and why is it important to highlight these errors (chapter 1)? Second, what have we learned about resolve and credibility from US coercive encounters with smaller powers over the last two decades (Bosnia-Herzegovina 1992–5; Kosovo 1998–9; Iraq 1991–2003), and how does this evidence directly challenge Press, Mercer, Hopf, and other standard criticisms of rational deterrence theory (chapters 2 and 3)? Third, what are the implications for US foreign policy, particularly in relation to the transferability of reputations for resolve, fighting for credibility, and Washington's application of coercive diplomacy in Syria as well as future asymmetric conflicts (chapters 4 to 7)? The book concludes, in chapter 8, with thoughts on confirmation bias in the field of international relations and the practice of selectively packaging and presenting international and foreign policy theory (and evidence) to privilege a specific US foreign policy agenda.

This book is unique in that it represents the first book-length, systematic, and comprehensive response to the proliferating contention that reputations are never worth fighting for because, the argument goes, adversaries never look at past behavior or judge resolve based on

---

68 Another potentially important lesson, which we discuss in chapter 6, has to do with the "credibility paradox," and the notion that *not* striking given the disarmament agreement reassured adversaries (including Iran) that the US was a credible negotiating partner.

behavior from other crises; the keys to credibility lie elsewhere. These views are not supported by the empirical evidence presented in the following chapters. This is an extremely important debate. In a world in which US deterrent and coercive capabilities undergird a significant measure of global security, the stakes are incredibly high.

The evidence in this book will show that, on the one hand, past actions are not definitive for reputations; because cases are often different in important ways, credibility is not perfectly transferable or inter-dependent. Alternatively, past actions are rarely completely irrelevant; in fact, in many instances the lessons learned from previous crises and/or encounters are incorporated into calculations of credibility. In other words, fighting for credibility makes sense in some cases, but would be foolish in others. Determining when and under what conditions coercive threats make sense, and when reputations matter, is likely to produce significantly more valuable (and policy-relevant) analysis with respect to credibility and international politics than simplified conten-tions that they are either *always* or *never* relevant.

This study uses comparative analysis of several asymmetric conflicts involving the US over the past two decades to defend a theory of crisis behavior grounded in rational deterrence theory (RDT). The book will show that the version of RDT dismissed by critics and skeptics of repu-tations in international relations is decidedly weak and one that few, if any, deterrence theorists actually embrace. This book fills a significant gap in theory and evidence through a careful and comprehensive treat-ment of reputations – not only for the purpose of building and apply-ing good theory, but in order to reveal the biases that plague ongoing efforts to narrow the gap between theory and policy in international relations.

A final point about what the book is *not* attempting to defend. Chal-lenging the notion that past behavior has no impact on future credibility should not be construed as an argument in support of "fighting wars for the sake of credibility," or that making good on your threats is suf-ficient reason, in and of itself, to expend significant material resources or risk American lives. This greatly oversimplifies the dilemmas facing leaders as they navigate complex foreign policy problems. Our objec-tive, by contrast, is precisely to move beyond such unhelpful either/or reasoning by offering a more balanced assessment of the role that reputations and past behavior play in the credible application of coer-cive diplomacy.

Chapter One

Reputations Research and Premature Closure of Inquiry

Our focus on the work of Press, Mercer, and Hopf is appropriate for two reasons. First, the case evidence and theoretical arguments presented by these authors collectively constitute an important challenge to conventional RDT. As noted by Huth, "reputation is the least developed component of deterrence theory";[1] as one of many constitutive components of RDT, reputation was often considered important intuitively rather than established as being so by explicit arguments and evidence. This assessment is echoed by Weisiger and Yarhi-Milo: "Orthodox reputation theory [RDT] gained widespread acceptance on the basis of its clear internal logic and strong policy recommendations rather than on the basis of empirical tests."[2] It is not surprising, then, that the challenge put forth by P-M-H has been a significant one, as reflected in a recent review article on reputation in international politics by Dafoe, Renshon, and Huth,[3] in which engagement with P-M-H figures prominently. Second, as discussed in the previous chapter, P-M-H research was central to policy debates during the Syria and Ukraine crises. Whether or not P-M-H truly represents the "current consensus" on reputations, as Christopher Fettweis[4] claims, is debatable (this is not the position, for example, that Dafoe, Renshon, and Huth take). Nevertheless, the record is very clear: many critics who rejected Obama's approach to Syria did so by embracing the P-M-H consensus and by dismissing concerns about reputations. For both its substantive theoretical challenge

---

1 Huth 1997, 97.
2 Weisiger and Yarhi-Milo 2015, 475.
3 Dafoe, Renshon, and Huth 2014, 384–9.
4 Fettweis 2012, 1130.

and its impact on prominent policy debates, therefore, understanding and engaging with the P-M-H consensus is crucial for scholars of deterrence and compellence, and for understanding the ongoing application of coercive diplomacy. If the debate on Syria is any indication, P-M-H research is likely to figure prominently in discussions about US policy in future international crises.

In this chapter, we outline several key problems with the P-M-H consensus that *should* have been apparent to those applying it to the Syria case. Several criticisms relate to the theory and methodology of the research itself, while others suggest logical problems in the application of the research to the Syria crisis. We similarly highlight extensive extant research on reputations that undermines the conclusions of P-M-H, pointing to a *premature closure of inquiry* by those invoking P-M-H during the Syria debate. To be clear, our intention is not to summarily dismiss the scholarly work of those who argue that reputations are irrelevant or that fighting for credibility never makes sense. As will become apparent in subsequent chapters, we take the theoretical and empirical arguments and implications of the P-M-H challenge very seriously in order to assess the quality of that case compared to our version of rational deterrence theory. We do take issue, however, with the manner in which P-M-H research is consistently invoked to support certain arguments with respect to American foreign policy.

The Press-Mercer-Hopf Consensus

The implications of P-M-H, if verified, are significant. As Weisiger and Yarhi-Milo point out: "From a policy perspective, the work of reputation critics [P-M-H] suggests that leaders are tragically mistaken when they commit to the use of force in the expectation of long-term benefits beyond any gains in the immediate dispute."[5] If P-M-H is correct, in other words, leaders must seriously re-evaluate long-held beliefs about the importance of following through on commitments or the dangers of being called on repeated bluffs. If the P-M-H consensus is wrong, conversely, leaders could face disastrous consequences for abandoning such principles.

The most surprising aspect of how the debate over reputations played out during the Syria crisis (and continues to unfold today) is how little

---

5 Weisiger and Yarhi-Milo 2015, 476.

attention scholars and analysts paid to carefully examining the underlying theories and evidence covered by Daryl Press, Jonathan Mercer,
and Ted Hopf. Journalists and political leaders engaged in debates over
US foreign policy rarely have the time or incentive to conduct comprehensive literature reviews when offering policy advice, but scholars of
international relations should be a little more circumspect; they should
take the time to check the research, evaluate the evidence, critically unpack the underlying theories being tested, and search for contradictory
or disconfirming arguments, theories, and evidence. In fact, academics
arguably have an obligation to do this, particularly when only a portion
of the relevant literature is privileged to support a preferred policy option. Research by P-M-H is typically cited without caveats, qualifiers, or
criticisms, and their findings are never balanced against other research
(e.g., on audience costs, coercive diplomacy, rational deterrence theory,
and deterrence successes and failures in recent crises) that directly challenges their conclusions. Yet those who cite P-M-H as sufficient evidence to dismiss reputations offer up these conclusions as if they *did*
perform a careful assessment of the relevant literature and research.

Those who subscribe to the view that P-M-H provide definitive proof
that reputations play no role in how adversaries assess US credibility
are, we believe, engaged in *premature closure of inquiry* – pushing conclusions about reputations in the absence of a thorough and balanced
evaluation of the relevant historical evidence and theoretical research.
Take, for example, the common refrain that adversaries would never
view US leaders as irresolute despite evidence from previous cases in
which Washington officials bluffed or retreated. Contrary to such expectations, Saddam Hussein seriously underestimated US resolve and
credibility in 2003 based on lessons he learned and reputations he assigned to US leaders from previous confrontations.[6] Hussein himself
admitted he did not believe that US/UK/coalition forces would attack Baghdad with ground troops *despite* all available evidence to the
contrary, because of mistaken assumptions that were reinforced after
the Gulf War (1991), Operation Desert Fox (1998), and again after the
Kosovo air campaign (1999). By logical implication, Saddam's assessment of US credibility in 2003 could not have been informed exclusively
by gauging US power and interests (as Press and Mercer conclude) –
he had no reason to dismiss US power and capabilities in light of the

---

6 Harvey 2011.

thousands of troops amassing at his border, a unanimous UN resolution (1441) threatening "serious consequences," a general consensus at the time regarding his WMD program, and strong bipartisan consensus after 9/11 that Washington had to deal with the evolving WMD-terrorism nexus. All of this was buttressed by dozens of statements from senior members of both political parties in Congress and the British parliament demanding full and complete compliance *and* a formal authorization to use military force. Hussein's own statements reveal that despite all the power and combined US/UK/coalition interests (commitments) playing out at the time, he still "underestimated" US credibility and the real threat to his regime – that is, reputations did form and were directly relevant to assessments of US credibility. This case is discussed in more detail in chapter 3.

The first question that should have been asked with respect to the Syria crisis is whether four cases of major power conflict from 1900 to 1911 (Mercer 1996) or three cases of superpower conflict from 1938 to 1939 and 1958 to 1962 (Press 2005) are entirely appropriate for drawing definitive conclusions about how contemporary adversaries interpret the credibility of US threats. Are there any significant structural (relative power), historical (previous interactions), regional (similar exchanges with other smaller powers), bilateral, domestic, political, economic, military, technological, or other factors that could conceivably raise legitimate questions about generalizations derived from a total of seven cases, many from the early 1900s? Should we not expect to find at least one clearly articulated explanation for why these cases remain perfectly appropriate for understanding the complexities of reputations and credibility in, for example, a US-Syria crisis fifty or one hundred years later? Are these seven cases supposedly more relevant than a series of recent asymmetric crises between the US and leaders in Iraq, Bosnia, Kosovo, Libya, and Afghanistan? How do we reconcile the findings from P-M-H with significant evidence from US deterrence cases over the past two decades that seems to contradict their conclusions about reputations? These latter cases show, indeed, that adversaries often underestimate US resolve because of commonly shared assumptions about the West's aversion to casualties, dismiss US credibility based on lessons learned from previous cases, and typically are deterred/compelled only after a reputation for resolve has been (re)established.

Copeland, for example, points out the following problem in his critique of Mercer: relying on cases from an earlier historical period ignores several important "boundary conditions" that fundamentally

alter the nature of strategic encounters – specifically, system polarity
and weapons technology. As he concludes: "Mercer supports his argument with evidence from three pre-1914 crises. By focusing on a mul-
tipolar period with conventional weaponry, however, Mercer limits
the applicability of his argument for the period that is the focus of his
policy conclusions, namely, the post-1945 bipolar system of nuclear-
armed great powers."[7]

With regard to Press, this criticism is reversed: lessons from Cold War
confrontations between nuclear-armed great powers are limited in their
applicability to post–Cold War asymmetric encounters between the US
and smaller powers like Syria. In both instances the logic is the same:
important differences exist regarding the international environment,
such that lessons from one era do not necessarily apply wholesale to
another.

Further, those applying the P-M-H consensus to Syria should have
noted that the evidence compiled by Press and Mercer in their seven
cases does not include any information about how US adversaries
viewed Washington's reputations for resolve or credibility. Mercer's
work focused on Britain's search for allies between 1901 and 1905; the
First Moroccan Crisis 1905–6; the Bosnia-Herzegovina Annexation Crisis of 1908–9; and the Agadir Crisis of 1911. Press studied the appeasement crisis of 1938–9; the Berlin crises from 1958 to 1961 (from the UK
and US perspectives); and US impressions of Soviet credibility during
the Cuban Missile Crisis, 1962. Hopf's (1994) study is an exception – he
does address Soviet impressions of US resolve and credibility after a
number of Cold War crises, but additional flaws in his research design
that undermine confidence in his conclusions have been noted elsewhere (these problems are discussed in more detail below).

A second key problem is what Dafoe, Renshon, and Huth termed the
"misspecification of the null theory." As the authors explain:

> Mercer tests a null model of deterrence theory in which assessments of re-
> solve vary deterministically and dichotomously based solely on behavior
> in the last crisis. This model generates strong, testable predictions. *How-
> ever, few theorists would argue that an actor will be perceived as resolved if and
> only if the actor stood firm in the last crisis.* Rather, reputational inferences are
> often probabilistic, continuous, and conditional on context, and relevance

---

7 Copeland 1997, 35.

could be a complex function of time, beliefs about the interdependence of commitments, conditions of the conflict, and other factors.[8]

Indeed, Mercer outlines his version of RDT in the simplest terms possible: "a state that yields should be viewed as irresolute and a state that stands firm should be viewed as resolute; however a state behaved in the last crisis should govern others' expectations of that state." Mercer contends that this formulation "fits with the beliefs of deterrence theorists (and of decision-makers) about how reputations form."[9] In other words, all that matters in this theory is how a state behaved in the last crisis. Press likewise begins his book by specifying the theory he plans to debunk: "The conventional wisdom – which I call 'Past Actions' theory – holds that decision-makers assess their enemies' credibility by evaluating their history for keeping (or breaking) commitments."[10] The same goes for Hopf's operationalization of RDT, in which adversary assessments of credibility hinge entirely on the "lessons" they learn from previous conflicts.[11]

Yet most deterrence theorists make no such claims. Even Thomas Schelling – the central proponent of the "conventional wisdom" on deterrence they claim to be refuting – would reject such simplistic arguments. In fact, Schelling's work,[12] often cited as representing the "strong-interdependence-of-reputations" position, never claims that fighting for credibility and resolve (to save "face") is justified under any and all conditions.[13] In Schelling's words: "It is often argued that 'face' is a frivolous asset to preserve, and that it is a sign of immaturity that a government can't swallow its pride and lose face. It is undoubtedly true that false pride often tempts a government's officials to take irrational risks or to do undignified things – to bully some small country that insults them, for example."[14] Far from arguing that fighting for credibility always makes sense, Schelling actually raises concerns about false pride and recommends protecting a more serious kind of "face" or "image," "consisting of other countries' beliefs (their leaders' beliefs,

---

8 Dafoe, Renshon, and Huth 2014, 388.
9 Mercer 1996, 43.
10 Press 2005, 1.
11 Hopf 1994.
12 Schelling 1960, 1966.
13 For a more thorough discussion of this point, see Mitton 2015.
14 Schelling 1966, 124.

that is) about how the country can be expected to behave. It relates not to a country's 'worth' or 'status' or even 'honor,' but to its reputation for action." As he explains,

> If the question is raised whether this kind of "face" is worth fighting over, the answer is that this kind of face is one of the few things worth fighting over ... "Face" is merely the interdependence of a country's commitments; it is a country's reputation for action, the expectations other countries have about its behavior ... *Still, the value of "face" is not absolute.* That preserving face – maintaining others' expectations about one's own behavior – can be worth *some* cost and risk *does not mean that in every instance it is worth the cost or risk of that occasion.*[15]

The argument is therefore considerably more nuanced than P-M-H allow. Schelling suggests that past actions and reputations are important but not sufficient, in and of themselves, to establish the credibility of a coercive/deterrent threat, and reputations are not perfectly transferable across cases regardless of capabilities and interests.

In sum, Press, Mercer, and Hopf all assess the importance of reputation in international crises by testing a seriously deficient version of deterrence theory that takes as its core logic the *complete* interdependence of commitments. That they find little to no support for this theory should be expected and is, in fact, consistent with much prior work in the field. As Huth summarized in his assessment of empirical findings of studies of deterrence, "there is weak support for the strong-interdependence-of-commitments argument."[16] This is significant, as the persuasiveness of the P-M-H challenge is ultimately contingent on the quality of the theory that is tested and found wanting; if this theory is one to which few actually subscribe, conclusions regarding the irrelevance of reputations are significantly undermined.

Third, as Weisiger and Yarhi-Milo have persuasively argued, P-M-H research has failed to consider the extent to which reputational considerations may operate through mechanisms other than explicit reference to past behavior. Specifically, the authors find support for

---

15 Ibid., 125, emphasis added.
16 Huth 1997, 91.

the possibility that "the effects of reputation ... act primarily through estimates of the opponent's interests."[17] As they argue, reputations are likely "folded into the general assessments of interests," meaning that "while it would not be inconsistent ... for leaders to reference past action in the context of an ongoing crisis ... the absence of such references is no guarantee that reputation is irrelevant."[18] That is, reputation and past behavior may help define the very parameters of the "interests" that subsequently feature in assessments of credibility. From the point of view of US adversaries struggling to gauge US commitments and willingness to use force in their particular case, past behavior under similar circumstances may help to *establish* what, precisely, constitutes US "interests." It signals what the US is or is not likely to accept under certain conditions. It is unlikely that adversaries would completely ignore US behavior in previous (similar) crises, because this would essentially strip away potentially useful intelligence about: (1) the conditions under which US military force is contemplated; (2) the strategic logic (sequence) tied to crisis escalation when explicit coercive threats are issued by Washington and ignored; and (3) the military, political,

---

17 Weisiger and Yarhi-Milo 2015, 474.
18 Ibid., 478. Perhaps the best way to conceptualize this critique is through an application of Stephen Van Evera's (1997) process tracing tests of causal inference. Press wrongly considers archival evidence of leaders referencing past behavior to be a "hoop test" for Past Actions theory. As James Mahoney (2012, 571) explains: "A hoop test proposes that a given piece of evidence ... *must be present* for a hypothesis to be valid. Failing a hoop test eliminates a hypothesis, but passing a hoop test does not confirm a hypothesis" (emphasis added). In his cases, Press argues that because no evidence of leaders referencing past behavior in assessing credibility were found (i.e., the hoop test was failed), Past Actions theory cannot be valid. In fact, references to past behavior constitute a "smoking gun" test: "Smoking gun tests ... propose that if a given piece of evidence ... is present, then the hypothesis must be valid. Passing a smoking gun test lends decisive support in favor of a hypothesis, *though failing a smoking gun test does not eliminate a hypothesis*" (Mahoney 2012, 571–2; emphasis added). Had Press found explicit reference to past behavior by leaders, Past Actions theory would have been confirmed (such evidence clearly constitutes a "smoking gun" for a theory that says leaders use past behavior to assess credibility). As a consequence, references to past behavior cannot be a "hoop test" for Past Actions theory, because "passing a hoop test does not confirm a hypothesis." But *not* finding any such evidence is insufficient for invalidating the theory ("failing a smoking gun test does not eliminate a hypothesis"), because there are ways *other* than explicitly referencing past behavior through which past actions can influence perceptions of credibility, as Weisiger and Yarhi-Milo point out.

and audience costs associated with Washington's options – namely, retreat, do nothing (status quo), or retaliate for noncompliance by demonstrating resolve.

Finally, and perhaps most importantly, the work by P-M-H stops short with respect to an important methodological principle: the search for discrepant evidence. A robust test of a given theory involves not only searching for and finding evidence that *confirms* the theory but also searching for, and *failing* to find, evidence that *disconfirms* the theory (this point is developed in greater detail, and put into practice, in chapters 3 and 4).

Each of these criticisms is expanded and explored in the following sections, which provide more detailed assessments of Hopf (1.1), Press (1.2), and Mercer (1.3). It is important to emphasize that the critiques outlined below should not be regarded as exhaustive summaries of each authors' arguments or as broad condemnations of the overall quality of their research. Quite the opposite – the logic, theory, and evidence of the P-M-H challenge is sufficiently compelling to warrant a balanced theoretical and empirical assessment vis-à-vis rational deterrence theory, a task that we undertake in subsequent chapters (2–7) of this book. Our purpose here, however, is to outline and summarize several key criticisms of P-M-H that were overlooked by many journalists, scholars, and others, who failed to consider their implications and whether or not they undermined the applicability of P-M-H to the Syria crisis. Section 1.4 offers a brief overview of *other* research on reputations that challenges the position of the P-M-H consensus (in other words, the type of assessment that was conspicuously absent from those championing P-M-H arguments vis-à-vis Syria).

1.1   Hopf (1994) "Peripheral Visions"

As mentioned, Hopf's research avoids one of the key problems noted above, as he explicitly investigates an adversary's (the Soviets') perceptions of US credibility. Nonetheless, as Press himself notes in his critique of Hopf's work, the findings are "highly suspect," because Hopf "did not systematically compare these views to Soviet opinions *before* each incident" (emphasis added): "Without this comparison it is impossible to know whether American defeats and withdrawals lowered US credibility. For example, Hopf reports that after the US withdrawal from Vietnam, Soviet observers were evenly divided about US credibility. But we cannot tell whether this reflects an increase or decrease relative to the Soviets' views before the Vietnam War."[19] Moreover, the fact that Soviet observers were "evenly divided" about US credibility suggests that US actions in Vietnam produced competing impressions of US resolve, enhancing perceptions of US credibility in the eyes of some officials but having the opposite effect for others. Of course, in the absence of information about Soviet impressions prior to these crises, the same limitations noted by Press apply to these conclusions as well.

Fukuyama points to another problem with Hopf's research: "Excessive attention to Soviet words rather than deeds flaws the author's major conclusions" that US military interventions did not deter the Soviets.[20] "Collapse of the American position in Indochina," Fukuyama reminds us, "was in fact followed by an upsurge in [Soviet] support for radical Third World clients, while the Reagan doctrine brought about a retrenchment of Soviet Third World commitments." The point is that Hopf's research on Soviet impressions of US credibility is far from definitive and, as many reviews of the book point out, represents a decidedly weak test of deterrence theory.

According to the dust jacket of his book, Hopf claims to have repudiated "the core assumptions of deterrence theory, one of the most central aspects of US foreign policy over the past half century ... The evidence in this book ... implies that military strength is not the only way – not even the most effective way – to deter an opponent." Yet rational deterrence theory does not claim that military strength is sufficient for deterrence – ignoring interests, commitments, and resolve cannot be regarded as a particularly effective way to establish credibility or deter / compel adversaries during international crises. The author goes on to point out that "the credibility of the United States in the Middle East, for instance, was not strengthened by US military actions, but rather by the adroit use of military and economic aid and diplomatic leverage."

---

19 Press 2005, 16.
20 Fukuyama 1995, 167. A similar criticism is made by Ralph Carter (1996, 132): "Throughout virtually the entire book, Hopf determines whether US deterrence efforts worked by noting what Soviet elites subsequently *said*, not by looking at what the Soviet Union subsequently *did*. Hopf acknowledges this weakness in the concluding chapter and provides a scorecard based on Soviet actions in the thirty-eight cases. Yet, in perhaps as many as ten of these cases, an overt US commitment to defend one of the parties is hard to identify. Questioning the validity of a quarter of the cases reduces the helpfulness of this scorecard" (emphasis in original).

But deterrence is agnostic about the specific kinds of pressures put on adversaries to force compliance[21] – it simply predicts success if the risks and costs of the retaliatory threat outweigh the risks and benefits of the consequences. As Quester observes, Hopf's book "is an example of what can be very intellectually valuable and stimulating about critiques of deterrence theory but also of what can be wrong with such critiques ... We have too many instances, in general, of authors 'disproving' the theory of deterrence but only by attacking something somewhat different. What Hopf refers to throughout this book as 'deterrence theory' is mostly 'domino theory.'" [22]

Richard Lebow, for his part, finds fault with Hopf's case selection:

> In all thirty-eight cases, he defines the Soviet Union as the challenger and the United States as the defender. In Vietnam and Nicaragua, to mention just two egregious examples, the United States might properly be considered the challenger, and there is little reason to consider either conflict a deterrence encounter. The overthrow of the shah of Iran in 1979 is coded as a Soviet victory and an American defeat, even though the Soviet Union never threatened or attacked Iran and the shah fell as the result of an internal revolution. His overthrow was a setback for the United States but was not a deterrence failure. Hopf nevertheless describes it as a "crucial case" for deterrence. Deterrence theory, he asserts, would predict that as a result of the shah's fall, the United States would lose its credibility to protect its interests in other parts of the world. To test a theory of commitments, a researcher would have to use cases in which commitments were made. As currently constituted, Hopf's data set and coding cannot be considered a fair test of Schelling, let alone of deterrence theory.[23]

Again, this critique speaks to the misspecification of the null theory identified by Dafoe, Renshon, and Huth[24] with respect to Press and Mercer. Hopf attributes to RDT certain arguments and inferences that simply do not correspond to the logic and theory of most RDT proponents.

---

21 See Quester 1995.
22 Ibid., 805.
23 See Lebow 1995, 320–1.
24 Dafoe, Renshon, and Huth 2014.

1.2   Press (2005) "Calculating Credibility"

In his book, Press examines the appeasement crisis of 1938–9, the Berlin crises of 1958–61 from Britain's perspective, the same Berlin crises from a US perspective, and US impressions of Soviet credibility and resolve during the Cuban Missile Crisis (CMC) in 1962. His argument is straightforward. The key question, identified at the outset of the book, is "How do countries assess the credibility of their adversaries' threats during military crises?"[25] The ultimate conclusion is that countries assess the credibility of threats by rationally weighing the power (whether an adversary is *capable* of following through on a threat) and interests (whether they are *willing* to do so) of the state issuing the threat. According to Press, states do not factor past behavior into their calculations of credibility. He argues that while calculating credibility based on past behavior is a convenient heuristic tool for use in day-to-day life (e.g., the credibility of a promise to show up on time from a friend who has been late repeatedly in the past is low), this "shortcut" is not used by decision-makers in high stakes, life-or-death military crises in international politics. The more high-pressure the situation, the more likely rational, strategic logic will be used to evaluate the probability an action (following through on a threat) will or will not be taken. As such, even if a state has repeatedly backed down in the past, if it has sufficient power and sufficient interest in a crisis, its threats will be considered credible.

To establish his case, Press focuses specifically on assessing the explanatory power of two opposing theories about how states calculate credibility: "Past Actions (PA) theory" and "Current Calculus (CC) theory." He then identifies two key assumptions of PA theory: (1) a country's credibility is affected by its record for keeping or breaking past commitments; and (2) a history of breaking commitments reduces credibility, while a history of keeping commitments increases it. He notes that different versions of PA theory exist, with varying degrees of specificity as to when past actions will be important. At the broadest level (the version that Press believes most policymakers adhere to) is the belief that past actions will be important even in completely different circumstances, with different adversaries, in different parts of the globe. Other versions are narrower, suggesting that past actions will be applicable only if occurring in the same geographic region; or in quick

---

25 Press 2005, 9.

succession (timing); or if there is a similarity of issues or stakes; or if the same countries are involved; or if the same leaders remain in office (on one or both sides). Press claims to disprove *all* of these variants. As noted, however, this raises the question of the "null theory" – most deterrence theorists would also *reject* the version of deterrence (PA) theory Press claims to be refuting.

Current Calculus theory, by contrast, "posits that a country's credibility is not tied to its past behavior; when leaders assess credibility in a crisis, they focus on the balance of capabilities and the interests at stake in the current confrontation."[26] As mentioned, the key consideration is whether the country issuing a threat has both sufficient power and sufficient interest to follow through. If so, the threat is credible, regardless of what the country may have done in the past.[27] The cases Press uses to test these opposing theories are selected on a "most-likely" basis – that is, cases that are most likely to provide evidence in support of PA. All of his cases "involve a series of crises occurring in quick succession, between the same set of countries, over the same set of issues, and in most cases involved the same set of leaders."[28]

According to Press, the evidence compiled from his four case studies "suggests that the blood and wealth spent to maintain a country's record for keeping commitments are wasted: when push comes to shove, credibility is assessed on the basis of the *current interests* at stake and the *balance of power*, not on the basis of past sacrifices."[29] In all four historical cases, he concludes that CC theory offers a better explanation than does

---

26 Press 2005, 20.

27 Ibid. Press predicts criticism stemming from the observation that leaders often look to past behavior to assess the capabilities of an adversary; this, however, does not refute Current Calculus theory. When looking at past behavior in this regard, states are assessing the power and effectiveness of an opponent, not their history of keeping commitments per se. The lesson, according to Press, is that when one *does* choose to fight, it is important to fight well (to send the message that one is effective and powerful), not that one must fight in order to maintain credibility (i.e., that one will follow through on threats in the future).

28 Ibid., 143. The criteria he uses to evaluate crisis decision making are: (1) statements of policymakers about an enemy's credibility; (2) the policies advocated in the crisis (as a proxy measurement – cautious policies suggest a perception of high credibility on the part of the adversary; assertive policies, low credibility); and (3) the reasoning provided for assessments of credibility (whether policymakers point to past actions or the current balance of power).

29 Ibid., 10, emphasis added.

PA theory. German perceptions of United Kingdom and French credibility leading up to the Second World War were not diminished by a series of capitulations in 1938, but instead reflected Hitler's perceptions of the shifting balance of power. Similarly, a series of bluffs over Berlin by the Soviets between 1958 and 1961 did not reduce their credibility in the eyes of either the British or the Americans; instead, as the overall nuclear balance shifted toward the Soviets, their credibility actually grew over this time period. Finally, during the CMC in 1962, Khrushchev's credibility was high, despite a history of backing down in Berlin, and was again a reflection of the (nuclear) power balance, not past behavior. As proof of these assertions, Press points to archival documentation of the deliberations by decision-makers and leaders during each crisis. He emphasizes that virtually no mention of past behavior is made during crisis deliberations, and that leaders instead assessed the immediate power and interests of their adversary.

Press anticipates the criticism that because two crises may be fundamentally different, it would be foolish to expect lessons drawn from one to be applied to the other. Past Actions theory, in this view, is only relevant in situations that are the same. Since Berlin and the CMC were fundamentally different, we would not expect lessons from Berlin (i.e., Soviets are irresolute) to be applied to the CMC. Press dismisses this criticism because it

> defends Past Actions theory in a way that strips the theory of its significance. If past actions only affect credibility in future crises when the future crises are virtually identical to the past ... then Past Actions theory is meaningless. It will almost never be worth keeping commitments for the sake of credibility if the credibility gained will only apply in identical cases. Identical cases are far too rare, if they exist at all.[30]

But this rebuttal oversimplifies the criticism. Of course no two situations are "identical"; this observation is self-evident. What Press misses is that in terms of international crises, there are categories that can help differentiate between like and un-like situations. In Berlin, for instance, the Soviets repeatedly threatened to change the status quo, but did nothing. In Cuba, they did change the status quo by installing missiles. A history of inaction in Berlin cannot be meaningfully applied to the

---

30 Ibid., 140.

CMC because the very initiation of the CMC itself was the result of Soviet action. This is not a trivial difference – it fundamentally alters the structure and dynamics of the deterrent/coercive encounter. Yet observing that the lessons from Berlin were (correctly) not applied in Cuba cannot be the basis for dismissing the importance of past behavior for credibility in other cases because no one, not even Thomas Schelling, would have expected them to be. The more relevant consideration is whether past behavior and reputations matter in fundamentally *similar* (but not, of course, *identical*) situations (this point is explored in more detail in chapter 2). As the cases examined in chapters 3 and 4 demonstrate, there is strong evidence to support this possibility.

Press also overlooks the fact that power and interests can pull in opposite directions. For instance, in confrontations in Somalia and Bosnia, the balance of power favored the US while the balance of interests favored Mohamed Farrah Aidid and Slobodan Milošević; what would Press's power/interests hypothesis predict? That the weaker state will back down when faced with a strong but less-interested opponent? Or that the less-interested stronger state will be challenged successfully by the weaker but more committed state? Press concludes that interests usually trump power but offers no theoretical justification for this belief. He admits that the combination of power and interests in his theory offers no consistent predictions but that "for a given level of 'interests,' fluctuation in power will affect credibility in a predictable way. And for a given balance of power, if the stakes in a crisis change, credibility will change, too."[31] This response raises questions of falsifiability.[32] After all, any outcome could be explained after the fact by reference to either dominating power or dominating interests; any change during protracted crises could be explained by "changing stakes." Also noteworthy is the endnote that accompanies this justification: "Current Calculus theory is also prescriptively useful. It suggests that the way to enhance credibility is to build power to defend interests so that they can be defended cheaply and effectively. This, rather than fighting wars to build reputation, will be the best method of enhancing credibility."[33] Press does not specify, however, what, precisely, constitutes "cheaply" and "effectively" in this context. Such considerations are, in fact, at the

---

31 Ibid., 28.
32 For a discussion of falsifiability in international relations theory, see Vasquez 1997.
33 Press 2005, 173, n. 73.

heart of casualty aversion; interpreting what the US considers cheap (or worthwhile) comes from assessments of what they have considered cheap (or worthwhile) in past situations – that is, what is their reputation for resolve in such circumstances. By bracketing "cheaply" and "effectively," Press's argument suggests that if a country is strong enough they will never be challenged, and their credibility will be absolute. This would make it difficult to explain challenges to the US during the 1990s or more recently, when US power and superiority was/is unquestioned and unprecedented. If there was ever a situation in which a preponderance of power would prevent challenges (which must logically be the desired outcome of any prescriptive policy of "building power" to enhance credibility), US dominance (particularly relative to powers like Iraq and Syria) was it – yet they faced repeated challenges. Indeed, as James Wirtz observes: "International history ... fails to support the intuitive deterrent effect a gross imbalance of power should have on the weak when they face a stronger competitor. Conflicts that the strong should hope to avoid and the weak cannot realistically hope to win populate the pages of diplomatic histories and are the stuff of current headlines."[34] Why is this the case? The answer may lie, in part, in reputation (in this instance, casualty aversion).

In his conclusion, Press touches on the first Gulf War, saying that Saddam Hussein's decision to invade Kuwait was not based on a lack of US credibility (due to past behavior; for example, Vietnam) – indeed, he argues that Saddam *expected* the US to intervene to help Kuwait, but simply thought he could win anyway. Press again oversimplifies the issue. The key question is not whether the US would act at all, but specifically *what* they might do (or more precisely, what would be the *extent* of their intervention)? Intervene to protect Kuwait, perhaps, but march all the way to Baghdad? Saddam certainly didn't think so, and this perception influenced his behavior. In subsequent crises (Operation Desert Fox in 1998 and the Iraq War in 2003), Saddam was convinced the US would do *something* (e.g., air strikes), but, once again, refused to believe officials in Washington and London had the stomach to actually invade the country and would almost certainly not move to Baghdad, despite US capabilities, support, interests, and threats.

Warnings about premature closure of inquiry associated with P-M-H research are particularly relevant when this work is cited as conclusive

---

34 Wirtz 2012, 16.

evidence to justify risky policies that could have serious consequences. Press acknowledges this very point: "Replication [of research] is *always* warranted before the results of any study are put into practice, especially when much is at stake [emphasis in original]. This is true for large-n quantitative studies, too: *no one should advise people to adopt potentially risky behavior on the basis of a single study*."[35] Obviously both the *number* and *type* of case studies should be expanded to test competing theories about reputations and credibility. Yet Press appears to have ignored his own advice when he offered very strong policy recommendations to the Obama administration during the Syria crisis. With references to *Calculating Credibility*, Press proceeded to admonish the president for issuing the initial red-line threat and recommended backing away from coercive diplomacy in the absence of any real US interests and no support for the use of military force. If bluffing carries no risks or costs, Press reasoned, then backing away from the red-line threat would be the more prudent strategy. Of course, we now know that his advice, and similar advice offered by Mercer, would have retained the regime's access to chemical weapons for use against rebels and, even more frighteningly, civilians, as had happened throughout the previous two years. Instead, coercive diplomacy succeeded in forcing Assad to dismantle the regime's stockpile.

1.3   Mercer (1996) "Reputation and International Politics"

Ironically, one of the strongest critiques of Mercer's work comes from Press:

> Mercer analyzes a set of military crises and discovers that when a country backs down, its enemies generally do not attribute its behavior to its character (or its leaders' characters). Instead they explain the decision to back down by attributing it to situational factors. Because reputation is a judgment about character, Mercer concludes that backing down does not lead to a reputation for being irresolute ... Unfortunately [this] does not fully answer the key question: whether backing down in one crisis reduces one's credibility in the future. Mercer's analysis shows that leaders tend to explain instances of backing down in situational terms, but he does not explore whether those situational explanations are then used as a basis for

---

35 Press 2005, 36, emphasis added.

future assessments of credibility. For example, Mercer notes that if a boy refuses to defend himself against a schoolyard bully and the bully attributes his pacifism to situational factors (e.g., he wears glasses), then the boy will not get a reputation for cowardice. True enough, but this misses the point: the bully now knows where to go for extra lunch money – the boy with glasses. Even though he explained the boy's behavior in situational terms, the bully may reasonably infer that the kid with glasses will not fight. In other words, Mercer's analysis leaves open the possibility that leaders make situational explanations when their adversaries back down, yet they nevertheless use the history of backing down to assess credibility in future confrontations.[36]

This logical problem raises important questions about Mercer's theoretical claims and is compounded by serious limitations with Mercer's evidence – as mentioned above, his cases focus exclusively on compiling information from the prior confrontation when testing whether a reputation for resolve matters. As Morgan points out in his comprehensive review of Mercer's work: "If A behaved irresolutely in 1906, then resolutely in 1910, only the latter counts for predicting A's reputation for resolve in 1912. This operationalization is too narrow. States are likely to consider many prior events and kinds of information in assessing resolve, including signals during the current crisis. They know better than to refer solely to the last case."[37] Consequently, as Morgan explains, "Mercer's argument might be carried too far. He concludes that a state's credibility rests less on reputation than on a calculation of its interests and capabilities," when in fact behavior from several previous cases could arguably have provided evidence that reputations and lessons learned from past actions matter a great deal. Mercer's evidence, in other words, is not sufficient to establish closure on the relevance of reputations.

In addition to these limitations, Mercer also faces the same problem as Press when concluding that only "interests" and "capabilities" matter, as if adversaries have access to all relevant information about these two components to be able to decipher US credibility whenever necessary. Interests are not always obvious (or consistent), and Washington's willingness to use force is never unequivocally clear or self-evident.

---

36 Ibid., 16.
37 Morgan 1997.

Adversaries often have a very difficult time assessing US credibility based exclusively on strict rationalist logic or cost-benefit/power-interest calculations. What is missing in this view is any attempt to explore the mechanisms through which adversaries measure US "interests" and "power" – adversaries' impressions of US actions in similar past cases often inform their impressions of US commitments, willingness to use capabilities, and, therefore, credibility (this point is discussed in more detail in chapter 2). As mentioned above, explicit reference to past behavior (essentially the only evidence sought by P-M-H to confirm RDT in the cases they examined) is not the sole indicator of the relevance of reputation (see the discussion of Weisiger and Yarhi-Milo [2015] above).

Mercer similarly misses the non-rational aspects of deterrence successes and failures. As Morgan explains, "Both case-studies literature and broad statistical studies of deterrence find that states often do not carefully calculate relative capabilities or the balance of interests (Huth and Russett 1984, 1990; Huth 1988; Lebow and Stein 1989, 1994). Motivated biases breed misestimates of one's own interests and resolve or of the opponent's, leading to surprises when opponents refuse to back down."[38]

As the evidence in chapter 3 will show, mistakes and miscalculations are very common, so the suggestion that reputations are irrelevant because adversaries have the capacity to rationally calculate US "interest" and "capabilities" misses a great deal of what makes credibility (and international relations) so complex. For better or worse, adversaries often rely on historical analogies that may or may not be appropriate when assessing current circumstances, and often rely on US or Western reputations (accurate or not) when selecting crisis management strategies.

But there is another, far more fundamental methodological problem with Mercer's research design – it is not well suited to testing the psychological theory it claims to confirm. Even accepting his detailed historical accounts, the evidence he compiled from his four cases is not sufficient to render any final judgments about how and why adversaries and allies assign *situational* or *dispositional* (reputational) attributes to their opponents' behavior. Mercer's psychological theory predicts that adversaries assign situational attributes when explaining "desirable" behavior, but they ascribe dispositional attributes when accounting for "undesirable" behavior. By logical implication and from the point of

---

38 Ibid.

view of US adversaries, Washington can get a reputation (i.e., a dispositional attribute) for being resolute, because opponents interpret these actions as *undesirable* (e.g., standing firm; fighting; launching an air strike), but Washington will never get a reputation from adversaries for lacking resolve when their behavior is interpreted as *desirable* (e.g., backing down; bluffing; failing to fight; conceding), because these actions are not assumed to indicate a dispositional routine, habit, or pattern. In sum, bluffing or backing down carries no costs in terms of US credibility in future crises. This is why so many of Obama's critics cited Mercer's work when recommending in 2013 that he should simply back down from his red-line threats against Syria.

Yet to produce a valid test of Mercer's psychology-based theory of attribution, one would need more evidence than the four cases in his study. In a perfect world with access to all available information about every US crisis, for example, we would hope to find examples of behavior predicted by Mercer's theory (much like the four cases in his study), but we would also need to search for and *fail to find* examples of behavior we would not expect (i.e., disconfirmations). Uncovering confirmations *and* failing to find disconfirmations constitutes a powerful test of the theory in question. Of course, Mercer caveats that his theory, like all others in the social sciences, is "probabilistic." A single discrepant piece of evidence would not therefore be sufficient for disconfirmation. This is a reasonable and generally accepted position. Yet *multiple* instances of discrepant evidence would be sufficient basis to seriously doubt the theory being tested.

The most obvious evidence to disconfirm Mercer's theory, or to challenge his policy recommendations on Syria,[39] would be cases in which adversaries *do* assign "dispositional" attributes (reputations) to US actions they deem "desirable" (e.g., backing down; issuing weak threats; bluffing; retreating; failing to follow through on a coercive military threat). Evidence that US adversaries assigned dispositional attributes to desirable behavior, or underestimated US credibility because they were guided by a strong belief (based on past actions) that Western leaders are casualty averse, would constitute powerful disconfirmation of Mercer's theory. The multiple US asymmetric deterrence encounters (1991–2013) covered in chapters 3 and 4 constitute such evidence. Moreover, these recent cases resemble, in important respects, the Syria crisis

---

39 See Mercer 2013.

and are likely to be the very cases Syrian officials should have been expected to learn from when drawing conclusions about how the US would have been likely to act in 2013. These cases are also more likely to be used by officials in Washington when drawing conclusions about what to do in Syria. Lessons learned from cases in the early 1900s, by contrast, will be far less relevant to theory and policy.

Premature Closure of Inquiry: An Illustration

Scholars, journalists, analysts, and others during the Syria crisis are not the only ones guilty of uncritically accepting and applying the evidence and implications of P-M-H. In this section, we offer two illustrations (one from political science, the other from law) in which respectable scholars, in well-known peer-reviewed academic journals, similarly advanced the P-M-H consensus as the settled science on reputations in international politics, then used it to extract even more definitive conclusions about the irrelevance of reputation, or firm policy recommendations with major practical implications, often without offering any new evidence or data.

Take first Shiping Tang's 2005 article published in a prominent journal specializing in international relations (IR) theory and security studies.[40] Tang begins his article by assuming that Press and Mercer have successfully debunked the "myth" of reputation. The starting point for Tang, in other words, is the "fact" that reputations for resolve do not and cannot exist, based on findings he cites from P-M-H. He even goes so far as to challenge Mercer for not taking the argument to its logical extreme – Mercer leaves open the possibility that reputations could form when adversaries view actions as undesirable (standing firm), a possibility Tang rejects (for reasons outlined below).

For Tang, the key issue is why politicians continue to believe in the importance of reputations and fighting for credibility when they should never assume that reputations for resolve matter: "There seems to be a gap … between politicians' persistent obsession with reputation and scholars' increasing doubt about reputation's importance, and that gap is widening."[41] Tang also highlights what he believes to be a gap in the existing literature. On one hand, there is work that focuses on

---

40 Tang 2005.
41 Ibid., 35.

politicians' belief in reputation, concluding that this concern has a major impact on states' behavior. The other line of work, taking a belief in reputation as fact, concludes that leaders are wrong to believe that reputation actually matters in international politics. Tang attempts to bring these two lines of argument together, explaining why politicians believe in reputation while also explaining why that belief is misguided.

In order to do so, Tang offers two main arguments: "First, there is a cult of reputation among politicians. Second, reputation for resolve cannot form in international conflicts because of anarchy."[42] As he explains,

> There is ... a fatal flaw in the cult's logic, for states rarely act according to the cult's logic even when the logic should most clearly apply: a state rarely underestimates its adversary's reputation even if the adversary has backed down in previous standoffs. In other words, although a state constantly fears that others may assign reputation to it based on its past behavior, the state never assigns reputation to other states based on their past behavior.[43]

Again, Tang provides no new evidence to support his claims and relies entirely on his conviction that Press's work dealt a "devastating blow to the logic of the cult."[44] Tang then tries to provide an overarching theoretical explanation for why a belief in reputation is unfounded, and why reputation for resolve cannot possibly form in international politics: anarchy. According to Tang,

> Reputation *cannot form in conflicts because of the anarchical nature of international politics.* Because of its simplicity, parsimony, explanatory power, and better fit with empirical findings, this explanation is superior to Mercer's ... Because a state's security ultimately depends on self-help, the worst-case mentality means that a state has to assume its adversaries to be resolute and its allies to be irresolute. Essentially, this worst-case assumption sets a baseline image for both adversaries and allies, and reputation becomes impossible to develop under anarchy. A state cannot lose nor gain reputation among its adversaries by either backing down or standing firm in a conflict, because its adversaries will always assume the state to be resolute

---

42 Ibid., 36.
43 Ibid., 42.
44 Ibid., 44.

(the baseline image) in the next conflict ... A state is assigned its baseline image by its adversaries and allies at the beginning of a crisis, and no past behavior can change that image ex ante.[45]

These sweeping generalizations and conclusions are offered without any new evidence to support them and despite the problems with P-M-H outlined above. Tang's contention that reputation has never mattered (and never will matter) in international politics is simplistic, to the say the least. Presumably only *one* case of reputations mattering would be sufficient to disprove his claim (given how strongly Tang emphasizes the implications of anarchy), and yet there are many cases of US interactions with smaller powers from 1991 to 2013 that directly challenge these claims – e.g., the Gulf War (1991), Bosnia-Herzegovina (1992–5), Operation Desert Fox (1998), the Kosovo air campaign (1999), the wars in Afghanistan (2001) and Iraq (2003), Libya air strikes (2011), and Syria (2013) (see chapters 3 and 4). For example, in 2002–3, Saddam Hussein seriously "underestimated" US-UK resolve and credibility, despite all evidence that he was facing a serious threat. Similarly, Slobodan Milošević mistakenly assumed in 1995 and again in 1999 that he could manage US-NATO air strikes because of his strong suspicion that Western leaders were casualty averse and would be forced to cave in the midst of a humanitarian crisis that Milošević perpetrated in the form of Operation Horseshoe. There is nothing about the nature of international anarchy that logically privileges or precludes one or another set of assumptions, perceptions, or conclusions that adversaries form about US capabilities, commitments, interests, resolve, or credibility.

Tang also confuses the "uncertainty" in anarchy and, ironically, imputes from it a form of certainty. According to Tang, uncertainty means states will always make the same prediction regarding an adversary's intentions: they will *always* assume that adversaries are resolute – case closed. This argument is difficult to accept. The concept of uncertainty is in fact the very thing that establishes the relevance of reputation and past actions when assessing US interests, Washington's willingness to use its capabilities, and, therefore, its credibility. Uncertainty and incomplete information, reputations, and lessons learned from past actions are often the only available tools to decipher pieces of the US credibility

45 Ibid., 50, emphasis added.

puzzle. Assessments of resolve and credibility *mitigate* uncertainty in the international system.

Next, consider the recent article by Vanderbilt law professor Ganesh Sitaraman in the *Harvard Law Review* (one of the top law journals in the United States).[46] Sitaraman essentially cites the Syria crisis as *confirmation* of the P-M-H consensus when he writes:

> For all the talk of credibility [from those advocating military action to enforce President Obama's red line on CW], political scientists have offered devastating critiques of credibility arguments in the context of military threats. They have demonstrated not only that the concept is often deployed in incomplete and illogical ways but also that as a historical matter, a country's "credibility" based on its reputation and past actions has little or no effect on the behavior of opponents in high-stakes international crises.[47]

His subsequent discussion of credibility arguments in IR is derived directly from P-M-H, even using Press's Past Actions theory as a stand-in for RDT (he calls PA theory "the most prominent" credibility argument, and "the one consistently invoked ... in foreign policy debates from Vietnam to Syria"; he then suggests that "the leading alternative to the past actions and reputation theories of credibility is [Press's] *current calculus* theory").[48]

In evaluating the "historical evidence" with respect to reputation in international crises, Sitaraman notes that "in a series of qualitative studies, political scientists have shown that past actions and reputation theories of credibility have little historical basis for support. When leaders evaluate their opponents, they assess threats based on current calculations, not on past actions."[49] He then offers brief overviews of the "qualitative studies" in question: Press's *Calculating Credibility*, Mercer's *Reputation and International Politics*, and Hopf's *Peripheral Visions*. No other studies on reputation in international politics are evaluated, although Gibler's article on "The Costs of Reneging" is afforded a footnote.[50]

---

46 Sitaraman 2014.
47 Ibid., 123.
48 Ibid., 125–6.
49 Ibid., 127.
50 Ibid., n. 22 – see Gibler 2008.

Sitaraman's overreliance on just three works (P-M-H) is particularly troubling given the powerful policy recommendations he extracts from them. First, he cites several examples (including Somalia [1992], Haiti [2004], and Libya [2011]) in which the preservation of United Nations Security Council credibility was considered a "national interest," justifying presidential authority to use military force absent congressional authorization. Subsequently, the evaluations of P-M-H described above are invoked to justify the following recommendation: "The credibility justification for the use of force should be removed from the constitutional law of presidential war powers. Incorporating credibility as one of the "national interests" that justify presidential use of force expands the President's war powers significantly without a legitimate policy justification."[51] This is a clear and concrete recommendation with potentially significant implications for legal justifications surrounding the president's war powers. Given the platform – the *Harvard Law Review* – Sitaraman's article is very likely to have at least reached (if not persuaded) those in a position to effect such change. Again, this recommendation is predicated entirely on the notion that "political scientists have demonstrated that in the context of military threats, credibility arguments are logically problematic and have little historical support."[52] The P-M-H consensus is taken as fact, and its implications are used to challenge existing legal justifications for the use of force.

1.4   Application of P-M-H Consensus Excludes Important Research on International Reputations

One of the more significant problems with the P-M-H consensus is the impression that less informed observers are likely to form based solely on descriptions by prominent IR scholars and journalists regarding research on reputations and the overwhelming consensus regarding its irrelevance to international (or US) credibility.

As discussed in the introduction (but worth summarizing here), the "emerging consensus" regarding reputations in international politics has been rather forcefully broadcast by many prominent scholars and journalists. Zakaria describes the political science research on credibility as "extensive" when criticizing the Obama administration's seeming

---

51 Ibid., 124.
52 Ibid., 136.

obsession with credibility in Syria.[53] Max Fisher cites Press to argue that "there's no historical evidence suggesting that backing down in a crisis ... reduces a country's future credibility."[54] Tang, as discussed above, claims that the evidence from Press has delivered "a devastating blow to the logic of the cult of reputation."[55] In his testimony before the House Committee on Homeland Security, Stephen Biddle referred to the results of "a generation of scholarship" suggesting that "statesmen often overestimate the degree to which reputation shapes others' behavior in future crises."[56] Matthews refers to a "severe lack of evidence" that credibility matters,[57] and Fettweis describes the "mountain of research from political science" confirming the irrelevance of reputations, and views credibility as an "illusion" because "credibility earned today does not lead to successes tomorrow and therefore is never worth fighting for."[58] Larison simply characterizes the obsession with reputations as a lot of "nonsense" and claims that Press's work "dismantle[s] the 'credibility' argument for intervention in Syria"; we are fixated on preserving credibility "that isn't in danger of being lost."[59] Larison goes even further, suggesting it would be wise to dismiss such claims as "just a pretext to cajole the administration into doing what Syria hawks have wanted to do all along."[60] Drezner finds the emphasis on credibility "odd" because the P-M-H research program confirms that "the trend in international relations scholarship has moved in the opposite direction."[61] If one works through the articles and blogs citing the P-M-H consensus, it would be difficult to arrive at any conclusion other than that the case is, rather definitively, closed.

THE MISSING SCHOLARSHIP

Compounding the problems detailed above regarding the applicability of P-M-H to the Syria crisis, those who cited P-M-H also excluded any references to relevant studies (available at the time) on reputations that

---

53 Zakaria 2013.
54 Fisher 2013a.
55 Tang 2005, 44.
56 Biddle 2013, 7.
57 Matthews 2013.
58 Fettweis 2014.
59 Larison 2013a. See also Larison 2013b.
60 Larison 2013c.
61 Drezner 2013a.

directly challenge their findings, including (but not limited to) Sartori, Guisinger and Smith, Lieberman, Harvey, Huth, Goldstein and Pevehouse, Danilovic, Downs and Jones, Crescenzi, Gibler, Walter, Tingley and Walter, Miller, Tomz, and Peterson.[62] A more thorough review of these contributions would have raised obvious concerns about whether the P-M-H consensus was sufficiently balanced and robust to serve as a solid basis for conclusions about reputations in general, or policy advice on Syria more specifically.

One obvious starting point would be Gibler's extensive overview of research on reputations and credibility. His review of relevant scholarship does not support the claims regarding a growing academic consensus on the irrelevance of reputation in international politics.[63] As Gibler notes,

> More sophisticated treatments of the reputation logic have been produced by formal theorists, both in economics and in political science. In economics, the ability of firm reputation to deter competition has been well analyzed … and political scientists have adopted these theories as tools in understanding the types of signals leaders can send … The sum argument of these statements and theoretical treatments is clear. Decision-makers argue and act, *at least in part*, based on reputations. Traditional deterrence theory suggests reputations should be pursued by leaders as important and manipulable tools, which are useful in future crises. Formal theorists agree; reputations provide valuable information when the costs of signaling are low.[64]

Gibler goes on to acknowledge that "these theoretical arguments often fail when tested empirically, generating, at best only *mixed support* for the proposition that reputations matter."[65] But "mixed support" is a far cry from the strong assertions by critics that reputations are irrelevant to an adversary's assessment of US credibility. Moreover, the empirical evidence Gibler cites when establishing "mixed" support relies

---

62   Sartori 2005; Guisinger and Smith 2002; Lieberman 1995a, 1995b; Harvey 1997, 1998, 1999, 2006, 2011; Huth 1997; Goldstein and Pevehouse 1997; Danilovic 2002; Downs and Jones 2002; Crescenzi 2007; Gibler 2008; Walter 2006; Tingley and Walter 2011; Miller 2012; Tomz 2012; Peterson 2013. See also Patrick Morgan's (1997) review of Jonathan Mercer, "Getting Respect Gets No Respect"; and Horst 2004.
63   Gibler 2008, 4.
64   Ibid.; emphasis added.
65   Ibid., 5, emphasis added.

heavily on the seven case studies by Mercer and Press. Gibler's own research, by contrast, directly challenges both Mercer and Press: "The results of this paper confirm that state reputations have an effect on state decisions to ally and initiate conflict ... Alliance reputations also matter in disputes. States with disreputable outside alliance partners are more likely to be targeted by rival states."[66] If reputations are worth fighting for in some cases, and can occasionally serve to control escalation in violence by reinforcing the credibility of military and diplomatic threats in regional rivalries,[67] or within the same protracted crisis over time,[68] then backing down could carry significant risks.

Sartori arrives at a similar conclusion in her research on deterrence, diplomacy, and honesty:

> Reputations for honesty play a key role in explaining the success of diplomacy. When a state has a reputation for honesty, it is better able to use diplomacy successfully to communicate that it is more resolved than an adversary previously had believed to be the case ... A state acquires a reputation for honesty when others observe it acting honestly. This happens when a state actually acts honestly, as well as when it bluffs and is *not* caught ... While traditional deterrence theory suggests that a state should fight or strengthen its military to increase its credibility, my work shows that there is another path: honest acquiescence, too, can increase a state's ability to use diplomacy in the future, by letting an opponent know that the state will threaten only when it really does intend to fight.[69]

In other words, bluffing, backing down, or retreating from a threat you have been explicitly defending as crucial to American and global security (e.g., Obama's red-line strategy vis-à-vis Syria in August–September 2013) is not particularly conducive to establishing an honest reputation and could damage credibility in future crises. Guisinger and Smith support Sartori's assertion that diplomatic honesty matters: "Diplomatic statements are believed only if a country's or leader's

---

66 Ibid., 22. Copeland (1997) makes a similar point in his review of the logical implications flowing from Mercer's findings. If states can get a reputation for being irresolute from allies, then there is an incentive to fight for credibility, in some cases, to avoid losing allies that might be required in future conflicts.

67 Huth and Russett 1988; Lieberman 1995a, 1995b.

68 Harvey 1998, 1999.

69 Sartori 2005, 13–14, emphasis added.

credibility is unmarred. Leaders keep their word so that they are believed in later crises."[70] The notion that backing down in Syria would
carry no serious consequences with respect to US credibility in this or
other cases – despite the diplomatic, domestic political, and military
resources already invested to enhance the credibility of the threat – is
not supported by this research.

In his critique of Mercer's research, Huth points to aggregate data
analysis that confirms the role of reputations in deterrence crises; past
actions are particularly relevant in regional contexts where defenders
and challengers engage in multiple interactions in the same geographi-
cal setting (e.g., enduring rivalries or protracted crises). Similarities in
relative capabilities, security threats, issues areas, and leadership establish the relevance of past actions, which explains why Huth found "a
consistent correlation between past defender retreats and subsequent
potential attacker challenges to deterrence."[71] In fact, even Mercer acknowledges Huth and Russett's[72] earlier empirical findings: "Past behavior and reputation are important only when the two combatants
have a continuing rivalry with prior confrontations ... A's past behavior
towards B, C, and D is irrelevant to E, which infers A's future behavior
only from A's past behavior toward E."[73] This distinction is basically
that between *specific* and *general* reputation (see chapter 2). Mercer apparently concedes that the former exists, but overlooks an important
logical possibility with respect to the latter: similarities *across* cases matter and could conceivably have an impact on the transferability of reputations within and across crises.

Consider the work by Danilovic[74] on extended immediate deterrence
between major powers. Calculating the credibility of a threat, she argues, begins with an assessment of the interests of the Defender – this
assessment establishes the parameters of the deterrence situation. If
the Defender has "inherent" or "intrinsic" (i.e., vital national) interests
in the region in question, it is more likely that the threat will be considered credible. This is an intuitive and logically plausible thesis, and
Danilovic finds strong empirical support for it. Importantly, however,

70 Guisinger and Smith 2002, 175.
71 Huth 1997, 94.
72 Huth and Russett 1984, 1988.
73 Mercer 1996, 22.
74 Danilovic 2002.

Danilovic also considers and tests for the influence of reputation – she,
like many others (as we outline in this book, see chapter 2), finds weak
support for the complete-interdependence-of-commitments position
(that reputation is all that matters and is perfectly transferable between
all crises no matter the important differences between them). Nonetheless, Danilovic *does* find support for the importance of reputation across
crises occurring in the same region; that is, she finds evidence that the
relevance of reputation is strong but qualified, and must be considered
in conjunction with interests (particularly inherent interests) as well as
capabilities. "In particular," she concludes, "a Challenger is more likely
to acquiesce to a Defender with a strong past record of honoring its
commitments in the same region."[75] Thus, while her initial thesis as to
the centrality of interests seems to place her in closer alignment with
P-M-H, her ultimate conclusion as to the multiple components of credibility (including qualified reputation) lends support to the arguments
and evidence we present in later chapters.

Evidence pointing to the transferability of reputations (across similar
cases), credibility, and diplomatic honesty appears in other scholarship
as well. For example, George W. Downs and Michael A. Jones address
the implications of reputation for cooperation and compliance with
international treaties, and provide a compelling explanation for why
the basic logic applies to both adversarial and cooperative scenarios.[76]
According to their evidence, states hold not one but many reputations
when it comes to compliance with treaty obligations, and the authors
draw on work outside of mainstream international relations theory to
explain differing compliance both within and across treaty regimes.

These findings are particularly insightful insofar as they directly
refute one of the key assumptions of P-M-H. Recall that Press's fundamental argument is that reputation doesn't matter. Implicit in this
argument is the notion that a state or leader cannot possibly possess a
single reputation that applies across different situations or be similarly
embraced by different adversaries. Downs and Jones also challenge
implicit assumptions about states possessing "a single reputation for
cooperation that characterizes its expected reliability in connection with
every agreement to which it is a party"[77] but, contra Press (who takes

---

75 Ibid., 158.
76 Downs and Jones 2002.
77 Ibid., 100.

this point to dismiss reputations altogether), the authors conclude that states possess multiple reputations depending on the circumstances, stakes, and/or putative partners (or adversaries) involved in a given situation. Thus, while the overall impact of reputation across different circumstances may be weak, the question of how reputations form is much more complicated and can, depending on similarities in context, adversaries, and issues, potentially be even stronger than has hitherto been appreciated. Their main argument is summarized as follows:

> The reputational consequences of a state's noncompliance with a given treaty are similarly limited by the history of its cooperative relationships with the other member states. While states have reason to revise their estimate of a state's reputation following a defection or pattern of defections, they have reason to do so only in connection with agreements that they believe (1) are affected by the same or similar sources of fluctuating compliance costs (or benefits) and (2) are valued the same or less by the defecting state. Over time, states develop a number of reputations, often quite different, in connection with different regimes and even with different treaties within the same regime.[78]

In other words, reputation is much narrower than conventionally conceived, yet, "at the same time ... reputational concerns are an important force for compliance in connection with certain agreements."[79] Similarities matter, and there is no logical reason to expect the same patterns would not apply to US adversaries assessing the credibility of coercive threats – they will look to the past and process their calculations on the basis of how proximate and similar past situations, events, experiences, and crises are to theirs.

Downs and Jones also show that iterated games, incomplete information, fluctuations in payoffs, treaty ambiguity, and other factors provide states with an incentive to let their reliability rates (reputations) vary, so the context of different commitments matters. Reputations for compliance are most relevant when the stakes and interests are high, but "reputational inferences" are conditional, localized, and segmented.[80] The authors go on to highlight the most relevant implication of this

---

78 Ibid., 97.
79 Ibid., 98.
80 Ibid., 109.

argument: "It follows that from the perspective of our model, the argument that a failure of NATO in an area like Kosovo or Macedonia will seriously erode NATO's credibility in connection with its commitments to Western Europe is wrong ... *The states that do have to worry about these sorts of commitment failures are smaller states that believe they are valued the same as the states that were abandoned.*"[81]

Reputations are relevant but conditional and often based on straightforward assessments of similarities across cases. As a hypothetical example, a small country (say, Togo) learns nothing by watching US–China trade negotiations, but it does pick up a few relevant clues by tracking US–Benin (or some other similarly sized nation's) negotiations. Similarly, China may learn very little about the US's deterrent efforts regarding Taiwan or Japan by watching the US response to Syria's chemical attacks, but Syrian and Russian officials are very likely to pick up many relevant clues from the US's deterrent interactions (and particularly the sequencing of US coercive airstrike threats) in similar crises with Milošević, Hussein, and Gaddafi over the last two decades. Similarly, withdrawal from Somalia did not cause states to infer that the US would abandon, for example, its commitment to South Korea, because a reputation for resolve in that sphere has been firmly established from previous commitments and deterrent threats. Syrian leaders are not expected to assign a single reputation to the US (and subsequently dismiss it) based on lessons learned from, say, the CMC, but instead look to US behavior in situations with circumstances similar to Syria's own – the country's leaders will look for the relevant reputation based on their impressions of similarities across cases like Vietnam, Somalia, Kosovo, and Iraq, in which a relatively weak state challenged the US. The "segmented" or "localized" reputation of the US in these types of situations suggests that reputations should not be defined in dichotomous terms as being either "present" or "absent." Reputation may not apply in the universal (completely interdependent and transferable) manner some might claim, but this recognition in no way confirms the P-M-H consensus that dismisses the importance of reputation altogether. As Downs and Jones point out, "to say that the power of reputation to enforce compliance is usually modest is no more a dismissal of reputation than the claim that many cooperative agreements are relatively shallow is

---

81 Ibid., 110–11, emphasis added.

a dismissal of cooperation. Reputation matters, just not so much as some might like."[82]

Mark Crescenzi, for his part, further shows that "states learn from the behavior of other nations, including the reputations states form through their actions in the international system."[83] "Using third-party states as proxies," Crescenzi observes, "states look for precedent and reputation in the extra-dyadic behavior of their dyadic partners. As opponents demonstrate hostility toward these proxy states across time, the likelihood of intra-dyadic conflict increases markedly."[84] Learning about US resolve and commitments from their behavior in other, similar crises is often the best way for adversaries to obtain relevant information about US interests, their willingness to use military force, and, more importantly, the costs they are willing to inflict on adversaries in retaliation for noncompliance. "Shortly after George W. Bush issued his ultimatum against Saddam Hussein's Iraqi regime," Crescenzi notes, "North Korea's Kim Jong II slipped into a rare level of seclusion. Daily reports of his activities disappeared from North Korea's official media."[85] The evidence suggests that reputations do matter and do travel – third-party states pick up signals from the behavior the US exhibits toward other states like them (or, as Downs and Jones put it, states they "believe ... are valued the same" by Washington).

Peterson's study of sanction threats provides additional support for the transferability of reputations across essentially similar interactions. The author found that targets of sanctions consistently looked to the sender's retaliatory actions in those prior cases in which other targets resisted: "When the sender has backed down recently, the target, inferring that the sender is prone to making empty threats, is less likely to acquiesce. Conversely, when the sender has recently imposed sanctions against a resistant target, the current target infers that sanction imposition is likely to follow resistance, and therefore, it is more likely to acquiesce."[86] The strong support for Peterson's findings was based on statistical analysis of US sanction policies over a thirty-year period, from 1971 to 2000.

---

82 Ibid., 113.
83 Crescenzi 2007, 382.
84 Ibid., 394.
85 Ibid., 382.
86 Peterson 2013, 672.

Similarly, Barbara Walter has shown that states actively and systematically build reputation in order to prevent future challenges from internal ethnic separatist movements. In studying when states were willing to accommodate ethnic minorities seeking self-rule and when they were not, Walter discovered that the presence of multiple potential *future* challenges from *other* minority groups in the same country precluded acquiescence, generating stiff and robust resistance from government forces. In other words, states were conscious of their reputation and sought to protect and reinforce it through displays of resolve in order to prevent future conflicts. Even more importantly, however, is that "this investment also appeared to pay off. *Governments that refused to accommodate one challenger were significantly less likely to face a challenge from a second or third group down the road.* It appears that governments use war not only to influence the behavior of one particular opponent, but other opponents as well."[87] These findings, as Walter points out, directly challenge the P-M-H consensus:

> The problem with these [P-M-H] studies is that they have examined the effects of reputation building across dissimilar contexts where different stakes were under dispute. Fighting to create a reputation for resolve might not have a significant effect when you look across different issue areas, geographic regions, or if you include a diverse set of players. But it does appear to have a strong effect when you look at similar players, fighting for similar stakes, against the same opponent over time.[88]

In her collaborative work with Dustin Tingley, Walter[89] further explored the importance of reputation by applying experimental techniques to examine the effects of repeated play on reputation building; this evidence is also directly relevant to exploring questions about the transferability of reputations across essentially similar cases: "Investments in reputation are likely to be made even in games that are repeated relatively few times. Uncommitted defenders will invest in reputation, and entrants will be influenced by reputation, even in games with only four iterations."[90] The implications of these insights are applied to

---

87 Walter 2006, 324, emphasis added.
88 Ibid., 325.
89 Tingley and Walter 2011.
90 Ibid., 361.

international relations, with obvious caveats about transferring lessons from experimental research to the world of foreign policy. According to the authors, the findings offer "strong empirical evidence that reputation building works":

> Studies by Mercer, Press, and by Snyder and Diesing have questioned the value of investing in a reputation for resolve; leaders who backed down in one crisis did not appear to suffer reputational costs for doing so. Our experiment suggests that backing down can have very negative effects if a game is expected to be repeated, and past behavior can be clearly observed. Indeed, backing down against the first entrant led to substantially lower earnings in subsequent periods ... Subjects clearly took into account how a defender behaved in the past and factored this into their decision about whether to challenge. If a defender had backed down, most entrants interpreted this to be a sign of weakness and most entrants chose to challenge more as a result. In this experiment, past behavior did matter, and investments in reputation building appeared to work.[91]

Finally, Michael Tomz offers some of the strongest evidence to date that history (past behavior) *does* matter and reputations *do* develop in international relations. In his award-winning examination of nearly three centuries of international finance, Tomz offers a "reputational theory" of debt repayment, which "offers new insight into relations between debtors [foreign governments] and [private] creditors."[92] For Tomz, traditional treatments of reputation in economics are limited insofar as they assume complete information, meaning an actor already knows the preferences of the party with which it is interacting. As a result, "there is no opportunity to develop beliefs – and therefore no opportunity to learn – about resolve, competence, and other attributes that could be relevant."[93] He goes on to develop a more sophisticated treatment in which "the reputation of an actor [is] the impression others hold about its preferences and abilities"; an impression that is formed, in part, by Bayesian updating in which behavior constitutes new "evidence" to either undermine or reinforce prior beliefs. In combination with context (specifically the economic environment at a given point

---

91 Ibid., 361–2, passim.
92 Tomz 2012, 4.
93 Ibid.

in time), a foreign government's decision to either service or default on debt serves as the basis for reputational inference and helps determine whether that government will receive access to more credit in the future and/or at what interest rate. As he concludes at the end of the book, his theory helps to

> explain how actors form beliefs and make decisions when information is imperfect and preferences can change. Participants in international relations update their beliefs, I argue, by studying behavior in context: they use data about past actions and – when available – external circumstances to learn about the disposition of a foreign government. The resulting beliefs summarize the government's reputation in foreign eyes and affect the course of international relations.[94]

Because governments are aware of the importance of their own reputation – and hence of the signals they send regarding their behavior – they have an incentive to follow through on repayment commitments (provided situational or environmental factors, such as economic crisis or domestic political shock, do not override this incentive and cause default to be preferred to long-term access to affordable credit). In this way, threats of retaliation and sanction in the form of high interest rates or lack of access to credit are rendered credible; reputation, Tomz argues, can help mitigate uncertainty and create continuity even under international anarchy.

While his theory relates specifically to international debt repayments, Tomz engages with the broader literature on reputations in IR, explicitly juxtaposing his own reputational theory against those of both Mercer and Press (which he labels "desire-based theory" and "current calculus theory," respectively). Importantly, he tests all three theories against his impressive collection of empirical evidence, concluding:

> The evidence ... not only supports my theory, but also casts doubt on alternative models of reputation in international relations. Contrary to [Mercer's] desire-based theory, investors make dispositional attributions even when the borrower behaves in desirable ways, and they take situational data (such as the Great Depression) into account when interpreting the behavior of foreign governments. Against [Press's] current calculus theory,

---

94 Ibid., 241.

investors regularly use past actions to predict future behavior. There is, therefore, a strong correlation between credit histories and access to capital, even after controlling for other indicators available to investors.[95]

Tomz's research is a valuable contribution to research supporting the relevance of reputations in IR – particularly the relationship between assumptions about "perfect information" and the probability of transferability of reputations and related information from past actions. In the absence of perfect information (a reasonable assumption in crisis situations), adversaries will look to past behavior to acquire what they believe is relevant information about US intentions, etc. P-M-H tend to assume perfect information about the various core elements of credibility (capabilities and interests), and are therefore more inclined to downplay/ignore the role of misperceptions and miscalculations. Our theory (outlined in the next chapter) accommodates these likely patterns. Relaxing assumptions about complete information is an important insight that applies to observations in this book and to problems with Press and Mercer, whose theories assume that adversaries can easily obtain information about interests and capabilities. US adversaries (like debtors and creditors) turn to reputations and lessons from past actions to decipher intentions and calculate the costs and benefits of specific actions. Reputations matter. There is no logical reason why the same patterns are not likely to play out in other contexts (something Tomz explicitly recognizes on pages 237–40 of his book), especially when the costs (military force) are likely to be viewed by adversaries as even more significant, or when the issues are immediately relevant to regime survival.

With respect to military confrontations, Lieberman's research[96] on credibility, reputations, and deterrence failure in the Arab-Israeli rivalry (1948–77) supports many of the points raised above, and reveals important policy lessons about reputation building in crises that are directly relevant to the Syria case. As Lieberman explains, "the phenomenon of deterrence, which is temporal, dynamic, and causal, has to be tested by a longitudinal research design and not by research designs that focus on 'snapshots' of single deterrence episodes."[97] When this approach is

---

95 Ibid., 35.
96 Lieberman 1995a, 1995b.
97 Lieberman 1995a, 2.

adopted, the evidence confirms that coercive diplomacy succeeds and fails over time and through stages, that resolve and reputations from previous interactions matter (as do capabilities and interests), and that all of this behavior is consistent with rational deterrence theory.

Lieberman's findings also challenge claims that Washington (or, in his case, Israel) cannot acquire a reputation from adversaries for being irresolute. In the absence of any response to an adversary's probes, defenders can (and often do) acquire a specific reputation for being irresolute that leads to an escalation in violence. Deterrence strategies, therefore, must be understood and evaluated through the prism of their long-term and cumulative impact over multiple exchanges. From this perspective, short-term deterrence failure (e.g., Syria's failure to comply with President Obama's red-line threat) is a necessary condition for deterrence success over time. Fighting for credibility occasionally makes sense, because "resolute defenders need to distinguish themselves from irresolute actors [by] maintaining control over the escalatory ladder of the conflict."[98]

Goldstein and Pevehouse point to similar patterns in crisis escalation. Their findings are particularly relevant to the Syria crisis and related debates over the wisdom of competing US foreign policy options: retreat, status quo (do nothing), or coercive military threats.[99] The empirical results from three distinct crisis periods during the Bosnia-Herzegovina conflict (1992–5) support the view that the international use of force induced Serbian cooperation. According to the authors, "robust NATO air strikes finally caused the Serb forces to cooperate with the Bosnian government."[100] Status quo strategies and reciprocity (cooperation through negotiation) often led Serb and Bosnian Serb leaders to embrace bullying tactics. Whenever the prerequisites for deterrence were met and a reputation for resolve established, credibility increased and the violence was contained (this case is discussed in greater detail in chapter 3).

These findings are supported by Harvey's work[101] on US deterrence encounters in Bosnia-Herzegovina (1993–5), Kosovo (1999), and Iraq (1991–2003), which again confirms that coercive threats succeed and

---

98 Ibid., 63.
99 Goldstein and Pevehouse 1997.
100 Ibid., 527.
101 Harvey 1998, 1999, 2006, 2009, 2011.

fail over time (and through stages) for reasons entirely consistent with
rational deterrence theory.[102] Harvey found – contrary to expectations
derived from P-M-H – that both general and specific reputations played
a significant role in Milošević's and Hussein's perceptions of US credibility. In each case, the absence of public and political support for
stronger military responses to an emerging threat, compounded by a
general reputation for casualty aversion, undermined the credibility of
the US deterrent threat in the early stages of the crisis. Initial support
for a stronger show of force was missing, primarily because of insufficient evidence that the crisis was serious enough to warrant the risks
to American troops. Consequently, weak US deterrent threats (consistent with President Obama's initial red-line warning to Syrian officials)
emerged as the only reasonable options available at the time (these
cases are discussed in more detail in chapter 3).

Space constraints preclude a more detailed review of the extant scholarship on reputations in international politics, but it is important to note
that many of these findings are supported by other work.[103] Put simply,
research on the importance of reputation in international politics is far
from settled. In a recent issue of the *Annual Review of Political Science*, for
example, Dafoe, Renshon, and Huth detail the extensive and ongoing
work being done on the subject (the above overview is focused primarily on the "strategic" literature on reputation; Dafoe, Renshon, and Huth
additionally summarize psychological and cognitive approaches while
offering definitional treatments of reputation, status, credibility, etc.).
As they summarize: "A large body of contemporary work – spanning
constructivist, realist, and rationalist approaches, formal and informal
theory, statistical and qualitative evidence, experimental (field, survey,
and laboratory) and observational designs – continues to investigate
reputation and status."[104] The central point to be extracted is that the
P-M-H consensus does not appear to be as definitive as its proponents
have been claiming and, by implication, policy advice on cases such as
Syria should more accurately reflect the state of the field. The policy
implications of the extant research are not as straightforward as many
have assumed, and a more balanced review of the literature and evidence on reputations in international politics is required.

---

102 See Harvey and Wilner 2012; Harvey 2011; Harvey and James 2009; Harvey 2006,
     1999, and 1998.
103 For example, Orme 1992; Shimshoni 1988.
104 Dafoe, Renshon, and Huth 2014, 372.

Conclusion

By invoking the "empirical evidence" and "academic consensus" they claim is represented by Press, Mercer, and Hopf, academics, bloggers, and journalists transform their own biases into something that appears to be objective, social scientific, and fact-based analysis. Ironically, this undermines the relevance (and credibility) of scholarly research on reputations and credibility in international relations. Perhaps the P-M-H (anti-reputation) thesis has gained such prominent status because of the ease with which its straightforward conclusions (reputations are irrelevant and P-M-H have provided "overwhelming" evidence to prove it) can be invoked to challenge any intervention on the basis of the non-transferability of credibility or reputations: fighting for credibility, or for any reason other than core national security objectives, can be easily portrayed as a serious mistake. How many of those reading these criticisms will take the time to do the kind of literature review included here? Obviously a balanced overview of the research on credibility, reputations, and coercive diplomacy in international relations is not conducive to being outlined in a brief op-ed or blog post. This is what makes the anti-reputation thesis so appealing – not necessarily its quality as a social scientific theory, but the simplicity with which the thesis, or its counterpart (i.e., reputations are everything), can be presented and sold through a selective discussion of social science research. One need not even agree or disagree with Zakaria's or Walt's political position to object to this approach to connecting theory to policy, a point to be discussed in more detail in chapter 8.

As we have detailed in this chapter, several clear problems exist with P-M-H, and no clear consensus has been reached with respect to the relevance of reputation in international crises. Despite the confidence placed on Press, Mercer, and Hopf that they have provided the final word on (or the definitive test of) reputations, or the only generalizable findings required to establish closure on these important questions (considering even the cursory literature review above), it is quite clear that we all share an obligation to expand both the *number* and *type* of case studies when testing theories about credibility, particularly when these theories are repeatedly used today to provide policy recommendations for how to handle crises like Syria and Ukraine.

The next chapter will focus on providing a fairer representation of the alternative theory of coercive diplomacy that connects interests, power, and reputations to explain behavior in US deterrence encounters from

1991 to 2013. Put another way, we will correctly specify the "null theory" (from the P-M-H point of view) that would need to be discounted if the conclusions from P-M-H were to be considered correct, before moving, in the subsequent chapter, to an evaluation of that theory against recent evidence from US asymmetric crises.

Chapter Two

Reputations Matter: Rational Deterrence Theory and Credibility Reconsidered

The previous chapter cautioned against drawing definitive conclusions about reputations that rely too heavily on the theories and case studies compiled by P-M-H. Although their research is certainly valuable and worthy of serious engagement, it is not sufficient to establish closure on this important subject. There is considerable scholarship that provides powerful contradictory evidence that reputations do form and regularly affect the outcomes of international crises.

This chapter outlines an alternative theory of credibility that stipulates the conditions under which reputations matter in the crisis deliberations of US adversaries, and why adversaries often rely on past actions when assessing US resolve. Where appropriate, we use critiques of P-M-H to clarify our arguments, juxtaposing the logic of our theory against the P-M-H consensus. As we will show, many of the critiques of P-M-H discussed in the previous chapter (e.g., the "misspecification" of rational deterrence theory; failure to consider past actions vis-à-vis "interests"; the importance of similarities across cases) are addressed by the theory outlined in this chapter. The theory's validity is reinforced by the case studies discussed in more detail in chapters 3–7.

There are at least six theoretical innovations (and clarifications) underpinning rational deterrence theory (RDT)[1] that directly challenge the

---

1 It should be noted that we do not explicitly differentiate between "deterrence" and "compellence" in this chapter. This distinction is discussed in the literature, with an early influential treatment offered by Schelling (1966). Nonetheless, the two categories of coercive diplomacy are virtually identical in terms of core prerequisites, though some theorists have argued that compellence is "harder" to achieve (for example, because of "loss aversion"; see Levy 1997). Yet the question of whether one or the

P-M-H consensus: RDT (1) *combines* communication, interests, capabilities, *and* resolve (reputations; past actions) in calculations of credibility; (2) assumes adversaries have imperfect information about US interests, capabilities, and resolve; (3) allows for the possibility of transferability of reputations across "similar" cases; (4) acknowledges the possibility of misperceptions and miscalculations on the part of US adversaries; (5) recognizes the mutually reinforcing impact of general and specific reputations; and (6) embraces the logical implications of reputations being "in the eye of the beholder." When combined, these theoretical innovations provide a much stronger account than P-M-H as to how adversaries calculated US credibility and their subsequent behavior in deterrence encounters from 1991 to 2013.

2.1   Four Core Prerequisites of Credible Coercive Threats

Contrary to the P-M-H consensus that credibility is a function of only *two* core variables – power and interests – rational deterrence theorists have shown that the credibility of a coercive threat, measured in terms of its ultimate success or failure, is a function of a defender's capacity to satisfy *four* core prerequisites.[2] Specifically, the standard, defender-oriented model of rational deterrence stipulates that a coercive retaliatory threat will be viewed by the adversary as credible if the defender: (1) clearly defines the behavior deemed to be unacceptable (*communication*); (2) conveys a commitment to protect these *interests*; (3) possesses the *capability* to defend these commitments; and (4) demonstrates (in the current crisis and/or in similar past crises) the *resolve* or willingness to deny the objectives sought (deterrence by denial) or to

---

other is more or less difficult has no bearing on the validity of the rational theory underpinning our take on coercive diplomacy; it simply means that leaders need to try that much more to satisfy the main elements of credibility when trying to compel opponents. Our point is that these higher standards were still met in Syria, for reasons we outline in this book (see chapters 4–7). An additional problem is differentiating between the two types of coercion in practice, as almost any encounter has elements of *both* deterrence and compellence (see chapter 3, n. 1). In sum, the distinction is not particularly relevant or necessary for testing the prerequisites for successful coercion, challenging conventional wisdom, or establishing the broader case for reputations in international politics.

2 See Harvey 1999 and 1998.

impose significant costs on adversaries who fail to comply (deterrence by punishment).[3] Huth makes the same basic argument regarding the logic underpinning rational deterrence: the theory stipulates that "the credibility of threats should be high when: a) the defender possesses the military capabilities to impose substantial costs and deny victory to the potential attacker; and b) the potential attacker believes that the defender will use his available military forces in a retaliatory strike."[4] That is, a state must have the capability to follow through on a threat, and the adversary must *believe* that it will do so and that the consequences would be unacceptable, all things considered. This version of deterrence theory also incorporates *capabilities, interests,* and *reputations.* It is the combination of these prerequisites that is expected to affect an adversary's perception of a defender's credibility, and accounts for the successes and failures of US deterrent threats in crises over the past two decades. If these prerequisites are satisfied, the expected net costs to the challenger should be greater than the expected net gains from non-compliance, and deterrence should work. The theory predicts failure if one or more of these conditions is absent. The relevant connection to reputations and past actions is found in the fourth prerequisite, resolve.

Measuring resolve is an inherently difficult process. A common error in the coding process is treating a challenge-response sequence (in which the defender follows through on a retaliatory threat following a challenge) as a definitive case of deterrence failure, thereby ending the search for case evidence. In fact, deterrence successes are often achieved as a result of short-term failures; probes from a challenger provide an opportunity for defending states to clearly demonstrate resolve (along with capability), leading to deterrence success in the long term.[5] Evaluating deterrence in the context of protracted crises (and not as a one-off phenomenon), therefore, provides a more accurate way to test core hypotheses regarding deterrence prerequisites, and helps underscore the relevance of reputation for resolve that is otherwise lost in more simplified "single-play" assessments.[6]

Resolve can be demonstrated through *costly signals* – that is, "any action, statement, or condition that increases the political, economic,

---

3 Harvey 1998, 1999, 2011.

4 Huth 1997, 74.

5 Lieberman 1995a.

6 For more on the sequential failure of deterrence over time and through stages, see George and Smoke 1974. An emphasis on the sequential nature of war more generally

or military costs assigned to the status quo, while lowering the costs of responding to a challenger's probes."[7] Specific actions (such as deployment of air, sea, or ground forces, or the evacuation of peacekeepers) or statements (public announcements of impending retaliation; explicit ultimatums and/or deadlines; public displays of unity among coalition members in support of a response or threat) help demonstrate and communicate commitment and resolve in the face of a potential challenge.[8]

In addition, however, adversaries are likely to look to previous stages of a protracted crisis for information as to how the interaction of these signals has played out in the past. Have signals translated into action following challenges/probes before? In other words, there is a dynamic interplay between signals (threats, commitments) and reputations (past behavior), which together help establish resolve and, ultimately (and in conjunction with capabilities and interests), credibility. This interplay is most prevalent in protracted crises (where lessons about past behavior are obviously and more immediately relevant), but can also have an impact on broader deterrence outcomes across separate cases. While the *specific* reputation of a defender is crisis-based and situational, a *general* reputation can also be established that is dispositional and behavioral, and therefore more broadly applicable from one distinct crisis to the next (the crucial distinction between specific and general reputation is discussed in greater detail below). There is no logical reason why adversaries would rely entirely on a single dimension of resolve when assessing credibility.

(and one that supports the conceptualization of the "protracted crisis" approach presented here) was articulated by Carl von Clausewitz in his seminal work *On War*. In a section entitled "War Does Not Consist of a Single Short Blow," he wrote: "If war consisted of one decisive act, or a set of simultaneous decisions, preparations would tend toward totality, for no omission could ever be rectified ... But if the decision in war consists of several successive acts, then each of them, seen in context, will provide a gauge for those that follow." See Von Clausewitz 2008, 18.

7   Harvey 1998, 676.
8   In this regard, we consider both "tying hands" and "sunk costs" as costly signals (see Fearon 1997). While each operates according to a slightly different logic, for practical purposes, "there are few examples of [a] pure case" of each; as Fearon (1997, 70) explains: "Building arms or mobilizing troops entails costs no matter what the outcome, but they also may affect the state's expected value for fighting versus acquiescing in a challenge (which may have something like a tying-hands effect)." Both types, therefore, ultimately help to signal resolve.

Despite their weaknesses, many US adversaries have come to believe that they have significant counter-coercion leverage; they assume, by raising US or coalition casualty numbers, they can pressure democratic governments to back off, and these expectations are largely informed by previous crises in which Western leaders did exactly that. Moreover, this assessment occurs *despite* the recognition that they are facing an unfavorable power balance. As James Wirtz explains:

> Although the leaders in weak states understand their inferior position, they believe that because of a variety of more pressing political and stra- tegic reasons, the strong will not be able to bring their full power to bear to interfere with the weak's initiatives ... They often seem to believe that international and domestic political constraints will prevent Great Powers from intervening effectively in limited wars or responding forcefully to provocations.[9]

Adversaries rationally expect and act upon the patterns they witness, because most reasonable opponents will come to believe that ignoring history is likely to carry enormous risks – states have no logical reason to ignore potentially valuable information (intelligence) about US re- solve based on past actions in similar cases. Nonetheless, this informa- tion is not definitive; that is to say, it works in conjunction with, and in- deed helps to inform, case-specific assessments of power and interests.

As Harvey explains, there is no logical reason to assign equal ex- planatory weights to the four prerequisites, which is why unpacking the main elements of communication, capabilities, commitment, and re- solve "facilitates more precise evaluations of the relevance and relative importance of these conditions as they change and interact in different contexts."[10] By implication, the four-variable model offers a better as- sessment of the very same factors (power and interests) stressed by the P-M-H consensus. Moreover, it provides clear and explicit theoretical justification for the inclusion of past actions and reputations as compo- nents of credibility. In contrast to the P-M-H perception that RDT posits reputation as being the definitive causal variable (the most extreme ex- ample of this is Press's Past Actions theory, which he predictably goes

---

9 Wirtz 2012, 16.
10 Harvey 2006, 142.

on to refute), our version of RDT recognizes that reputations are only part of the puzzle – potentially of greater or lesser importance depending on the specific circumstances of the coercive encounter in question. Any researcher who assumes that deterrence theorists are preoccupied only with resolve or reputations is simply wrong – credibility has never been exclusively about reputations alone.

Harvey's re-analysis[11] of the evidence compiled across multiple deterrence data sets[12] supports the view that the interrelationships among the core prerequisites for successful coercion are far more complex than Mercer and Press acknowledge.[13] By extension, the suggestion that reputations for resolve are *never* relevant, because states *never* acquire a reputation for being irresolute, is not supported by the evidence. An adversary's assessment of resolve is often derived from past actions in previous crises – for example, in enduring rivalries[14] or within a protracted crisis over time[15] – and these assessments are fundamentally linked to credibility and deterrence success. By combining interests, capabilities, *and* resolve (i.e., lessons learned about general and specific reputations that adversaries acquire from previous cases and past actions), RDT offers a more accurate account of how reputations are connected to credibility, and a stronger explanation for the success and failure of coercive diplomacy in several recent asymmetric conflicts involving the US from 1991 to 2013.

RDT and Necessity and Sufficiency

This robust, four-condition version of RDT introduces additional complexities with respect to theory testing that P-M-H overlook. Deterrence models that conceptualize credibility in terms of only two variables aren't so much *wrong* as they are incomplete.

---

11 Harvey 1998, 1999.
12 This includes Huth and Russett 1984, 1988; Lebow 1981; and Lebow and Stein 1989, 1990.
13 For standard references on the logical foundations of deterrence theory that helped shape the field of coercive diplomacy, see Zagare 1990 and 2004; and Zagare and Kilgour 2000. For excellent treatments of the conceptual foundations of deterrence, see Morgan 1983 and 2003; and Paul, Morgan, and Wirtz 2009.
14 Lieberman 1995a, 1995b.
15 Harvey 1998, 1999.

First, the four-condition version of RDT generates thirty-two possible case study profiles (or "response sets") that would be relevant for testing the theory against expected outcomes.[16] That is, there are thirty-two different possible combinations of the various prerequisites that constitute possible "recipes" with respect to different deterrence encounters. Second, there are important interaction effects among the four (rather than only two) core prerequisites.

As a result, there are many logical, theoretical, and empirical errors critics can make when examining what they assume is all relevant data for rejecting deterrence theory. Press's test of Past Actions theory, for example, stipulates that reputations *alone* determine deterrence success/failure. This means that to properly test for PA theory, one must look for *confirming* evidence corresponding to response sets in which the presence of a reputation for resolve leads to success. Because the model includes four conditions, however, this outcome is possible under *multiple* scenarios and in various combinations (the presence of resolve but absence of the other three prerequisites, the presence of resolve and capabilities but absence of communication and commitment, etc.). This supporting evidence would then have to be balanced (weighed) against *disconfirming* evidence corresponding to all response sets in which the presence of a reputation for resolve led to deterrence failure (which again includes multiple possible combinations of the other prerequisites) and, finally, combined with the evidence across all response sets in which the absence of a reputation for resolve led to deterrence success. The evidence would then have to be assessed in relation to various necessary- and sufficient-condition hypotheses[17] in order to accurately test the underlying logic of the theory. Press's study, by contrast, examines only a few select cases that represent but a small fraction of the evidence required to test any of the theories he claims to be testing in his book.

Similarly, by focusing exclusively on the somewhat watered-down version of the two-variable model of deterrence – interests and capabilities – P-M-H assume that the only response sets worthy of consideration are those in which "interests" and "power" favor the defender and lead to success, and cases in which "interests" and "power" favor the adversary and lead to failure. Again, the evidentiary requirements for

---

16 See, for example, Harvey 1998.
17 See Harvey 1998.

testing a four-variable version of RDT are considerably more complex, because there are so many theoretically relevant combinations of cases and corresponding hypotheses that should be tested before making any definitive conclusions about reputations. Given all of this, a total of only seven cases combined across two studies by Press and Mercer is not sufficient to establish closure on this important subject.

Finally, consider some of the important findings from Harvey's 1999 study, in which the four-condition version of RDT is processed through existing deterrence data sets and related hypotheses:

Capability ... affects both resolve and communication. The capacity to demonstrate resolve is usually enhanced when leaders of the defending state have access to (and control over) a large, easily mobilized military force.

Effective and timely communication often depends on the quality of political, diplomatic, and bureaucratic capabilities.

Communication and commitment are also related. Defenders are more likely to mount a serious diplomatic effort to define the unacceptable behavior and communicate intentions to challengers when the balance of interests, which tend to drive commitments, favors the defender.

Resolve may be less important during situations in which the defender's capabilities are so overwhelming, and the costs of retaliation so low, that the deterrent threat remains credible even if resolve is questioned ...

The lower the costs of retaliation to the defender, the more resolute the defender is likely to be perceived, and the more credible the defender's threat.

The absence of certain prerequisites is more or less likely to provoke a challenge depending on the status of other variables in the model. According to Lebow's data, for example, the absence of resolve is more likely to provoke a challenge when defenders clearly communicate a threat of retaliation. That combination is particularly susceptible to failure for two reasons: the probability of a successful challenge increases when defenders are not resolute, and challengers are likely to gain more by successfully challenging in these situations than they would if the defender made no public pronouncements or was never fully committed to the issue or protégé in the first place. The victory, in other words, would not be as sweet.

Military mobilization is more likely to be perceived by the challenger as a bluff when the issue is unimportant to the defender or political, military, and economic ties between defender and protégé are insignificant. These types of failures occur even when a defender's capabilities, on balance, outweigh those of the challenger. In this context, challengers may gain more by provoking a strong, resolute defender who is not entirely committed to the cause.[18]

High levels of capabilities, in other words, can actually provoke a challenge – more is not necessarily better.[19] The presence and absence of core prerequisites in different combinations and degrees explains the success and failure of coercive diplomacy, and all of these results are logically consistent with expectations derived from a standard, rationalist model of deterrence theory, one that is significantly more complex than the version that is dismissed by P-M-H.[20]

Reassessing Fearon

Another benefit of applying necessary- and sufficient-condition logic to tests of rational deterrence theory is that it raises some interesting questions about James Fearon's widely cited reassessment of deterrence and bargaining. According to Fearon, "Conventional wisdom holds that in international disputes, a state's military threats are more likely to work the more the state is favored by the balance of power *or* the balance of interests."[21] Fearon goes on to state that "mainstream rationalist theories characterize international crises as contests decided by *a* critical factor – the side with more military capabilities, more resolve, *or* stronger intrinsic interests is predicted to prevail."[22] The clear implication is that we can test each prerequisite independently, and that conclusions about success and failure tied to these independent tests reveal important and unanticipated logical flaws with the theory and its expectations: "The core idea is that (1) having more of the relevant critical factor (capabilities, resolve, etc.) allows a state to make a more credible threat to escalate a crisis to military conflict, and that (2) the side not favored by the

---

18 Harvey 1999, 857–61 passim.
19 Zagare and Kilgour (2000), for example, offer formal proof that mutually increased capability might actually provoke a challenge, as high costs diminish mutual credibility.
20 The relationship between context and causation has been neglected in the literature on coercive diplomacy, with the following exceptions: Lieberman 1994; Fearon 1994; Mercer 1996; Schaub 1996; Goertz 1995; and Braumoeller 2003.
21 Fearon 1994, 236, emphasis added.
22 Ibid., 244, emphasis added.

balance of the critical factor will realize its disadvantage and so is more likely to back down."[23]

As the preceding discussion makes clear, however, Fearon's interpretation of deterrence is *not* entirely consistent with the underlying theoretical tenets of RDT (though it does bear a strong resemblance to the claims of P-M-H). Again, RDT actually stipulates a variety of different necessary and sufficient conditions that are all relevant to testing, and most of these variations *combine* interests and capabilities, along with other prerequisites, to explain success and failure – we are not dealing, in other words, with an either/or proposition.

The specific hypotheses Fearon is testing are derived from assumptions about *independent* necessity or *independent* sufficiency, but this approach overlooks dozens of other relevant hypotheses suitable for adequately testing RDT. The more robust version of RDT stipulates that it is typically the side with relatively more capabilities *combined with* a perceived willingness to use them (resolve; reputations) *and* stronger interests/commitments that will prevail. The absence of one or more of these factors will likely lead to failure.

Moreover, stronger tests of RDT should not only consider multiple hypotheses derived from the general theory, but should also include both confirming and disconfirming cases in which factors are present and/or absent in different combinations. Some of Fearon's findings may very well reveal evidence to confirm/disconfirm some core hypotheses, but it is not clear that these cases are sufficient in and of themselves to reveal significant logical flaws in the theory. Instead, the flaws may be a product of testing a model that isolates only a few key prerequisites, treats them as "independently" necessary or sufficient, and compares their impact against general and immediate deterrence successes and failures. As with other critiques of deterrence, Fearon's approach represents only a partial test of a far more complex bargaining theory.[24] For example, the ratio of the defender's capabilities is not expected to be relevant unless it is combined with interests – this is why probes are common, as adversaries attempt to develop ex post assessments of resolve; interests, similarly, are important but are less likely to lead to immediate deterrence success if no capabilities are deployed as a costly signal; and, finally, credibility is often tied to existing commitments and

23 Ibid.
24 Harvey 1999.

evidence of some willingness on the part of the defender to fight for similar interests in the past, as discussed above.

Another key problem with Fearon's interpretation as it relates to the importance of reputations and past behavior (in conjunction with the other prerequisites) has to do with his treatment of the perceptions and beliefs of the challenger. As he observes:

> Rational challengers will select themselves into a crisis according to their beliefs about the defender's preference for war versus concessions, and will do so in a manner that influences the probability of immediate deterrence success. When the defender is initially expected to prefer war to backing down, only highly motivated, hard-to-deter challengers will choose to threaten in the first place. When the defender is initially expected to probably prefer concessions to war, then the incentive for "opportunistic," probing challenges is increased; in this set of cases, the challengers will tend on average to have low values for conflict and so will be relatively easily dissuaded by an immediate deterrent threat.[25]

Yet establishing an adversary's perception of the defender's preferences is not as straightforward as Fearon implies – adversaries rarely have sufficient knowledge of a defender's capabilities, commitments, or resolve to "rationally" select themselves into or out of a crisis, regardless of whether we are dealing with general or immediate deterrence. This is why probes often occur even when ex ante information indicates strong "interest" – capabilities may be low, and adversaries never know if these interests (including commitments to allies) are always and forever strong enough to elicit a significant response. It is the response of the defender to these probes that reinforces (or diminishes) credibility and leads to deterrence success or failure.

In other words, and contrary to Fearon, it is not the challenger's sudden realization that it has inferior capabilities that generates the immediate deterrence success; it is the defender's demonstrated willingness to use the capabilities the challenger already knew the defender had but assumed it would not use. We agree with Fearon – challengers who select themselves into a crisis where the defender has fought in the past are highly motivated, and immediate deterrence failure might be predicted. However, deterrence failure is *more* predictable when there is no

---

25 Fearon 1994, 245–6.

response from the defender to the initial probe; failure may have less to do with stronger motivation on the part of the challenger than with their (mis)perceptions of the defender's motivation – the causal mechanism linking actions to failure is very different. Deterrence can still be achieved in this scenario if the defender clarifies its commitments through reinforced threats and costly signals. Again, the key consideration for understanding the conditions of deterrence success and failure is the interplay between *all* four prerequisites of RDT in the context of protracted crises (see chapter 3).

2.2   Reputations and Imperfect Information

One of the more significant problems with the P-M-H consensus is that, despite the general agreement that power and interests are essential to calculations of credibility, none of the authors explain *how* adversaries actually go about measuring their opponents' interests and capabilities, or how these specific elements of credibility can be calculated without any reference whatsoever to an opponent's past actions or reputations. With respect to Press's approach to measuring power, for example, he simply notes that military capabilities can be measured in a variety of ways, most often combining tangible (size of forces, weapons technologies, size of economy, etc.) with intangible qualities (morale of soldiers, quality of leadership, and "the society's willingness to suffer casualties in pursuit of national objectives").[26] Press notes that scholars often create composite scores on the basis of these factors, but decides for his own part to adopt a "third" approach:

> I argue that decision makers are not interested in abstract measures of national power; when they confront threats during real crises they ask themselves: Can the adversary do what he threatens to do and achieve his objectives at a reasonable cost? To answer this question, they evaluate the specific instruments of military and economic power that will determine whether the threats can be carried out successfully, and at what cost.[27]

Yet there is no clear indication of the process through which adversaries actually measure or interpret these components of power when

---

26 Press 2005, 24.
27 Ibid.

calculating their opponent's credibility. Surely it is not simply the mere existence of specific instruments of military and economic power that accounts for an adversary's perceptions; what matters is the adversaries' assessment of the defender's *willingness* to use these tools in light of comparative interests, commitments, risks, and costs. These estimates, moreover, are never straightforward – states send mixed signals, engage in deception, don't have the facilities or resources to acquire complete information about an opponent's capabilities and commitments, or are plagued by organizational constraints that preclude getting sound advice or intelligence from acolytes who fear retribution if they challenge their authoritarian bosses.[28] For smaller states engaged in asymmetric confrontations with the US, therefore, past actions play an important role in assessing US capabilities and the resolve (or willingness) to use them.

The same limitations apply to measuring adversaries' interests. Press begins by noting that in any crisis, "the antagonists may have innumerable interests at stake."[29] These range from material interests, such as resources or territory, to non-material stakes with cultural and ideational value (e.g., Jerusalem for Jews, Muslims, and Christians). He then explains: "Current Calculus theory accommodates all these components of interests – material and nonmaterial – and what it tells us is simple: leaders assess the credibility of threats by comparing the expected costs of carrying out those threats (based on power) against the interests at stake (an amalgam of all the factors listed above)."[30] For the purposes of theory testing, Press simplifies the concept of "interests" by dividing them into three broad categories:

In the simplest terms countries have "vital interests," "important interests," and "concerns." Vital interests are those related to a state's survival.

---

28 Harvey 2011. Critics might protest leaders' discounting intelligence assessments of interests and capabilities in favor of personal opinions gleaned from interpretations of past actions as hardly a rational application of reputations for the purposes of calculating credibility. This objection misses the point. Decision-makers occasionally make serious *errors* by relying on experiences from prior similar crises (in addition to Hussein in 2003, Slobodan Milošević incorrectly assessed US resolve in the 1998–9 Kosovo campaign based on US behavior in Bosnia), but whether or not assessments are accurate or inaccurate does not obviate the fact that past actions *were* used to make assessments about US intentions/resolve.

29 Press 2005, 25.

30 Ibid.

Important interests is a broad category; it encompasses crises over stakes with real material value that do not significantly threaten the state's survival. Concerns, on the other hand, relate to a state's values and ideals but do not involve significant material stakes.[31]

The entire discussion is framed as a set of guidelines on how *scholars* should think about collecting relevant information, long after these crises, to operationalize the interest categories for each case. Again, this says very little about how *adversaries* might actually piece together relevant information, for example, about US interests during the crisis, or how and why they are likely to accept or dismiss US credibility once these calculations are finalized. Press seems to assume that relative power and interests in any given case are rationally self-evident to both scholars and adversaries; presumably they have access to any information they need to perform the utility-maximizing cost-benefit calculations required to effectively manage the crisis and, therefore, don't need information from past actions, even when facing similar opponents over the same types of security threats.

Leaving aside questions about how different permutations and combinations of vital and important interests are logically connected to perceptions of credibility and subsequent behavior, the more serious problem with this approach is that any outcome can be explained ex post facto with reference to prevailing interests – for instance, "less" US interest in the Syria WMD crisis throughout 2012 (as demonstrated by Washington's failure to respond to several Syrian chemical attacks despite the red-line threat), and "more" US interest in 2013 after the Ghouta attacks, hence Assad's capitulation. But this raises serious concerns about falsifiability: any outcome can be explained after the fact with references to shifting interests. Press explicitly acknowledges this problem:

> Although the theory is straightforward, testing it is far from simple. With so many elements contributing to the concept of interests, falsification is impossible because virtually any result could be rationalized with an ad hoc weighting of the factors that contribute to interests. While the logic of Current Calculus theory suggests that leaders should consider the nuances of the situation – and all the components of [material and non-material]

---

31 Ibid., 25–6.

interests described above – when they calculate the interests at stake, testing the theory requires creating a simple framework for measuring interests in a consistent way.[32]

Logically, if interests are self-evident and easily categorized, we would not expect many crises to escalate out of control – both sides would (presumably) be able to produce a reasonably accurate prediction of actions and reactions based on a rational assessment of the balance of interests and power. But crises do happen and frequently escalate, often because it is very difficult for adversaries to decipher comparative interests and commitments. Understanding the mechanisms through which adversaries assess interests, commitments, and resolve accounts for why reputations and past actions are relevant in many cases.

Obviously an adversary's perceptions of US power and interest are important, but it is equally obvious that no regime can possess perfect information about these important factors. As Tomz[33] convincingly demonstrates through his extensive research on reputations and cooperation in the financial realm, if the assumption of perfect information is relaxed, then reputations and related lessons learned from past cases become more relevant. Of course, core national interests that are connected to securing the state from direct military attacks against its citizenry typically come with very credible retaliatory threats, but the larger set of security interests and priorities that most states attempt to balance are less clear-cut and often prone to changes, adjustments, and intentional deceptions (something that is particularly true for a global power such as the United States, a dynamic discussed in greater detail below). This is why past behavior (e.g., whether an opponent has a record of keeping or breaking commitments in similar circumstances) is an important mechanism through which adversaries overcome the problem of uncertainty and imperfect information in international relations. By logical extension, attempting to reinforce credibility by demonstrating resolve or by keeping commitments (rather than repeatedly bluffing) can serve to enhance the credibility of coercive threats across similar cases (transferability); conversely, weaknesses demonstrated in other cases are often interpreted by US adversaries (correctly or mistakenly) as indicating a lack of resolve.

---

32 Ibid., 25.
33 Tomz 2012.

If this is a reasonable account of how US interests evolve and change, and if adversaries have imperfect information about US interests and related commitments to impose significant costs, then we could reasonably expect states to look for as many relevant signals and pieces of intelligence as possible when assessing US credibility and the potency of Washington's commitments, often by testing US resolve, probing for weaknesses, and by looking for information from previous interactions during similar crises. There are no obvious political, psychological, or military-strategic reasons why adversaries would be disinclined to rely on past US behavior in similar crises or circumstances, precisely because this information is directly relevant to an adversary's assessment of US interests and Washington's willingness to deploy forces.

There is an added challenge adversaries face when judging the credibility of US threats that reinforces the relevance of past behavior – the *depth* and *breadth* (reach) of US power. Given its place in the international system, US security interests are not as narrowly defined as those of smaller states concerned primarily with survival or territorial integrity. As Danilovic points out, "unlike other states … major powers' security concerns are much more expansive, reaching beyond their borders and immediate surroundings."[34] In almost every confrontation, the US has a clear preponderance of military power. Imputing what Washington *can* do does very little to mitigate ambiguity about what US leaders *will* (or *might*) do. Reliance on information obtained from past actions (reputations) thus serves as a helpful heuristic device, supplying information about variables (particularly "interests") that cannot be easily measured.[35] Logically, of course, reputation continues to perform this function even in situations in which "interests" and "power" are more evident, because interests are not static and a willingness to deploy force is never consistently high or low – circumstances change and these variations matter. As such, the importance of reputations is best viewed along a continuum and in gradation rather than through the prism of their presence or absence, or as completely relevant or entirely irrelevant.

---

34 Danilovic 2002, 164.
35 Weisiger and Yarhi-Milo (2015) make a similar point when they argue that reputational considerations are likely already "folded into" perceptions of an adversary's interests; explicit reference to past behavior is not the *only* way reputation can be relevant, it may also inform basic perceptions about willingness to use force, etc.

One final point about interests and the difficulty adversaries face when assessing *what* they are and how *strong* they might be: political officials are often divided over what US "interests" actually are or should be. Comparative interests may seem like a straightforward variable that belongs in theories about credibility, but in addition to the general problems Press and others have had in defining precisely what interests are and how we expect adversaries to see them, there are many complexities related to specific cases that make adversaries' judgments about US interests, as Stein emphasizes, "extraordinarily difficult ... [even] after the fact."[36]

Consider the Syria case (although the same complexity will apply to any of the cases we examine in this book). Ezra Klein[37] provides an excellent summary of the various competing interests at play and the problems one might face when trying to decipher US interests in the late summer of 2013. As one works through Klein's list of the various interests and justifications for intervening (or not intervening) tied to these objectives, one begins to see the problem adversaries might have and why they might look to past actions for additional insights and intelligence to help predict US actions. For each and every putative "interest" and related response and/or policy option, there were arguments and counter-arguments, supporters, and dissenting voices. What for some was a clear and vital interest (punish Bashar al-Assad for using chemical weapons) was for others not worth the potential risks associated with action (civilian casualties, mission creep, continued chemical weapon use). Conversely, what most would agree would be a desirable outcome (stopping the bloodshed) was limited by what could be feasibly done to achieve it (full commitment of US troops).

The point is that understanding and defining a states' "interests" is incredibly difficult and complex, even for those within the state itself! Each "interest" comes with a series of competing risks and costs, and there is often significant disagreement as to whether they should or should not be pursued. If *we* have a hard time resolving these debates, how likely is it that adversaries will have a relatively straightforward time looking at "interests" and "capabilities" to assess the credibility of a US coercive threat? To suggest that past actions will be completely ignored by adversaries trying to work through this complexity makes little sense. In the absence of perfect information, adversaries are compelled to compile as much available information as possible –

---

36 Stein 2013, 369.
37 Klein 2013a.

past actions form an important part of this tableau, particularly given their relative clarity (known and documented activity) in the face of often ambiguous and contradictory debates regarding, in particular, the "true" nature of national interests.

2.3   Similarity and Transferability of Reputations and Credibility

Are reputations and credibility transferable across crises or are they entirely independent of past behavior? In an effort to preempt meaningless criticisms that blame the absence of reputational effects on minor differences across cases,[38] Press selects "similar" cases that are "most likely" to illustrate the role of reputations in support of Past Actions theory. He scores each of his cases along several dimensions of similarity,[39] and emphasizes that "if leaders were *ever* going to make judgments about the enemy's credibility from his past actions, this would be the time."[40] He concludes that no such transfer of reputations occurred

---

38 One could, of course, offer numerous dimensions by which *any* case differs one to the other, and become frustrated by what appears to be the selective invocation of similarities and differences such that, apparently, falsifiability is rendered impossible (i.e., any instance in which past behavior appears not to matter can be explained away by highlighting cherry-picked differences; any case in which it appears to matter could be claimed by highlighting cherry-picked similarities). This does present challenges, but none that are insurmountable. As long as one is clear that the relevant similarities between cases relate to key and core elements of the coercive encounter (e.g., proximity in time, adversary, regime, leadership, issue area, security threat, strategic imperatives, deterrent/compellent strategy, crisis management techniques, threat-counter-threat sequence, etc.), one can confidently and consistently dismiss "trivial" differences in making assessments of whether cases are like or un-like situations. Moreover, the "lessons" learned and applied may vary depending on the relevant dimensions of similarity in question. For example, Saddam Hussein may apply lessons about US resolve and casualty aversion based on Vietnam, Somalia, Kosovo, etc., which were similar to his own encounter in some but not all dimensions *so long as the lessons learned and applied relate to the dimensions of similarity.* That is, similarities in adversary and threat-counter-threat sequence can impart lessons as to what an adversary may do in the context of that sequence, but this does not mean that more general lessons will necessarily be applicable if there are important differences regarding other dimensions of the crisis.

39 The dimensions are: region, timeframe, issue, stake, actors, leadership, and pattern of behavior. See the table on page 40 of Press's 2005 *Calculating Credibility*.

40 Press 2005, 5.

in the cases he studied (despite their similarities), so transferability is impossible. We have already addressed the problems of relying exclusively on a relatively small collection of "similar" cases to establish closure on transferability, and have previously challenged the assumption that interests and power are sufficient in and of themselves for adversaries to assess credibility. As noted above, these concepts cannot be adequately measured in the absence of past actions – the variables are intimately linked.

But there are other issues connected to questions about similarities, differences, and transferability that the P-M-H consensus sidesteps. Press claims, for example, that similarities across cases are very rare, because

> leaders understand that no two crises are sufficiently alike to be confident that past actions are a reliable guide to the future. Crises can be compared along many dimensions, and there will always be differences along some of them. In the unlikely event that decision makers have a recent and very similar crisis to use as a comparison they are still wary of drawing conclusive parallels because the results from the previous crisis may have triggered changes that invalidate the comparison.[41]

According to this view, adversaries will forgo drawing any conclusive parallels – that is, refuse to use history as a guide to action – because it is the more rational and risk-averse approach to assessing an opponent's true intentions and credibility. Mercer makes a similar point: "Decision-makers do not consistently use another state's past behavior [whether in the same region or a different region] to predict that state's behavior."[42] The main problem with transferability, according to both authors, is that foreign policy crises are too different to be meaningfully informative, so the transfer of credibility is virtually impossible and, by logical implication, reputations are irrelevant to calculations of credibility.

Yet how exactly does one work through the caveats included in these quotes? If there are differences (and presumably similarities) along *some* dimensions of a crisis, or if decision-makers "inconsistently" use past behavior to draw "inconclusive" but still informative parallels to predict US resolve and credibility, then reputations and past actions might

---

41 Ibid., 22.
42 Mercer 1996, 227.

be said to *occasionally* matter. The more relevant theoretical challenge is to figure out when and under what conditions similarities are more or less likely to affect the prospects of transferability. How similar does a crisis have to be for an adversary to pick up (or dismiss) dispositional/reputational signals about US resolve?

First, any valid conclusion about the extent to which two or more crises are similar/different requires some measure of empirical evidence and a sufficient number of crises to confidently confirm or refute the case for comparability or transferability. Simply proclaiming that no two crises are identical is not sufficient for concluding that reputations cannot form or that lessons cannot possibly be applied to other cases. Press dismisses this important point by misinterpreting it: "If past actions only affect credibility in future crises when the future crises are virtually identical to the past … then Past Actions theory is meaningless. It will almost never be worth keeping commitments for the sake of credibility if the credibility gained will only apply in identical cases. Identical cases are far too rare, if they exist at all."[43] This rebuttal oversimplifies the criticism. *Of course* no two situations are identical – this is self-evident. A more reasonable interpretation of the point, however, is that reputations based on past actions are neither completely transferable (given key differences across international crises) nor completely irrelevant (in light of the possibility that important similarities exist).

Second, there is no question that adversaries will inevitably see differences across cases, but these difference are likely to be less pronounced if, for example, the US was recently engaged in a similar crisis, in the same region, against another smaller, authoritarian regime over the same set of security issues (e.g., weapons of mass destruction). If cases are similar enough on key dimensions of a crisis (proximity in time, adversary, regime, leadership, issue area, security threat, strategic imperatives, deterrent/compellent strategy, crisis management techniques, threat-counter-threat sequence, etc.), and differ in other, less significant ways, then analogies and parallels would arguably serve as the basis upon which adversaries could conceivably pick up relevant information[44] or mistakenly perceive (miscalculate) a reputation based on past actions. Logically, if differences matter, then so should similarities, but the relative importance of whatever variations apply should

---

43 Press 2005, 140.
44 Tomz 2012; Crescenzi 2007; Harvey 2006.

be measured in gradations, not absolutes.[45] By implication, the notion that reputations either do or do not exist is too simplistic to be policy relevant.

Third, if reputations are in the eye of the beholder, as both Mercer and Press proclaim, then we should expect perceptions of similarities to be as well, which logically implies the possibility that lessons from past US actions are transferable. Perceived similarities can lead adversaries to (either correctly or mistakenly) interpret a strong reputation for resolve and be deterred (Syria 2013), or reinforce perceptions of US weakness (irresoluteness) and escalate (Kosovo 1999; Iraq 1991 and 2003). The assertion that a US reputation for repeatedly bluffing, backing down, or retreating is unlikely to transfer does not flow logically from the premise that reputations are in the eye of the beholder. If they truly are, then similarities and differences matter a great deal, and managing and manipulating perceptions of the core elements of US credibility should remain an important part of US strategy (more on this below).

Fourth, there is no *policy-relevant* reason to privilege an assumption of differences across cases, nor any reason to expect one assumption to be any more useful than the other when contemplating how adversaries are likely to make decisions about US credibility in any given crisis. Nevertheless, Press attempts to draw out a clear-cut, policy-relevant conclusion based on his assumption: "In the unlikely event that decision-makers have a recent and very similar crisis to use as a comparison they are still wary of drawing conclusion parallels because the results from the previous crisis may have triggered changes."[46]

---

45 This is an important point. As has been argued, reputation for resolve is only one
    component of a broader equation with regard to determining the credibility of a
    coercive threat. Presumably, its relative weight within such a calculation may be
    linked to the number of key similarities and/or differences between the cases being
    invoked for the purposes of establishing reputation in the immediate case. That is,
    in cases that are similar on most or all of the important dimensions (proximity in
    time, adversary, regime, leadership, issue area, security threat, strategic imperatives,
    deterrent/compellent strategy, crisis management techniques, threat-counter-threat
    sequence), the relative weight of past actions and reputations for calculations
    of credibility is likely to be higher than when cases have only one or two key
    dimensions of similarity. Even more important, however, is the connection between
    what types of lessons are learned and the *particular dimension of similarity* between the
    two (or more) cases (see n. 38 above).
46 Press 2005, 22.

However, the relationship between risk propensity and the (unproven) tendency for decision-makers to embrace differences rather than similarities makes no practical sense, nor is there any logical reason why we should always expect US adversaries to err on the side of assuming only differences matter. Ignoring potentially relevant information from similar cases is just as risky as assuming that crises are sufficiently distinct in every instance to ignore any and all parallels. When it comes to using or dismissing historical analogies of the past, most adversaries are rational enough to understand the risks of adopting either of these two extreme positions. Of course no two crises are identical enough to make lessons about credibility perfectly transferable, but it is conceivable that some adversaries will assign a much *higher* risk to a strategy that completely dismisses past US behavior or ignores parallels that may provide useful when gauging US interests, resolve, and credibility. In fact, the tendency for adversaries to apply lessons from the past to inform current strategies is well documented in existing research (see chapter 1), and has been reconfirmed through multiple US deterrence crises over the past two decades (see chapter 3).

None of the preceding analysis should be taken to support the extreme version of the transferability argument. A recent example of this position is the argument put forth by Anne Marie Slaughter regarding the connection between (in)action in Syria and credibility in Ukraine.[47] As both Beinart and Zakaria point out,[48] that kind of total transferability simply does not take place. We agree with their criticisms – Syria is not related to Ukraine, and Putin's decision to invade Ukraine had very little to do with whatever signals he picked up about Obama's lack of resolve in Syria (leaving aside the fact that deterrence actually worked in Syria because of the threat of air strikes). The differences between these two cases, on a variety of levels, were too significant to overcome. We do, however, reject the other extreme, derived from the P-M-H consensus, that reputations and past actions are always completely irrelevant. Both sides make the same fundamental error – arguing in favor of absolutes when the evidence supports a more balanced interpretation of how reputations and credibility work. Indeed, Beinart, in arguing against the transferability of reputations, appears to contradict himself when he says: "In assessing America's likely response to attacks on the

47 Slaughter 2014.
48 Beinart 2014; Zakaria 2014.

Senkaku (Diaoyu in Chinese) islands, China will likely draw on what it knows – from America's public statements, private messages, *past actions*, and military deployments – about how much the United States cares about islands in the East China Sea."[49] Exactly! Past actions are part of the puzzle, but not the totality of it. If past actions matter, then reputations are relevant.

2.4   Reputations and Miscalculations

Of course, one difficulty with assessing reputation for resolve as a component of calculating credibility is the persistent possibility of misperception – adversaries can mistakenly interpret a strong reputation for resolve where none exists and avoid behavior that leads to war, or mistakenly assume irresolution when the defender is actually committed to protecting their interests.

This possibility is particularly relevant to the Syria crisis of 2013, as well as the other cases examined in this book. Smaller powers (with fewer intelligence resources) are inclined to need more information about US intentions and, therefore, are more likely to rely on past actions, or probe for additional intelligence regarding US commitments. Smaller powers have organizational impediments that could undermine the search for balanced advice (or perspectives) on US commitments; specifically, authoritarian regimes with highly centralized power structures are susceptible to miscalculating US interests and commitments based on lessons learned from other cases. Saddam Hussein's use of strategic ambiguity prior to the 2003 Iraq War, for example, is described at length by Harvey:[50]

> While strategic ambiguity was becoming less acceptable to the United States and UK, Saddam was incapable of re-evaluating his insights about American post-9/11 fears (and interests) to fully understand the implications of the domestic political debates playing out at the time. He failed to understand the sense of urgency US officials (on both sides of the aisle) felt to finally address Iraq's WMD threat, or the serious misperceptions in Washington regarding Iraqi WMD. Nor did Hussein appreciate the logic of coercive diplomacy, the political costs to the United States and UK of

---

49 Beinart 2014, emphasis added.
50 Harvey 2011, 252.

backing down after issuing credible threats, or his real proximity to war after the unanimous endorsement of UNSCR 1441. None of the requisite information that would have enhanced Saddam's capacity to consider the costs and risks of his actions (or how they were perceived in Washington) was available to him or members of his regime, a point so clearly noted by his chief adviser, Aziz. Saddam not only refused to collect and use relevant evidence and intelligence on the United States but admonished his chief advisers to leave these kinds of interpretations to him. In discussing this issue with his advisers in 1990, Saddam explained:

"America is a complicated country. Understanding it requires a politician's alertness that is beyond the intelligence community. Actually, I forbade the intelligence outfits from deducing from press and political analysis anything about America. I told them that [this] was not their specialty, because these organizations, when they are unable to find hard facts, start deducing from newspapers, which is what I already know. I said I don't want either intelligence organization [the Iraqi Intelligence Service or the General Military Intelligence Directorate] to give me analysis – that is my specialty ... We agree to continue on that basis ... which is what I used with the Iranians, some of it out of deduction and some of it through invention and connecting the dots, all without having hard evidence."[51]

Saddam Hussein seriously underestimated US interests and Washington's willingness to use overwhelming force, primarily because of the impressions he'd formed from past US actions and exchanges in 1991 (Gulf War) and 1998 (Operation Desert Fox). Hussein mistakenly assumed throughout 2002–3 (as he and his advisers later admitted) that US actions would look very much like their responses in previous cases. These mistakes were compounded by an authoritarian regime in which information and intelligence was analyzed almost exclusively through the prism of Hussein's biased perceptions of the threat (this case is discussed in more detail in chapter 3).

Finally, although the cases covered in the following chapters offer strong evidence that smaller powers have relied heavily on past actions when assessing US credibility and resolve, there is no logical reason to discount the possibility that reputations also exert influence on larger powers with massive intelligence-gathering organizations, and that

---

51 Quote from Woods, Lacey, and Murray 2006, 12.

similar miscalculations and misperceptions can occur. For example, Slobodan Milošević (mistakenly) expected US and NATO officials to capitulate during the 1999 Kosovo campaign based on expectations about casualty aversion he formed from previous US foreign policy crises (especially Bosnia 1992–5 and Iraq 1998). On the other hand, US and NATO officials similarly expected Milošević to quickly capitulate during the early stages of the air campaign based largely on lessons they learned about him during the war over Bosnia-Herzegovina between 1992 and 1995 – when threatened with air strikes, Milošević had repeatedly backed off. The "widely shared" view among Western allies at the time was, as then secretary of state Madeline Albright remarked, that "Milošević would probably back down after a few visible targets were hit."[52] President Clinton was even more explicit: "The reason we went forward with the air actions is because we thought there was some chance it would deter Mr. Milošević based on two previous examples – number one, last October in Kosovo, when he was well poised to do the same thing; and number two, in Bosnia, where there were 12 days of NATO attacks over a 20-day period."[53] Both sides (including the US and its massive intelligence apparatus) relied on the reputations they assigned to their opponents and applied these lessons to inform their (ultimately mistaken) judgments about the other side's interests and capabilities.

The key consideration is that adversaries do not assess reputation (and therefore credibility) in a deterministic way, as P-M-H allege. From a theoretical perspective, the fact that states can and do "get it wrong" is not as important as the fact that they nonetheless *use* past behavior to make inferences about credibility (reputations matter). From a policy perspective, the possibility of misperception underscores the importance of satisfying the four prerequisites of rational deterrence so as to maximize the probability of success. Demonstrating resolve does not *guarantee* coercive success, but along with the other prerequisites (clear communication, commitment, and capabilities) it can greatly reduce the likelihood of misperceptions and miscalculations. Of course, if one or more of the other prerequisites are *absent*, merely fighting for the sake of demonstrating resolve will not be enough (therefore, importantly,

52 Quoted in Burg 2003, 93.
53 Quoted in Daalder and O'Hanlon 2000, 92.

we do not recommend in this book that fighting for reputation *always* makes sense).

2.5   General versus Specific Reputations

Another important distinction between P-M-H and our version of RDT is the former's undifferentiated treatment of "reputation" itself. By contrast, we distinguish between two types of reputation: *general* and *specific*. General reputations relate to habitual features or characteristics of a state's foreign policy that are perceived by adversaries as patterned and consistent, and repeatedly inform expectations about its behavior. General reputations rarely change and are typically based on widely accepted (though occasionally mistaken) impressions of the opportunities and constraints that adversaries believe influence a state's foreign policy preferences and priorities. Perhaps the clearest illustration of a general US reputation, one that has regularly affected the way adversaries assess Washington's resolve, is the Western (liberal democratic) aversion to military and civilian casualties. Again, these commonly shared perceptions are not decisive enough to define an adversary's overall impression of US intentions, but there is evidence to suggest that these perceptions do play a role when adversaries evaluate important pieces of an opponent's credibility. Evidence supporting the relationship between rising casualty numbers and an inevitable decline in domestic political and popular support for interventions has received detailed treatment in the literature.[54]

Given these consistent trends, it is understandable that adversaries occasionally exploit such pressures. In fact, explicit efforts to increase casualty numbers – for example, through ethnic cleansing, exacerbating a humanitarian refugee crisis, or deploying human shields – are examples of strategies used by Slobodan Milošević and Saddam Hussein to establish counter-coercion leverage by exploiting Washington's reputation for casualty aversion.[55] Of course, adversaries often miscalculate by overestimating Washington's aversion to casualties, and as a result have occasionally underestimated US resolve to sustain an operation despite a significant decline in popular support, but these

---

54 See Mueller 2005; Gelpi and Mueller 2006; Gelpi, Feaver, and Reifler 2009.
55 Harvey 2006; Harvey and James 2009; Harvey and Wilner 2012; see also Byman and Waxman 1999, 2002.

strategic errors simply add further confirmation that general reputations play a role in adversaries' assessment of US credibility (as previously discussed).[56]

Specific reputations for US resolve evolve over a much shorter period
of time and typically emerge as a direct consequence of specific interactions and exchanges during different stages of a protracted military-
security crisis or enduring rivalry. Unlike general reputations, specific
reputations for resolve can change relatively quickly. In the context of
a US deterrence encounter, for example, resolve is best demonstrated
through the use of US military force in retaliation for the failure of an
adversary to comply with the demands stipulated in a deterrent threat.
However, if retaliation is not forthcoming, and in the absence of perfect
information about US intentions, adversaries often probe for concrete
evidence regarding US interests and credibility, usually by mounting
challenges at various points in the crisis. If US officials fail to respond
to these probes, for whatever reason,[57] adversaries are likely to interpret
this as a partial clarification of Washington's (un)willingness (resolve,
or lack thereof) to deploy military capabilities to enforce the deterrent
threat. Consistent with RDT, maintaining credibility often requires
demonstrations of resolve to reduce uncertainty about US commitments. Fighting for specific credibility, in other words, is occasionally
prudent regardless of whether the demonstration of resolve has any
direct bearing on reinforcing general credibility with other adversaries
in other crises.

---

56 Both Jervis (1976) and Lebow (1981) have shown that leaders often use inappropriate
    analogies of the past when designing responses to current crises, and, as a result
    of cognitive and motivational biases, often select historical reference points that
    confirm pre-existing biases about resolve and credibility, something that might
    help explain the consistency with which casualty aversion has been invoked in
    confrontations between the US and smaller powers. Again, even if these impressions
    are "wrong," they point to the relevance of reputation in a theoretical sense;
    practically, they reinforce the *difficulty* – but, importantly, not the *impossibility* – of
    demonstrating a reputation for resolve as well as the importance of satisfying *all*
    deterrence prerequisites in order to achieve success.
57 Washington's crisis-based resolve can quickly change for a number of reasons: other
    foreign policy crises can become more central to US priorities; domestic public and
    congressional opposition to military intervention could increase (reinforcing a general
    reputation for casualty aversion); military or political support from key allies, or from
    UN Security Council members, could vanish; realities on the ground could change
    (e.g., an influx of al-Qaeda supporters among the Syrian opposition); etc.

As Jon Western points out, the Syria crisis generated real concerns about *specific* reputation, regardless of whether a general reputation was at stake. In this and other cases, the relevance of reputation cannot and should not be entirely reduced to whether or not reputations transfer across cases. As Western observes:[58]

> It's pretty clear that the primary objective here is to punish the Syrian regime and deter a future chemical weapons attack in Syria. The Obama administration is focused on a very limited strike and doesn't want to see an outright rebel victory. The logic of this strategic objective makes sense to me. I am persuaded by Daryl Press and Jon Mercer's respective works that precedent effects, reputation, and credibility concerns are often overstated. But, their works look at how third-party leaders infer or read other actors' responses elsewhere – not at how actors respond to bluffs in a particular case. It seems pretty clear that if the US does not punish the perpetrators of this attack, *these same perpetrators almost certainly will calculate that they can act again with impunity*. And, as we've seen in the past week, the use of chemical weapons quickly changes the international political dynamics. In other words, if there is no action now, there will almost certainly be events on the ground that provoke international action later. It's probably not a question of whether, but when, the international use of force happens.

In particular crises, specific reputations do matter and do explain why, on occasion, fighting for credibility makes sense. Western's insights also explain why the distinction between specific and general reputation is particularly important when the *primary* goals of coercive diplomacy reside *within* a crisis (as they almost always do) – reputations matter in the short term and against the same opponent, independently of whether they will matter to another adversary, elsewhere, over the long term.

Finally, in summarizing and synthesizing extant treatments of reputation, Huth asserts that reputation must also be understood in the context of three questions: (1) reputation for what? (2) reputation for whom? and (3) reputation based on what?[59] The first, reputation *for what*, refers to the characteristics from which challengers derive their perceptions for reputation. For instance, the reputation for a willingness to

---

58 Western 2013b, emphasis added.
59 Huth 1997.

use force to protect a state's interests; or reputation for having powerful military capabilities and a willingness to use them under certain (common) circumstances (a reputation for resolve). The key issue in regard to reputation *for whom* is whether an adversary assigns a reputation to the state, to the political system (e.g., democratic institutions), or to a specific individual leader. Huth suggests that all are possible, though reputation for military strength is more likely to be conferred to the state itself than to individuals.[60] Finally, and perhaps most important, *what* is reputation based on? That is, how far back in the past are incidents considered? Does it matter who was involved, where, and under what circumstances? Huth suggests that different logical arguments can be made for different time frames and circumstances, which relate to the issues surrounding similarities and differences raised in section 2.3 above. All of these points reveal a much more complex and nuanced understanding of reputations, one that is often missing in simplified dismissals of the relevance of past actions and behavior.

2.6   Reputations, Credibility, and Transferability Are in the Eyes of the Beholder

Imperfect information, perceptions of – and prudent reliance on – similarities across cases, the probability of miscalculations, and the relevance of both general and specific reputations are all vital for understanding any decision to accept or challenge a US deterrent threat. These factors must also, however, be viewed through the prism of the adversary's unique perception of US credibility. Credibility is not something that is entirely present or absent (in contrast to common assumptions in much of the literature); it ranges from very strong to very weak, and its potency is a function of the adversary's assessment of the degree to which the core prerequisites – communication, interests (commitments),

---

60 While the evidence in this book suggests reputational inferences can be (and are) made vis-à-vis all three units of analysis, we defer making theoretical or analytical statements regarding these distinctions (in this sense, we generally agree with Huth's [1997, 78] assessment that "reputations for resolve could be plausibly associated with either [an individual or state] unit of analysis"). Determining to whom (or at what level) US adversaries assign reputation (state, democratic institution, or specific leader) is a fascinating subject, but ultimately beyond the scope of our argument. Our intent is to establish the broad relevance of reputation (wherever assigned) in US asymmetric encounters over the last several decades.

capabilities, and resolve – are present or absent.[61] These perceptions, moreover, are always balanced against the adversary's own interests, capabilities, and resolve to withstand US retaliation, and their willingness to impose counter-coercive costs (e.g., casualties).

Reputations are not owned – they are assigned to states by their allies and opponents for a variety of reasons, as discussed earlier. Reputations, in other words, are in the eyes of the beholder and, therefore, are highly variable and unpredictable (but not entirely random). This recognition features particularly prominently in the work of Jonathan Mercer, who emphasizes a psychological and therefore subjective model of threat perception. Stein, in referencing a later work by Mercer on emotional beliefs and cognition, summarizes the implications well: "The credibility of threats, an essential component in theories of deterrence, compellence, and bargaining, is not only a property of the sender, as some formal models of signaling suggest, but also a function of the beliefs of the receiver."[62] As Shannon further points out, reputations are "to a substantial degree in the hands of others … Different people perceive intentions, means, and consequences differently. Jervis (1976) notes that the way actions are read is determined by the perceivers' needs, theories and expectations."[63] If we apply these observations to the Syria case, Shannon postulates, then "inaction likely does affect our reputation with some, namely the Syrian rebels. But it also reminds us that not everyone, and not even every ally, learns the same 'lesson' from American behavior." Pach agrees:

> The central problem is that it is extremely difficult to send messages about resolve and determination that will be understood in the way you want

---

61 In contrast to Press's conceptualization of credibility as being either present or absent, in reality credibility is far more complex – its presence or absence should be viewed on a continuum of potential responses ranging from most severe (war) to least severe (nothing). Similarly, an adversary's interpretation of US credibility is likely to fall along a similar continuum. For example, Saddam did not believe a US ground invasion into Baghdad was a credible enough threat to worry about and was prepared to suffer the consequences of another US air campaign. Assad, by contrast, believed that a US air campaign was very likely and was not prepared to accept the risks, so he complied. Credibility is based on the magnitude of the potential US response, which is a product of past behavior in similar situations. This is why Press's continued assertion that the US should not "fight wars for the sake of credibility" is somewhat misleading; the choice is far more nuanced than that.
62 Stein 2013, 382 – see Mercer 2010.
63 Shannon 2013 – see Jervis 1976.

them to be understood. States don't own their reputations; friends and foes are free to draw their own (often conflicting) interpretations of events. To clarify this a bit, consider the interaction of resolve and capabilities, both of which are necessary to make deterrence successful. Even if the United States has the resolve to establish its credibility with respect to red lines in Syria, doing so may detract from its capability to enforce similar promises in East Asia ... If Washington is wasting time and attention trying to establish "credibility" in Syria, it may not be paying sufficient heed to events around the Pacific ... The bottom line is that we don't actually know how Pyongyang or Beijing will interpret [the Syrian CW] deal, or how what they "learn" will matter for policy six months or six years down the road.[64]

Shannon and Pach provide excellent illustrations of a standard critique of reputations embedded in the P-M-H consensus: if reputations are in the eye of the beholder, then different adversaries could conceivably assign different reputations to (or extract different lessons from) the same behavior; consistency and predictability is virtually impossible. By logical implication, as P-M-H argue, reputations are not transferable (or fungible) across cases, so fighting to establish resolve, reinforce (manipulate) reputations, or maintain credibility makes no sense.

Yet consider the serious logical inconsistency between the observation that reputations are in the eyes of the beholder and the associated conclusion that "a state *rarely* underestimates its adversary's reputation even if the adversary has backed down in previous standoffs [and] the state *never* assigns reputation to other states based on their past behavior."[65] How exactly can we simultaneously establish a strong a case for variability, *inconsistency*, and non-transferability, yet still arrive at the conclusion (and confident prediction) that reputations and past actions are *consistently* never relevant when adversaries estimate credibility? In this sense, P-M-H uses an assumption of inconsistency to predict very patterned and consistent behavior across cases.[66] If reputations and their corresponding relevance to decision making are indeed in the eyes of the beholder, then, in some cases, adversaries could conceivably: rely on

---

64 Pach 2013.

65 Tang 2005, 42, emphasis added.

66 Or, in methodological terms, it could be said that P-M-H use a constant to explain a variable.

past actions from similar cases to gauge/interpret US interests, commitments, and resolve; occasionally perceive similarities across cases (whether misperceived or not) and use these historical analogies to inform present circumstances; be expected in some cases to assign a reputation (or dispositional attribute) to an opponent's behavior; and occasionally conclude that credibility is indeed transferable in light of these similarities. In sum, if reputations are inconsistent, there is no reason to conclude that adversaries will consistently refuse to rely on past actions to acquire information about US commitments, or repeatedly reject the possibility (despite numerous bluffs) that their adversary is irresolute. For example, both Milošević and Hussein discounted US resolve and Washington's willingness to impose unacceptable costs (i.e., credibility) precisely because US officials tended in past crises to rely exclusively on air strikes. This decision can be explained, at least in part, with reference to their interpretation of US behavior in past cases – these adversaries concluded that recent history was relevant.

To make things slightly more complicated yet realistic, it is not exclusively the eyes of a single individual or leader but the impressions and consensus emerging from broader debates and discussions in the decision-making apparatus of the state that dictate how the "eye" beholds past actions and translates them into inferences about reputation – it is the feedback and intelligence provided to leadership by advisers that is most often responsible for balancing different, often competing (and occasionally shifting) interpretations of US credibility. As Keren Yarhi-Milo concluded: "Decisionmakers' own explicit or implicit theories or beliefs about how the world operates and their expectations significantly affect [the] selection and interpretation of signals. Decisionmakers in the British Cabinet, the Carter administration, and the second Reagan administration debated what to make of different indicators of intentions."[67]

The key feature of Yarhi-Milo's "selective attention" thesis is the variegated interpretations of credibility that result from the subjectivity of individual perceptions (on the part of leaders and their advisers) and the organizational biases of the intelligence community. She points to, for example, the intense internal debates during the Carter administration as to Soviet intentions: "Carter and his advisers did not agree

---

67 Yarhi-Milo 2013, 46.

on the informative value of Soviet costly actions. Rather, they debated the importance of various indicators in inferring intentions, and interpreted costly Soviet behavior markedly differently from one another."[68] While not entirely unproblematic (e.g., she also artificially separates "capabilities" and "behavior" in testing for alternative hypotheses of credibility calculation), Yarhi-Milo's analysis helps illustrate the inherent unpredictability of decision-maker perceptions.[69]

To this end, we should not be viewing Syria, Iran, or North Korea as single entities with a common and shared view of US credibility – just as there are multiple debates and competing positions (beliefs) within the US or Canada regarding adversaries' actions and the consequences of various responses, there are likely to be very similar debates and competing interpretations running through deliberations by opponents – some of which will almost certainly reference and rely on reputations assigned to the US based on past actions. To conclude that only one of these groups will consistently prevail in all crises is not plausible. Rarely does a clear consensus exist, which is why it is partially the responsibility of the defending state to satisfy the key prerequisites of coercive diplomacy to increase the probability that credibility will be perceived as strong. In the end, however, these signals can be misperceived and credibility under- (or over-)estimated.

Successfully signaling a reputation for resolve is certainly *difficult* as a result, but, crucially, not *impossible*. Schelling recognized this possibility when he wrote:

> The principle is at work all over the world; *and the principle is not wholly under our control*. I doubt whether we can identify ourselves with Pakistan in quite the way we can identify ourselves with Great Britain … "To identify" is a complex process. It means getting the Soviets … to identify us with, say, Pakistan in such a way that *they* would lose respect for our commitments elsewhere if we failed to support Pakistan … In a way, *it is the Soviets who confer this identification*; but they do it through the medium of their expectations about us and our understanding of their expectations. *Neither they nor we can exercise full control over their expectations.*[70]

---

68 Ibid., 22.
69 See also Yarhi-Milo 2014.
70 Schelling 1966, 56–7, emphasis added.

The notion that past actions never play a role in any of these delibera-tions makes no intuitive sense, is not supported by the evidence pre-sented in this book or in numerous other studies of deterrence, and does not flow logically from the assertion that credibility is in the eye of the beholder.

Conclusion

This chapter has presented six key – and interrelated – theoretical com-ponents of RDT that are misunderstood or missing in the critiques of conventional deterrence theory put forth by P-M-H and their propo-nents. First, the credibility of a coercive threat is tied to four (not simply two) prerequisites: communication, commitment (interests), capability, and resolve. Reputations and past actions are linked to credibility pri-marily through the fourth dimension, resolve, but, crucially, each di-mension is *combined* such that the theory predicts failure if one or more is absent. Second, adversaries – like all actors in international politics – suffer from imperfect information. Assessing an adversary's power and interests is not a straightforward process (particularly when states occa-sionally send deceptive or mixed signals) – reputations and past actions can help mitigate some of this uncertainty. Third, and as a consequence, states can misperceive and make mistakes, attributing reputations for resolve where none exist or vice versa. Fourth, contrary to the P-M-H consensus, similarities across cases *do* matter and reputations *can* trans-fer from one crisis to another. No two cases are identical (obviously), but similarities across key dimensions can provide potentially impor-tant insights and lessons as to how states have behaved in similar situ-ations in the past. Fifth, an important difference exists between *general* (patterned, consistent, dispositional, and relevant between cases) and *specific* (situational, short-term, and relevant primarily within protract-ed crises) reputation; any treatment of reputation as an undifferentiated concept loses vital nuance, ignoring the variegated influence of linked behavior (and lessons learned) in both the long and short term. Finally, reputations are in the eye of the beholder. While this does mean (as P-M-H suggest) that one cannot dictate exactly what one's reputation will be, it also underscores (contrary to P-M-H) the logical inconsisten-cy of suggesting that adversaries *never* assign a reputation for resolve based on prior behavior.

Chapter Three

US Reputation Building in Deterrence Encounters, 1991–2003

This chapter explores three case studies of US reputation building in protracted (asymmetric) military-security crises from 1991 to 2003: Bosnia-Herzegovina 1992–5, Kosovo 1998–9, and Iraq 1991–2003. Our objective is twofold. First, in keeping with the theoretical arguments presented earlier, we investigate the relevance of past behavior and reputations as they relate to specific deterrence/compellence encounters and associated outcomes. It should be noted that these three protracted crises encompass multiple exchanges that combine to provide considerable evidence to support RDT and, more specifically, highlight three principles guiding our collection of case evidence: deterrence succeeds and fails through time and in stages; reputations evolve through these exchanges (specific reputations); and past actions inform perceptions/decisions across crises (general reputations). We believe these cases and associated exchanges constitute sufficient evidence to *disconfirm* the P-M-H consensus that reputations never matter in international politics.

Second, when compared with the crises examined by P-M-H, our cases are significantly more policy-relevant vis-à-vis Syria in 2013 and will remain relevant to future asymmetric crises involving the US. As mentioned, one of the most striking aspects of the repeated invocation of P-M-H research during the Syria crisis was the fact that none of their cases focused specifically on how and why deterrence succeeds or fails during protracted international crises or how different opponents might react to Washington's coercive threats in predictable and consistent ways under essentially similar circumstances. Put simply, the cases in P-M-H look nothing like Syria. If similarities across cases affect the probability of reputations forming, then those who offered policy advice on Syria should at least have acknowledged relevant lessons from

US encounters over the last two decades, rather than relying solely on cases from the early 1900s or Cold War.

In contrast with P-M-H, the evidence from our cases shows that US adversaries often relied on experiences from previous confrontations when assessing US credibility. We draw on primary, archival, and secondary sources to identify when and under what conditions past behavior was relevant to an adversary's calculation of US credibility. Our discussion focuses on identifying in each case the presence of both general (dispositional, across-case) and specific (within-case) reputations. As we shall see, both types of reputation were relevant (though not necessarily decisive) to adversaries' calculations and subsequent deterrent/compellent outcomes.[1]

These findings strongly support the four-condition model of RDT and, by logical extension, reveal the consistent role of reputation as a component of the broader theory. Our evidence also complements recent quantitative work by Weisiger and Yarhi-Milo, in which the authors, in testing expectations derived from both P-M-H and RDT, found that "contrary to the predictions of reputation critics ... a strong relationship [exists] between a country's past action and the probability of a new dispute [i.e., deterrence failure]."[2] Finally, our evidence disconfirms P-M-H by indicating precisely the type of reputational inferences dismissed by these authors.

Four additional points are in order prior to presenting the case evidence. First, for reasons noted in the previous chapter, RDT is agnostic

---

1 There are elements of both deterrence and compellence in almost every exchange, and most exchanges can be interpreted as either deterrence or compellence encounters, which complicates efforts to draw out these distinctions for the purposes of testing/evaluation. For example, compelling the Assad regime to dismantle chemical weapons does in fact accomplish deterrence as well – logically, Assad will be deterred/prevented from using weapons he was forced to relinquish. It is very difficult to decipher or separate the two in the context of the protracted crises we examine in this and subsequent chapters, precisely because there are multiple exchanges, strategies, and responses over time. Consider, for example, the stage of the crisis when Obama is reinforcing his coercive threat to deter Assad from using chemical weapons (prior to Assad's decision to dismantle): is the US deterring the use of these weapons or compelling Assad to move munitions outfitted with chemical weapons back into storage? As such, though we attempt to be as clear and precise as possible in our case discussions, the reader should not be preoccupied with such terminology.

2 Weisiger and Yarhi-Milo 2015, 474.

about whether an adversary's perception of US interests, capabilities, or reputations (i.e., credibility) is accurate, or whether their response to US pressure is procedurally or substantively rational; mistakes and miscalculations will be made. The central point is that regardless of whether US deterrence succeeds or fails, or whether the adversary prevails or loses by challenging the deterrent threat, reputations and past actions can be found to have played a role in calculations on both sides, as the evidence will show.

Second, the test we conduct with respect to RDT versus P-M-H does not require that we provide proof that past actions *alone* determine an adversary's behavior and/or crisis outcomes – we have already provided several reasons why such a weak version of deterrence theory should be rejected. Our position is that interests, capabilities, *and* reputations (both general and specific) *combine* to provide a better account of the perceptions, strategies, and successes and failures we explore in this and subsequent chapters.

Third, deterrence encounters should not be viewed as single data points but as exchanges in a protracted crisis. As Lieberman explains, "The phenomenon of deterrence, which is temporal, dynamic, and causal, has to be tested by a longitudinal research design and not by research designs that focus on 'snapshots' of single deterrence episodes."[3] Deterrence strategies, therefore, must be understood and evaluated through the prism of their long-term and cumulative impact over multiple exchanges. From this perspective, short-term deterrence failure (e.g., Syria's failure to comply with President Obama's red-line threat) is a necessary condition for deterrence success over time. Fighting for credibility occasionally makes sense, because "resolute defenders need to distinguish themselves from irresolute actors [by] maintaining control over the escalatory ladder of the conflict."[4] This "protracted-crisis" approach is reflected in our case studies.

Fourth, the more apparent the similarities across cases, the more likely it is that adversaries will rely on information from past actions to gauge Washington's willingness to use sufficient military force to impose high costs. With respect to evaluating President Obama's (and President Assad's) strategic calculations in August–September 2013, for example, there are a number of historical precedents, including several

---

3 Lieberman 1995a, 2.
4 Ibid., 63.

asymmetric crises between the US and smaller powers, which were far better suited to generating policy-relevant findings on US coercive diplomacy. The contemporary cases discussed below reveal patterns of reputation building that directly disconfirm conclusions from P-M-H, lead to a different set of policy recommendations (ones President Obama ultimately embraced and successfully implemented), and provide a theoretically informed explanation for why Bashar al-Assad and Vladimir Putin capitulated to what they perceived to be credible US coercive threats.

Case 1 – Bosnia-Herzegovina (1992–5)[5]

Between 1992 and 1995, a series of coercive encounters between the US (supported by NATO and the UN) and Bosnian Serbs occurred in Bosnia-Herzegovina. As in Syria in 2013, these encounters involved a series of threats by the US and its allies to deter and/or compel a smaller power in the course of a violent and protracted conflict. The general pattern relating to coercive US action in Bosnia-Herzegovina is quite clear. Whenever US officials failed to respond to probes and challenges, the violence escalated. When resolve was demonstrated through mobilizing military forces or air strikes, escalation was controlled. If not buttressed by credible threats over time, adversaries continued to probe for weaknesses in resolve and commitments, and began to contemplate the utility of challenging again. This pattern repeated itself in over a dozen separate exchanges in the two-year period, which provides evidence consistent with expectations derived from rational deterrence theory.[6] When conditions were met, deterrence succeeded. In the absence of one or more core prerequisites, deterrence failed. Reputations and resolve were central to these successes and failures.

In the summer of 1993, for example, mounting pressure for a more robust international effort (in part because of the Serb shelling of a French-staffed UN base in Sarajevo) led the US to declare its willingness to employ unilateral air power in an effort to increase pressure on Bosnian

---

5 This case discussion draws on Harvey 1997. However, the discussion here,
   supplemented by additional primary and archival documents, places greater
   emphasis on evidence relating to reputations as opposed to the other prerequisites of
   RDT (while nonetheless recognizing that all prerequisites must be present to predict
   deterrence success).
6 See Harvey 1997.

Serb military leader Ratko Mladić. US demands were clear: end attacks on Muslim safe havens, create safe passage for UN relief convoys, and negotiate a peace settlement. NATO similarly (and under pressure from the Americans) issued a warning that it would conduct a series of strategic bombing raids against the Serbian military if the latter did not cease attacks on Sarajevo.[7] Importantly, these threats were explicit and well communicated, with NATO specifying its demands and outlining how the air strikes would be coordinated. Initially, Serb leaders were defiant, threatening retaliation against UN peacekeepers on the ground should the strikes be conducted. A deterrent counter-threat from the US specified the destruction of 1500–2000 Serbian guns should any attacks on UN peacekeepers occur. While fighting in other parts of Bosnia continued, artillery attacks on Sarajevo stopped within hours of the ultimatum.[8] Subsequently, an explicit US threat to Mladić specifying that air strikes would ensue unless heavy artillery was removed from Sarajevo by 13 August succeeded, marking the first time since the war had begun that the Serbian general relinquished previously occupied territory.[9]

These clear examples of deterrent (no attacks on UN personnel) and compellent (removal of artillery from around Sarajevo) successes stand in stark contrast to subsequent outcomes in which US, NATO, and UN threats were ignored and violence continued to escalate. In October 1993, for example, the Serb military renewed its artillery attacks on Sarajevo. Unlike the exchange over the summer, however, the resulting coercive threats from the US were weak and unspecified: no schedule was established, nor were the threats backed by official statements (costly signals) from the US State Department or NATO.[10] The attacks on Sarajevo began as minor probes to test US/NATO resolve, but increased in number and intensity over the next two months as no significant retaliatory threat was mounted. Any potential response was hampered by differences among Western allies, with the UK, France, and other EC members opposing air strikes.[11] On 11 January 1994, NATO issued

---

7 Whitney 1993.
8 Burns (1993) writes, for example, that "the silence of the guns today bolstered those who have argued that it may not be necessary for air strikes to be carried out, only for the threat of them to be made credible."
9 Jehl 1993.
10 Binder 1993.
11 President Clinton was publicly critical of them for this (see Binder 1993; see also Devroy and Smith 1993).

another warning to end the siege, but the threat was undermined by regulations and limitations that diminished its potency.[12] The Bosnian Serbs ignored the ultimatum and continued to shell Sarajevo through January.

On 5 February a Serb military attack on the crowded Markale central market killed sixty-eight civilians and wounded more than two hundred others. Western leaders unanimously condemned the massacre, vowing in numerous public statements to expand efforts to deal with the siege.[13] The ensuing coercive threats from US/NATO were detailed, specific, and robust – end the siege, withdraw all forces and heavy weapons to positions behind a 20-kilometer exclusion zone, and place all other heavy weapons in the area under UN control, or face direct attacks from NATO bombers – and were accompanied by a firm and clearly communicated 21 February deadline for compliance.[14] On the day of the deadline, UN observers confirmed that Serb leaders had acquiesced to virtually all NATO demands, meaning there was no need for air strikes.[15] As on previous occasions, however, the Serbs began to probe US/NATO resolve shortly thereafter, just as peace talks appeared to be heading in the right direction. Unlike previous occasions, the US/NATO response to these probes was decisive: on 28 February, four Serb warplanes were shot down by NATO aircraft, a clear demonstration of resolve and commitment to enforce the UN's no-fly zone (NFZ).[16]

Ultimately, the market attack of 5 February was a tipping point – news of the massacre bolstered domestic support in the West for more assertive action in Bosnia-Herzegovina, and galvanized the international community more generally, allowing US/NATO leaders to establish and communicate a robust and credible coercive threat to Serb leaders regarding the siege of Sarajevo. Decisive responses to subsequent probes confirmed US/NATO resolve, and violence was contained. Successful coercion in this exchange hinged primarily on increased international interest in containing and curtailing violence following the market massacre. But success was not a product of invigorated interest alone – only when *added* to the prerequisites of clearly communicated

---

12 Apple, Jr 1994.
13 New York Times 1994.
14 Sciolino 1994a; Cohen 1994.
15 Kifner 1994.
16 Gordon 1994a.

threats and sufficient air power (capability) to effectively punish Serb forces, and *reinforced* by the subsequent action (responding to probes) to affirm resolve did the US and NATO achieve their objectives.

Nor was this success long lived, as Mladić again began to probe just a few months later, in April 1994, around the town of Goražde (a formally declared Muslim "safe area"). This breakdown in deterrence was precipitated, in part, by statements from the US defense secretary William Perry and chairman of the joint chiefs of staff General John Shalikashvili to the effect that "the United States is not prepared to use force to stop the Serbs from overrunning the threatened Muslim safe area."[17] President Clinton and his national security adviser, Anthony Lake, quickly attempted to walk these comments back by reiterating US commitments to the area, but the damage had largely been done.[18] (Peter Jakobsen suggests that Perry "gave the [Bosnian Serbs] the green light" to continue attacks.)[19] By 9 April 1994 the Serbs had "overran strategic high ground above ... Gorazde ... with tanks, artillery and infantry attacks."[20] A threat to control the fighting from UN secretary-general Boutros Boutros-Ghali (not the US or NATO) lacked a specific deadline for Serb withdrawal and failed to draw explicit ultimatums specifying consequences if compliance was not forthcoming.[21] The Serbs ignored the warning and continued shelling the city. A limited bombing campaign on 10 April produced little effect, with the Serb Army conducting another major offensive against the town the following day, 11 April. In the course of this attack, UN commander Michael Rose issued direct warnings to General Mladić to stop shelling immediately or face additional air strikes. The retaliatory threat was not carried out and Mladić's forces continued to fire for an additional two hours.[22]

Ultimately, the effects of the 10 April sorties were negligible, little more than a "symbolic shot across the bow."[23] Mladić pressed on, believing further damage of a similar magnitude was manageable and victory in Goražde well worth the costs and risks associated with continued

---

17 Lewis 1994.
18 Ibid.
19 Jakobsen 2000, 13.
20 Sudetic 1994a.
21 Lewis 1994.
22 Sudetic 1994b.
23 Gordon 1994b.

defiance. On 22 April NATO issued another ultimatum modeled after the successful Sarajevo exchange detailed above. Unlike earlier threats in the Goražde exchange, this ultimatum was buttressed by expanded discretionary powers for NATO commanders with respect to bombing decisions.[24] Russia's decision to drop its objections to the potential NATO bombing campaign also appeared to have an impact: shortly following statements from Russian foreign minister Andrei Kozyrev that "the only alternative to air strikes is compliance by the Bosnian Serbs with their commitments," Serb forces gradually began to withdraw from around the city.[25]

This exchange highlights, again, the complex interplay between each RDT prerequisite; not the inadequacy of RDT as a theory for explaining coercive outcomes, but rather the difficulty of *achieving* deterrence success in practice given the prerequisites outlined in RDT and the protracted nature of most international crises. Effective communication was undermined by the discordant messages from Secretary Perry and General Shalikashvili, on one hand, and President Clinton and NSA Lake, on the other. Contradictory French and British proposals as to how to deal with the Serb attack further undermined NATO's ability to, in the beginning, communicate as a unified voice (international consensus was further undermined by Russian obstinacy).[26]

US/NATO capabilities, similarly, were initially questioned, largely as a result of the "dual-key" approach to air strikes (whereby both UN and NATO commanders had to simultaneously agree to and authorize air strikes, often causing logistical delays and problems) that had characterized air force operations to that point in Bosnia. Finally, the weak, "symbolic" air strikes of 10 April were insufficient for re-establishing US/NATO resolve to inflict punishment on the Serb Army. Only after a much clearer and specific threat was articulated, with an expanded target list and broader international consensus, did the Serbs pull back.

Once again, however, it wasn't long before the Serbs began probing, this time around Sarajevo. As a declassified intelligence briefing from the director of central intelligence (DCI) Interagency Balkan Task Force on 19 May 1994, reveals: "The Bosnian Serbs continue to test the UN's resolve to control the zone [around Sarajevo] ... The Serbs appear to

---

24 Whitney 1994.
25 Specter 1994.
26 Burg and Shoup 1999.

be systematically challenging the UN's control of Sarajevo, particularly since the NATO airstrikes around Gorazde ... Bosnian Serb violations of the 20-kilometer exclusion zone seemed to be *an effort to assess the UN's threshold for action.*"[27] This is precisely the type of behavior anticipated by RDT. Lacking complete or perfect information as to UN and US/NATO commitments and/or capabilities over time, the Serb Army could not simply "calculate" (given "power" and "interests," à la P-M-H) their "threshold for action"; instead, this threshold was *revealed* (at least from their point of view) by UN/NATO responses to Serb attacks/violations. The point at which the threshold was crossed (the "tipping point") served to re-establish resolve. In other words, how the UN/NATO behaved (whether by acquiescing or producing weak responses to probes; or, alternatively, by responding with enhanced threats in the form of costly signals or military strikes) served as the basis for Serb inferences about UN/NATO behavior moving forward. Past actions mattered; specific reputations formed.

The importance of maintaining a reputation for resolve is further illustrated by the events of spring and summer 1995. In May 1995, NATO responded to an increase in heavy shelling and the use of phosphorous grenades in Sarajevo by issuing a formal ultimatum demanding that all heavy weapons inside the 20-kilometer exclusion zone around the city be removed or surrendered to UN forces.[28] On the day of the deadline, NATO aircraft (predominately US-led) struck a Serb ammunition dump near Pale, destroying two weapons bunkers in the process. A second round of air strikes the following day destroyed an additional six weapons bunkers. Although lauded by British and American officials, both the French and Russian ministries condemned the attacks. The newly elected French president, Jacques Chirac, re-issued warnings that France would withdraw its troops if the United Nations could not adequately protect its peacekeepers. Russia, meanwhile, once again intervened on the Serbs' behalf in an attempt to negotiate an end to the strikes.[29] The rift in UN consensus undermined both the credibility and the capability of NATO for enforcing its ultimatum. Motivated by their ability to defy UN demands, the Serbs retaliated by shelling five UN "safe havens" and conducting a massive bombardment of the

---

27 Clinton Digital Library 1994, emphasis added.
28 Cohen 1995a.
29 Whitney 1995a.

northeastern town of Tuzla. In one of the worst atrocities of the war, seventy-one civilians were killed and many more injured, with images of "the severed limbs of youths who had been enjoying coffee on the terrace of a Tuzla café" being captured on television. The Serbs, as a *New York Times* headline noted, had "call[ed] and raise[d]" NATO's bluff.[30]

Shortly thereafter, in July 1995, an encounter between UN/NATO and Serb forces occurred over the town of Srebrenica. There were two retaliatory threats issued in this exchange: a relatively weak NATO offensive (which failed), and a subsequent Bosnian Serb retaliatory threat to kill hostages (which succeeded).[31] Although two air strikes were carried out by Dutch and US military aircraft under the auspices of NATO, a third sortie was abandoned after the Bosnian Serbs threatened to kill Dutch soldiers.[32] NATO had the capability to continue with the offensive, but its resolve in pursuing the mission was compromised when the hostages were taken. With a breakdown in resolve, the success of the UN/NATO's (compellence) strategy was unlikely. From the Bosnian Serb perspective, however, the threat to kill hostages satisfied all four prerequisites for deterrence and succeeded in preventing further NATO air strikes. The subsequent massacre at Srebrenica, in which more than 8000 Bosnians were killed by Serb Army troops, was one of the worst mass atrocities to befall Europe since the Second World War.

The relevance of these last two exchanges is particularly evident in the context of the next several encounters. Following the atrocities at Srebrenica and Žepa, international will for more robust intervention increased. In late July, a warning was issued to Mladić that any attack on Goražde would be met with significant air strikes.[33] This threat was subsequently expanded, on 1 August, to include other UN "safe areas."[34] Just as peace prospects in the Balkans were improving,[35] however,

---

30 Cohen 1995b.
31 Hedges 1995a; see also Cohen 1995c.
32 Hedges 1995b.
33 Hedges 1995c.
34 Whitney 1995b.
35 On 9 August 1995, the US unveiled a new peace initiative, outlining a territorial division that would have preserved the ratio of 49 percent of Bosnian territory for the Bosnian Serbs and 51 percent for a Muslim-Croat federation. While the Bosnian Serbs would be able to retain control of the recently conquered towns of Srebrenica (11 July) and Žepa (25 July), the Muslims would be compensated with land around Sarajevo. The plan, introduced by Richard Holbrooke, US assistant secretary of state

another mortar attack on the Markale market in Sarajevo, in which thirty-seven people were killed and another eighty or so injured, effectively derailed negotiations. Two days later, on 30 August, NATO launched Operation Deliberate Force (ODF), a massive military operation (nearly 300 sorties) involving five countries (France, the Netherlands, Spain, the UK, and the US) hitting Serb targets across Bosnia. Following the initial round of attacks, Western leaders were clear that air strikes would continue until NATO demands were met. On 1 September, a pause in ODF was announced and a new round of peace talks initiated (this time with the Serbs [Mladić, Karadžić, and Milošević] negotiating as a single team). Even in the face of the massive NATO bombing campaign, however, Mladić was willing to accept only two of the three major NATO demands. Though he was prepared to stop shelling UN "safe areas" and to open routes into Sarajevo, he was not prepared (at that point) to pull heavy weapons from the outskirts of the city. As a result, NATO resumed air strikes four days later – on 5 September – and, along with the UN's Rapid Reaction Force, continued attacking Serb targets, making it clear to Mladić that only pulling the heavy weapons would end the bombardment. On 14 September, nearly two weeks after it had initially begun, ODF was suspended as Serb leaders (including Mladić) finally agreed to withdraw their heavy weapons from the exclusion zone around Sarajevo. By 21 September, some 250 heavy weapons had been removed, and UN monitors were given unimpeded access to the area. The fighting had stopped, and the peace process was well under way.

US intelligence assessments of Mladić during this exchange relied explicitly on perceptions of his past behavior. As a declassified CIA memo from 6 September 1995, entitled "Mladic Running True to Form," explains: "Mladic's decision about withdrawing heavy weapons will be determined by both his perception of military and political "realities" *and by his familiar patterns of thinking and behaving.*"[36] The memo goes on to cite "recent media appearances" by Mladić that suggested that he also had made reputational inferences regarding UN/NATO action. According to the memo, Mladić's "facts and tactical considerations" as he "has indicated he perceives them" include his "past experience with UN/NATO forces: Mladic's reactions to past NATO strikes suggest he

---

for European and Canadian affairs, was gaining favor among the warring factions. See New York Times 1995; also Holbrooke 1998.

36 Clinton Digital Library 1995b, emphasis added.

may judge that he can outlast international willingness to pursue military action and that he can manipulate the allies and put them off with token actions."[37]

Continued pressure through ODF, moreover, was recognized as the best way to convince Mladić to capitulate, an assessment similarly revealed through reference to his past behavior. A declassified intelligence briefing from the DCI Interagency Balkan Task Force on 5 September 1995 first notes that Mladić, "unlike the Bosnian Serb political leadership[,] ... is refusing to accept the demand ... that heavy weapons be withdrawn from the exclusion zone around Sarajevo." It then concludes: "Various reporting and past experience make clear, however, that Mladic responds to changing circumstances, mostly credible military pressure. He backed down and withdrew some of his forces from the Sarajevo region in 1994 when it appeared NATO was prepared though airstrikes to enforce the UN-imposed heavy weapons exclusion zone."[38]

Additional archival material suggests that bombing was recognized at the time as necessary for re-establishing UN/NATO resolve vis-à-vis the Serbs. In a state department cable to Secretary Perry, NSA Lake, Ambassador Madeline Albright, and General Shalikashvili on 4 September, Richard Holbrooke discussed the progress of negotiations after "some fifty hours of discussions with Milosevic." He argues, in part, that "a resumption of the bombing tonight is an essential component of our negotiating strategy ... Its value in both Belgrade and Sarajevo is becoming increasingly clear." The cable finishes by saying: "In conclusion, bombing this week while we go to Geneva [for further negotiations] will be a plus in the talks themselves, in strengthening our overall image in Europe, with Sarajevo, *and in partially restoring some of the events of recent years.*"[39] As it turns out, Holbrooke's assessments were more or less right – continued pressure through ODF was essential to "restoring" a reputation for resolve that had been gradually eroded in previous exchanges, and was a necessary component of the broader diplomatic strategy that was able, eventually, to bring the war to a close.

The exchange of August/September 1995 can be seen as having two distinct stages. Stage one included the Markale attack and its immediate

---

37 Ibid.
38 Clinton Digital Library 1995a.
39 United States Department of State 1995, emphasis added.

aftermath, as ODF was launched and UN/NATO demands (stop shelling UN "safe areas"; open routes into Sarajevo; remove heavy weapons from around the city) were articulated. With Mladić refusing to capitulate even in the face of a massive military campaign (ODF constituting at the time the largest military operation in NATO's history), this initial stage represents a clear failure of coercive diplomacy. The Bosnian Serbs were neither compelled to comply with, nor deterred from committing further infringements against, UN demands. This failure is perplexing, given that several key prerequisites for successful coercive diplomacy were clearly met: UN/NATO demands were explicitly and unequivocally communicated; the mobilization of force for ODF was overwhelming and, along with international condemnation of the market attack, demonstrated a strong commitment to achieving the outlined objectives; and the execution of the initial strikes showcased the continued capability of UN/NATO forces to deliver a devastating bombardment. Why, then, did coercive diplomacy fail? The answer lies in perceptions of UN/NATO resolve on the part of Mladić (as detailed above); after nearly four years of fighting, and numerous instances in which the UN/NATO either backed down entirely (as in the July 1995 exchange) or ended bombing campaigns prematurely (e.g., the May 1995 exchange), Mladić had real reason to doubt whether ODF would persist long enough or with enough force to achieve all of its demands. This *reputation* undermined the positive presence of the other prerequisites, and caused Mladić to persist in the face of significant coercive pressure. The Serb military leader, with very little to lose, assumed that it was only a matter of time before the air attacks would end, particularly given Russian threats of intervention if the strikes continued (Russian and French opposition had played a key role in undermining the air campaign of May 1995 – see above). Thus, the first stage of the crisis resulted in coercive failure largely because of past actions and behavior by the UN and NATO in previous exchanges during the war.

Stage two occurred when NATO resumed air strikes on 5 September, backed by artillery attacks from the Rapid Reaction Force and the launching of thirteen Tomahawk cruise missiles from the USS *Normandy* stationed in the Adriatic Sea. In the face of this renewed coercive pressure, Mladić and the Bosnian Serbs capitulated to UN demands by withdrawing their heavy weapons from the 20-kilometer exclusion zone around Sarajevo. After nearly four years of bitter war, peace was finally within reach, with the subsequent signing of the Dayton Peace Accords widely acknowledged as a significant achievement of coercive diplomacy. This success at stage two is intimately linked with initial failure at stage one. As has been argued, a short-term deterrence/compellence failure is often required to demonstrate (or *re-establish*) a reputation for resolve, and is therefore necessary for long-term coercive success. How else would Mladić know that the alliance was committed to following through on their threats? Again, breaking a crisis down into extended threat/response sequences is important. Not only does it offer a more accurate depiction of the actual history with regard to a particular crisis, it similarly allows for the gathering of more data for the purposes of empirical testing. In terms of testing RDT, identifying multiple data points within a single crisis reflects the possibility that the four conditions of successful deterrence can actually change throughout the crisis. Re-establishing resolve by recommencing air and artillery strikes on 5 September – though initially an apparent failure of deterrence/compellence – was necessary for the peace process that began on 14 September, and for the subsequent long-term deterrence success embodied by the Dayton Accords.

Overall, Harvey[40] assesses fourteen exchanges (1993–5) between the US/NATO/UN and Bosnian Serbs for necessity and sufficiency as it relates to the four RDT prerequisites. His results support the hypothesis that all four prerequisites were necessary for deterrence success, as well as the related claim that the absence of any one prerequisite was sufficient for failure. Further, when testing for *independent* necessity and sufficiency, Harvey found that "resolve consistently performed well relative to other factors, implying that the presence or absence of different prerequisites (or combination of prerequisites) does not have a uniform impact on the probability of success."[41] While this in no way implies that a reputation for resolve alone can account for deterrence success (the simplified argument against which P-M-H stakes its claim), it does highlight the relative importance of resolve vis-à-vis the other prerequisites in enhancing the probability of achieving effective deterrence/compellence.

Goldstein and Pevehouse, in their study of coercive bargaining in the Bosnia-Herzegovina conflict, point to similar patterns in crisis escalation.[42] Their empirical results from three distinct crisis periods during

---

40 Harvey 1997, 1998.
41 Harvey 1998, 702.
42 Goldstein and Pevehouse 1997.

the conflict (1992–5) support the view that the international use of force induced Serbian cooperation. According to the authors, "robust NATO air strikes finally caused the Serb forces to cooperate with the Bosnian government."[43] Status quo strategies and reciprocity (cooperation through negotiation) often led Serb and Bosnian Serb leaders to embrace bullying tactics. "Clearly, such 'nice' strategies as Axelrod's tit for tat or Osgood's GRIT [Graduated Reciprocation in Tension Reduction] do not work well against bullies."[44] Whenever the prerequisites for deterrence were met and a reputation for resolve established, credibility increased and the violence was contained.

Jakobsen's case study on coercive diplomacy in Bosnia-Herzegovina lends further support to the notion that a specific reputation for resolve mattered, particularly in the final stages of the crisis:

> The initial failure of NATO's 1 August [1995] threat was inevitable given the reputation that the Western powers had established for failing to execute their threats or limiting their use of force to a symbolic level. In the year preceding the threat, non-compliance had brought the BSA [Bosnian Serb Army] more gain than pain as the West had kept punishment to a minimum and tried to obtain Serbian co-operation by scaling down demands and offering carrots instead.[45]

As he concludes, "Operation 'Deliberate Force' induced the BSA to reassess its image of the West, and NATO forces deployed to oversee the implementation of the Dayton Peace Agreement were treated with respect. The West no longer had the reputation for backing down and letting non-compliance go unpunished."[46]

The brief case evidence provided here is sufficient to establish the central claim that specific reputations mattered over the course of the Bosnia-Herzegovina crisis. The record is clear: across multiple exchanges, a reputation for resolve (in conjunction with clear communication, commitments, and capabilities) was essential for successful deterrence; even when the other three prerequisites were present, moreover, a perceived lack of resolve based on inferences from past behavior precipitated

---

43 Ibid., 527.
44 Ibid., 528.
45 Jakobsen 2000, 17.
46 Ibid.

failure (as occurred in the August–September 1995 exchange detailed above). Further, both sides in the crises appeared to make reputational inferences – US intelligence estimates assessing Mladić's likely responses to UN/NATO ultimatums, for example, explicitly referenced his pattern of behavior in previous exchanges. These findings provide support for RDT while simultaneously undermining confidence in the P-M-H consensus.

Case 2 – Kosovo (1998–9)

The Kosovo crisis, though shorter in duration, was similarly composed of repeated and evolving exchanges between the UN/US/NATO and a smaller adversary: the Federal Republic of Yugoslavia (FRY) under the leadership of Slobodan Milošević. Following a series of international condemnations and punitive sanctions against the FRY in the early months of 1998, international concern over growing violence in the province of Kosovo led to a more vociferous and threatening Western posture. At a meeting of European foreign ministers on 8 June, the UK's foreign secretary, Robin Cook, strongly hinted that Milošević's continued aggression in Kosovo would not be without consequence: "I hope Milosevic is listening. This is the last warning. He should back off now."[47] Calls from the Contact Group – the international body tasked with spearheading the West's approach to the former Yugoslavia, composed of the US, the UK, France, Germany, Italy, and Russia – for a ceasefire, international monitoring, and talks toward a political solution followed shortly thereafter.

On 15 June, as a result of mounting concern over the situation, NATO conducted major aerial exercises over Albania and Macedonia as a show of strength. Eighty-five aircraft from thirteen countries flew in "Operation Determined Falcon," designed to, in the words of US defense secretary William Cohen, "demonstrate ... that NATO is united in its commitment to seek a cease-fire and a cessation of hostilities [in Kosovo] and demonstrate its capacity to rapidly mobilize some very significant lethal capability."[48] Shortly after the exercises, Milošević, following talks with Russian president Boris Yeltsin, agreed to meet with ethnic Albanian leaders, echoed a pledge to permit foreign diplomats

---

47 Keesing's Record of World Events 1998, 42356.
48 CBS News staff 1998.

to observe the situation, and promised Moscow (a traditional ally of the Serbs) that his government would try to assist the thousands of refugees generated by the crisis.[49] Later that month, US envoy Richard Holbrooke – stating that the crisis was in a critical stage – failed to persuade Milošević to reach a peaceful solution to the conflict.[50] On 24 June 24, UK prime minister Tony Blair warned that there remained the possibility of employing NATO air strikes against Serbia unless Milošević withdrew from Kosovo, as the alliance began to draft plans for the use of military force as a "final ultimatum." Nonetheless, reports from observers determined that NATO's show of force had little to no impact on the activities of Serbian security forces, who continued their crackdown on ethnic Albanians in the province.[51] Although the demonstration of NATO air power on 15 June was ample evidence of its capability to launch air strikes against the FRY, the Western powers only half-heartedly communicated real, credible threats to Milošević. Furthermore, disagreement within the Contact Group over air strikes – namely from Russia – blunted the coherence of Western demands and resolve, and thus the effectiveness of the threat of force. At the end of the exchange, even while the violence continued in Kosovo, NATO air strikes were not considered by the Western powers as a serious option at that time.

In early September, it was evident that Serb military, paramilitary, and police units remained heavily engaged in "counter-insurgency" operations in Kosovo. Particularly distressing to the international community were reports of atrocities committed by Serb forces, including the razing of entire ethnic Albanian villages and a number of massacres, which were forcing tens of thousands to flee their homes. As a result, on 23 September, the UN Security Council adopted Resolution 1199, which demanded a ceasefire, condemned violence by "any party," and also expressed "grave concern" over the "excessive and indiscriminate use of force by Serbian security forces."[52] The resolution

---

49 Gordon 1998. The ethnic Albanians' rejection of Milošević's overtures to hold talks further destabilized the situation, leading to a tightening of Belgrade's grip on the region. Archival evidence indicates the extent to which the Clinton administration recognized the importance of Moscow's role in the Kosovo crisis. See, for example, Clinton Digital Library 1998 and 1999a.
50 New York Times 1998c.
51 Keesing's Record of World Events 1998, 42356.
52 United Nations Security Council 1998b.

invoked Chapter VII of the UN Charter, which hinted that further action was possible.

The threat of NATO intervention came soon after. The United States argued, contrary to Russian and Chinese claims, that NATO did not require additional UN authorization to use military force. Further, a number of NATO officials remarked that the alliance was completing plans for air strikes against Serbia. On 24 September, the alliance approved an "activation warning," which authorized the Supreme Allied Commander Europe (SACEUR) to request the necessary forces to conduct military operations of a "limited" and more extensive "phased" nature against Serbia.[53] Later in the week, on 28 September, Milošević announced that his forces were "victorious" in Kosovo and were returning to barracks. In response, Secretary Cohen said that there had been no evidence Serbia was beginning a strategic withdrawal or ending its military campaign against ethnic Albanian separatists.[54] He warned Belgrade that failure to do so would result in NATO strikes.[55]

In early October, a massacre in which an estimated thirty-six ethnic Albanian civilians were killed by Serb forces resulted in further condemnation by the international community and shed doubt on Milošević's claims that his forces were ending their operations in Kosovo. NATO faced a decision on whether to commit to air strikes after UN secretary-general Kofi Annan's report on the situation, and a number of officials made clear signals that the alliance was willing to use its considerable military strength in the region to affect an outcome. As the US advised Americans to leave the FRY in anticipation of NATO military action, Secretary Cohen was reported as saying that military strikes would begin "soon." Secretary of State Albright mentioned that while the Western powers hoped for a negotiated solution to the crisis, the best way to press the issue was to back up diplomatic initiatives with the threat of the use of force.[56]

On 6 October, the Security Council reported that the FRY was not in full compliance with UN resolutions despite reports of a Serbian

---

53 BBC 1998a.
54 A declassified US intelligence assessment of compliance with UNSCR 1199 reveals that, as of 1 October 1998, the Serbs were complying with only one ("provide security for international monitors") of the 10 provisions. See Clinton Digital Library 1999b.
55 Erlanger 1998a.
56 BBC 1998b.

withdrawal from Kosovo. Furthermore, US special envoy Richard Holbrooke reported continuing failure to persuade Milošević to accept a political solution. At this juncture, President Clinton made the most explicit statement of Western demands and threats to that point: Milošević was required to unconditionally comply with Security Council demands by declaring an immediate ceasefire, pull out Serbian security forces, allow unhindered access to Kosovo for international relief organizations, and begin negotiations with Kosovar Albanian rebels toward a political solution to the conflict. Clinton's statement that "NATO was prepared to act"[57] was reinforced by Secretary Cohen's statement that NATO possessed sufficient capability to inflict "substantial" losses on Yugoslav military capabilities from the air.[58] NATO secretary general Javier Solana further stated that the alliance stood ready to launch air strikes against the FRY in a matter of days, as the planning process was complete, and that an "activation order" would clear the way for the use of force. However, Solana refused to give a specific date for such an event.[59] Last-ditch meetings between Holbrooke and Milošević were reported to yield no progress and Western countries began to advise their nationals to leave the FRY in advance of possible NATO action.

NATO's activation order came on 13 October and centralized NATO assets under the command of SACEUR, allowing for a limited program of strikes. (Although Italy and Germany – between governments at the time – had expressed their reservations on using force, their subsequent endorsement of the policy at the North Atlantic Council meeting that gave the order sealed alliance unity.) Reports subsequently emerged suggesting that Milošević was soon to agree to international requirements on the crisis in Kosovo, which were expanded to include allowing refugees to return to their homes as well as cooperation with the international war crimes investigators.[60] The next day an agreement was formally reached that called for the deployment of 2000 unarmed observers under the aegis of the Organization for Security and Cooperation in Europe (OSCE) to verify Serb withdrawal, NATO reconnaissance overflights to supplement the OSCE mission, full refugee repatriation, and eventual negotiations between Milošević and the ethnic

57 Myers and Erlanger 1998b.
58 Myers and Erlanger 1998a.
59 Cohen 1998a.
60 Cohen 1998b.

Albanians, whose militant wing, the Kosovo Liberation Army (or UCK, its Albanian acronym), was committed to independence. The observers' safety and freedom of movement was also guaranteed. Milošević responded by claiming that Serb units were withdrawing. He also told the Serbian public that military intervention had been averted and that the agreement would only lead to autonomy for Kosovo, not the full independence demanded by ethnic Albanian separatists. The threat of air strikes remained, however, as NATO gave Belgrade ninety-six hours to comply.[61]

Despite the last-minute agreement between FRY and the Western powers over the crisis, continuing violence and evidence of another Serb crackdown in Kosovo renewed NATO's threats to use force unless Milošević came into full compliance. Western powers stated that they were not satisfied with the extent of Milošević's withdrawal from Kosovo, and reminded Belgrade that NATO's activation order remained in force and gave it the authority to launch air strikes if it saw fit. SACEUR General Wesley Clark and US envoy Christopher Hill gave Milošević until 27 October to fully comply with the provisions of the agreement or risk NATO strikes.[62] Satisfied with Milošević's "substantial compliance," NATO subsequently lifted the immediate threat of strikes on that date, but did not cancel it outright in order to "extend indefinitely the threat of strikes should Milošević resume the campaign [in Kosovo]."[63]

The alliance's commitment to the threat of force to reinforce diplomatic initiatives succeeded in this (October 1998) exchange – albeit, in a somewhat disjointed fashion – as Milošević was given a clearly communicated set of coherent, realizable objectives, engaged by a credible threat of force from a highly capable military presence, and faced with enough Western resolve (notwithstanding Russian and Chinese objections)[64] to sign on to the agreement brokered by Holbrooke. Although the situation lurched from crisis to crisis at first, steadily increasing, credible NATO resolve (to push Milošević to the brink), and enough time and incentives to accept a political solution (to ensure that he did not step over the edge), assured that Belgrade would agree to the proposals on the table.

61 Perlez 1998.
62 Whitney 1998.
63 Facts on File Yearbook 1998.
64 Ibrahim 1998.

Intensifying conflict between Serb forces and UCK rebels, however, precipitated another crisis on 17 January after the discovery of the mutilated bodies of forty ethnic Albanians outside the village of Račak. The massacre, and subsequent Serb attempts to hinder a verification mission, resulted in swift international condemnation. More importantly, NATO held an emergency meeting to discuss its response to the mass killing.[65] It was identified as a clear violation of Serbia's commitments to NATO, and as a result the alliance demanded that the perpetrators of the massacre be brought to justice and war crimes prosecutors be permitted to conduct an investigation, in addition to reiterating the provisions of the agreement struck between Serbia and NATO in October. The dispatch of two senior NATO generals and other officials to Belgrade soon after the massacre was intended to impress upon the Serbs the importance of living up to their commitments with NATO in addition to providing a "final" warning to both Milošević and the increasingly unified and emboldened ethnic Albanian resistance.[66]

The military option had thus been renewed: warnings that NATO would resort to air strikes to contain the situation and bring the Serbs into an acceptable level of compliance began to resound from various NATO and government officials. In addition to the statements made by Secretary General Solana and Secretary Albright to the effect that the Serbs faced NATO action should Milošević not comply with the October agreement, SACEUR noted after meeting with the Yugoslav leader that he only understood the language of force, and thus it was incumbent upon the alliance to produce a credible military threat to the FRY.[67] As more NATO assets assembled in the region for possible use against targets throughout the FRY, the West ratcheted up the pressure on Milošević, warning that his maneuverings to stay ahead of NATO air strikes left critical issues unresolved and risked the very action he was attempting to skirt.

At the same time, the situation was complicated by the growing strength and legitimacy of the UCK in Kosovo among ethnic Albanians. In order to engage this group of hard-line Kosovar separatists, the Clinton administration pressed them to support a realistic political settlement – one that gave Kosovo autonomy, not independence.

---

65 Perlez 1999a.
66 Perlez 1999b.
67 Perlez 1999c.

Realizing that a political solution was necessary to avoid a deepening spiral of violence in Kosovo, the Contact Group struggled to bring the various parties to the negotiating table. To this end, threats of force were extended to the UCK as NATO warned both sides that they had "reached the limit."[68]

The turning point came on 29 January, after two weeks of constant threats by NATO against both Belgrade and the UCK. The Contact Group gave the various sides three weeks (until 13 February) to reach a political solution to the conflict during talks in Rambouillet, France, and then another week to implement an agreement based on a Contact Group proposal calling for a "self-governing Kosovo" as well as demands that international verifiers and war crimes tribunal investigators receive full cooperation to maintain the ceasefire and ask questions regarding atrocities.[69] To that effect, NATO issued an ultimatum consisting of a clear and direct warning of military intervention against both Serb and ethnic Albanian forces in Kosovo unless their respective negotiating parties came to an agreement on time.[70] The next day, NATO removed the last constraints against military force to increase pressure on the warring parties. Soon after, both parties agreed to send high-level representatives to Rambouillet for talks, but Milošević and several hard-line UCK officials refused to attend, sending aides to the negotiations instead. Despite this setback, however, a united front for urgent and comprehensive talks among the parties from the Contact Group, and a credible, capable, and constantly communicated threat of force to bolster the Contact Group's diplomatic pressure succeeded in bringing the various sides to the table.

Meanwhile, violence continued in Kosovo, as did Western threats of military intervention. Threats were especially leveled against Milošević, who was under the most pressure to accept the Contact Group's proposals. Kosovo's autonomous status, the question of independence, and the deployment of an estimated 30,000-strong NATO implementation force remained the contentious issues. Milošević, who categorically refused to permit foreign troops to operate on Yugoslav soil, vigorously

---

68 CNN 1999. The Contact Group was temporarily split on this matter, but the American position of extending the threat of force to both sides in order to compel negotiations won out in the end.
69 BBC 1999a.
70 Ibid.

opposed the latter stipulation.[71] As the deadline for a solution neared, NATO stepped up threats to conduct military operations against the parties, backed them up by bringing more military assets into the region, and began planning for strikes. The US in particular was pushing for immediate strikes should Belgrade block the agreement. The threats intensified as the deadline loomed, and included direct warnings from Secretary General Solana and President Clinton that strikes were imminent. A clear signal was the evacuation of Western diplomatic and relief staff from the FRY.[72]

Intense negotiations through February and early March failed to produce an agreement.[73] While the Kosovar Albanians were eventually persuaded to accept a provisional agreement, Milošević and the Serbs remained steadfast in their refusal. Richard Holbrooke and Ambassador Christopher Hill (the architect of the peace plan) made a two-day trip to Belgrade on 10 March in another attempt to persuade Milošević, but again could not secure his acceptance.[74] Hill communicated to Secretary Albright that the odds of Serb acceptance of the proposal stood at "zero point zero."[75] A resumption of the Rambouillet talks in Paris on 15 March was similarly ineffective. While the Kosovar Albanians signed the agreement on 18 March, Milošević flatly refused.[76] A renewed FRY offensive against the UCK further eroded peace prospects, with the assault seemingly aimed at "crushing the forces of the ethnic Albanians."[77] Over the subsequent days, NATO continued to ratchet up the threat of air strikes, promising "widening" and "sustained" attacks on expanded FRY military targets.[78]

A final overture to Milošević from Holbrooke was rebuffed on 22 March.[79] On 24 March, the bombing campaign began, as "scores of Serbian military bases and depots, aircraft and munitions factories were ... hit by NATO forces equipped with more than 400 bomber aircraft from

---

71 BBC 1999b.
72 Becker 1999. See also BBC 1999c.
73 For an overview of the Rambouillet conference, see Weller 1999.
74 Gall 1999.
75 Quoted in Burg 2003, 91.
76 Whitney 1999a.
77 Perlez 1999d.
78 Myers 1999.
79 Perlez 1999e.

European bases, and missile weaponry aboard a half dozen warships in the Adriatic region."[80] As Daalder and O'Hanlon summarize:

> The failure of the Rambouillet talks left the United States and NATO with little choice but to follow through on their frequent threats of force and commence military operations against Serbia. In doing so, Washington and its allies were convinced that a demonstration of NATO's military prowess was all that was needed to force Milosevic back to the bargaining table. As events showed, this did not happen. Instead, Milosevic escalated the conflict.[81]

The air campaign (Operation Allied Force) would go on to last seventy-eight days, until Milošević finally capitulated on 10 June and the bombing stopped.[82] The reasons for this capitulation remain contested (more on this below), but it is clear that US/NATO coercive diplomacy (deterrence and compellence) initially failed, despite clearly communicated threats and ultimatums, sufficient capabilities to inflict significant damage on FRY forces, and a strong commitment to resolving the Kosovo crisis.

Why, then, did Milošević fail to comply? Many pointed to the history of bluffs from US/NATO since the crisis began in 1998. As NATO threats (and their associated ultimatums) continued to be ignored, *New York Times* journalist Jane Perlez recounted a conversation with NATO officials: "[They] described the history of the threats made by the alliance but not carried out against Mr. Milosevic since last summer when Serbian forces embarked on a major offensive against the ethnic Albanian guerrillas."[83] Anthony Lewis, also of the *Times*, described what he called the "Credibility Gulch" of the US and NATO, whereby "Milosevic has treated the [repeated] threats [over Kosovo] contemptuously, as bluffs."[84] While earlier exchanges (e.g., in October 1998) had seen the successful use of coercive threats, the efficacy of their issuance had gradually eroded. As General Klaus Naumann explained to a US Senate committee: "We were sent to Belgrade [in October 1998] with a clear stick in our hip pocket, the ultimatum." But eventually "this stick had been transformed into a rubber baton since our threat was not as

---

80 Clines 1999.
81 Daalder and O'Hanlon 2000, 65–6.
82 Whitney 1999b.
83 Perlez 1999d, 17.
84 Lewis 1999.

credible as it used to be in October. *We had threatened too often and hadn't done anything.*[85] Following the Račak massacre, for example, NATO's "final" warning to Milošević again stopped short of the use of force as preparations were made for negotiations at Rambouillet. By March, this specific reputation for not following through on threats of punitive military action helped undermine, in part, the credibility of NATO's coercive strategy. Given the string of "frequent threats, failed ultimatums, and feeble deadlines that were immediately reset once passed," Daalder and O'Hanlon write, it is not "surprising that Milosevic might have come to believe NATO would not strike or, when it did, that the allies would not be able to sustain the effort for long."[86]

In addition to specific, within-crisis credibility concerns, however, there is also evidence that general, dispositional (across-case) reputations were relevant in the Kosovo crisis. That is, Milošević based his decisions in Kosovo, in part, on assessments of the behavior of US and NATO officials elsewhere (including but not limited to Bosnia-Herzegovina and Iraq). The general reputation of the US and NATO helped inform two aspects of Milošević's decision-making calculus: first, how long and severe he believed the bombing campaign would be; and second, the tactics he believed he could employ to undermine the US/NATO's willingness to continue strikes in order to secure a preferable deal (compared to the one offered at Rambouillet) for the FRY.

With respect to the first dimension, Stephen Hosmer notes that "while Milosevic apparently expected to be bombed, his intelligence sources and *perceptions of recent US and NATO behavior* may have encouraged him to believe that any NATO air strikes would be of limited duration and severity."[87] This behavior, moreover, extended beyond the immediate crisis in Kosovo to include US/NATO actions in other crises. As Steven Burg observed: "Milosevic's estimate of the probable potency of the NATO threat was likely to have taken into account the relatively limited air campaign conducted in Bosnia in 1995 and the similarly limited action taken by the United States and Britain against Iraq in December 1997."[88] Hosmer likewise makes the connection between Kosovo and Iraq:

A brief bombing campaign may also have appeared credible to Milosevic because of the precedent set by the December 1998 Operation Desert Fox

85 Quoted in Burg 2003, 92; emphasis added.
86 Daalder and O'Hanlon 2000, 95.
87 Hosmer 2001, 19; emphasis added.
88 Burg 2003, 93.

air campaign, in which US and UK forces attacked Iraq for its refusal to permit UN inspections of suspected weapons of mass destruction (WMD) sites. The operative lesson for Milosevic was that even though Saddam refused to yield, the bombing was terminated after four days. In this respect, Milosevic may have expected that any NATO bombing would be more akin to Operation Desert Fox than to Operation Desert Storm.[89]

As do Daalder and O'Hanlon:

American and British air strikes against Iraq the previous December suggested that the Clinton administration itself did not have the stomach for a sustained military effort. If anything, Operation Desert Fox demonstrated that air strikes designed to "degrade" an opponent's military capability – even that of an opponent as feared and loathed as Saddam Hussein, ruling a country in a region of critical interest to the United States, and possessing the capacity to produce weapons of mass destruction – would likely last only a few days.[90]

Indeed, available evidence indicates that Milošević was aware that the NATO threat to bomb was real, but nonetheless remained confident that NATO would not escalate strikes to levels that were unsustainable (from the FRY point of view) nor conduct any ground invasion into Kosovo.

Milošević made these feelings known in communications with Western officials. Sell recounts a conversation between Milošević and Richard Holbrooke: "During a ceremonial dinner in late 1998, Holbrooke reminded Milosevic that he faced the prospect of massive bombing if he did not agree to the US proposal. And Milosevic, in an extraordinary scene, leaned back and replied 'Yes, Dick, I understand, but I'm sure that the bombing will be very polite.'"[91] Later, in the 21 March meeting with Richard Holbrooke noted above (which constituted the final attempt by US/NATO to secure an agreement to avoid air strikes),

89 Hosmer 2001, 21–2.
90 Daalder and O'Hanlon 2000, 95.
91 Sell 2002, 303.

Milošević was similarly resigned to the prospect of a *bombing* campaign (not an invasion). As described by Holbrooke:

> I said to him, "You understand that if I leave here without an agreement today, bombing will start almost immediately." And he said, "Yes, I understand that." I said, "You understand it'll be swift, severe, and sustained." And I used those three words very carefully, after consultations with the Pentagon. And he said, "You're a great country, a powerful country. You can do anything you want. We can't stop you." ... I said, "Yes, you understand. You're absolutely clear what will happen when we leave?" And he said, very quietly, "Yes. You'll bomb us."[92]

Milošević was thus quite clear – NATO would bomb (not invade) and the bombing would be "very polite" (i.e., survivable, as it was for Hussein in Iraq in 1998). While it is important to recognize that such perceptions did not *wholly determine* Milošević's decision to ignore the coercive threat (additional reasons may have been – and likely were – relevant, including the symbolic importance of Kosovo, domestic political pressures, Russian undermining of UN consensus, and so on), it is nonetheless clear that past behavior (in Kosovo, but also in other crises, such as Bosnia-Herzegovina and Iraq) contributed to his calculation that air strikes could be outlasted. Reputations mattered.

The second dimension of Milošević's calculus – the tactics he believed he could employ to overcome NATO's coercive campaign – were similarly influenced by a general reputation attributed to US/NATO; specifically, Milošević's perceptions of Western *casualty aversion*. Milošević assumed (and publicly stated) that US/NATO leaders lacked the intestinal fortitude to sustain a bombing campaign. In comments to German foreign minister Joschka Fischer, Milošević stated (in March 1999): "I can stand death – lots of it – but you can't."[93] During NATO's bombing campaign, Milošević predicted: "You are not willing to sacrifice lives to achieve our surrender; but we are willing to die to defend our rights as an independent sovereign nation."[94] These perceptions were tied, again, to Milošević's understanding of Western behavior in past crises (including Vietnam, Somalia, Haiti, Iraq, and Bosnia-Herzegovina; for

---

92 Quoted in Hosmer 2001, 20.
93 Quoted in Daalder and O'Hanlon 2000, 94.
94 Doder and Branson 1999, 263.

a general discussion of American casualty aversion with regard to these crises, see Gelpi, Feaver, and Reifler).[95] As a result, Milošević believed he could *counter-coerce* NATO into stopping or limiting its military campaign.

Byman and Waxman offer a good overview of the counter-coercion thesis as it pertains to the Kosovo case:

> Rather than simply minimizing the effect of coercive threats, an adversary may try to impose costs on the coercing power; it can escalate militarily or attempt to drive a diplomatic wedge between states aligned against it, perhaps convincing the coercer to back down and withdraw its own threat to impose costs ... Any assessment of air power's effectiveness should focus on the perceived costs it creates in an adversary's mind. But, viewing coercion dynamically, that assessment should incorporate the adversary's ability to neutralize those costs (or its belief that it can) as well as the set of other threats bearing down on the adversary at any given time.[96]

Given perceptions as to Western casualty aversion, Milošević believed he could overcome the NATO campaign by, as Wilner explains, "increasing the number of civilian and NATO military deaths."[97] The most obvious example of this strategy was the existence of Operation Horseshoe, which involved the ethnic cleansing (through forcible expulsion) of Albanians from Kosovo (thus creating a refugee crisis and humanitarian disaster). Harvey elucidates: "It stands to reason that NATO's guiding principles would generate obvious counter-moves by Milosevic to increase innocent suffering (e.g., Operation Horseshoe), undermine alliance cohesion, create counter-alliances (with Russia and China), and increase actual or prospective US or allied casualties."[98] Hosmer offers a similar assessment:

> Milosevic [believed] that the NATO governments would not remain steadfast in their support of the bombing and that they could eventually be persuaded to accept terms close to those being offered by Belgrade. He was no doubt encouraged in this view by the irresolution NATO had

---

95 Gelpi, Feaver, and Reifler 2009.
96 Byman and Waxman 2000, 10–11.
97 Wilner 2015, 25.
98 Harvey 2006, 150.

displayed in past dealings with the FRY over Kosovo and the apparent differences of opinion that existed among the allies about the use of force. Furthermore, it seemed clear that Milosevic assumed that the FRY could promote the erosion of NATO unity and resolve by (1) engaging in ethnic cleansing, (2) undermining support for the war among NATO and other foreign publics, and (3) exploiting Russia's support for the FRY.[99]

What Milošević misunderstood, of course, was that NATO's sustained bombing campaign (and the alliance's crystal clear commitment to circumvent an uglier ground war) was designed precisely to avoid US/NATO military casualties (while limiting Kosovar and Serb civilian deaths), thus stripping from Milošević's toolbox any countercoercion leverage that would have come from exploiting the West's aversion to casualties. When faced with mounting military failures and increasingly costly US/NATO attacks on high-value targets in Belgrade, and without any corresponding successes to point to, Milošević was forced to capitulate, accepting a deal that was demonstrably worse (from the FRY point of view) than the one that had been on the table in Rambouillet.

Contrary to those who attribute Milošević's decision to settle to an imminent threat of a NATO ground invasion[100] or domestic political pressures,[101] it was precisely NATO's decision to apply coercion *exclusively* through air power that served to end the crisis.[102] It took seventy-eight days of bombing (and the increasing intensity of air strikes over the final few weeks) to convince Milošević that countercoercion would not (or could not) deliver the deal he had hoped to achieve. While other factors (including, again, the symbolic importance of Kosovo and domestic political pressures) were obviously important in pushing Milošević to hold out, NATO's general reputation for casualty aversion (compounded by examples of limited bombing in Iraq and a specific reputation for irresolution in prior exchanges of the Kosovo crisis) formed the basis of a counter-coercive strategy that prolonged the crisis.

---

99 Hosmer 2001, 24–5.
100 For example, Daalder and O'Hanlon 2000; Byman and Waxman 2000.
101 See Lake 2009.
102 Harvey 2006; see also Stigler 2002/3.

Finally, it must be noted that US/NATO leaders *also* drew on past behavior and reputations to inform their perceptions of what Milošević was likely to do in Kosovo. As Hosmer describes:

> The calculations of some allied leaders that Milosevic would come to heel and accept the terms of the Rambouillet Agreement after a few days of bombing seem to have been predicated on a misestimate of how Milosevic would view his options. Their miscalculations seem to have been influenced at least in part by the effectiveness of limited NATO bombing in bringing the conflict in Bosnia-Herzegovina to a close in 1995 and by the Dayton negotiation experience, where Milosevic conceded on most of the demands being made of the Bosnian Serbs. The NATO leaders may also have been misled by Milosevic's apparent readiness to yield under a NATO bombing threat in October 1998.[103]

The "widely shared" view among Western allies at the time was, as then secretary of state Madeleine Albright remarked (and as referenced above), that "Milosevic would probably back down after a few visible targets were hit."[104] President Clinton was even more explicit: "The reason we went forward with the air actions is because we thought there were some chance it would deter Mr. Milosevic based on two previous examples – number one, last October in Kosovo, when he was well poised to do the same thing; and number two, in Bosnia, where there were 12 days of NATO attacks over a 20-day period."[105] While these assessments turned out to be incorrect, they nonetheless contradict the P-M-H consensus, which suggests that past actions are never used to calculate credibility (in this instance, the US inferred from past behavior that Milošević would be irresolute in the face of air strikes, despite his insistence during crisis negotiations that he would stand firm and fight to the end).

Indeed, the evidence from the Kosovo case points to multiple instances in which both specific and general reputations were relevant to assessments of an opponent's behavior in a crisis situation. Most strikingly, US/NATO threats following the breakdown of the Rambouillet negotiations were unsuccessful despite satisfying three (communication,

103 Hosmer 2001, 17–18.
104 Quoted in Burg 2003, 93.
105 Quoted in Daalder and O'Hanlon 2000, 92.

capability, commitment) of the four prerequisites for successful deterrence as stipulated by RDT. As in the Bosnia-Herzegovina case, perceptions as to a lack of resolve undermined success. Critics might point to an asymmetry in "interests" (i.e., several of the stipulations in the Rambouillet proposal were so unacceptable to the Serbs that agreement was not possible) in this case; this may very well be true, but Milošević's decision to defy US/NATO threats (and to hold out for as long as he did) was clearly predicated on an assessment of "asymmetric interests" that suggested to him that the US/NATO would back down or not bomb for very long – that is, his belief that military action could be overcome (which ultimately undermined the credibility of the threat) led him to hold out, which led to war. This belief, moreover, stemmed from his perceptions of US/NATO past behavior. Thus, while it would be correct to highlight the Serbs' strong interest not to acquiesce to the Rambouillet deal, the specific strategic sequence of the crisis (the practical *outcome*) was, in large measure, the result of reputations.

Case 3 – Iraq (1991–2003)[106]

Between the Gulf War in 1991 and the Iraq War in 2003, the United States and Iraq were engaged in an ongoing international rivalry involving multiple crises and confrontations, some rising to the level of overt military conflict. While space constraints preclude an exhaustive discussion of these exchanges here, we again focus on evidence of reputational inference in order to assess the relevance of past behavior for deterrence and compellence outcomes. The pattern in Iraq is clear. As Jon Alterman suggests, the "iterative nature" of the rivalry led to "repeated cycles of violence short of all-out war."[107] "Over time," Alterman writes, "Iraq learned how to deal successfully with the international community. It adopted policies of 'cheat and retreat,' testing limits and then quickly stepping back from the brink when punishment seemed imminent."[108] This pattern played out repeatedly over the twelve-year time span from 1991 to 2003.

---

106 This case discussion draws on Harvey and James 2009. Again, however, the discussion here, supplemented by additional primary and archival documents, places greater emphasis on evidence relating to reputations as opposed to the other prerequisites of RDT (while nonetheless recognizing that all prerequisites must be present to predict deterrence success).

107 Alterman 2003, 295.

108 Ibid.

In April of 1991, not long after the end of the Gulf War, the UN Security Council passed Resolution 688, condemning Iraqi repression of its Kurdish population in the north.[109] The US and several Western allies subsequently established a "no-fly zone" (NFZ) over northern Iraq, and further demanded an end to Iraqi incursions into Kurdish territory.[110] Plans to establish a Kurdish safe haven were vociferously rejected by the Iraqi government, with officials arguing that "the proposal to set up a zone under United Nations supervision inside Iraq to deal with the so-called refugee problem is a suspicious proposal that Iraq categorically rejects and will resist with all means."[111] In response, the Bush administration issued a direct warning to Baghdad not to use military force in northeastern Iraq. The warning was "the most explicit American demand on any Iraqi use of military within its borders since the war ended."[112] It was also clear, specifying that "'no ground or air forces' would be allowed to function in the area involved."[113]

The credibility of the threat was undermined, however, by caveats from President Bush that no American troops would become involved in Iraq.[114] Not surprisingly, therefore, Iraq pushed back by launching attacks on Kurdish forces around the city of Erbil on 12 April, a direct violation of US warnings.[115] While initially reiterating his reluctance to "interfere,"[116] a few days later, in response to growing concerns for the safety of Kurdish civilians, President Bush announced a joint US-European plan to send US troops into northern Iraq to build refugee camps and guarantee protection for the Kurds.[117] This action superseded the earlier caveats and bolstered the credibility of the threat against Iraqi military action. Two days later, on 18 April, Iraq and the United Nations signed a memorandum of understanding providing for a UN humanitarian presence in Iraq and the stationing of 500 UN security guards in northern Iraq to protect the relief operations, with an agreement to remain in force until 31 December 1991, with the possibility for

---

109   For the full text of the resolution, see United Nations Security Council 1991.
110   Krauss 1991.
111   Ibrahim 1991.
112   Sciolino 1991a.
113   Ibid.
114   Bush 1991.
115   Cordesman 1994, 19.
116   Dowd 1991.
117   Sciolino 1991b.

renewal.[118] Additional probing occurred on 22 April around the city of Zakho, but Iraqi forces subsequently withdrew to several kilometers from the city following additional US warnings.[119]

The northern NFZ was joined by a southern NFZ in August of 1992, as the US, Britain, and France responded to, in the words of President Bush, "Saddam's use of helicopters and ... fixed-wing aircraft to bomb and strafe civilians and villages" in southern Iraq – a clear indication, he added, that Iraq was "failing to meet its obligations under United Nations Security Council Resolution 688 ... demand[ing] Saddam Hussein end repression of the Iraqi people."[120] Iraq was given twenty-four hours to comply. While Baghdad vowed to eliminate the NFZ through the use of force, the Pentagon reported that Iraqi forces had begun removing their helicopters and airplanes north of the 32nd parallel by the evening of 26 August.[121] Over the next several months, Iraq complied completely with the "no-fly" restrictions, and coalition forces controlled the airspace south of the 32nd parallel.

In December 1992, however, a confrontation between US and Iraqi fighter jets in the southern NFZ resulted in an Iraqi MiG being shot down.[122] American officials commenting on the incident argued that Baghdad's decision to breach the 32nd parallel was a deliberate move by Iraq to "test the willingness of the United States" to uphold the NFZ, especially in light of American involvement in Somalia and Bosnia-Herzegovina.[123] In early January 1993, Iraqi ground forces had begun deploying surface-to-air missiles (SAMs) south of the 32nd parallel, weapons capable of destroying coalition airplanes patrolling the zone.[124] An ultimatum was issued from the US, UK, France, and Russia to remove the SAM systems, with the threat that a failure to comply would result in a "decisive" response.[125] Baghdad was initially defiant, citing Iraq's sovereign right to deploy the missiles within its territory.[126] Nonetheless, with additional international pressure (including increased

---

118 Sciolino 1991c.
119 Sudetic 1991.
120 New York Times 1992.
121 Schmidt 1992.
122 Gordon 1992.
123 Ibid.
124 Gordon 1993a.
125 Gordon 1993b.
126 Gordon 1993c.

coalition flights over the NFZ), Iraq "backed down," and dismantled and removed several missile batteries in the NFZ before the deadline.[127]

On 11 January, however, Iraq continued its provocative actions by relocating several dismantled SAM sites to the northern NFZ and sending several hundred armed Iraqi soldiers across the border into Kuwaiti territory, ostensibly to retrieve six anti-ship missiles left behind when Iraqi forces were driven from the country in 1991. The US and UNSC strongly condemned the incursion, warning of "serious consequences" if any further action along the border took place.[128] The following day, 12 January, Iraqi forces again entered Kuwait; combined with continued ambivalence regarding the removal of SAM sites in the southern NFZ, this Iraqi behavior prompted a stronger response from the Bush administration. American officials noted that a plan to attack Iraq had been made "in principle," adding that it was "just a matter of when to pull the trigger."[129] On 13 January, more than one hundred coalition planes conducted a thirty-minute bombing raid on Iraqi targets inside the NFZ.[130] American ground troops were deployed to the Kuwait-Iraq border as a further deterrent against Iraqi provocations.[131] The US, UK, and France all reiterated their resolve to enforce the NFZ and warned that further military action against Iraq would be taken if it continued its pattern of "cheat and retreat" in violating UN-sanctioned restrictions.[132] Additional coalition attacks were conducted on 17 and 18 January;[133] these strikes were limited in scope but nonetheless sent a strong political message to Iraq that allied forces were prepared to continue enforcing the UN mandate. Subsequently, on 19 January, Baghdad announced that it had ordered a cease-fire against allied jets in the NFZ, a move observers called a "major concession."[134]

Although tensions remained high (and minor incursions and confrontations over the NFZ occasionally occurred but did not escalate),

---

127 Gordon 1993d.
128 Ibrahim 1993.
129 Gordon 1993e.
130 Apple, Jr 1993.
131 Schmitt 1993.
132 Gordon 1993f.
133 On 17 January, US Navy ships positioned in the Persian Gulf and Red Sea launched 40 cruise missiles at an Iraqi military complex in the suburbs of Baghdad – see Gordon 1993g; on 18 January, a daytime raid struck SAM sites in the NFZ – see Gordon 1993h.
134 Gordon 1993i.

the exchange ended in a clear victory for the US and its allies. Iraq was compelled to accept the southern NFZ and was ultimately deterred from continuing its attacks against Shiites in southern Iraq. Moreover, this exchange established a clear pattern of Iraqi behavior: first a rhetorical rejection of UN resolutions, then a challenge to US resolve to enforce said resolutions and associated ultimatums, followed by a period of military entrenchment against Western military attacks, then a reversal of policy in order to adhere to Western demands, and eventually renewed Iraqi rejections of various UN/US demands.

Following the January 1993 exchange, the next major confrontation between the US and Iraq occurred in October 1994. Known as Operation Vigilant Warrior, the crisis was a direct result of Iraq's hostility toward Kuwait and was answered by swift and forceful action on the part of the US and allied forces from Europe. A significant buildup of Iraqi troops near the Kuwaiti border prompted a response from the Clinton administration that "it would be a grave mistake for Saddam Hussein to believe for any reason that the United States would have weakened its resolve" on issues similar to those that had developed in 1990.[135] The provocation was accompanied by Iraqi demands at the UN for an end to crippling US-led economic sanctions.[136] As a response, the US repositioned various naval assets into the region, stepped up reconnaissance flights over the southern NFZ, and ordered 4,000 US Army troops into Kuwait.[137] Officials both in the US and at the UN reiterated their commitment to protecting Kuwait and condemned Iraqi behavior.[138] Undeterred, Baghdad augmented its troops in the region to number 80,000 – a force considered large enough for invasion. President Clinton responded on 9 October by dispatching 36,000 troops and an additional 51 combat planes to Kuwait.[139] Over the following several days, Iraqi troops began withdrawing northward to positions near Basra, and tensions eased somewhat (though American deployments to the Gulf continued).[140] Subsequent American proposals for an "exclusion zone" in southern Iraq (in order to prevent Iraqi military forces from

---

135 Gordon 1994c.
136 Crosette 1994.
137 Gordon 1994c and 1994d.
138 United Nations Security Council 1994a.
139 Jehl 1994.
140 Gordon 1994e.

being positioned within striking range of Kuwait) were undermined by French and Russian resistance.[141]

Nonetheless, the US maintained diplomatic and military pressure on Baghdad; on 13 October, Secretary of Defense Perry announced a revised plan to deter Iraq that involved increasing "the American military presence in the Persian Gulf region," including the positioning of American warplanes and a division's worth of tanks and armor on the borders of Iraq – mainly in Saudi Arabia, the United Arab Emirates, and Kuwait – even after the immediate crisis had passed.[142] The following day, 14 October, the Clinton administration (along with the British government) introduced (and subsequently passed) UNSC Resolution 949, condemning Iraqi military deployment along the Kuwaiti border and demanding continued withdrawal along with a commitment not to redeploy to the south.[143] On 16 October, the Iraqi government signaled its intention to comply fully with the provisions of UNSCR 949.[144]

In August 1996, Baghdad again began probing, this time in the north. On 30 August, reports indicated the mobilization and deployment of significant numbers of Iraqi troops toward Kurdish districts.[145] The Clinton administration communicated a clear warning to the Iraqi regime that it would "consider any aggression by Iraq to be a matter of very grave concern."[146] The following day, 31 August, a major Iraqi armored force invaded the provisional Kurdish capital of Erbil – a move many observers interpreted as a clear attempt to test US resolve. As the *New York Times* reported: "Whatever else Saddam Hussein may be up to in northern Iraq, he is probing to see if the United States and its allies are still prepared to enforce the tight limits they imposed on Iraqi military activity following the Persian Gulf War."[147]

On 1 September, the Clinton administration issued explicit military threats to punish the Iraqi regime for its blatant violation of several UNSC resolutions.[148] On 3 September these threats were buttressed by the launching of twenty-seven cruise missiles at military targets in

---

141 Sciolino 1994b.
142 Gordon 1994f.
143 United Nations Security Council 1994b.
144 Ibrahim 1994.
145 Myers 1996a.
146 Ibid.
147 New York Times 1996.
148 Myers 1996b.

southern Iraq.[149] American actions were met with ambivalence from major allies and outright hostility from other key nation-states:

> Britain expressed strong support in words but kept the planes it has in the region out of operation ... France did not take part either, and did not endorse the American decision to take military action, even after President Clinton called President Jacques Chirac before the missile attack in an appeal for support. Russia and China both sharply condemned American intervention, and those Arab states that had supported the multinational operation to drive Iraqi occupiers out of Kuwait in the 1991 Persian Gulf war were critical or silent about today's strikes.[150]

Despite these fissures in the international community, American military actions and related threats appeared to succeed. On 4 September, President Clinton announced that the US action had achieved its goals related to Iraqi withdrawal from the north.[151] A week later, on 13 September, the Iraqi government announced that it would no longer attack coalition fighters enforcing the NFZs in northern and southern Iraq. Pentagon officials also reported that Iraq had halted repairs to its air-defense sites, in response to specific US demands.[152] Nonetheless, continued resistance from Russia, China, and France to any US/UK military and diplomatic strategies in the region threatened to undermine the credibility of US/UK deterrent threats.

In January 1998, the Iraqi government announced its intention to ban United Nations Special Commission on Iraq (UNSCOM) weapons inspectors from eight presidential sites on Iraqi soil – a move that was immediately followed by explicit threats of military force from the US and UK.[153] But disagreements among the five permanent members of the Security Council persisted. Russia, China, and France maintained that existing UNSC resolutions did not provide sufficient justification for renewed military attacks, while American and British officials insisted that existing resolutions were sufficient. As before, these divisions made it difficult for the US and UK to mount credible threats vis-à-vis

---

149 Myers 1996c.
150 Whitney 1996.
151 Weiner 1996.
152 Shenon 1996.
153 Crosette 1998a.

Baghdad. Over the next several months, negotiations – largely brokered by UN secretary-general Kofi Annan – proceeded amid US and Russian disagreement as to the best strategy to deal with the issue of weapons inspections.

The crisis was resolved, for the time being, on 23 February, when Annan secured an agreement from the Iraqi government to resume full cooperation with UNSCOM and the International Atomic Energy Agency (IAEA).[154] The resulting memorandum of understanding was endorsed in UNSC Resolution 1154, passed on 2 March.[155] Washington and London had pushed for a more explicit threat but, once again, met with resistance from the other permanent members. On 5 March, UNSCOM inspectors returned to Iraq; although inspections were conducted without interference, questions arose as to subsequent access to the disputed sites – the Iraqi government claimed it had not agreed to any further inspections of the sites, whereas inspectors believed the initial visits had only served to establish the right of access prior to future visits.[156]

Despite initial signs of cooperation, relations between UNSCOM and Baghdad regarding the inspections process broke down in August 1998. On 5 August, Iraq announced it was suspending all cooperation with UNSCOM and the IAEA inspection teams, and restricting monitoring activities to existing sites.[157] In contrast to the response to the February 1998 crisis, the international community (even the US) was relatively muted in its condemnations of Iraqi behavior (on 26 August, UNSCOM inspector Scott Ritter resigned in protest at what he perceived to be a weakening of US and UK policy toward Iraq).[158] Negotiations proceeded through September (Baghdad was initially keen on a potential compliance review because of the prospect of sanction relief, but the US refused to consider any potential relief until full compliance was achieved and verified).[159] On 31 October, Iraq declared an end to all cooperation with UNSCOM and the restriction of the IAEA to monitoring activities only.[160]

---

154 New York Times 1998a.
155 United Nations Security Council 1998a.
156 New York Times 1998b.
157 Crosette 1998b.
158 Miller 1998.
159 Crosette 1998c.
160 Crosette 1998d.

This decision by Baghdad prompted another round of explicit US/ UK threats. On 2 November, UK prime minister Tony Blair warned Saddam Hussein: "If the use of force is necessary that is the course that will be taken." UK defense secretary George Robertson similarly warned Hussein to stop obstructing UN weapons inspections or "face the consequences."[161] These threats were followed on 5 November with the passage of UN Security Council Resolution 1205,[162] condemning Iraq's behavior as a "flagrant violation of resolution 687 [the cease-fire resolution of 1991] and other relevant resolutions," and demanding that Iraq provide "immediate, complete and unconditional cooperation" with UNSCOM and the IAEA. The threat of military action was reinforced on 11 November with the removal of all UNSCOM personnel from Iraq (on the recommendation of the US).[163] The final component of the threat was issued on the afternoon of 14 November – the American and British governments authorized "substantial military action" against Iraq and an initial wave of strike aircraft was readied.[164] Mere hours before strikes were due to begin, however, Baghdad announced it was willing to comply with UN demands. The US and UK called off the attacks, but warned that their forces would remain ready to act.[165]

UNSCOM inspectors returned to Iraq on 17 November 1998.[166] The victory was short lived. On 8 December, the chief UN weapons inspector, Richard Butler, declared that Iraqi officials were still impeding inspections.[167] In a report released on 15 December, moreover, Butler stated that Iraqi compliance with disarmament obligations required further verification. It stated that the Iraqi government had provided some clarifications sought by the commission, but that in general Iraq had "not provid[ed] the full cooperation it promised on 14 November 1998." The report concluded: "Iraq's conduct ensured that no progress was able to be made in either the fields of disarmament or accounting for its prohibited weapons program."[168]

---

161 BBC 1998c.
162 United Nations Security Council 1998c.
163 Crosette 1998e.
164 Erlanger 1998b.
165 Shenon and Myers 1998.
166 Jehl 1998.
167 Crosette 1998f.
168 For the full text of the report, see Federation of American Scientists 1998.

In response, on 16 December, American and British forces initiated military action against Iraq. In a televised address, President Clinton declared that the action, code-named Operation Desert Fox, was "designed to degrade Saddam's capacity to develop and deliver weapons of mass destruction, and to degrade his ability to threaten his neighbors."[169] In keeping with recent diplomatic patterns, Russia and China vigorously criticized the action. Russian president Boris Yeltsin demanded an end to the US/UK strikes.[170] The general reception at the UN was similarly critical.[171] The strikes ended on 19 December with the US and UK declaring the mission's objectives achieved.[172] Iraq was defiant, declaring UNSCOM would never be allowed to return.[173]

Periodic talks collapsed over the next several years – on 5 July 2002, Iraq-UN talks in Vienna broke down without agreement.[174] On 12 September 2002, President George W. Bush issued a formal threat to Iraq if it failed to comply with seventeen existing UN resolutions. The next week, on 16 September, Iraq agreed to the "unconditional" return of UN inspectors.[175] Formal negotiations began soon thereafter, but broke down when Iraq insisted on leaving certain sites off limits.[176] On 8 November, the UNSC voted unanimously to endorse Resolution 1441, declaring Iraq in "material breach" and reinstating inspectors after a four-year absence.[177] Saddam Hussein issued a formal reply a week later to the UN secretary-general, accepting the conditions outlined in the resolution. Weapons inspectors from the United Nations Monitoring, Verification and Inspection Commission (UNMOVIC, which had replaced UNSCOM) soon arrived in Baghdad.[178]

The subsequent events, which ultimately culminated in the American-led invasion of Iraq in March 2003, are documented in Harvey 2011. The failure of American compellence in this final crisis was the product of multiple factors across various levels of analysis. Crucial to

---

169 For a transcript of Clinton's remarks, see CNN 1998.
170 BBC 1998e.
171 BBC 1998d.
172 Myers 1998.
173 Kinzer 1998.
174 New York Times 2002a.
175 Preston and Purdum 2002.
176 Purdum and Preston 2002.
177 United Nations Security Council 2002.
178 New York Times 2002b.

this outcome, however, were Hussein's misperceptions as to American resolve based on his prior experiences with the US (including in the exchanges detailed above). To Saddam, US/UK threats in 2002/3 were considered in the context of over a decade of similar threats and related crises. Hussein admitted that he did not believe US/UK/coalition forces would attack Baghdad with ground troops *despite* all available evidence to the contrary (the "serious consequences" promised in UNSCR 1441, the significant deployment of US/UK military assets in theater, etc.), because of "mistaken" assumptions that were reinforced after the Gulf War (1991), Operation Desert Fox (1998), and again after the Kosovo air campaign (1999). Disagreement in the UNSC over the implications of UNSCR 1441 and the absence of support for a second resolution, moreover, led Hussein to discount the threat of invasion. Considering the numerous instances in which permanent members of the Security Council undermined American efforts to proceed with more robust military and diplomatic strategies (as noted above), Hussein likely expected a similar outcome in the 2003 crisis. Likewise, the limited nature of US attacks following the Gulf War led him to anticipate more modest military action. As George Piro (the FBI agent charged with interrogating Hussein following his capture) explained: "[Saddam] thought the United States would retaliate with the same type of attack as we did in 1998 under Operation Desert Fox ... He survived that once, [so] he was willing to accept that type of attack. That type of damage."[179]

Tariq Aziz (Hussein's chief adviser) offers further details regarding Hussein's impression of US resolve in 2003: "Of course he was aware, it was all over the television screen. He thought they would not fight a ground war because it would be too costly to the Americans. He was overconfident."[180] The US decision to avoid moving into Baghdad in 1991/2 confirmed Hussein's suspicions regarding Washington's general reputation for being casualty averse. This reputation was reinforced by another significant deterrence encounter in 1998 – Operation Desert Fox – in which the Clinton administration launched a series of air strikes, but no ground war, in retaliation for Hussein's refusal to comply with UN disarmament resolutions. As Alterman explains: "Saddam Hussein apparently used his series of confrontations with Western coercive diplomacy as an educational opportunity. He was more difficult

179 Pelley 2008.
180 Deulfer 2004.

to coerce in 1998 than he was in 1991 because he understood well the limits of Western resolve and the ways to determine that resolve."[181]

Past experiences, in other words, reinforced Hussein's impressions of US resolve and led to perhaps the most serious underestimation of US credibility in the period leading up to the 2003 Iraq War. Relying on Washington's general reputation for being casualty averse, and more specific (crisis-based) reputations for relying exclusively on air strikes in previous encounters, Hussein was convinced that US officials would use the same strategy in 2003 – air strikes but no invasion (as per 1998), and if an invasion, no push to Baghdad (as per 1991).[182]

Hussein himself repeatedly issued statements confirming his impressions of Washington's general reputation for casualty aversion, based on US actions in other crises. For example:

Their outcome [in Vietnam] is known to you. How would they do then if they were to confront Iraq under completely different circumstances, except for that the people, including the Vietnamese and Iraqi people, have in common: the determination to face the invaders?[183]

We are sure that if President Bush pushes things toward war and wages war against us – his war of aggression which he is planning – once five thousand of his troops die, he will not be able to continue war.[184]

When the battle becomes a comprehensive one with all types of weapons, the deaths on the allied side will be increased with God's help. When the deaths and dead mount on them, the infidels will leave and the flag of Allahu Akbar will fly over the mother of all battles ... Not a few drops of blood, but rivers of blood would be shed. And then Bush will have been deceiving America, American public opinion, the American people, the American constitutional institutions.[185]

Going back, such perceptions also clearly colored his impressions of the likely American response to an Iraqi invasion of Kuwait. In a

---

181 Alterman 2003, 295.
182 Harvey and James 2009.
183 Quoted in Bengio 1992, 143.
184 Quoted in Haselkorn 1999, 52.
185 Quoted in Freedman and Karsh 1993, 36.

meeting with his Revolutionary Command Council on 29 December 1990, Saddam asked and answered the following question: "[Can anyone tell me] why America has not ventured to a war [*sic*] for a long time now? Because they see our preparation and realize that they will suffer a great [number of] human casualties. After that, the decision maker would say that he does not want to remain."[186] Indeed, Janice Stein found that US deterrence efforts in the period leading to the 1991 Gulf War failed for reasons tied to misperceptions – Saddam Hussein seriously underestimated American resolve to follow through with air strikes, and miscalculated the impact of US air power on Iraq's ability to outlast coalition forces.[187] Once hostilities began, moreover, Hussein continued to subscribe to the belief that even relatively minor American casualties would offer significant leverage. When an adviser (in a February 1991 meeting) suggested that 5000 American deaths might be enough to achieve victory, Hussein quickly interjected: "Five hundred."[188] Consider also the comments by Tariq Aziz on 24 February 1991: "They [the Americans] have been striking us for 38 days and they have not suffered any losses ... Let us pray to God to grant us success to slaughter any number of them. This is what is going to help us get results."[189]

Harvey and James compiled evidence from six major exchanges during the 1991–2003 period to test rational deterrence and compellence theory. "Dissecting the United States–Iraq rivalry" into its component parts, the authors point out, "reveals a series of separate (though interrelated) encounters" that highlight the "exact sequence within which appropriately designated deterrent or compellent threats, countercoercive strategies and retaliatory responses unfold over time" – failures at one stage can provide relevant information for interpreting and explaining successes later on.[190] Each of these interactions provided updated information regarding changes in US resolve and credibility. In conjunction with perceptions of US casualty aversion, this specific reputation – developed in over a decade of diplomatic and military exchanges – played a crucial role in Hussein's calculations and, as a result, his behavior vis-à-vis US coercive threats.

---

186 Conflict Records Research Center 1990, 16.
187 Stein 1992.
188 Conflict Records Research Center 1991b, 4.
189 Conflict Records Research Center 1991a, 4.
190 Harvey and James 2009, 222.

Conclusion

The evidence in this chapter disconfirms the P-M-H position as to the complete irrelevance of reputations and past behavior in calculations of credibility. As has been argued, a crucial component of theory testing is not only the search for (and discovery of) evidence that supports the theory but also, concomitantly, the search for (and inability to find) evidence that undermines it. In the case of the P-M-H consensus, any and all evidence that either general (dispositional) or specific (crisis-based) reputations mattered in the context of coercive crises is disconfirming. In the three cases examined above, smaller US adversaries repeatedly drew on their perceptions of US past behavior and reputations to make assessments as to the credibility of US coercive threats. Adversaries operate under conditions of imperfect, incomplete information; they cannot simply "calculate" the precise level of US interests in a particular confrontation. As such, they often probe for information as to the precise location of the US's "threshold" for action. This pattern occurred in Bosnia-Herzegovina (1992–5), Kosovo (1998–9), and Iraq (1991–2003). It also occurred in Syria (2013), a case to which we now turn.

Chapter Four

The Strategic Logic of US Coercion: Explaining Deterrence Failures and Successes in Syria, 2011–13

The theory and evidence presented in the previous chapters leads to conclusions directly relevant to understanding the strategy and rationale underpinning US foreign policy in Syria from 2011–13. Patterns common to the cases discussed in chapter 3 played out in Syria. As expected, the initial red-line threats issued by President Obama were weak and failed to satisfy the core prerequisites of successful coercion.[1] There was very little support, when the initial threats were issued, for anything approaching a much stronger intervention, simply because there was no clear, actionable intelligence of a devastating enough chemical weapons attack that would warrant an escalation in US coercive diplomacy. Imperfect information about US interests and commitments reinforced the assumption held by Syrian officials that Washington was not motivated to respond to these violations and that further attacks were unlikely to provoke military action. In essence, Syrian officials underestimated Obama's resolve, continued to probe for weaknesses, and, in the absence of any response, launched additional chemical attacks until a tipping point was reached. The Ghouta attacks provided US leaders with the evidence they needed to bolster the credibility of their retaliatory threats – essentially by acquiring the added public, political, and international support necessary for a more forceful and effective deterrent threat, leading to the UN-sanctioned disarmament agreement.

---

1 This initial threat was weak because it was not backed up by other elements of credible coercive diplomacy (i.e., no mobilization/deployment of US airpower to the region, no specific air strike threat, no request for congressional authorization, etc.); in the absence of these factors, even a robust reputation for resolve would be insufficient to achieve deterrence success.

This chapter proceeds as follows. First, the case for deterrence and compellence "success" in Syria will be established, an important starting point for any effort to explain that success. Once the case for a successful outcome has been made, the remainder of the chapter will compare P-M-H against RDT explanations. The evidence will show that, in contrast to P-M-H predictions (but in keeping with the findings of the previous chapter), both general (dispositional) and specific (crisis-based) reputations and lessons learned from previous US crises over the past two decades played a crucial role in how Bashar al-Assad and Vladimir Putin assessed the credibility of Washington's threats and ultimately why they decided to relinquish Syria's stockpile of chemical weapons.

4.1   Defining Success in Syria

With respect to testing RDT and comparing its predictions against P-M-H in the Syria case, success is defined exclusively in terms of the specific objectives sought and the strategies implemented to achieve those objectives. The success or failure of deterrence should not be defined in relation to the failure to achieve an expanded set of otherwise very laudable goals, especially if these goals were never central to the core strategy being pursued – for example, regime change, an expanded military operation to facilitate a decisive military victory for the rebels (it was never clear which rebel group the operation would have helped), an end to the civil war in Syria, an end to the regime's conventional military attacks against civilians, or criminal prosecution of those responsible for the chemical attacks. In fact, many of these far more challenging goals were explicitly (and repeatedly) *excluded* as objectives. As Goddard explains: "If compellence is going to be effective, the US must be crystal clear in defining the behavior that Assad must cease. On the face of it, this seems to be something that the Obama administration has achieved: it has gone out of its way to explain that Assad must stop using chemical weapons. Thus 'the use of chemical weapons' is the bright red line that must not be crossed."[2]

From the start, the president and his senior officials were very careful to tie their core objectives to the chemical weapons issue, primarily to manage expectations after the Ghouta attacks and gain some measure

---

2 Goddard 2013.

of political support for a limited military operation to punish the Syrian regime for using chemical weapons against their own civilians, deter any further use of these weapons, and reinforce the long-standing international norm against the use of chemical weapons. "In defining our military objectives," noted then secretary of defense Chuck Hagel, "we made clear that we are not seeking to resolve the underlying conflict in Syria through direct military force. Instead we are contemplating actions that are tailored to respond to the use of chemical weapons. A political solution created by the Syrian people is the only way to ultimately end the violence in Syria."[3] In Obama's words:

> The chemical weapons ban that has been in place is not something that only protects civilians. It also protects our own troops. You know, they don't have to wear gas masks even in tough battlefields because there is a strong prohibition and countries generally don't stockpile them. And if we see that ban unravel, it will create a more dangerous world for us and for our troops when they're in theater as well as for civilians around the world. It is worth preserving.[4]

These sentiments were repeated in almost every official statement, interview, and press conference throughout the period. As Miller notes: "Indeed, at the end of the day, the president's bottom line is to restore some credibility when it comes to his own red lines on chemical weapons and keep on the right side of history in the face of the largest deployment of those weapons since Saddam Hussein used them against the Kurds and Iranians."[5]

There is no question that administration officials were also concerned that a failure to follow through on their more explicit red-line threats (issued after Ghouta) would undermine perceptions in Tehran of US resolve and credibility on other red lines issued with respect to Iran's nuclear weapons program. Yet these concerns were never the primary justification for deterrence in Syria; they were secondary considerations that were relevant to debates surrounding the costs of bluffing and the transferability of reputations to Iran and North Korea. A more detailed discussion of the real and imagined costs of bluffing

---

3 Washington Post staff 2013.
4 MSNBC staff 2013.
5 Miller 2013a.

and transferability with respect to these and other crises is addressed in chapters 6 and 7.

Many well-respected military analysts, including Anthony Cordesman, argued that chemical weapons should not have been the main issue – the goal should have been a forced military resolution of the entire crisis. Cordesman offered several reasons why this outcome was more important than a deal to rid Syria of its chemical weapons;[6] however, his policy recommendations excluded details on how the US could achieve this outcome through a massive military operation without exacerbating the humanitarian catastrophe in Syria, or without repeating the Iraq and Afghanistan experiences. There is little doubt the Syrian regime would have retained its chemical weapons, as an added feature of its own defense and deterrence strategy, had the Obama administration followed Cordesman's advice.

But these loftier objectives were never central to Obama's plans; emphasizing them mistakenly shifts the criteria for establishing a clear measure of deterrence failure and success relevant to the specific red lines issued in this case, and the attendant exercise of coercive diplomacy vis-à-vis the Syrian regime. Obama's stated objectives (punishment and deterrence), while open to criticism, were always clearly articulated – changing the regime was explicitly rejected as a reasonable, politically palatable, or achievable goal. Cordesman (and others) may be upset by Obama's approach to Syria, but such preferences are irrelevant to testing rational deterrence theory, unpacking the reasons for the success and failure of coercive diplomacy, or assessing the role of reputations and credibility in international crises.

Other critics set an even higher standard for assessing success or failure in Syria: "Rather than asserting that American credibility is at stake in Syria," Qazi argued, "we must ask the crucial question: Are American allies looking at the situation and questioning US commitment to preserve and enforce a Western-led international system and its norms? The answer, as seen through western [sic] public opinion, is negative."[7] Again, questioning whether Washington's credibility for preserving the entire "Western-led system" is being eroded may be the standard that Qazi and others would like to see prioritized, but it is not an appropriate standard for testing deterrence theory or for understanding the role and importance of reputations and credibility in this case.

---

6 Cordesman 2013b.
7 Qazi 2013.

Many will no doubt argue that defining "success" so narrowly sets the coercive diplomacy bar very low, as the WMD deal is all Obama managed to achieve while violence in Syria continues and Assad remains in power (and likely continues to use chlorine as a weapon, a chemical that is not subject to the CWC and therefore not part of the stockpiles Assad was required to declare and dismantle as part of the agreement). But none of these critics came close to predicting that, without firing a shot, the US could get the Assad regime (with Russia's support) to acknowledge Syria's chemical stockpiles, accede to the CWC, accept a unanimously endorsed United Nations Security Council disarmament resolution demanding that he dismantle his weapons, and then proceed to relinquish his stockpiles, all in the face of an air strike threat from Washington. As Klein summarized:

> Remember: The White House's aim here wasn't to topple Assad, or even hurt him. It was to affirm and reinforce the international norm against chemical weapons ... Assad is now agreeing to preserve and strengthen that norm. He's agreeing to sign the treaty banning chemical weapons – a treaty Syria has been one of the lone holdouts against. He's creating a situation in which it would be almost impossible for him to use chemical weapons in the future, as doing so would break his promises to the global community, invite an immediate American response, and embarrass Russia. This is, in many ways, a better outcome than the White House could have hoped for. Punishing Syria may or may not have actually reinforced the norm against chemical weapons – particularly if the strikes went bad and the American people punished members of Congress who voted for them. But Syria joining the treaty against chemical weapons definitely, almost definitionally, reinforces the ban.[8]

The Assad regime's decision to dismantle their weapons in the face of these military threats is the most obvious indication that coercive diplomacy worked and the objectives were achieved, perhaps even beyond the expectations of most (if not all) officials and observers at the time. As Freilich concluded:

> On paper, the Russian proposal to dismantle Syria's chemical weapons looks like the optimal outcome, a result of American coercive diplomacy

---

8 Klein 2013b.

at its best. A military attack to punish Syria for its use of chemical weapons was never the objective, but a means to an end, which was to firmly establish the principle that the use of chemical weapons will not be tolerated in the modern world. If – and this is a very big if – even part of the Syrian chemical arsenal is actually placed under international supervision and ultimately dismantled, the United States will have achieved far more than it set out to do, and the Obama administration will be able to claim a major foreign-policy success.[9]

Nor were Klein and Freilich the only ones to argue that even if the plan was not "perfectly" implemented, it should nonetheless be regarded as a significant success.[10] As such, the fact that 98 percent or more of Assad's chemical stockpiles have been dismantled is remarkable; similarly, accusations regarding chlorine use, although troubling, do not obviate this accomplishment.[11]

When asked to comment on the red-line controversy and the UN disarmament deal a few months after the crisis, Israeli president Benjamin Netanyahu stated: "[I think this is] the one ray of light in a very dark region. It's not complete yet … We are concerned that they may not have declared all of their capacity. But what has been removed has been removed. We're talking about 90 percent. We appreciate the effort that has been made and the results that have been achieved."[12] In a separate statement, Netanyahu had earlier acknowledged to Senator Kerry:

We have been closely following – and support – your ongoing efforts to rid Syria of its chemical weapons. The Syrian regime must be stripped of all its chemical weapons, and that would make our entire region a lot safer. The world needs to ensure that radical regimes don't have weapons of mass destruction because as we've learned once again in Syria, if rogue regimes have weapons of mass destruction, they will use them … What the past few days have shown is something that I have been saying for quite some time, that if diplomacy has any chance to work, it must be coupled

---

9 Freilich 2013.
10 Fortna 2013.
11 Also see the comments made by the OPCW director general ambassador, Ahmet Üzümcü, in the second annual Justice Stephen Breyer International Law Lecture hosted by the Brookings Institution on 9 April 2015; see Brookings Institution (2015).
12 Quoted in Goldberg 2014.

with a credible military threat. What is true of Syria is true of Iran, and, by the way, vice versa.[13]

Max Fisher of the *Washington Post* offers a similar assessment of the outcome in relation to the objectives sought:

> The deal probably helps Assad stay in power. But it also makes it far less likely, and perhaps someday soon makes it impossible, for him to use chemical weapons against his own people. That's good for Syrians, although ending the war would be better. More to the point of both the deal and of the initial US plan to strike Syria, it helps uphold the international norm against the use of chemical weapons. That, and not ending the war, was Obama's clearly stated mission all along. That's not a mission that does a whole lot to help Syrians, or much of anything to resolve Syria's civil war, but it does at least appear to be so far achievable. And that's something.[14]

Again, the key consideration is recognizing the clear objectives of Obama's coercive strategy, and evaluating success or failure in relation to these limited, but noteworthy, goals.

Nonetheless, success in this case does go beyond the specific disarmament deal in certain respects; it should also be measured in relation to (1) the very strict demands that the UN resolution placed on Syria, all of which were accepted by Russia through several rounds of negotiations;[15] and (2) the periodic reports confirming significant disarmament progress.[16] The true measure of success (and the credibility and potency of the coercive threat), in other words, is not simply the *fact* of an agreement but the *extent* to which Syria and Russia embraced the UN resolution and the subsequent pace of disarmament and destruction – all taking place in a war zone where Syrian officials are fighting for regime survival. These were not straightforward and easy concessions, especially in light of the importance Assad placed on these weapons as a deterrent against Israel. These successes, in other words, should be viewed against the overwhelming consensus among Obama's critics

---

13 Quoted in Gradstein 2013.
14 Fisher 2013d.
15 United States Department of State 2013b; for a review of the negotiations, see United Nations Security Council 2013b.
16 See, for example, the Organisation for the Prohibition of Chemical Weapons 2015.

(on the left and right) that Assad and Putin would never live up to the deal.

Finally, there are broader, regional benefits to the agreement that should be considered when assessing success in this case, as Freilich nicely sums up:

> The United States and its Western allies achieve their objectives without recourse to force, Obama is spared an embarrassing defeat in Congress[;] Russia ... almost desperately wants to prevent a further display of America's singular might and role in the world ... Iran, which showed a surprising appreciation of the consequences of Syria's use of chemical weapons, turned on its ally, demanded that Damascus accept the Russian proposal and came off looking like a responsible player ... Syria's neighbors, including Turkey, Jordan and Lebanon, are spared the possible destabilizing effects of an American attack, including even greater refugee outflows from Syria, [and] Israelis will breathe more easily.[17]

To be clear, these benefits do not constitute core requirements of "success" in the Syria case (e.g., not achieving them would not have been grounds for "failure" in a limited test of RDT), but instead constitute additional fruits (along with the reinforcement of the prohibition on the use of WMD) of a successful coercive strategy. As such, recognition of such benefits is important for countering the criticism that the scope of coercive action was too limited and therefore not worth the effort – defining the success or failure of RDT in precise terms does not prevent subsequent assessment of the ramifications of either a successful or failed coercive strategy, a distinction that is too often blurred by analysts writing about contemporary crises.

Testing RDT requires careful attention to the behavior deemed unacceptable and the extent to which that behavior was repeated following the retaliatory threat. Resolving the larger conflict, on the other hand, has nothing to do with testing the prerequisites for deterring the use of chemical weapons. The red line and subsequent coercive threats following the Ghouta attacks were always intended to address that specific threat and should be judged accordingly. Those who were demanding

---

17 Freilich 2013.

much more or much less from the president should consider this: neither a larger (threatened) attack nor a retreat would have produced the WMD deal.[18]

Now that the Syria case has been defined in terms of RDT, the remainder of the chapter will focus on providing a clear explanation for success in Syria, with specific references to the core prerequisites of RDT, general and specific reputations for resolve, and how adversaries' perceptions of US interests, commitments, capability, and credibility evolved during the crisis.

4.2   Syria: RDT versus P-M-H

From the perspective of proponents of the P-M-H consensus, the Syria crisis is an easy case to interpret and explain – all that is required is a straightforward assessment of relative interests and capabilities. Early on in the crisis, as long as the chemical attacks were not too severe, the US did not have an interest in fighting, so its threat to punish chemical attacks was not credible. Later, when the killings escalated and became more public, US interests changed. At that point, US threats became more credible and Assad signed the deal to relinquish his chemical weapons. This review of the Syrian case does not seem at all inconsistent with, for example, Press's Current Calculus theory, which would argue ex post facto that the threat was credible enough to compel Assad to relinquish his weapons because, when compared with Syrian and Russian interests and capabilities, US interests and capabilities, once again, were simply *higher* following Ghouta.

But where should one look for evidence confirming an explanation that relies exclusively on higher "interests" or Washington's stronger commitment to use its capabilities (power) to impose its will? Oddly enough, both Press and Mercer forcefully argued at the outset of the Syria crisis that the US had *no* real strategic interests in Syria (despite the humanitarian catastrophe), which is why fighting for credibility made no sense to them and why they believed US officials should back down. Both Press and Mercer also argued at the time (along with Stephen Walt and Fareed Zakaria) that the threat of an "unbelievably

---

18 For a good discussion of Obama's balanced approach to the crisis in light of less
     appealing alternatives, see Easley 2013.

small" strike was not particularly credible or potent and would not be sufficient to compel Assad to capitulate – Obama, they counseled, should simply back away from the initial red-line threat, cease and desist in his administration's efforts to reinforce coercive diplomacy, and admit to a bluff – because, based on their research, bluffing carries no reputational costs (a point to be addressed in more detail in chapter 7).[19]

Friedman's take on the crisis illustrates this very common interpretation of Obama's comparative weaknesses:

> When President Barack Obama threatened military action in retaliation for what he claimed was the use of chemical weapons by the Syrian government, he intended a limited strike that would not destroy the weapons. Destroying them all from the air would require widespread air attacks over an extensive period of time, and would risk releasing the chemicals into the atmosphere. The action also was not intended to destroy Syrian President Bashar al Assad's regime ... Instead, the intention was to signal to the Syrian government that the United States was displeased. *The threat of war is useful only when the threat is real and significant. This threat, however, was intended to be insignificant [and] the president chose to frame the threat such that it would be safe to disregard it.*[20]

Friedersdorf arrived at the same conclusion: "In Syria, the US faces significant risks and meager rewards in a matter *peripheral to our interests*. Foreign observers understand how that shapes our actions."[21] Stephen Walt similarly pointed to an absence of US interests:

> A US attack on Syria is unwise for several reasons. First, the United States has no vital strategic interests there ... Second, the moral case for intervention is not compelling either ... The likely use of chemical weapons by the Syrian government does not justify war either ... Lastly, wise leaders do not go to war without robust international and domestic support. Neither is present in this case.[22]

---

19 See Press and Lind 2013; Mercer 2013.
20 Friedman 2013, emphasis added.
21 Friedersdorf 2013b, emphasis added.
22 Walt 2013c.

As many critics ultimately argued with respect to potential strikes, there was: no support from the public; no support from key allies, including the UK; no support from Congress; no support from the UN or UNSC; no significant global backlash against Syria's use of chemical weapons, but significant backlash against the threat of US intervention; no apparent pressure on the US to respond with force to eleven previous chemical attacks; no interest in supporting al-Qaeda elements in the Syrian opposition/insurgency; and no interest in fighting another Mideast war or attacking another Muslim state after a decade of costly wars in Afghanistan and Iraq.

All of this points to an *absence* of plausible US interests and commitments, and an *unwillingness* on the part of the US administration, Congress, and the public to support a military attack that would risk drawing the US into another prolonged conflict. Presumably, these factors constituted the significant barriers US officials faced when trying to mount a credible threat of punishment. Stephen Biddle's congressional testimony at the height of the crisis encouraged this interpretation of a weak threat with little credibility to impose sufficient costs on the Assad regime:

> The more limited the strike, moreover, the greater the odds that Assad discounts our threat and continues to use CW. One way to read a small US use of force is that it signals American willingness to escalate if Assad defies us. But it could also be read just the opposite way: as a signal of US unwillingness to strike massively (if we were really willing to use massive force, why haven't we?), and a sign that the US is reluctant to commit. The very emphasis the Administration now places on the limited nature of our prospective attack is a very plausible indication of Presidential ambivalence and unease with the use of force in Syria; Assad would not have to be crazy to read this as a sign that the US lacks the will to intervene decisively. Limited attacks send ambiguous signals that can be read as commitment or reluctance; the more limited the attack, the more ambiguous the signal and the lower the odds that an audience subject to cognitive, cultural and institutional blinders will read it the way we want them to.[23]

---

23 Committee on Homeland Security 2013, 20.

Biddle goes on in his testimony to outline other domestic and regional factors Assad would likely have considered when assessing his options:

Assad also needs to worry about others' perceptions of his resolve. To survive, he must convince his officers and his soldiers that he is resolute and capable of winning the war – if he looks weak or irresolute, lieutenants who fear getting stuck on the wrong side of a losing war might jump ship and defect or flee early while they still can. He might well regard a limited US airstrike as a test of his own ability to project an image of toughness and commitment to his own officers and thus refuse to back down. He is also presumably wary of signaling weakness to the rebel alliance in a way that could embolden them or encourage them to hold out for maximalist ambitions of ousting or trying him. Just as we worry about the effects of backing down on perceptions of our toughness and credibility ... so Assad has the same worries or even more so – and this could lead him to defy our wishes and continue CW use simply to demonstrate his own toughness and resolve.[24]

Logically, if Vladimir Putin and Bashar al-Assad were convinced that the US threat was not credible, because of minimal US interests and significant domestic pressure to avoid another costly intervention, then Assad would not have relinquished any of the weapons the regime had repeatedly relied on to accomplish their military objectives, especially when these same weapons served as a deterrent against Israel. In addition, the domestic and other regional pressures Biddle outlines would have increased Assad's reticence to give up CW, lest doing so erode his own reputation among key supporters and regional players. And yet, despite the obvious incentives on the part of Assad and Putin to prevail in this crisis, and the widely perceived limitations with the US threat (and credibility), Washington's coercive diplomacy ultimately succeeded. Why?

The Syria case reveals serious problems with the P-M-H focus on "interests" and "capabilities" alone – the P-M-H consensus provides no clear guidelines for deciphering what US interests Assad and Putin would have included in their estimation of US credibility, and what information they would have used when deciding to hand the US

---

24 Ibid.

government a victory by relinquishing the chemical weapons. Even a cursory review of the case shows that officials in Washington were balancing multiple (often competing; occasionally mutually exclusive) interests and commitments, all of which could conceivably have been relevant to an adversary's calculations and decisions. Depending on which US interest an adversary determines to be most relevant, their choices will be quite different. For example, US officials may have been highly motivated to strengthen the prohibition on the use of chemical weapons by reinforcing their commitment to the original red-line threat. But after a decade of war in Afghanistan and Iraq, officials were also highly motivated to avoid another prolonged and very costly military campaign, which would seriously diminish the probability (and credibility/potency) of a prolonged series of air strikes in an effort to avoid mission creep and appease strong domestic opposition. Again, depending on which of these two perfectly reasonable yet competing US interests an adversary determines to be more relevant, their assessment of US credibility and responses will be quite different. Moreover, ongoing and at times quite heated debates that played out in Congress, the media, and across public-opinion polling would produce mixed signals at best, so the standard P-M-H assertion that "interests" determine an adversary's assessment of US credibility is not particularly helpful.

P-M-H also misses another major dimension of the complexity related to gauging US interests in this or any other case. The mere act of issuing a red line had the effect of changing the scope of US interests in the Syria crisis, as did the later decision to reinforce that threat when the red line was crossed in a significant way. US interests in this case, in other words, evolved over time, which is why Assad had to search for information to get a clearer sense of the scope and intensity of US commitments, resolve, and interests, often through probes, challenges, and (eventually, in Ghouta) tipping points. As Biddle explains, Obama's red line "created a US national security interest in preserving our credibility that did not exist before-hand, and to back down now, in the aftermath of this commitment, is to incur a cost in diminished credibility going forward. That will indeed reduce our deterrent leverage for hard cases like Iran, and our ability to reassure allies."[25]

---

25 Ibid.

P-M-H, of course, would counsel against the issuing of the red-line threat in the first place, and subsequently argue that there is no basis for the perception that credibility is worth preserving (and therefore no actual reason to consider it a national interest), but even they, along with other reputation critics, are forced to admit that policymakers continue to believe that it is worth preserving and that, as a result, once a red-line threat is issued, state interests do in fact shift (which is true even if, as Tang suggests,[26] it is only because of a misguided "cult" of reputation, though we argue that the evidence in this book points to a more legitimate basis for such a perception on the part of policymakers).

Consider, furthermore, several additional problems with the logic underpinning an approach that links credibility exclusively to interests and power. On one hand, those who cited P-M-H research on reputations argued that Obama should not fight for credibility, because an adversary's relatively straightforward assessment of "low" US interests and power are sufficient for them to assess US credibility and act accordingly (low interests, so defy the threat). The US threat to keep the strikes "limited" (and bearable) should have been credible, therefore, because of the obvious absence of US interests or willingness to deploy expanded force. So why, in the absence of a credible threat to impose much more serious costs on the regime, did Assad and Putin capitulate? P-M-H provide no clear answers to that question, and no guidelines for answering any of the following important questions: how exactly did Assad and Putin navigate through this complexity to decipher their estimates of US credibility or the risks tied to available responses? What information did Assad and Putin use to elevate the probability of more potent strikes, while downplaying the credibility of Obama's promise to keep the strikes "unbelievably small"?

US Reputations and Past Actions

The answer is that the threat was credible and potent *enough*, in the absence of clear US interests or evidence of a strong commitment to use significant power, because of US *reputation* and *past behavior* in similar crises. In direct contrast to expectations derived from the P-M-H consensus regarding the irrelevance of past actions, lessons learned from similar cases of US asymmetric deterrence encounters in Kosovo 1999,

---

26 Tang 2005.

Iraq 2003, and Libya 2011 informed the strategic choices both Assad and Putin were considering at the time. With these cases in mind, it was virtually impossible for officials in Damascus and Moscow to know with any certainty whether US officials would be able to limit the threatened air attacks to an "unbelievably small" campaign, given US reputations from previous cases (e.g., bombing in Kosovo lasted seventy-eight days; the Senate Foreign Relations Committee granted Obama ninety days for the operation in the draft authorization resolution). Based on previous cases, Assad and Putin understood the risks – if air strikes produced no clear signs of progress, if the regime retaliated by using chemical weapons again, or if humanitarian conditions on the ground continued to deteriorate (e.g., Kosovo, Libya), the pressure on Washington to sustain the bombing campaign would have been significant. Biddle's discussion of US credibility highlights the risks:

> If our strike fails to deter Assad, and we detect further Syrian CW use, what then? Do we double-down and escalate to heavier attacks to prove that we meant it? If not, would this not be at least as damaging to our credibility and reputation for resolve than if we decline to attack in the first place? After all, the declared purpose of the attack would presumably have been to deter CW use – if the purpose has not been met, would standing down not send the message that anyone who simply rides out initial, limited US airstrikes is off the hook, devaluing the currency of small-scale attacks and making it less likely than before that we can signal resolve through the limited use of force in some future crisis? If we are not actually willing to follow through and carry out the implicit threat of escalation inherent in a limited strike then the limited strike amounts to a bluff; if we are caught bluffing we reduce our ability to succeed without follow-on escalation the next time, even if the next time we really are willing to escalate.[27]

Stokes's discussion of a "credibility spiral" raises similar concerns and warnings that were likely understood by Assad and Putin, particularly in light of many recent examples of mission creep involving the US and smaller powers in asymmetric crises:

> Credibility spirals have an inherent tendency to escalate, especially when there is an absence of a clearly defined strategy to help check ever

---

27 Committee on Homeland Security 2013, 5.

larger commitments to maintaining credibility … If the US were to bomb Syria … it is very likely that the Assad regime would survive an initial round of strikes. Then what? In the absence of significant diplomatic resolution, the credibility spiral would predict that the US would need to escalate, especially if Assad cocks a hoop at the US, itself quite possible given his international backers, all of whom have a stake in hastening a post-unipolar world order.[28]

Once started, the argument goes, intervention in Syria would be difficult to stop absent significant and tangible achievements, such as the removal of Assad or the stabilization of violence more generally. Several foreign policy analysts arrived at the same conclusions and offered identical warnings, as follows.

Escalation and Mission Creep

"It's possible that strikes won't actually deter Assad from using chemical weapons and could even make him more likely to use them if he panics and fears he might lose otherwise. Strikes could also inflame anti-Americanism in Syria or the region more generally, leading more people to rally behind Assad. It also could kill innocent civilians – cruise missiles do miss sometimes. The biggest concern, though, is that the United States could get sucked into a war it's worked hard, rightly or wrongly, to avoid. Mission creep happened after the US invaded Iraq and Afghanistan; it also happened in Libya in 2011, when a 'no-fly zone' grew into an all-out intervention against Moammar Gaddafi. The danger that limited strikes will become something more open-ended is real."[29]

"Even a 'tailored' attack against what is a chaotic, fragile and war-ridden country could have unanticipated and destabilizing consequences – ones that the United States would be unable to contain short of deeper involvement."[30]

"Airstrikes are unlikely to end the clamor about US credibility. A volley of cruise missiles or conventional bombs will not win the war, but it will

---

28 Stokes 2013; see also Schelling 1960 and 1966.
29 Fisher 2013b.
30 Menon 2013a.

embroil us more deeply in it. Those that would fight now for credibility will then advocate the military escalation needed to achieve victory."[31]

"Even if the administration is genuinely committed to only minor military action, Washington would find it hard to be only half in. Inconsequential missile attacks still would represent increased US investment in the Syrian civil war. Pressure on Washington to do more would steadily grow, with a warlike Greek chorus intoning 'US credibility' at every turn."[32]

"If we have no positive effect on the long-term outcome in Syria, despite what the president and the secretary of state have said about the limited nature of the attacks, what credibility we do establish by making this attack I think gets eroded over time."[33]

"America cannot stand losing wars. The hegemon simply doesn't lose wars. No hegemon loses wars. In a few days' time, the current hegemon will most likely 'lose' against Syria, however. That is unacceptable, so the US will likely strike yet again. For reasons of prestige. And they will continue striking until they have won – or at least 'avoided defeat.' That will take a long, long time. In Washington they call this 'mission creep,' and they fear that even more than they fear chemical weapons."[34]

These analysts joined many others offering similar arguments about the prospects for credibility spirals, mission creep, escalation ladders, the law of unintended consequences, and the power of failure to dominate perceptions of progress in any intervention. The common policy recommendation was for the US to stand down, for reasons Biddle sums up nicely: "Sooner or later we are thus likely to face a choice between standing down with important aims unmet or escalating to levels of commitment that outstrip our interests in the conflict. If so, it is better to stand down sooner, and more cheaply, rather than later, and more expensively."[35]

Biddle, like others who raised the same concerns and offered the same advice, were right about the high costs of intervention, but they

---

31 Friedman 2013a.
32 Bandow 2013.
33 Col. Jack Jacobs, quoted in Tillman 2013.
34 Jakobsen 2013.
35 Committee on Homeland Security 2013, 18.

misinterpreted the effects on Assad and Putin's calculations, particularly their assessment of the many imperatives driving the administration's strategy and the role of domestic and international *audience costs*.[36] As Fearon explains, "The greater the escalation, the more humiliating the acquiescence, and the greater the audience's dissatisfaction."[37] Democratic leaders are particularly susceptible to these audience costs, which explains why their threats of escalation are more likely to be interpreted as credible, all else being equal; costly signals (such as the public "red-line" announcement in August 2012) risk significant public backlash if the leader fails to follow through (in this case, with the reinforced retaliatory threats after Ghouta). Anything approaching a significant retreat by the US would almost certainly have been criticized by both parties in Congress (regardless of whether they endorsed authorization), the media, and the American public, all pointing to the disastrous consequences for American credibility. If Syrian officials did not fully appreciate the domestic pressures Obama was facing to follow through with some form of punitive air strikes, or the risks of escalation if strikes failed to achieve any significant sign of progress, Russian officials certainly did; they understood how the crisis was playing out, because they faced the same escalation sequence (and dilemma) when trying to prevent air strikes against Slobodan Milošević, Saddam Hussein, and Muammar Gaddafi.

Schmitt draws even more direct parallels between the Bosnia case and Syria.[38] Like Ghouta, the 5 February 1994 attack by Serbs on the Markale market in Sarajevo killed scores of civilians and generated significant international backlash. The US/NATO threat of air strikes persuaded Russia to help negotiate the withdrawal of Bosnian Serb heavy weapons away from Sarajevo and into UN-monitored storehouses. As time went on, however, the Bosnian Serb military probed for weaknesses in the air strike threat by retaking the weapons, positioning them around the Bosnian capital, and launching a series of devastating attacks against Bosnian Muslims. This tipping point set the stage for strengthening the resolve to carry through with US/NATO air strikes in response to the atrocities, which then set the stage for Dayton (see chapter 3).

---

36 See Fearon 1994.
37 Ibid., 580.
38 Schmitt 2013.

With these experiences in mind, it is perfectly understandable why Moscow jumped at Kerry's statements (or offer) regarding the require- ments for avoiding a US strike; evidently, the promise to keep the campaign limited was *not* credible, but the threat and probability of escalation *was* – Russian officials wanted to avoid losing their fourth ally in the last decade.[39] Obama's decision to approach Congress with a commitment to limit the strikes did little to alleviate concerns about escalation, because Putin would have interpreted Obama's overture as a veiled attempt to get any resolution passed that authorized military force (this is discussed in more detail in chapter 5). Regardless of how watered down the resolution was, Obama could use it to justify escalat- ing the bombing, particularly if there were few signs of progress after the initial wave of strikes. In other words, the threat did not have to indicate a commitment to extended air strikes to raise concerns about escalation.

US reputations extracted from previous crises (and recent history) had a significant impact on how adversaries in this case assessed the credibility and probability of military force. In the past, and under simi- lar circumstances, faced with the same threats (air strikes) to deal with a WMD or humanitarian crisis, costly signals issued by Washington were ignored until an escalation in the violence provoked a series of reinforced deterrent threats and a stronger show of force.

If proponents of P-M-H are correct – that is, that truly accurate as- sessments of US credibility are simply a function of an adversary's rela- tively straightforward reading of US "interests" and Washington's will- ingness to apply its "power" to protect those interests – then the Assad regime would never have escalated the use of chemical weapons in the first place, Russian officials would have been far more vigilant about pressuring Assad to avoid the use of chemical weapons, and the regime would still have this capability in its arsenal. If information about US in- terests and power was that easy to compile, they would have calculated the risks and costs and acted accordingly. But they obviously underes- timated US resolve, because they either misread the information about US interests, miscalculated the probability of military escalation, or, in the midst of trying to gauge US interest and resolve through probes, reached a tipping point where US officials were forced to reinforce the threat (as predicted by RDT). For reasons covered in earlier chapters,

---

39 Baczynska and Gutterman 2013.

US interests are not static, unchanging facts waiting to be calculated by adversaries as they evaluate their crisis management options. Interests can change in the course of a crisis depending on circumstances and moves by the adversary. At best, adversaries can piece together some information about US interests, commitments, reputations, and resolve through probes and challenges, but none of this information will be perfect – every option carries risks.

4.3   Protracted Crises, Probes, and Tipping Points

As detailed in chapter 3, adversaries engaged in conflicts with the US over the last two decades repeatedly probed for weaknesses in US deterrent threats, because they were unclear about US interests and needed to obtain more information about Washington's resolve. The failures and successes of coercive threats must be evaluated in the context of multiple exchanges in these protracted crises.

With regard to Syria, it was perfectly reasonable for any US president to issue some form of coercive (red-line) threat against the Assad regime to deter its military from using chemical weapons. Few at the time criticized Obama for being irresponsible, unreasonable, or reckless,[40] and key allies in the region, including Turkey, Israel, and Jordan, expected nothing less. Following Ghouta – that is, having failed to deter the regime from using sarin nerve gas to kill over 1400 civilians (added to approximately 100,000 casualties from conventional attacks over the previous two years) – the only rational, politically acceptable option for the president was to re-establish the resolve necessary for a more credible US deterrent threat by demonstrating a willingness to respond to Syria's noncompliance. The strategy was directed primarily at Syria, not Iran or North Korea (for reasons explained in chapter 7), and backing away from the crisis at that point in time, based on recommendations from scholars pointing to case studies on reputations in the early 1900s and Cold War, was not likely to change many minds. The more relevant practical lessons of how to effectively apply coercive diplomatic threats were based on perceptions of the effects of US threats in deterrent encounters over the last two decades.

---

40 Exceptions include Press and others who were critical even in these early stages of any policy that set the stage for any possible action or intervention down the line.

The same action-reaction sequence had unfolded in prior crises in Bosnia-Herzegovina (1993–5), Iraq (1991–2003), Kosovo (1998–9), and Libya (2011). In each case, particular interventions (Operation Deliberate Force – Bosnia; Operation Desert Fox – Iraq; Operation Allied Force – Kosovo; Operation Iraqi Freedom – Iraq; Operation Unified Protector – Libya) were typically preceded by a weak threat, an escalation in violence, and an almost identical set of domestic and international pressures that compelled the US and key allies to subsequently threaten military strikes. Officials in Washington began by issuing preliminary deterrent threats, hoping to convince the regime in question to de-escalate their attacks against a growing insurgency, or to comply with some UN no-fly zone or disarmament resolution. But these initial threats almost always failed because many of the preconditions for successful deterrence were not present, namely: public/political support for a clear commitment to address the crisis; the capability and willingness to enforce serious consequences for noncompliance (e.g., by positioning US military assets in the region); and evidence of the resolve to follow through with retaliatory strikes if clearly articulated demands were not met. The crisis in Syria followed the same path-dependent script, except for the ending.

Weak (red-line) threats not only failed to control these crises, they often led to an escalation in violence; in Syria, this took the form of more significant chemical weapon attacks by the Syrian regime on the civilian population. Obama may have issued a red-line warning, but it was never clear to Syrian leaders whether he was committed to the deterrent threat, or what the red line actually meant, especially after repeated chemical attacks over the previous year produced no retaliatory response. In addition to the damage caused by a specific reputation for backing down in the face of these violations, the initial red-line threat was also undermined by a general US reputation for casualty aversion, a reputation compounded by the fatigue of a decade of war in Afghanistan and Iraq. But in addition to the challenges Obama faced with respect to mobilizing sufficient support for more robust threats earlier in the crisis (in the absence of clearer evidence of significant CW casualties), there were other problems with mounting stronger threats at such a juncture, as Knopf explains: "If the Obama administration had thought more carefully about what it most wanted to deter and better communicated its true red lines, developments so far would not have appeared so damaging to US credibility."[41]

---

41 Knopf 2013.

Knopf then raises concerns about the significant downside to this approach: "It invites targets of deterrence to engage in actions just below the red-line threshold set by the deterring state. In such a scenario, Assad might still use chemical weapons in a limited fashion because he would think that he could get away with it." On the other hand, the downside to defining red lines too broadly is that adversaries will probe for information about the defender's real interests and resolve by challenging the threat, which can, according to Knopf, "damage the deterrer's reputation and lead observers to conclude that certain regimes are impossible to deter, when in reality those regimes can be and probably are being deterred from higher-level provocations."

Knopf raises several valid points about the unintended consequences of issuing either more precise or broader deterrent threats. In hindsight, perhaps a clearer set of red-line conditions would have prevented the escalation to the level of the August 2013 attack, but Obama had little support for issuing a stronger threat prior to the images of mass casualties from Ghouta. As Knopf concludes, "Policymakers can be tempted to ask both more and less from deterrence than they should [but] even where deterrence is appropriate, there is still a risk it will fail." Rational deterrence theory provides the best theory for understanding (and predicting) successes and failures in this regard, particularly when these cases are studied in the context of imperfect information, general and specific reputations (and past actions), probes, and tipping points during multiple exchanges in a protracted crisis.

Much as in past cases, as images of atrocities began to filter through broadcast and social media, political leaders, including the president, began to support a more explicit, coercive diplomatic approach to the crisis. The options were pretty straightforward. US officials could have continued to simply ignore the attacks (the advice from many critics), an (in)action that would have likely been interpreted by Syrian officials as additional evidence of an absence of US resolve and further proof that the red line was a bluff. This new benchmark for acceptable behavior would almost certainly have resulted in additional chemical attacks at, below, or just above (to probe) the newly established threshold. Alternatively, the administration could have reinforced deterrence by issuing clearer statements supported by explicit plans to launch retaliatory strikes for noncompliance. The president selected this second strategy, backed by much clearer and increasingly more vocal commitments to impose at least some costs on the Syrian regime through strikes that could potentially *escalate* (whatever the administration's insistence otherwise). Secretary Hagel was then tasked with updating military plans for a Syria operation, and Secretary Kerry began the process of building a coalition-of-the-willing by engaging in talks with NATO allies, the United Arab Emirates, Saudi Arabia, and Jordan.

Obama responded to the combined effects of several previous failures by re-establishing the credibility of his red line in several ways: he clearly communicated the behavior deemed to be unacceptable, established a commitment to the cause by linking it to core US interests in protecting norms against chemical weapons, highlighted the obligation to punish violations (in this case, through air strikes), demonstrated a willingness to use military capabilities by deploying military assets to the region (a costly signal and an indication of US resolve), and planned openly for the air strikes by approaching Congress for authorization and, initially, obtaining support from the Senate Foreign Relations Committee for a sixty-day operation with an extension of another thirty days. When pieced together, and combined with a credible threat of escalation, these actions satisfied the four conditions for successful coercion and the threat worked. Once these explicit threats were issued, both Assad and Putin understood that the US backing off, retreating, or accepting the status quo became increasingly more difficult and less likely, because the audience costs for the Obama administration were viewed as too high.[42]

Assad's Miscalculations

The mistake by Syrian officials was not in misreading US resolve – it *was* weak for most of the crisis. The regime's mistake was failing to control the violence as they attempted to probe for information about US resolve and credibility. They miscalculated the tipping point beyond which US officials would be compelled to impose credibility-reinforcing costs on the regime for noncompliance. Every US deterrence encounter over the past two decades has had its respective tipping point. The Srebrenica massacre of 8000 Bosnian Muslims in July 1995

---

42 For a discussion of costly signaling and audience costs, see Fearon 1994 and 1997. For recent reviews of the literature on audience costs and the challenges associated with providing definitive empirical proof that they exist and matter, see Levy 2012 and Trachtenberg 2012.

led to a much stronger US intervention in the Bosnia-Herzegovina crisis and ultimately the signing of the Dayton Accords; the Kosovo air campaign was precipitated by the massacres of forty-five Kosovar Albanians in Račak in January 1998; rapid escalation of civilian casualties in Misurata led to the 2011 war in Libya; the 9/11 attacks provoked the invasion of Afghanistan in 2001. The tipping point pushing US officials over the line in Syria was the chemical attack in Ghouta in August 2013.

In addition to these tipping points, presidents are required to construct credibility by piecing together different elements of the support they require for an effective and potent coercive threat; they need support from their own national security team, senior (and hopefully influential) members of their own party and members of the congressional opposition, votes in key congressional committees to support authorization (if they go that route), support from the House and Senate (numbers for and against authorization matter), support through public opinion, political support from key allies in NATO, the EU, and regional powers (e.g., key members of the Arab League), military commitments from key allies and supporters, endorsement from the UN Security Council, and, with any luck, a strong UN resolution with a Chapter VII mandate to impose "serious consequences" if the state fails to comply.

Bashar al-Assad rationalized, for good reason, that US acquiescence to earlier chemical attacks was in part a function of Washington's dispositional aversion to casualties, compounded by a decade of war in Afghanistan and Iraq. He was right, but only to a point – namely, 1400 well-documented and highly visible casualties from the sarin attacks. For Assad, the initial probes appeared to be working, providing important information about the lack of US resolve to get more heavily involved in the crisis. In comparison with the August 2013 attacks, however, the limited nature of these earlier attacks made it very difficult for the Obama administration to confirm the regime's culpability. Assad misunderstood the difference.

Dilanian and Cloud provide an excellent overview of the investigative challenges the administration faced in their efforts to justify a stronger response to previous challenges.[43] The first indications of chemical

---

43 Dilanian and Cloud 2013.

use were processed in July 2012, over a year before the August 2013 attacks and a month prior to Obama's official red-line warning:

> It was the beginning of a stream of intelligence documenting what US officials say was a yearlong escalation in the use of the banned weapons by the government of President Bashar Assad, a far more extensive record of the incidents than previously known. The Obama administration did not publicly acknowledge the attacks for months, and declared in April that it believed Syria had used chemical weapons.

As the authors further explain in their extensive reporting,

> Administration officials say the evidence for previous chemical attacks wasn't as compelling, and critics acknowledge it would have been even harder to make the case for a military response to more limited use of the banned weapons. But some current and former officials say the slow response by the White House raises questions about whether earlier, clearer warnings by Obama – and perhaps limited actions such as providing sophisticated weapons to Syrian rebels – could have deterred last month's attack in Damascus suburbs.

When asked by reporters why the president failed to respond to earlier attacks, Kerry replied: "The president didn't believe it was a compelling enough case to win the support of the American people and the world." Dilanian and Cloud continue: "As reports of chemical weapons attacks accumulated in 2012 and early 2013, some officials within the government felt that the White House, recalling the intelligence failures that led to the Iraq war and reluctant to get involved in Syria, was insisting on an unrealistic standard of proof."

As a result, it was very difficult to piece together the support required to move forward with a more robust and credible threat that satisfied the core prerequisites for successful deterrence. Despite additional reports of chemical attacks over the next year, administration officials were never convinced the case was strong enough in light of lingering concerns about intelligence errors prior to 9/11 and the Iraq War. As the authors explain, investigating such attacks was hard, "because of the difficulty of obtaining tissue and soil samples and other evidence before it disappears. And some of those incidents may have involved crowd-control agents that are not banned, such as tear gas, or diluted chemical weapons."

In their review of the same sequence of chemical attacks throughout the previous year, Entous, Malas, and Abushakra noted that US and Israeli officials were convinced that "Mr. Assad settled into a pattern of using small amounts of chemical weapons, believing the West wouldn't intervene." Doctors on the ground understood "they needed to supply Western nations with proof of chemical-weapons use," and, unless the attack produced significant casualties, administration officials would not consider these smaller attacks as evidence that the "red line" was crossed.[44] Their report went on to point out that in July, a month prior to the August Ghouta attack,

> American and Israeli spy agencies for the first time intercepted fragmentary intelligence about regime forces using chemical weapons on a small scale. The evidence wasn't conclusive – there were no physical traces – but some top military officials say they found it persuasive and wanted to make it clear right away to Syria the US wouldn't tolerate even small attacks. The then White House Deputy National Security Adviser Denis McDonough and other officials told their agency counterparts that the top-secret information shouldn't be made public, but congressional committees were briefed, according to officials. Mr. McDonough also decided to restrict the distribution of such "raw" intelligence inside the government because of its sensitivity, these people say. White House officials didn't want to set off a chain reaction that would restrict their ability to decide how active a role to play, senior US officials say.

In fact, the larger August attacks required weeks of intelligence gathering to mount a strong enough case, and even that evidence was not sufficient to convince many skeptics still worried about another intelligence error: the post-Iraq standard of proof remained almost impractically high. Eventually, however, the case was made. On 4 September 2013, Secretary of State Kerry confirmed eleven prior attacks, "more than double the number the administration had divulged previously," resulting in about 150 deaths.[45]

The sequence of interactions throughout the year provides additional confirmation of Obama's hesitancy to establish clearer coercive diplomatic signals and threats earlier in the crisis. As expected, and consistent

44 Entous, Malas, and Abushakra 2013.
45 Dilanian and Cloud 2013.

with other deterrence encounters since 1991, the violence escalated, because Assad underestimated US interests and commitments, assumed US leaders were casualty averse in the face of significant pressure to avoid foreign intervention, and would therefore tolerate ever-increasing violations of the red line against CW. As in the past, the adversary miscalculated US resolve, with their actions eventually reaching an unacceptable tipping point. Once reached, US coercive strategy changed, along with its interests and commitments to protect international norms against the use of chemical weapons.

4.4   Credibility Paradox – Punishments and Promises

Credibility is not exclusively tied to threats of punishment. Bargaining success in deterrence cases also requires credible reassurances that retaliation will *not* occur if the adversary complies.[46] Success in Syria, in other words, required credible signals from President Obama and Secretary of State Kerry that strikes were not inevitable. This difficult balancing act often leads to what Abrahms describes as the *credibility paradox* in international politics: "The very escalatory acts that add credibility to a challenger's threat can subtract credibility from his promise" not to attack.[47]

Abrahms's work on the credibility paradox raises several important points about the unintended consequences of mounting a credible threat of serious punishment. The main problem with most bargaining theories of violence, the author reminds us, is the prevailing assumption that there is a direct and straightforward relationship between higher levels of threatened punishment (military escalation) and the probability of compliance by an adversary – logically, as the cost and probability of the threatened violence increases, so should credibility and the likelihood of success. Yet stronger and more credible threats also create a sense of inevitability, in which the probability of violence is almost guaranteed: significant mobilization of troops, definitive statements about strategic imperatives, repeated references by officials to serious security threats, and so on can create the impression that the attack is almost inevitable, because backing away from the attack after issuing such strong threats could be considered very costly by the defender. If the adversary perceives the attack to be virtually

---

46 Stein 1991; Kydd 2000; Davis 2000; Lebow 2001.
47 Abrahms 2013, 1.

guaranteed, why comply? An adversary has nothing to lose by rejecting the demands laid out by the defender in the hope that civilian casualties and collateral damage imposed on the adversary by air strikes
could create a public backlash forcing the deterring/coercing state to
stand down. This guiding assumption was explicitly acknowledged
by Saddam Hussein and Slobodan Milošević in their respective battles
with the US and NATO.

Abrahms credits Schelling for the idea that deterrence requires a
credible threat to impose unacceptable costs *and* "a credible promise to
remove the pain in the event concessions are forthcoming. Otherwise,
no incentive exists for complying with the demands."[48] The dual nature
of credibility also highlights the important role of "communication" in
deterrence exchanges: effectively communicating a clear and credible
threat by defining the unacceptable behavior that needs to stop, communicating the punishment and costs if it does not, and communicating
a credible promise to hold off on imposing the punishment if the adversary complies. This is precisely why John Kerry's statements about the
conditions for holding off on the strikes were so important – they communicated (intentionally or not)[49] that attacks would not occur if Assad
dismantled the regime's chemical stockpiles and production facilities.
Once Russian officials picked up on Washington's "credible" promise
not to attack Syria if the regime dismantled its chemical weapons program and tied this commitment to a UN resolution, the prospects for
effective deterrence improved significantly.

Perhaps the clearest indication of a US commitment to stand by its
"promise" was the decision by US negotiators to pass on the French
draft resolution (which pushed for a Chapter VII mandate) in favor of
the US draft, which took an automatic strike off the table.[50] The concern
in Russia was that the US might abuse various challenges and delays
during the disarmament process to justify an attack, a lingering effect
of the Iraq War and another pretty clear indication of how reputations
matter in international relations. Why include a Chapter VII mandate,

---

48 Ibid. – see Schelling 1966, 75–6.
49 Whether Secretary Kerry's remarks were preplanned and coordinated or, as
    many suggest, off-the-cuff and spontaneous is irrelevant. Either way, they served
    precisely the same function: clearly articulating to Assad and Putin the minimum
    requirements for avoiding a strike.
50 For the full text of the French Resolution, see Telegraph staff 2013; for the text of the
    US resolution, see United Nations Security Council 2013b.

Putin reasoned, if you are truly committed to a diplomatic solution to the disarmament problem? US officials were asking the same question when making the case for *including* a Chapter VII mandate – why should officials in Syria or Russia be concerned about an attack if they are indeed committed to diplomacy and honest disarmament? In the end, US officials conceded the point but remained committed to signaling that military force was still on the table. The US concession went a long way toward resolving the credibility paradox – it was interpreted as a sign that Washington was willing to credibly negotiate with Syria for the primary objective of getting rid of CW.

4.5   Summary and Conclusions

Extremes Are Wrong

Extreme views on each side of the Syria debate (i.e., reputations are everything; reputations are nothing) were wrong, particularly when offering advice on how Obama should have handled the crisis. As Fearon judiciously pointed out at the time:

> Credibility, or following through on previous diplomatic commitments, should clearly not be the only consideration but neither should it be completely disregarded. If a prior commitment or threat implies that, the way things play out, you would have to take an action that is incredibly costly and not at all in your current interest, then, fine, take the hit and don't do it. No one will infer that you are no longer willing to fight for anything that's important to you. At worst you will face more challenges than you otherwise would have on some foreign policy margin. But neither does the position that credibility should be completely irrelevant in a decision to use force make much sense.[51]

Fearon does an excellent job of highlighting the inconsistency in the two "Diplomatic Commandments" being issued by many of the administration's strongest critics during the Syria crisis:

> 1) Never make a commitment to use force (set a red line) that you aren't willing to actually follow through on. 2) Never fight a war or carry out

---

51 Fearon 2013b.

a military action just for the sake of credibility. Use force only if it is in your national interest, all things considered, at the time of decision. If you think about it, there is a pretty strong tension between these two commandments, because (2) implies that any prior public commitments you make are essentially meaningless – you are going to use force according to whether it makes sense at the moment, regardless of what you said in the past. So what would the point be of making public statements concerning what you might be willing to use force over? ... Do you really want to say that leaders should never try to indicate what they might view as an important interest that they might be willing to use force over when this isn't already 100% clear? States certainly want to be able to communicate credibly on the question of what they would use force over, and on average it is probably a good thing – in terms of avoiding unnecessary conflicts – if they can. But there is an inevitable downside. The cost of credible communication is that there is sometimes a cost for not following through, and that cost can be a consideration inclining a leadership towards using force when they otherwise wouldn't have.

Fearon's observations are particularly relevant in light of the many problems noted earlier regarding imperfect information about US interests, commitments, and resolve in most crises. These limitations explain why past actions and statements, along with general and specific (crisis-based) reputations, do occasionally matter, in some cases a great deal. And, if they do matter, then credibility is, on occasion, worth fighting for, because credible, resolute, and costly signals that a state is committed to escalating the violence and raising the stakes can successfully deter and compel. In fact, the critics' strongest case against military intervention in Syria is perhaps the most compelling reason why Assad and Putin capitulated – fear of escalation and the risks of yet another war in the Middle East that would have expedited regime change.

Relevant Reputations (and Credibility)
Are in the Eyes of the Beholder

Rational deterrence theory provides a strong foundation for explaining and predicting outcomes and behavior in the Syria case. In the end, both Bashar al-Assad and Vladimir Putin concluded that support from Russia and China in the UN Security Council would not be a sufficient guarantee against a US attack on Syria, and that there was no way to know for sure whether US officials would be able to limit the attacks to an "unbelievably small" campaign. Faced with the prospect of US air strikes, and no ability to impose significant counter-coercion costs on the US by exploiting the public's aversion to casualties (as Milošević learned in Kosovo), both Assad and Putin decided that the risks were too high; thus, the threat worked. Critics failed to appreciate the difference between their "expert" assessments of Obama's credibility, on one hand, and Assad's and Putin's perceptions and calculations, on the other. Credibility, as proponents of P-M-H argue, is in the eyes of the *beholder*, not the scholars or strategic analysts trying to decipher credibility based exclusively on their intimate knowledge of US domestic politics or their convictions about what US interests and commitments *should* be.

As noted in earlier chapters, although proponents of P-M-H embrace the notion that credibility is in the eyes of the beholder, they failed to appreciate the logical implications of their own argument. Assad and Putin understood the implications of US threats, particularly after what happened to Milošević and Hussein, and in so doing they agreed with the most pessimistic predictions put forward by critics of bombing – it would be difficult to control the crisis, and the likelihood of regime change would substantially increase as time went on and the crisis continued to escalate. The Obama administration's threat worked because the costs to Assad outweighed any potential benefits associated with the continued use of CW or showing toughness vis-à-vis the US.

Similarities, Differences, and Relevant Cases

Finally, when offering policy recommendations for a case like Syria, it is vitally important to look at relevant cases rather than form conclusions from case studies that bear very little relationship to the issues, players, historical context, and strategic imperatives relevant to a crisis in 2013.[52] If similarities across cases are likely to facilitate the transfer of lessons and reputations, then crises from the last two decades are considerably more relevant to constructing meaningful policy advice for Syria than those examined by P-M-H. In his *Foreign Policy* blog posting on Syria, Press suggested that the US should not be at all concerned about reputations because of the work he did on US perceptions of Soviet credibility during, for example, the Cuban Missile Crisis. Yet reputations

---

52 For an interesting take on a similar issue, see Fearon 2013a.

between superpowers during the Cold War clearly have *very little* to do with Syrian perceptions of US credibility today (a critique that similarly applies to the cases examined by Hopf), which is why Syrian officials likely looked for lessons about *relevant* US reputations from cases such as Kosovo and Iraq, in which a relatively weak state challenged a superpower. Similarly, officials in Washington are likely to look at recent history involving similar actors over similar security issues rather than rely on findings from Mercer's research on four cases from the 1900s and 1930s, especially when making judgments about how coercive diplomacy, reputations, and credibility are likely to work in Syria.

Chapter Five

RDT, Domestic Politics, and Audience Costs

When President Obama decided to delay the air strikes in favor of approaching Congress for authorization, the projected votes were not in his favor – both the House and Senate were unlikely to come close to providing majority support for the draft resolution tabled at the time by the Senate Foreign Relations Committee.[1]

On 3 September 2013, the US Senate Committee voted in favor of a draft resolution authorizing the president to "use the Armed Forces of the United States as he determines to be necessary and appropriate in a limited and tailored manner against legitimate military targets in Syria, only to: (1) respond to the use of weapons of mass destruction by the Syrian government in the conflict in Syria; (2) deter Syria's use of such weapons in order to protect the national security interests of the United States and to protect our allies and partners against the use of such weapons; and (3) degrade Syria's capacity to use such weapons in the future."[2]

The resolution gave the president up to sixty days to complete the initial operation, and another thirty days if required. Some favored a significantly shorter period of time and demanded more control to prevent mission creep. Others argued that focusing primarily on the WMD issue was not enough and pushed for stronger references to regime change and a more explicit commitment to supporting the opposition. Advocates of intervention had a very hard time drafting a congressional resolution that successfully balanced these two seemingly

---

1 Andrews et al. 2013; Volsky, Legum, and Leber 2013.
2 United States Congress 2013.

incompatible objectives. One side was pushing for limited air strikes to punish the Assad regime, but only enough to deter Syrian officials from repeating the same atrocities. Those in favor of a more robust mandate were convinced that the air campaign should impose significantly higher costs on the regime to enhance the credibility of Washington's deterrent threat. They argued that extended air strikes would degrade the Syrian military's capacity to launch subsequent chemical attacks, and provide meaningful support to "upgrade" the Syrian opposition – in other words, it would facilitate regime change.

The tension between these two positions was illustrated in the president's remarks to the press on 3 September, immediately before meeting with members of Congress to discuss the draft resolution and possible vote:

> This is a limited, proportional step that will send a clear message not only to the Assad regime, but also to other countries that may be interested in testing some of these international norms, that there are consequences. It gives us the ability to degrade Assad's capabilities when it comes to chemical weapons. It also fits into a broader strategy that we have to make sure that we can bring about over time the kind of strengthening of the opposition and the diplomatic and economic and political pressure required so that ultimately we have a transition that can bring peace and stability not only to Syria but to the region. But I want to emphasize once again: What we are envisioning is something limited. It is something proportional. It will degrade Assad's capabilities. At the same time, we have a broader strategy that will allow us to upgrade the capabilities of the opposition, allow Syria ultimately to free itself from the kinds of terrible civil wars and death and activity that we've been seeing on the ground.[3]

Those in favor of limited, tailored (cosmetic) strikes wanted to accomplish three objectives using Tomahawk cruise missiles: (1) undermine the regime's ability to launch further chemical attacks; (2) illustrate resolve to impose serious consequences; and (3) deter another chemical attack (full stop). Those in favor of more significant attacks over a longer period of time (consistent with the 60–90 day authorization in the draft Senate resolution) wanted to accomplish much more: (1) damage Syria's capacity to launch chemical attacks; (2) punish

---

3　White House 2013b.

the regime and deter it from using chemical weapons again (limited strikes, they argued, would fail to accomplish this objective); and (3) degrade the Syrian military and "upgrade" the opposition in its battles with the regime.

Both sides believed their strategy was ideally suited to re-establishing US credibility and accomplishing their respective core objectives, so the main challenge for the Obama administration was finding the right balance between "limited" and "extended" strikes to get the required number of "yes" votes. Many of the "no" or "leaning no" votes were actually in *favor* of some form of punitive air strikes but felt Obama's specific plans threatened to do too little or too much. The issue was not the rejection of the president's preference for punitive strikes – it was the absence of support for a "perfect" strategy the majority would accept. The president was losing support among advocates of intervention who believed the draft resolution carried significant risks of tipping the balance in the wrong direction.

Many of the "no" votes were inevitable and immovable: anti-war Democrats opposed to US involvement in any conflict, members of both parties exhausted by a decade of costly and painful wars in Afghanistan and Iraq, hardcore realists on both sides who dismissed the administration's assertion that bombing Syria would serve America's core strategic interests, libertarians and isolationists opposed to wasting military and economic resources on wars that are unconnected to the country's self-defense, and Tea Party Republicans whose default position is to oppose whatever the Obama administration supports.

Congressional Republicans were prone to defend multiple, often confusing and contradictory, views on the strikes. Occasionally these mutually exclusive recommendations came from the same member of Congress.[4] As Milbank pointed out:[5]

Some protested when Obama threatened to bomb Syria without congressional approval; others then criticized him for seeking congressional approval. They complain that Obama's use-of-force resolution is too broad; they argue that it would amount to only a "pinprick." They assert that he should have intervened long ago; they say that he has not yet made the case for intervening. They told him not to go to the United Nations; they

---

4 Richter 2013.
5 Milbank 2013.

scolded him for not pursuing multilateral action. They told him to arm the rebels and, when he did, they said he had done it too late and with insufficient firepower. Genuine disagreements within the GOP can explain some of the contradictions. And it's a fair criticism to say that Obama waited too long to act, even if there was never a consensus for action. But the one thing that seems to unite the opposition is the belief that Obama is wrong, no matter what.

The most compelling explanation for why so many Democrats and Republicans were unlikely to endorse the president's request for authorization is pretty clear: the *political* benefits attached to a "no" vote were so much higher and obviously more appealing. Consider the counterfactual political consequences of "yes" and "no" votes, respectively. If the president obtained congressional authority to use force, any member who voted "no" would suffer none of the political consequences of the air campaign. Interventions involving dozens (possibly hundreds) of air sorties rarely achieve anything significant during the first stages and typically make a crisis much worse before things begin to improve, if at all. There would have been no "mission accomplished" banners claiming an early victory, and anyone who rejected authorization would have been in a much stronger political position to exploit the failures, mistakes, and civilian casualties that would have overpowered public perceptions of progress – an important lesson from recent (and largely unsuccessful) air campaigns against ISIS in Iraq and Syria from 2014 to 2016. Failures dominate perceptions of progress in most conflicts, because it is easier to identify what has gone wrong in the midst of a humanitarian catastrophe than it is to point to what has gone right (particularly as people continue to die). In sum, the politics of a "yes" vote were "lousy," as Douthat explains: "The bases of both parties are opposed, the public in general is skeptical, and the president isn't popular enough to provide cover for legislators worried about how another military adventure would play back home."[6]

On the other hand, if the president failed to obtain authorization, it was entirely reasonable for those in Congress to expect the air campaign to move forward anyway. Given the very powerful statements issued over the previous three weeks by the president and

---

6 Douthat 2013.

members of his national security team, the administration appeared to be absolutely convinced that doing nothing would seriously damage US credibility and security, jeopardize the security interests of key allies in the region, render obsolete an important international norm against the use of chemical weapons, and embolden the Assad regime to escalate the violence by continuing to use chemical weapons against the opposition. The president and his advisers appeared all but convinced that a failure to follow through with some form of punitive air strikes would damage domestic and international credibility and, by extension, seriously undermine US security. It was pretty obvious at the time that President Obama and his national security team believed that fighting for credibility made sense in this case. Anyone in Congress who was convinced the president was going to strike with or without authorization would rationally conclude that voting "no" made more sense, and carried fewer political risks, regardless of whether they wanted Assad to be punished for the chemical attacks on Ghouta. These calculations go a long way toward explaining the congressional polling numbers described at the outset of the chapter.

5.1   Domestic Politics, US Credibility, and the Eyes of the Beholder

Obviously the president was on the verge of losing congressional support for authorization and, for many critics, a vital part of the domestic political support he required to strengthen his resolve.[7] Going to Congress, they argued, was the wrong move at the wrong time that destroyed whatever credibility the president had left. These critics turned out to be wrong. It was their failure to appreciate the credibility (and potency) of the threat from the point of view of Assad and Putin that explains why they tended to overstate the implications of a "no" vote for US credibility. Take Douthat's warning as an example:[8] a "no" vote "wouldn't just be a normal political rebuke of President Obama. It would be a remarkable institutional rebuke of his presidency, with

---

7 Mark Shields and David Brooks provide an excellent assessment of the congressional politics and implications of a post-"no" vote on various aspects of credibility. See Shields and Brooks 2013.
8 Douthat 2013.

unknowable consequences for the credibility of American foreign policy." He goes on to argue:

> The global system really does depend on other nations' confidence that the United States means what it says – that the promises the White House and the State Department make are binding, that our military commitments aren't just so much bluster, and that when the president speaks on foreign policy he has the power to live up to his words ... But if he loses that vote, the national interest as well as his political interests will take a tangible hit: for the next three years, American foreign policy will be in the hands of a president whose promises will ring consistently hollow, and whose ability to make good on his strategic commitments will be very much in doubt.

But this would be true only *if* Obama lost the formal vote *and* backed off from the air strike threat. In fact, the very reasons Douthat lists for why Obama's credibility and US national interests would be jeopardized if he failed to obtain authorization *and* launch punitive strikes are the very same audience costs pushing Obama to move forward with the attacks regardless of the vote – Assad and Putin expected as much. They understood the pressure Obama was facing to reinforce US credibility – they did not expect Obama to bluff, because a bluff at that stage would have seriously damaged US credibility and interests. They got it, even if Obama's critics didn't. Consider several other examples.

Loyola correctly points out that Syria was not a threat to US national security, it was about "an 'international norm' that matters mostly to ... the academic Left."[9] But this particular group did not have sufficient influence "to provide Obama with a solid majority in favor of strikes, so Obama ... had to go looking for support among proponents of the old Bush doctrine [and] [t]o get their support, the administration [expanded] the target list." Although Loyola gets the congressional politics right, he, much like Douthat, misinterpreted the negative impact on the president's credibility, which he believed at the time was "already zero."

Anthony Cordesman made the same miscalculation about US credibility when assessing Obama's decision to delay the strikes in search of congressional authorization:[10] "The President's decisions have reinforced all of the doubts about American strength, and our willingness

---

9 Loyola 2013.
10 Cordesman 2013a.

to act, of both our friends and foes." Obama "rushed into the kind of rhetoric you only use if you actually intend to act regardless of domestic and international support," Cordesman argued, and the decision to go to Congress raised serious doubts about his intention to act.

Simons's assessment of US credibility follows the same logic and arrives at similarly mistaken predictions:[11]

> So, here we are: Washington has been equivocating covertly from the outset. Nonetheless, now those in favor of a strike seem to think that if only we make the signaling public (and splashy), we will deter the actors we want to deter. How sadly ironic that what this actually exposes is the extent to which Washington misreads other people's sophistication and underestimates other regimes' ability to read our signaling for what we actually communicate: we don't have a principled foreign policy or a national strategy.

All three analysts (and many others) were convinced that Obama had no credibility left. They also assumed that Syrian and Russian officials would interpret US resolve and credibility in exactly the same way they did, see through Obama's empty threats, and continue to ignore the president's red line with or without a limited air strike. They were wrong on each count.

The best point of departure for understanding the adversaries' perception of US resolve and credibility is the outcome – a deterrence success, a unanimously endorsed UN resolution, capitulation by Assad and Putin on key demands regarding Syria's chemical weapons, and the dismantling of over 98 percent of the regime's stockpiles over the following months. Critics' predictions about deterrence failure, based on *their* impressions of Obama's "zero credibility" were mistaken because they overlooked the central point about credibility – it's in the eyes of the beholder and stems from the strategic calculations of the regime's leaders and *their* understanding of US domestic politics, the high probability of a strike, and the implications of escalation and mission creep.

Domestic Politics, Past Actions, and Reputations

Everything related to perceptions of US reputations for resolve and credibility, or perceptions of similarities and differences across

---

11 Simons 2013.

previous cases, or the probability of transferring lessons learned from these earlier (similar) crises, or mistakes and miscalculations about US commitments and intentions must be understood from the perspec-' tives of Assad and Putin. This is the only way to fully understand an outcome that almost no one expected or predicted.

To highlight the relevance of past actions in the Syria case, take as an example the strong impressions many US adversaries are likely to have formed about the power and influence of US leaders in asymmetric deterrence encounters over the last two decades, using widely accepted explanations of the 2003 Iraq War to illustrate the point. The most popular account of the Iraq War (arguably the accepted history, appearing in hundreds of books and articles on the subject) is pretty clear: all of the blame for the onset of hostilities should be placed on a small group of neoconservatives who managed to push the country into a war of choice – democratic institutions essentially failed to check the abuse of power in this case. Despite the absence of weapons of mass destruction in Iraq, these unilateralists framed Iraq as a serious threat and proceeded to fabricate intelligence on Iraq's WMD to serve their ideological objectives. They succeeded in accomplishing this outcome, many US adversaries are likely to conclude, because: the American public is malleable or gullible; the US media is controlled by US leaders and can be exploited to fabricate a WMD threat narrative or proliferate images of a humanitarian catastrophe to justify intervention; intelligence can be spun to justify the imperative to strike or intervene, regardless of the validity of the estimates; Congress can be persuaded to support a resolution based on flawed intelligence; and US leaders can ignore domestic and international public opinion if they are committed to attacking another state. In other words, if a few neoconservatives can take the most powerful country on the planet over the brink to war in Iraq based on a decidedly weak WMD case, then the same neoconservatives or liberal interventionists could easily accomplish the same feat in Syria in light of a similar threat or humanitarian crisis – as they did in Bosnia, Kosovo, Iraq, Afghanistan, and Libya.

It is difficult to be definitive about how Assad and Putin processed information about US domestic politics, and there were likely multiple debates across various factions within these regimes regarding the relevance of recent US history. But it is not unreasonable to argue that the dominant account for the Iraq War (notwithstanding its fundamental weaknesses as a plausible theory) would inform an adversary's calculations under similar circumstances.[12] Assad and Putin believed that even minor air strikes were very likely, despite domestic opposition, and expected the crisis to escalate (chapter 4). Lessons learned about the power of US administrations to control the agenda or to generate sufficient support for their idiosyncratic foreign policy priorities arguably enhanced the credibility of the US threat (and provide yet another useful illustration of why reputations matter). The votes may not have been there, but Assad would have assumed the president could simply adjust the wording of the resolution, bargain with those on the fence to get the votes he needed (as Bush did in 2002), or simply attack without authorization.

Dissension in Congress was not a barrier to credibility if the debates themselves enhanced the prospects of at least some form of military attack – the details of how the pre-vote positions were playing out, or what kind of strike the president would initiate, may have been significant to analysts, bloggers, politicians, and journalists immersed in US domestic politics, but, given the outcome, they were apparently far less relevant to Assad and Putin, who were understandably worried about the prospects of any attack and crisis escalation.

It is conceivable that significant delays associated with postponing unilateral air strikes in favor of approaching Congress may have damaged some aspects of US credibility by diminishing the potency of the military threat,[13] but there are at least two problems with this assertion. First, the key question, again, is whether US adversaries believed the delay would have a significant impact on US operations, particularly given repeated assertions by the chairman of the Joint Chiefs of Staff, General Martin Dempsey, that the US military would be ready under any conditions to attack relevant targets. Moreover, avoiding earlier strikes provided an opportunity for a diplomatic resolution in the form of the disarmament agreement, whereas striking earlier would have exacerbated the *credibility paradox* – balancing a credible military threat

---

12 For a comprehensive critique of conventional wisdom, see Harvey 2011.
13 Pavel and Ward 2013.

with a credible promise to avoid attacks if the adversary complies (see chapter 4).

McManus even suggests that approaching Congress may have *enhanced* US credibility in the eyes of adversaries:

> If Congress does approve military action, it will be extremely obvious to Syria that Obama has the ability to follow through in the present and in the future. The fact that Congressional approval would also mean approval by at least a portion of the opposition party would make the signal that Obama has the ability to follow through even clearer. Indeed, it appears that the tactic of seeking Congressional approval may already be working even before a full Congressional vote. The very act of seeking approval has signaled Obama's confidence that he has the ability to follow through and prompted more politicians, including Republicans, to speak up in support of him. Based on this analysis, it is probably no coincidence that Syria's suggestion that it is open to giving up its chemical weapons came only a few days after the Senate Foreign Relations Committee voted to authorize military action.[14]

Again, the key to understanding the outcome is to unpack the relevance of these domestic political signals from the point of view of Assad and Putin, and then piece them together with other important components of credibility – communication, interests, capability, and resolve. The domestic political obstacles and related audience costs (and risks) associated with diminishing Obama's resolve to follow through with strikes, in the absence of congressional support, are only relevant if the adversary sees these pressures as more powerful than the incentives to actually follow through. The incentives to strike would have been viewed as more relevant if both Assad and Putin believed that domestic opponents could be persuaded to support some kind of resolution to accommodate the president's preference for strikes – Obama could tweak the resolution with sufficient caveats or simply buy the votes he needed.

---

14 McManus 2013.

Chapter Six

Reputations, Credibility, and Transferability: Reconsidering Syria's Relevance to Iran, North Korea, and Beyond

In addition to overlooking the theory (chapter 2), history (chapter 3), and contemporary empirical evidence (chapter 4) illustrating the important role of reputations and credibility in international politics, many critics of Obama's Syria policy also mistakenly framed the "credibility" and "reputation" arguments in simplistic and easily refutable terms without ever addressing the reputation-based imperatives underpinning the actual policy. According to Zakaria, Walt, Mercer, and Press and Lind,[1] for example, Obama's primary justification for threatening to strike Syria was to send credible signals of Washington's resolve to Iran and North Korea. It is foolish, they all argued, for Obama to think that striking Syria (or backing off) would have any bearing whatsoever on Iran's uranium enrichment plans or North Korea's nuclear proliferation calculations, because that is not how reputations or credibility work – they are not transferable across security crises, and only case-specific interests and capabilities matter. Once these extreme versions of transferability are presented as the "core" justification for Obama's Syria strategy, critics proceeded to cite P-M-H research as proof positive that such exaggerations are silly and disdainful.

It is true that administration officials frequently raised concerns about linkages and transferability across cases, as illustrated in Secretary of Defense Hagel's 2013 testimony before the Senate Foreign Relations Committee:[2] "A refusal to act would undermine the credibility of America's other security commitments – including the president's

---

1 Zakaria 2013; Walt 2013b; Mercer 2013; Press and Lind 2013.
2 Quoted in Stewart 2013.

commitment to prevent Iran from acquiring a nuclear weapon ... The word of the United States must mean something."

Daniel Byman, among the most widely cited experts on the application of coercive diplomacy and deterrence strategy, offered a similar warning:[3]

> When deterrence fails, the United States looks weak and indecisive. Moreover, not acting after issuing ultimatums harms America's reputation. As Mr. [Mike] Rogers [R-MI] and others have argued, inaction makes it more likely that American red lines elsewhere in the region will be questioned, especially in Iran, which is facing pressure on its nuclear weapons program and watching Syria closely.

In his speech to the Berkeley Chamber of Commerce in September 2013, Senator Lindsey Graham's (R-SC) comments are perhaps the clearest and most explicit illustrations of the same "extreme" transferability arguments: "Chemical weapons in Syria today means nuclear weapons in the US tomorrow."[4] He also warned, "If you're worried about the Iranians getting a nuclear weapon, as I am, the last card to play to stop that is how we handle Syria."[5] These arguments deserve to be challenged, for very good reasons noted by many skeptics, including Friedersdorf:[6] "There is no reason to believe that failing to intervene in Syria would affect, for example, the global system's understanding of how the United States would react to a North Korean attack on the demilitarized zone, or an Iranian attack on Israel, or aggressive moves by China to assert more power in the Pacific Ocean." Matthews agrees (quoting Press):[7]

> "When Iran's leaders are trying to figure out if we'll really mess with them if they interfere with tanker traffic in the Strait of Hormuz, they'll ask, 'Does the US really care about global oil flows?' and 'Can the US Navy really keep those sea lanes open?,' and the answers are 'Yes, we care deeply,' and 'Yes, the Navy can,'" Press says. "*It would be foolish in the extreme to think that our willingness to intervene in a civil war in which we have no allies*

---

3 Byman 2013.
4 Brown 2013.
5 CNN 2013.
6 Friedersdorf 2013b.
7 Matthews 2013, emphasis added.

and no friends is a good indication to how we'd respond to attacks on genuine national interests."

Although both Friedersdorf and Matthews are correct, their critique is only relevant if Obama, Kerry, and Hagel believed at the time that the *only* reason to defend the red line and strikes in Syria was to send a signal to Iran or North Korea. There is obviously an important distinction between drawing out the connections to Iran and North Korea to help "sell" a policy, and relying exclusively on these connections to adopt or justify that policy.

Transferability was not the central justification for Obama's Syria policy – the administration's primary strategic objectives were far more numerous: (1) to establish credibility vis-à-vis Syria and Russia; (2) to reinforce the red lines regarding the use of chemical weapons in *this* crisis against *these* civilians; and (3) to correct past failures to address the eleven previous chemical attacks from 2011 to 2013. These deterrence failures collectively (and incrementally) reinforced a US reputation for weakness and irresolution that increased the probability and magnitude of subsequent chemical attacks. Once the credibility of the US deterrent threat was strengthened from 21 August to early September, backing off from these now-reinforced threats, administration officials warned, would seriously damage US credibility to punish violations in this case, and would virtually guarantee an ongoing and well-established pattern of further chemical attacks. This was always about punishing the Assad regime for escalating the use of chemical weapons in the Ghouta attack and credibly deterring Syrian officials from using such weapons again. The draft resolution tabled by the Senate Foreign Relations Committee made these objectives very clear (see chapter 5).

Jon Western[8] does a good job addressing the misplaced criticisms stemming from P-M-H:

> It's pretty clear that the primary objective here is to punish the Syrian regime and deter a future chemical weapons attack in Syria. The Obama administration is focused on a very limited strike and doesn't want to see an outright rebel victory. The logic of this strategic objective makes sense to me. I am persuaded by Daryl Press and Jon Mercer's respective works that precedent effects, reputation, and credibility concerns are often

---

8 Western 2013b.

overstated. But, their works look at how third-party leaders infer or read other actors' responses elsewhere – not at how actors respond to bluffs in a particular case. It seems pretty clear that if the US does not punish the perpetrators of this attack, these same perpetrators almost certainly will calculate that they can act again with impunity. And, as we've seen in the past week, the use of chemical weapons quickly changes the international political dynamics. In other words, if there is no action now, there will almost certainly be events on the ground that provoke international action later. It's probably not a question of whether, but when, the international use of force happens.

The primary focus of Obama's strategy was always Syria; this was never really about Iran or North Korea, despite the administration's political rhetoric to the contrary (a rationale for which is explained below). As Max Fisher acknowledges,

> By every indication, from its own rhetoric to its decision to possibly act on this seemingly egregious attack but not on previously reported chemical attacks, the Obama administration would launch strikes against Syria to punish the Assad regime for apparently using chemical weapons. The two big goals would be to deter Assad from using chemical weapons again and to deter any future military leader from using them, either.[9]

Seib agrees that the administration's central objectives were directly tied to Syria:[10]

> The biggest risk in the credibility game may well be to America's Syria strategy itself. Though the administration has failed to convey this message particularly well, its underlying goal in launching a military strike would be to shake up the balance of power enough to push Syria and its Russian benefactors back toward a diplomatic solution. Without more military pressure, it's likely Syria and Russia won't see much reason to negotiate anything. And the Syrian opposition, sensing it doesn't have America at its back, might well see diplomacy as a trap that could bring about its demise.

Deterring Assad from using these weapons required a strong and credible threat, regardless of whether those same threats sufficiently

---

9 Fisher 2013a.
10 Seib 2013.

transfer credibility to other adversaries or security issues. The utility of threatening some level of intervention to protect a chemical weapons ban and related norm in Syria should not be assessed exclusively in terms of how likely the strategy is to accomplish a complex array of strategic objectives elsewhere in the world.

Critics are likely to push back by referencing dozens of speeches and statements by senior administration officials and congressional leaders explicitly drawing linkages to Iran and North Korea, but that is not evidence that these considerations were the *primary* justification for the strategy, which is why the following observation by Zakaria misses the central point:[11] "If keeping your word, intervening and staying the course help in deterring rogue nations, the United States' decade-long interventions in Iraq and Afghanistan should have stopped the Iranian and North Korean nuclear programs. In fact, those interventions did not even deter our allies in the Pakistani government from aiding the Taliban." The problem with Zakaria's argument is his selective application of various (often absurd) aspects of different cases to summarily reject the entire transferability argument without ever addressing the more reasonable aspects of transferability and interdependence that are connected to pieces of US credibility in other cases.

It is important not to conceptualize transferability exclusively through direct linkages between Washington's strategy in Syria and Iran's or North Korea's calculations regarding their nuclear programs. US actions in Syria are likely to convey far more than a single message about US interests and commitments – credibility is complex. Some aspects of US signaling can reasonably be expected to transfer across essentially similar cases, while other aspects of the case are less relevant; transferability, therefore, should be understood in terms of degrees and not as an absolute (present/absent), as we have demonstrated in earlier chapters.

Like Zakaria, Takeyh offers another version of the "perfect" transferability argument before summarily dismissing it:[12]

Credibility is a prized word in international politics. Countries that keep their promises and enforce their red lines can be counted on to deter their enemies and assure their allies. Nations, as with human beings, develop

---

11 Zakaria 2013.
12 Takeyh 2013, emphasis added.

reputations, and those that break their pledges are impossible to trust. As such, the failure of the United States to bomb Syria is bound to empower Iran and reinforce its quest for nuclear arms. The only problem with such assertions is that the *historical record* suggests that the so-called credibility argument rests on a very thin intellectual rail.

Chapman makes the same point:[13] "What should be plain to Iran is that Washington sees nuclear proliferation as a unique threat to its security, which Syria's chemical weapons are not. Just because we might let Assad get away with gassing his people doesn't mean we will let Iran acquire weapons of mass destruction that would be used only against other countries." Not surprisingly, Daryl Press and Jennifer Lind concur:[14]

> If Kim Jong Un is trying to figure out whether or not the United States would defend South Korea, he will notice that Washington and Seoul have been allies for more than six decades, and that with the rise of China, the United States is increasing its focus on East Asia. The notion that Kim would interpret US reluctance to stop a humanitarian disaster in Syria as a green light to conquer a major US ally strains credulity.

The preceding arguments suffer from at least three errors. First, they bias the case against a poorly operationalized version of "perfect" transferability that can be easily dismissed, precisely because that level of interdependence of threats "strains credulity." Second, the approach overlooks a far more reasonable and balanced representation of complex credibility that allows for some meaningful transferability across cases (examples are described below). Third, in terms of policy relevance, the authors' rejection of "perfect" transferability is not sufficient to establish the cost-free utility of the alternatives they recommend – that is, bluffing, retreating, or backing away from the red-line threat.

We believe no event or associated reputation is perfectly transferable across every dimension of Washington's multiple relationships. But the extent to which similarities encourage the transferability of lessons depends on the adversaries' perceptions – the probability of transferability is in the eyes of the beholder, as discussed in chapter 2. To conclude that nothing about a previous case or past actions of a state is ever

---

13 Chapman 2013.
14 Press and Lind 2013.

likely to be transferred, or will never be considered by any adversary to be relevant when calculating US credibility in a current case, "strains credulity" and is certainly not supported by the evidence compiled in the previous chapters. Both extremes are wrong – the notion that transferability never occurs is just as mistaken as the view that credibility is perfectly transferable and transportable. If dozens of US foreign policy experts can disagree on whether Washington has lost or gained credibility with Iran, the issue is evidently more complicated.

Like many critics of Obama's Syria strategy, Takeyh defended his analysis by repeating the P-M-H refrain: "America's enemies put premium on its capabilities rather than indications of its resolve," so why bother worrying about the presence or absence of resolve in other cases? But surely no sane enemy would challenge the "fact" of US power – crises erupt precisely because enemies question the willingness of US officials to use that power to impose costs. And, as the evidence presented earlier illustrates, adversaries have a hard time accurately gauging US interests, commitments, resolve, and credibility; wars happen as adversaries probe for information about Washington's commitments to apply force. These adversaries are not probing for information about whether the US has the military capabilities to impose costs; they are wondering about US resolve. Oddly enough, Takeyh goes on to point out that "just because Tehran recognizes the reality of American strength that does not mean that Iran will readily acquiesce to its mandates." Precisely. Yet when one explores the reasons Iranian officials might or might not acquiesce to American power, perceptions of US resolve to employ its capabilities to impose significant military (or economic) costs on the regime are surely an important consideration in Tehran.

6.1   Why Transferability Matters

There are ten very good reasons why the Obama administration explicitly connected their credibility in Syria with their policy objectives in Iran and North Korea. Some of those reasons are political, others strategic.

First, establishing linkages to other cases reinforces prerequisites for credibility in the Syria case. As noted earlier, a credible deterrent threat requires communication (clearly defining and communicating to an adversary the behavior deemed to be unacceptable), clear interests and commitments, capability (the power to impose costs), and resolve (a willingness to see those costs imposed). If these conditions are met, the credibility of the threat is enhanced and the theory predicts success. The theory also predicts a higher probability of failure if any one or more of these prerequisites is missing. By logical implication, if Obama can convince Assad and Putin that there is far more at stake for him than Syria and chemical weapons – for example, by linking US commitments and interests in Syria to strategic objectives vis-à-vis Iran and North Korea – then that particular prerequisite for credibility (expanded commitments/interests) is enhanced in the Syria case. The question is not whether Press, Mercer, or any other American analyst or expert sees credibility as transferable across these cases; the relevant question is whether Assad and Putin believe that Obama thinks the cases are connected. The point critics miss is that these statements have less to do with Iran and North Korea than they do with sending signals to Assad and Putin. If officials in Syria and Russia believe that Obama and Kerry are convinced US credibility is on the line with other states as well, whether or not officials in Iran and North Korea buy the argument, the added measure of commitment is likely to have an impact on calculations regarding the probability of strikes in Syria and related risks of noncompliance. Notwithstanding the critics' arguments about the non-transferability of credibility and reputations (a position refuted in earlier chapters), explicit claims that reputations *are* transferable can serve an important role in deterrence. See, for example, Mitton's explication of Schelling's emphasis on the commitment of reputation (by pointing to loss of credibility in future hypothetical negotiations with other parties) as an important and effective tactic vis-à-vis the *present* negotiation (or crisis), regardless of whether subsequent adversaries actually make any such calculation.[15]

Second, there are other, domestic political reasons why it makes sense to link US credibility in Syria with other cases: (1) the public is likely to believe that such linkages exist; (2) members of Congress are inclined to draw the same connections and conclusions about the transferability of credibility and reputations; and (3) those members of Congress who reject the linkages will still exploit generally held assumptions about transferability to their advantage, particularly if the president fails to act. In other words, even if administration officials or members of Congress are not entirely persuaded by the interdependence argument, they are still likely to exploit the transferability assumption to buttress

---

15 Mitton 2015. See also Schelling 1960, especially chapter 1.

support for a policy that can be justified for reasons tied exclusively to enhancing credible deterrence in Syria. In fact, despite Obama's efforts to establish the link in his statements and speeches, he obviously understands the logic of coercive diplomacy better than his critics are willing to admit:

> I think what the Iranians understand is that the nuclear issue is a far larger issue for us than the chemical weapons issue, that the threat ... against Israel, that a nuclear Iran poses, is much closer to our core interests. That a nuclear arms race in the region is something that would be profoundly destabilizing ... My suspicion is that the Iranians recognise they shouldn't draw a lesson that we haven't struck [Syria] to think we won't strike Iran.[16]

Nevertheless, many critics of Obama's Syria policy seemed to have confused the politics associated with drawing linkages to Iran and North Korea with the strategic imperatives driving the use of coercive diplomacy.

Third, in his discussion of the research program on credibility and reputations, Drezner suggests that policymakers and academics "might be saying the same word but thinking about it differently."[17] We agree.

> Academics have the advantage of thinking about the long term; for policymakers, the long term is two weeks (for the Middle East, it's two days). Because of these different perspectives, they look at credibility differently. Academics usually make the country the unit of analysis: does the United States show resolve or not, for example. They care about the role that credibility plays over the span of years. For foreign policymakers, all politics is personal ... They care about whether they or their boss is perceived by others inside the Beltway as credible or not immediately after a crisis ... International relations academics might well be correct in observing that what happens in Syria now will not affect what happens in Iran a year from now. Still, policymakers might well be correct in noting that if Barack Obama fails to follow through on his Syria pledges, his personal credibility might take a short-term hit inside the corridors of power.

---

16 Quoted in Borger 2013.
17 Drezner 2013a.

It is obviously difficult to gauge the relative weight assigned to these different components of credibility, or whether Obama actually believed there was a direct, automatic, and easily transferable linkage between the Syria and Iran cases, but he certainly understood the *political* costs of backing off from his now-reinforced threats against Syria. Again, Iran and North Korea were not the primary justifications, but they certainly served as convenient selling points for a policy most likely guided by other strategic and domestic political imperatives. Moreover, whatever the long-term implications for US credibility and the transferability of reputations between Syria and Iran (or North Korea), the personal/political reputation of "President Barack Obama" was likely to be damaged by unenforced threats and called bluffs. In negotiations between world leaders, these kinds of personal reputations are not entirely irrelevant (though they are far from definitive). Stephen Cohen, for example, suggested during the early stages of the Ukraine crisis that "Putin doesn't trust or like Obama. He thinks he's weak, irresolute and doesn't keep his word. Putin trusts [Angela] Merkel, the chancellor of Germany."[18] This is *not* to suggest that Obama's personal reputation for resolve (or lack thereof) was responsible for the Ukraine crisis (a notion so simplistic as to preclude further comment), but rather that, as Drezner points out, academics and analysts sometimes overlook the powerful incentives politicians face to maintain personal reputations for being tough, trustworthy, and/or resolute.

Fourth, while fighting for credibility in Syria *exclusively* to compel Iran to disarm its nuclear program is a policy worthy of contempt, rejecting the application of coercive diplomacy in Syria based on the conviction that there are *absolutely no transferable linkages whatsoever* between US credibility in Syria and Iran is equally simplistic and potentially dangerous as a guide to policy. This is particularly true when this extreme position is derived almost exclusively from Mercer's and Press's seven case studies from the early 1900s and 1960s, respectively. Indeed, it is not unreasonable to argue that explicit statements by administration officials drawing out connections between Syria and Iran can arguably achieve some limited strategic benefits in the latter case, and potentially other security crises as well. If US officials can convince adversaries that the country remains strongly committed to enforcing its red-line threats (because of significant audience costs), or that US officials honestly believe that the credibility of Washington's coercive threats is a core strategic

---

18 Cohen 2014.

interest in and of itself (despite the risks, costs, and dangers), these actions could send relevant signals to Iranian officials regarding US red lines in that dispute (or to future adversaries regarding US red lines in general). It is certainly not inconceivable to expect Iranian officials to assign a higher level of credibility to the US red-line threat against Tehran if they believe Washington is convinced that credibility is worth fighting for, even in cases that do not include a nuclear threat. This is *not* to suggest that defending a red line in Syria directly affects Iranian perceptions of US resolve to defend red lines established for that crisis, nor are US actions in Syria directly relevant for gauging the credibility of US threats to retaliate against an Iranian attack on Israel (nuclear or otherwise). But Iranian leaders can certainly pick up some meaningful reputational signals if Obama is having a hard time getting political support for an "unbelievably small" attack against Syria despite the regime's use of chemical weapons and the deaths of some 1400 civilians – this hesitancy does indicate a significant measure of public discomfort with foreign interventions, regardless of the widely subscribed international norm being violated. Iranian officials are certainly more inclined now to assume that, all else being equal, the same challenges would apply to a US administration contemplating military hostilities against a much more powerful adversary in the Middle East for simply "deploying" rather than actually "using" a nuclear weapon, or for getting much closer to the point of being able to rapidly deploy that capability. Critics may seize on this argument to counter that we are making the same perfect-transferability argument we have claimed elsewhere to reject, and therefore that we are suggesting that fighting for credibility is *always* prudent and warranted. Once again, that critique relies on a strict either/or interpretation of transferability that fails to capture the complexity and nuance of reputations vis-à-vis coercive diplomacy.

Fifth, if a reputation for resolve and associated credibility are in the eyes of the adversary – and both Mercer and Press agree that they are – then so is transferability and the requisite perceptions of similarities that facilitate transferable lessons and expectations across cases. As outlined in chapter 2, each dimension of credibility, including an adversary's assessment of US interests, commitments, resolve, and capabilities (as well as similarities across cases and, by logical implication, transferability) are in the eyes of the beholder. There is no logical reason to assume that there is *nothing* about the Syria case that transfers to Iranian or North Korean officials. There are likely to be multiple perceptions and corresponding debates playing out in Iran and North Korea regarding the meaning of US actions in Syria, and there is no reason to believe that no one in these capitals sees any relevant linkages to their interactions with Washington. The notion that everyone in Tehran agrees that nothing of relevance can be learned about US interests from the Syria crisis requires considerably more proof than proponents of P-M-H have provided to date. Even under non-democratic regimes, competing perspectives can exist among ruling elites, such that internal policy debates – and the competing and contrasting perceptions and perspectives of key players – can influence how an Ayatollah Khamenei or a Kim Jong-un perceives the lessons and implications of American past behavior.

6.2   Complex Credibility and Transferability

Sixth, and as a logical consequence of the preceding points, any serious effort to establish whether credibility is transferable must first unpack the complex nature of credibility in any given case and ask the relevant question: what aspects of credibility (and what lessons) are more or less likely to transfer given similarities across the relevant cases? When viewed from this perspective, it becomes immediately apparent why extreme views – for instance, that credibility is perfectly transferable, or that transferability is completely irrelevant (P-M-H) – are both wrong. Consider the multiple (often competing) dimensions of credibility in the Syria case.

Complex Credibility in Syria

Credibility of US coercive threats to deter Syria from using chemical weapons:

– from Russian perspective;[19]
– from Syrian perspective;

Credibility of US coercive threats to compel Syria to dismantle their stockpiles:

– from Russian perspective;
– from Syrian perspective;

---

19 Because reputation is in the eye of the beholder, it is certainly possible that Russia and Syria (or Putin and Assad) held *different* perceptions as to the implications of

Credibility of US commitment to diplomacy and the UN disarmament resolution;
Credibility of US threats to deter ongoing attacks on Syrian rebels and civilians;
Credibility of US commitments to provide arms to the rebels in support of regime change;
Credibility of US commitments to protect allies (Israel, Turkey, Jordan);
Credibility of the president in the eyes of domestic audiences;
Credibility of the president in the eyes of foreign leaders;
Credibility of US commitments and resolve to manage and deter related security threats:

- Iran's acquisition of material supporting a nuclear weapons program;
- Iran's production and enrichment of weapons-grade uranium;
- Iran's research and development, short of actual deployment of nuclear weapons;
- Iran's deployment of nuclear weapons;
- Iran's use of nuclear weapons;

Credibility of US commitment to enforce international norms against chemical weapons;
Credibility of US commitment to the principles of responsibility to protect;
Credibility of US commitment to the principles of state sovereignty and non-intervention;
Credibility of US commitment to multilateral consensus.

---

past US behavior. It is possible, then, that Russia may have had to *convince* its protégé (Syria) to accept the disarmament deal because Moscow viewed the threat of air strikes as credible, while Assad did not (in which case, the deterrence/compellence encounter is "between" Putin and Assad and, therefore, rational coercion applies, as do the research questions regarding core prerequisites and the relevance of reputations). Absent access to the archival material and diplomatic correspondence between Moscow and Damascus, it is impossible to know for certain how divergent Russian and Syrian perceptions were in this regard (though the Syrian regime's escalating behavior prior to the August 2013 attacks suggests it was rationally probing for information about US resolve), but this possibility further underscores the multifaceted and complex nature of credibility considerations in this case.

As Farley explains in his account of the complex, interconnected, complementary, and often contradictory dimensions of credibility:[20]

> States don't own their reputations; friends and foes are free to draw their own (often conflicting) interpretations of events. To clarify this a bit, consider the interaction of resolve and capabilities, both of which are necessary to make deterrence successful. Even if the United States has the resolve to establish its credibility with respect to red lines in Syria, doing so may detract from its capability to enforce similar promises in East Asia.

Similarly, a commitment to strike Syria to enhance the credibility of a US commitment to defend a widely recognized international norm necessarily detracts from the credibility of US commitments to UNSC multilateralism or the principle of non-intervention, which may exacerbate the problem by convincing other adversaries to acquire the capabilities to deter similar interventions into their affairs. Intervention in Syria, for example, could provoke the very proliferation nightmare in Iran the Obama administration is trying to deter. Iranian perceptions of US commitments to defending red lines in Syria may influence some of the debates playing out in Iran regarding Obama's red lines issued against their nuclear program, but US actions in Syria are not likely to convince Iran to relinquish (or rapidly speed up) its nuclear weapons program. On this point, Miller highlights the right factors in relation to Iranian perceptions of US credibility in the context of Obama's Syria policy:[21]

> Preventing Iran from acquiring nuclear weapons has been the policy of three American administrations. The factors that would impel a US president to attack Iran would be fundamentally different, as would the domestic and international environments in which a debate about the use of force would be conducted ... The idea that if you respond forcefully to less egregious criminal acts, you can prevent more serious crimes – the "broken-windows" approach – may apply to cities, but it isn't necessarily germane to deterrence in the Middle East, particularly when you have two different perpetrators.

---

20 Farley 2013a.
21 Miller 2013b.

Miller is right; there are many issues that will inevitably come into play when Tehran contemplates their next moves in relation to their ongoing relationship with the US and the continuing implementation/ enforcement of the Joint Comprehensive Plan of Action (JCPOA). But it would be a mistake to assume non-transferability based on the observations that Syria and Iran are different. For example, dithering by Obama and debates in Congress do send some relevant signals that would likely be picked up by some factions within Iran – as discussed above, we have no control over how these signals are interpreted or exploited in Tehran. Do the signals from Syria amount to sufficient weakness to propel Iran toward immediate nuclear weapon development and deployment? Obviously not, but this oversimplifies the calculus with respect to Iran's decision making around its nuclear program. As *part of* that calculus (i.e., neither irrelevant nor definitive), it would be just as dangerous to assume that Iranian officials pick up no lessons or completely dismiss any transferability of information from Syria to Iran.

How do we go about assessing Iranian perceptions of US interest in Syria if those interests have changed and evolved over time? Consider some of the questions Iranian officials might be asking in relation to a decision by Obama, in the absence of the WMD disarmament agreement, not to follow through with strikes. Obviously, there is still a credible threat of significant military retaliation if Iran uses (or even threatens to use) nuclear weapons against the US or its allies, but does that credibility apply in the same way to suspicions about the deployment of a single nuclear weapon? Does US credibility with respect to their retaliatory threat apply to Iran coming close to but not crossing the line to deployment? Does it apply to Iran crossing the line to processing weapons-grade uranium (which it has already done)? Tehran has to gather as much relevant information as it possibly can to determine where the precise US "tipping point" lies – at what juncture does America's commitment kick in and when does the use of force to protect American interests occur? Like Assad with respect to CW, this may involve gradual escalation through limited probes designed to gauge US commitment and resolve. Iranian officials, like those in Washington, are likely to have ongoing debates about all of these policy options, and assessing credibility from the lessons learned about US "interests" in Syria is not as clear-cut as P-M-H imply. Analysts interested in providing a balanced take on transferability need to establish what aspects of the Syria crisis apply to what aspects of the Iranian situation.

In light of this complexity and the tensions associated with protecting one dimension of credibility at the expense of another, scholars and pundits should be very careful when formulating definitive generalizations about the presence or absence of credibility, or determining whether reputations and lessons are completely transferable or entirely irrelevant. It is likely to depend on the specific aspects of credibility one is referring to and the extent to which the adversary is more or less likely to draw relevant (transferable) linkages. It is important to note, however, that this kind of complexity is virtually ignored by proponents of P-M-H.

Seventh, building on the theme of complex credibility and transferability, there are many other, more subtle dimensions of transferability that critics miss when they frame the problem in its most simplistic terms. Consider these possibilities, described by Seib:[22]

> Would American failure to act on Syria also make it more likely that Israel would decide to launch its own, unilateral strike against Iran's nuclear facilities, because the Israelis will conclude they can no longer count on the US in the face-off with Tehran? It's also possible that failure to act would further diminish American influence on the Egyptian military, which recently tossed out that country's elected Muslim Brotherhood government. If the US appears to be retreating from the front-line role it has played in the Middle East for the past four decades, Egypt's new leaders may decide they have less incentive to heed American pleas that they temper their crackdown on Islamists in their streets. There also is the danger that the already-strained effort to work out an understanding with Afghanistan's government over security cooperation as American troops leave could become more difficult. How readily would Afghan President Hamid Karzai lean on cooperation with the US if the US isn't seen as a reliable actor? ... And would Iraq also conclude it can't rely on US security guarantees and instead make a more overt cohabitation deal with Iran next door?

Former Middle East negotiator Dennis Ross raises similar concerns about the higher probability of an Israeli attack on Iran's nuclear

---

22 Seib 2013.

facilities if they have serious reservations about Washington's resolve to defend red lines:[23]

> For all the tough talk about what would happen if the United States struck targets in Syria, the Syrian and Iranian interest in an escalation with the United States is also limited. Can the same be said if Israel feels that it has no choice but to attack the Iranian nuclear infrastructure? Maybe the Iranians will seek to keep that conflict limited; maybe they won't. Maybe an Israeli strike against the Iranian nuclear program will not inevitably involve the United States, but maybe it will – and maybe it should. If nothing else, it is time to ask the opponents of authorization of strikes in Syria if they are comfortable with a position that is very likely to rule out any diplomatic outcome on the Iranian nuclear program. Even in their eyes, the costs of inaction may then not appear so low.

Takeyh makes the same point:[24] "Prime Minister Benjamin Netanyahu and his hawkish advisers may yet conclude that any forceful resolution of the Iran crisis requires Israel acting alone. Whatever the probabilities of Israeli bombing Iran's facilities may have been prior to the Syrian crisis, those numbers have only gone up."

Analyses of different dimensions of transferability by Seib, Ross, and Takeyh strike us as entirely reasonable and raise important questions about how different dimensions of a crisis can produce transferable lessons that affect strategic calculations. The P-M-H view that interests, power, and credibility are somehow hermetically sealed and exclusively relevant to the specific case and actors at the center of a particular crisis seems, in this context, a tad too simplistic to be embraced as a valuable guide to theory or policy.

Eighth, and somewhat related to the previous point, proponents of P-M-H tend to conceptualize otherwise complex and nuanced variables in very stark (present/absent) terminology: relative interests and power determine the presence or absence of credibility; reputations are irrelevant; differences outweigh similarities; credibility is not transferable across cases; and so on. But if *all* of these things are ultimately in the eyes of beholder, then it is entirely appropriate to view these variables on a continuum, not in terms of absolutes. In the context of imperfect

---

23 Ross 2013.
24 Takeyh 2013.

information and an adversary's constant search for relevant signals to clarify US credibility, learning and applying lessons from past behavior (i.e., transferability) are entirely reasonable expectations. Credibility must be viewed in terms of a complex set of interconnected pressures that would not preclude the possibility that lessons from past cases may be picked up and applied. This is one of the more important lessons of intelligence failures leading to the 2003 Iraq War – for reasons outlined in chapter 3, Saddam Hussein underestimated US credibility because of lessons about Washington's aversion to casualties he transferred from previous crises. Credibility, in other words, is not as simple as calculating comparative interests and power, both of which *should* have been very clear to Saddam Hussein from 2002 to 2003.[25] Similarly, Iran or North Korea may largely *misread* US credibility as a result of lessons they believe they have learned through US action (or inaction) in Syria and elsewhere. This is not an indictment of the importance of reputation or the possibility of transferability – rather, it underscores their continued relevance to international politics, even as it undermines the availability of simple, clear-cut policy prescriptions such as those intimated by the P-M-H consensus ("don't fight or follow through, because it never matters one way or the other").

Ninth, Drum raises a common argument against transferability based on the observation that crises are different. We have already dealt with the theoretical implications of similarities and differences in chapter 2, but the point is relevant to the Syria case as well. According to Drum:[26]

> In foreign affairs, it's very seldom that you see *identical scenarios unfold over and over*. Everyone accepts that the United States has certain interests, and it's not hard to recognize that our interests in Syria are somewhat different than they are in Iran. Thus, the fact that we changed course on bombing Syria over a very specific violation of international norms regarding chemical weapons says very little about how we'd eventually react to Iran building a nuclear bomb. Sure, they both involve WMDs in some way, but the similarity ends there. Syrian chemical weapons simply aren't a big priority for America. Iranian nuclear bombs are. Everyone knows this.

This is true. One can easily find clear examples of very poorly constructed arguments about reputations transferring from one case to

---

25 See Harvey 2011.
26 Drum 2013b, emphasis added.

another; for example, Anne Marie Slaughter's attempt to establish a clear link between (supposed) US failures in Syria and Russia's moves on Ukraine.[27] Yet one can readily accept Drum's point, and acknowledge the serious weaknesses in Slaughter's analysis and policy recommendations, without arriving at the other extreme position that there is nothing about past cases that matters, or that cases are always different enough to render any reputational transfer irrelevant or inconsequential. Finding "identical scenarios" (a literal impossibility) should not be the standard for contemplating the possibility that lessons are transferred – again, these are not either/or questions, because cases are not identical or completely different.

Drum is correct that "similar situations are very uncommon in international relations. Situations separated in time are almost always different enough that it's hard to draw any firm conclusions about patterns of behavior, which is why it takes a very long time for credibility to be either established or lost."

But these are empirical questions that demand exposure to much stronger evidence confirming that differences across cases are consistently (and inevitably) viewed by all adversaries (forever) as far more relevant to their strategic calculations than any similarities. Again, there is a serious contradiction in the belief that credibility is in the eyes of the beholder (an argument for agency, subjectivity, and variation) and the alternative view that every single beholder will inevitably and consistently reject any similarities across even very recent cases when contemplating their crisis management strategies (an argument against agency and in favor of structure and patterned consistency). One view assigns the power of perception to adversaries, the other strips it away in favor of a law-like generalization about the factors adversaries will inevitably ignore when forming their perceptions.

The real question is, How similar does a case have to be to increase the probability of transferability? For example, Iraq 2003 and Syria 2013 are different in some ways, but very similar in others, and these similarities speak to the prospects that past actions may become relevant, as we argue in chapter 4. Differences across certain dimensions may very well inhibit reputational transfer, and, given that there will always be *some* differences between cases, wholesale transfer is unlikely. However, this does not preclude transfer along those dimensions that *are* similar;

---

27 Slaughter 2014.

whether such similarities can overcome broader differences between cases to impart lessons about reputation is not a question for the scholar or analyst to determine ex post facto, but rather an immediate consideration for the relevant international actor (Iran, North Korea, etc.). In the end, it is only their perception of similarities and differences that matter.

6.3   Iran, Transferability, and the Credibility Paradox Revisited

Tenth, and finally, there is another important dimension to the transferability-of-credibility argument that critics overlook, one that is directly relevant to understanding the relationship between the Syria crisis and US–Iran relations. Drezner was one of the few analysts to observe that Iranian leaders may have interpreted the Syria outcome as an important indication of US bargaining credibility (reassurance) and an opening to renewed dialogue on Iran's nuclear weapons program:[28] "Rather than accommodation on Syria signaling a weakening of resolve to Iran, it might have signaled something very different – a willingness of the United States to accept the negotiations track," and a more credible US commitment to move forward on sanctions relief in exchange for limitations on Iran's nuclear program. Fisher picked up on the same theme:

> There's a strong case to be made, though, that Obama's pragmatic handling of Syria has sent exactly the right signals to Iran, particularly at this very sensitive moment … Seeing Assad's deal with Obama work out (so far) sends the message to Iran that it can trust the United States. It also sends the message that making concessions to the United States can pay off … Obama's decision to back off Syria strikes … boosts the credibility of his stated position that he isn't seeking Iran's destruction and that he will seek detente with Iran if it first meets his long-held demands on uranium enrichment.[29]

Obama appeared to understand the paradox and the requisite policy corrective: "My view is that if you have both a credible threat of force, combined with a rigorous diplomatic effort … you can … strike a

---

28   Drezner 2013c.
29   Fisher 2013c.

deal."[30] The fact that the US, Iran, and five other world powers signed a deal curbing Iran's enrichment program only two months after the UN resolution on Syria adds considerable weight to this argument. It also provides a compelling indication that bargaining reputations from one case to another *are* transferable and that the credibility paradox, discussed in detail at the end of chapter 4, can be resolved. Just over two years later, the significant nuclear arms deal of July 2015 (the Joint Comprehensive Plan of Action) lends further support to this possibility, though few (if any) analysts seem to have made the connection.

---

30 Quoted in Borger 2013.

Chapter Seven

Responding to Critics: Alternative Explanations and Competing Policy Recommendations

With the preceding analysis in mind, this chapter addresses other explanations for the Syria outcome and evaluates a set of competing policy recommendations that consistently emerged from those citing P-M-H research. Specific emphasis will be placed on evaluating the core recommendation that Obama should back away from the coercive threat and essentially concede to a bluff on his red lines, because reputations are irrelevant, credibility is not transferable, and bluffing carries no costs or risks in international politics.

7.1 Alternative Explanations for the Syria Disarmament Deal

We begin with a brief review of the alternative explanation Peter Feaver provides for the outcome of the Syria crisis:[1]

> For about 10 days prior to that abrupt reversal, everyone thought the United States was about to attack. Heck, even Obama's senior staff thought the United States was about to attack. During that time ... there was ample back-and-forth diplomatically about possible deals of the sort that arose suddenly in the last 48 hours. But there was no progress. There was, however, a steady erosion in credibility of the strike. As political opposition at home mounted, it went from a near certainty of happening to a near certainty of not happening ... How could a threat, which when credibly imminent was producing defiance suddenly produce a breakthrough when

---

1 Feaver 2013, emphasis added.

it seemed least credible? ... *Putin and Assad acted not because they feared the imminent strike. They acted at the moment when they least had to fear the strike in order to get the most from Obama.*

This explanation directly contradicts the rational deterrence interpretation we present in this book. We believe – in keeping with this interpretation and the attendant evidence of consistent behavior in similar deterrence encounters over the previous decade – that Assad and Putin acted when they most feared escalation, for reasons we outline in chapters 4, 5, and 6.

Drezner's assessment of Russia's "victory" serves well as a concise summary of the problems with Feaver's position:[2]

> As a result of the past week's worth of supposedly brilliant machinations, Russia has managed to bolster ... a very wobbly ally with a government that is a shell of its former self, a pariah of the international community, under heavy United Nations Security Council sanctions, and about to be overrun with chemical weapons inspectors to destroy its WMD stockpiles. Even if this agreement improves the odds of Assad staying in power, he's in charge of a radically depleted asset. So, in other words, compared to where Russian influence in the Middle East was at the start of 2011 to now, I'm not terrifically impressed. And it's not like Russia's prospects improve when you look elsewhere, I might add.

The logical implication of Feaver's interpretation is that Assad and Putin preferred the disarmament outcome to one in which they (1) retain their chemical weapons (as a modest deterrent against Israel and a useful weapon against the opposition); (2) force Obama to admit he was bluffing (as Feaver implies he was), thereby seriously damaging the president's credibility at home and undermining his relations with key allies (including Israel); (3) deliver a serious blow to the Syrian opposition; and (4) emerge from the crisis with their respective positions in the region not only intact but buttressed by the fact that they stood up to the US. This alternative scenario would have served Assad's interests far more than the humiliation he suffered from having to acknowledge the existence of and then systematically dismantle his chemical weapons. To argue that the scenario outlined above is

---

2 Drezner 2013b.

somehow less appealing to Assad than the disarmament deal is, in a word, puzzling.

Our explanation is entirely consistent with the logic and expectations underpinning RDT. If Assad and Putin believed that strikes were likely (based on past US actions in similar situations), then giving up the chemical weapons was a rational response to avoiding an outcome (strikes, military escalation, and possibly regime change) that would have been far more costly to the regime. The principles of Occam's razor (parsimony and succinctness) apply here. The theory we offer is a relatively straightforward rational deterrence account of behavior, an account based on a widely accepted theory supported by considerable historical and case-specific evidence – it should be preferred to an alternative account/hypothesis that requires serious contortions of strategy and logic (or some "godly" intervention, as posited by Jeffrey Goldberg)[3] to explain the same behavior and outcome.

Nevertheless, Feaver goes on to argue: "By late Sunday and early Monday of this week, the credibility of the threat was at the lowest point it had been since the crisis began. The House was almost certainly going to vote against Obama. The Senate was a likely no, too. And Obama's advisors had said it was 'unthinkable' that the president would strike Syria in defiance of that expected congressional rebuke."

For reasons we outline in chapter 5, US domestic and congressional politics actually enhanced the credibility of US deterrence from the adversaries' perspective. If, as Feaver claims, Assad had no reason whatsoever to see Obama's threat as credible and that it had in fact "a near certainty of not happening," there would have been no reason for Assad to dismantle his weapons, the same arsenal he repeatedly denied even existed. The disarmament outcome is far easier to explain with reference to sufficient US credibility, not its absence. The mistaken assumption underpinning Feaver's account is that you either have credibility or you don't, and, according to Feaver, Obama had no credibility left with respect to his resolve to defend the red-line threat. As we have explained, however, credibility and deterrence outcomes unfold over time and through stages – so the real question Feaver neglects to address is *how much* of a threat was enough to force Assad and Putin to capitulate.

---

3 See Goldberg (2016, 75) for comments relating to the "deus ex machina" of the Russian offer to broker the disarmament deal.

If the bombing was unlikely to occur or was too limited to have any significant effect on Syria, then why not let the US get tangled in yet another Middle East war they were destined to lose? Why save Obama from suffering the consequences of issuing the initial red-line threats that had turned the situation into a crisis in the first place? The more reasonable interpretation, and the one that requires fewer leaps of logic (i.e., no non-sequitur, out-of-the-blue "acts of god"), is that Putin was desperate to prevent yet another attack on a key ally that would reconfirm Russia's ongoing decline as a significant global power and patron. With the benefit of hindsight acquired from several previous (similar) encounters with the US, Assad and Putin decided to avoid another Bosnia, Kosovo, Iraq, Afghanistan, and Libya.

Feaver concludes with a "final" interpretation of what transpired in Syria that makes much more sense to us, because this part of his argument directly contradicts his earlier views about the absence of US credibility.[4] "For coercion to work," he correctly points out, "you have to simultaneously threaten bad outcomes if the target defies you *and promise good outcomes if the target acquiesces.*" This is entirely consistent with the points we raise in chapter 4 (section 4.3) regarding the prerequisites for resolving the *credibility paradox*. In offering this explanation, Feaver is forced to concede a crucial point – successful coercion *requires* a "credible" threat of punishment *and* a "credible" promise to make concessions. In the absence of one or the other, you have no agreement. In light of the disarmament agreement, it is apparent that both aspects of coercion were satisfied.

Arena's excellent analysis of the Syria outcome also highlights the problems with Feaver's logic, particularly in relation to the "successful" application of coercive diplomacy in this case:[5]

That Putin proposed a deal only after it became clear that nothing more than an "incredibly small" US intervention was forthcoming, if one was at all, is only puzzling if we assume that what kept Putin from pushing Assad to offer concessions up until that point was a belief that the US wasn't going to use force ... But it strikes me as perfectly possible that Putin assumed much the opposite. That all talk of enforcing global taboos was mere pretense for a wider war that would end with regime change. After

---

4 Feaver 2013, emphasis added.
5 Arena 2013.

all, the US invoked lofty liberal principles when justifying its intervention in Libya, but rather than simply preventing a massacre, the US ended
up playing the role of rebel air force. And when Saddam Hussein finally
started to comply fully with UN weapons inspectors, the US showed no
interest in negotiating. One can see how Putin might have come to the
conclusion that you can't believe the US when it says "all we want to do is
stop this bad thing from happening; we promise we won't keep bombing
the crap out of you until your government falls and one that's willing to
let us write their constitution for them takes over. Pinky-swear."

Escalation *was* a serious concern, which is why Obama's "promise" to
limit the strikes to an "unbelievably small" campaign was not credible
to Assad or Putin – they learned certain lessons from past deterrence
encounters with the US (over similar issues), each of which followed
the same path with a very patterned sequence of weak threats, counter-
threats, tipping points, escalation, and regime change.

7.2   The Real Costs of Bluffing on Syria

There are two common but mutually exclusive (and equally mistaken)
conclusions about the impact of bluffing in international relations. The
P-M-H view maintains that bluffing is irrelevant or cost-free, because
reputations for being irresolute (weak) never form, and because any
credibility concerns associated with bluffing (or standing firm) are not
transferable across cases.

The other view, dismissed by proponents of P-M-H, holds that bluffing is always dangerous precisely because states can acquire a reputation for being weak, these reputations are interdependent, and credibility is perfectly transferable across cases.[6] To summarize both extremes,

---

6 For a more nuanced treatment of bluffing in international politics, see Sartori 2005.
   Sartori focuses on the power of diplomatic "honesty" in helping states pursue an
   effective foreign policy, meaning the natural corollary of her theory is the deleterious
   consequences of diplomatic "dishonesty" – i.e., bluffing. She concludes that a state that
   has been recently caught in a bluff develops a "reputation for bluffing" and is "less
   able to communicate and less likely to attain its goals" (p. 43). While Sartori explicitly
   differentiates reputation for honesty from the more widely debated reputation for
   resolve along a variety of dimensions (see pp. 44–9), her theory and subsequent
   empirical testing support the notion that bluffing carries costs. At the very least, states
   caught in a bluff reduce their maneuverability and leverage in subsequent interactions.

bluffing is either irrelevant or catastrophic. Chapman provides a good illustration of these two positions:[7]

> The United States boasts the most powerful military on Earth. We have 1.4 million active-duty personnel, thousands of tanks, ships and planes, and 5,000 nuclear warheads. We spend more on defense than the next 13 countries combined. Yet we are told we have to bomb Syria to preserve our credibility in world affairs ... On the surface, American credibility resembles a mammoth fortress, impervious to anything an enemy could inflict. But to crusading internationalists, both liberal and conservative, it's a house of cards: The tiniest wrong move, and it collapses.

The problem with these extreme views is that both sides are engaged in a form of confirmation bias designed to either completely reaffirm the absolutely essential nature of credibility for global politics or US foreign policy writ large, or to completely dismiss as exaggerated any and all claims about reputations and transferability. Common sense and face validity dictate that the truth falls somewhere between. It would be wrong to expect any action to result in the immediate collapse of US credibility in all of its multiple dimensions, but it is equally mistaken to remain convinced that reputations are *irrelevant*, or that adversaries *never* assign a reputation for being irresolute to their enemies (no matter how many times they back off from a threat), or that a US decision to retreat from red lines in Syria would have absolutely no effect whatsoever on any aspect of US credibility in other cases, or that bluffing carries no risks or costs.

Now, if common sense and empirical evidence dictate that reputations for resolve can occasionally transfer across similar cases, then our objective should be to determine what those occasional circumstances might be. The remainder of this chapter will challenge the P-M-H policy prescription that bluffing is risk-/cost-free.

P-M-H Consensus: Reputations Are Irrelevant, so Bluffing Is Costless

According to P-M-H, crisis decision making is all about power and interests, nothing more (Press); adversaries never assign a dispositional

---

7 Chapman 2013.

attribute (reputation) to their opponents for being irresolute or backing down (Mercer); and a state's credibility in any given crisis is independent of past actions and never transferable to future exchanges or other cases (Hopf). In sum, reputations either do not exist or, if they do linger, they are irrelevant. If we accept these conclusions, and ignore the many serious theoretical, logical, and methodological problems outlined in earlier chapters, then it stands to reason that fighting for credibility is never prudent or justifiable, and bluffing carries no risks or costs. As Friedersdorf explains in his defense of bluffing as a legitimate policy option:[8]

> Presidents of the United States say things that they don't mean all the time. The White House and the State Department break promises all the time. This has been so through all the decades that we've led the current global order ... It's also important to remember that remarks by the president, off-the-cuff or otherwise, aren't the only or even the primary way that other states gauge the likelihood that America will or won't act to back up what we've said we're going to do. America's actions flow from our *interests*, the risks and rewards of pursuing them in a given situation, and the absolute and relative *power* that we enjoy.

Highlighting the essentially benign nature of bluffing was a central argument put forward by many of those who repeatedly cited Press and Mercer during the Syria crisis – that was the point they were trying to make while criticizing Obama for worrying far too much about fighting for credibility in Syria or protecting some general US reputation for defending red lines that should never have been issued in the first place. Don't worry about appearing irresolute, critics argued, because adversaries will judge credibility exclusively on the basis of power and interests. If the US can't get a reputation for being irresolute, then backing away from the red-line threat would not only be prudent but would carry no short- or long-term risks or costs to US credibility when dealing with Iran, North Korea, or any other potential future adversary.

But what if Press and Mercer are wrong, for all of the reasons outlined in earlier chapters? What if reputations and past actions do matter? What if credibility is considerably more complex than reputation-critics

---

8 Friedersdorf 2013b, emphasis added.

imagined? What if lessons about credibility are transferable across cases, because, in light of imperfect information during a crisis, perceptions of interests, power, resolve, and credibility are ultimately in the eyes of the beholder? What if adversaries suffer from the cognitive and motivational biases Jervis identified three decades ago,[9] and what if they do rely on their perceptions of similarities from previous cases, or the general and specific reputations they assign to the US when assessing Washington's interests and commitments? What if fighting for credibility does make sense in some cases? And what if the evidence presented in this book raises serious questions about premature closure of inquiry, as well as related problems with the theory, logic, and evidence underpinning the P-M-H consensus, much of which is derived from great-power cases in the 1900s and 1930s that bear no relationship to an asymmetric conflict between the US and Syria in 2013? And what if the evidence compiled from deterrence encounters over the last two decades, all from protracted, asymmetric crises that look very similar to Syria, disconfirms the central claims about reputations from Press, Mercer, and Hopf?

Analysts who continue to cite P-M-H typically do so without ever engaging any of the potential problems with this research program. Western offers a useful example of the policy advice offered by those who referenced (and explicitly subscribed to) the P-M-H consensus, specifically as it relates to the dangers – or lack thereof – of bluffing in international relations:[10]

> Does the United States really look weak and indecisive if it fails to follow through on a bluff? The United States uses force at a rate that is several times greater than others – it has already toppled regimes on Iran's western border and on Iran's eastern border – and somehow it is the lesson of Syria that is more salient for Iran? More broadly: why should an occasional bluff matter? Well, actually it doesn't … Jon Mercer's excellent book on reputation shows that we've spent far too much blood and treasure over the folly of preserving our credibility. Daryl Press spent years trying to demonstrate the costs of lost credibility when a state fails to follow through on its threats. His finding? The conventional wisdom on credibility "is wrong" … Make the threat. Sell it and try to dissuade the Syrians

---

9 Jervis 1976.
10 Western 2013a, emphasis added.

from using chemical weapons. *If they call our bluff, so be it* – at this point it's really the best in a set of really weak/bad options.[11]

Biddle raises the same point in defense of his "bluffing" recommendation to Congress at the height of the Syria crisis:[12]

> It would have been better if we had never begun this escalatory process by issuing "red line" threats that were not in our interest to enforce; nevertheless it is wiser to cut our losses while these losses are still relatively limited rather than doubling down and, in all likelihood, increasing the eventual price of failure. Although there are important costs in backing down, this is ultimately the least-bad course even so.

In light of the case evidence presented in chapters 4 through 6, however, it is clear that both Western and Biddle misjudged the adversary's perceptions of US credibility and therefore got their policy advice dead wrong – if Obama had bluffed and backed away from the red lines, there is no logical reason why Assad would have read this as a credible deterrent threat and stopped using chemical weapons. And in light of Assad and Putin's decision to capitulate when faced with the reinforced threat, it is clear that the escalation of violence in the form of chemical weapons *was* controllable and was not a product of some "set of other factors." These analysts misunderstood the logic of coercive diplomacy in this case, the utility of reinforcing the deterrent threat, and the role of reputations in convincing Assad and Putin that strikes were inevitable and that mission creep was very likely. A strong coercive threat was necessary for the disarmament agreement; bluffing was *not* the "best in a set of really bad options," or the "least-bad course" of action, and would *not* have achieved the same or a better outcome. Western and Biddle are certainly free to discount the costs of chemical attacks,

---

11 Western also noted that "Robert Jervis demonstrated four decades ago that signaling is complex business," but the author never explains what he means by "complex business," how this complexity supports his views on costless bluffing, and provides no details with respect to Jervis' misperception theory, its effects on an adversary's receptivity to coercive diplomacy or likely response(s) to bluffing, and the implications for coercive diplomacy more generally. Simply citing a well-respected author like Jervis does nothing to connect his theory and evidence to the arguments Western is attempting to defend.

12 Committee on Homeland Security 2013.

because these weapons have not been directed at American citizens, but there are nevertheless significant costs to bluffing if Syria retains chemical weapons and continues to use them. In the absence of any response by the US, Assad's regime would likely have escalated the use of these weapons, and the international norm against their use would have suffered a serious blow.

Western's and Biddle's policy recommendations were also fundamentally mistaken, because their understanding of reputations (they both cite Press and Mercer) and corresponding theories of coercive diplomacy, credibility, and the implications of bluffing are incomplete and underdeveloped. We know from the case evidence that in the *absence* of a clearly articulated and credible retaliatory threat undergirding the red line, the US acquired a crisis-based reputation for being irresolute, which led to repeated violations of the red line and several chemical weapons attacks against Syrian civilians. The largest attack, against Ghouta, was followed by an escalation in the tone and substance of Washington's retaliatory threats and led to one of the most sweeping and successful disarmament agreements in history. Backing down in Syria would simply have confirmed assumptions (and reputations) about casualty aversion and convinced the regime that the US had no interest in preventing further uses of chemical weapons. Consistent with patterned behavior in similar cases over previous decades, a bluff would have led to an escalation in the violence.

There are several additional problems with the "theory" and logic of bluffing extracted from the P-M-H consensus.

7.3   Bluffing and Bad Poker Analogies: What the Critics Miss

Why Bluffing Matters

First, the most obvious policy contradiction is found in the critics' admonition that Obama should never have issued the weak red-line threat in the first place and should never have reinforced the threat later on when the red line was crossed with the Ghouta attack. The US, according to many critics, had few interests and demonstrated no apparent willingness to use sufficient force to change the course of the war or to impose significant costs on the regime. Yet if bluffing carries no risks or costs, why worry about issuing red-line threats, anywhere or at any time? If Obama could simply have backed away from the initial or reinforced threat at any point in time without suffering any damage to his credibility in this or any other case, then where is the harm in bluffing with the initial red-line threat? It makes perfect sense to do this, especially if proponents of P-M-H are correct and there are no costs, because the red-line threat and subsequent efforts to outline the strategic imperatives driving US priorities in this case stood at least some small chance of deterring chemical use. If Mercer is right that states can't get a reputation from adversaries for being irresolute, even after repeatedly bluffing or backing down, then why not continually bluff, even when interests and capabilities are not in your favor? If there are no costs to bluffing, then give it a shot – reputations don't form, so there are no reputational costs to worry about. If reputations are irrelevant and if credibility is not transferable, then why not encourage the president, secretary of state, and secretary of defense to exaggerate the strategic importance to the US of any WMD use and repeat these threats at every opportunity? Of course, the reason Biddle and others think the original red-line threat was a mistake, and are not inclined to recommend the more assertive approach to bluffing outlined above, is precisely because they *do* understand at least some of the potential costs of bluffing.

Farley makes a similar logical error when presenting his take on the effects of bluffing:[13]

> But the notion that the US needed to go to war in order to send a message has always been a bit silly. Washington cannot force any other country to learn any particular lesson; observers are always free to make their own conclusions ... Bluffing is an important tool of diplomatic statecraft, and there's no reason to believe that a called bluff over Syria means that the US is bluffing with respect to its other international commitments.

There is an obvious contradiction here between claiming that adversaries are "free to make their own conclusions" and Farley's judgment that "there's no reason to believe that a called bluff over Syria means that the US is bluffing with respect to its other international commitments." Of course there is a reason, *because* adversaries are "free to make their own conclusions" and therefore could conceivably draw linkages between past US actions and similarities in their current situation. Of course there is a reason, because of imperfect information

---

13 Farley 2013b.

when adversaries assess US interests and resolve to use force – once again, it is entirely conceivable that past behavior in similar cases will help adversaries acquire some information about US credibility and commitments. The notion that evidence of repeated bluffing in the past and in other cases has no bearing whatsoever on how adversaries might choose to calculate US interests in a present crisis is not only bad theory but is disconfirmed by an abundance of evidence from the last two decades.

Now, if Mercer is right about adversaries never assigning a reputation to US leaders for being irresolute, or never underestimating US resolve based on past experiences, then Assad would not have raised the stakes by launching a more devastating chemical attack. The fact that he did speaks volumes about how leaders probe for information about US resolve, and why it is so important to signal resolve and defend credibility in some cases. Adversaries cannot make decisions exclusively on the basis of straightforward calculations of interests and power, because US interests and willingness to use capabilities are never that clear-cut or straightforward – they don't have perfect information and must rely on other signals and indicators of intentions, and these often require references to past US actions in similar situations. Moreover, adversaries have no way of confirming whether the information they do obtain from probes is sufficient to lead them to the right decisions. In fact, if officials in the Assad regime (or Assad himself) had the capacity to correctly predict Obama's response to the Ghouta attacks, based exclusively on tracking US interests and power, they likely would not have launched the attacks in the first place (assuming that the limited tactical gains of that particular strike did not outweigh the costs of losing an important deterrent capability in the long run; even simply considering the "psychological" impact of the attack can't explain the decision in these terms – given that smaller chemical attacks had gone unpunished, the psychological fears associated with such weapons could have been steadily exploited, on a smaller scale, moving forward).

The argument that Obama loses nothing by backing away after Ghouta is simply not plausible, for many of the reasons related to complex credibility and transferability outlined in chapter 6. Western retreat in Syria would have provided a clear signal to aspiring chemical weapons states that there is some value (and security) in acquiring this capability. One can certainly downplay these costs when compared with the costs of US intervention, but it would be difficult to deny the probability of further chemical use if the president accepted the recommendation to bluff. Ghouta would then have become the new benchmark for acceptable behavior, raising the probability of escalation as the regime continued to probe for additional information about Washington's real red line and tipping points.

When Bluffing Matters

Second, most discussions of the merits of bluffing rarely ask or answer some of the most relevant questions: bluffing on what specific issues and at what point in the crisis? Surely the costs of failing to respond to Syria's violations of the red line in 2012 are not the same as the costs of bluffing (backing down) after investing considerably more time, energy, and political capital reinforcing the deterrent threat following the Ghouta attacks in August 2013. There is a qualitative distinction between the costs of not following through on the initial red-line threat and the costs of failing to follow through after a much larger chemical weapons attack and dozens of speeches by senior White House officials explicitly extolling the many strategic imperatives compelling the US to respond. The costs and risks of bluffing at these two points in time are obviously different, yet no such allowances are noted by proponents of P-M-H to accommodate the policy implications of these differences. Leaders repeatedly say things they don't mean, but rarely do they issue so many clear and forceful statements about the need to act, replete with explicit references to strategic imperatives and a full-court public relations campaign by the secretaries of state and defense, and the chairman of the Joint Chiefs of Staff, to sell the policy and solicit support from leading opposition members (many of whom were very concerned about the effects of their decision on their mid-term election prospects). Instances of strong and forceful deterrent threats are rare, for obvious reasons – they require enormous political capital and carry significant audience costs if commitments and declarations are proven to be a bluff. To compare this or any similar situation with the typical broken promises a president makes on a semi-daily basis misses too much of what makes the reinforced red-line threat (and bluff) so different from, say, a decision to back away from building a road in some senator's constituency, or a failure to close Guantanamo. Using sweeping generalization to draw out the relatively benign nature of bluffing at the final stages of the Syria crisis simply ignores too many aspects of international and domestic politics that explain why credibility and reputations in these cases were and are so important.

Why Bluffing in International Politics Is Not Like Poker

Third, the common use of poker (or chess) analogies to explain why bluffing is rational and normal usually fall flat when applied to US foreign policy or international crisis bargaining. Take as an example Matthews's discussion (in which he directly quotes Press) of bluffing in Syria:[14]

> Perhaps the best case for the irrelevance of past US behavior to future geopolitical disputes, though, is that if bluffing really did destroy US credibility, that would make international politics the only kind of competition on Earth that works like that. "In every domain of competition – business, finance, sports, war, games – smart strategic actors use feints," Press says. "Nobody plays chess and adopts the position that, 'Once I move a bishop forward, I'd never move it back.' … Anybody who says that it's bad strategy to bluff has an open invitation to poker night at my house."

First, poker and chess bear only a distant, ephemeral, and at best incredibly superficial connection to international politics or interactions in a foreign policy crisis. For this reason alone, using analogies of poker and chess to provide policy guidance on Syria, or to justify an argument that past behavior is "irrelevant" to an adversary's calculations of US credibility, or that repeatedly bluffing cannot possibly push an adversary to assign a reputation to US leaders for being irresolute is not only silly but potentially dangerous, for reasons that will become apparent below.

Just for the sake of pushing the poker analogy to its logical extreme, however, it should be pointed out that repeatedly bluffing carries enormous risks in both poker and international relations, because it inevitably sends a reputational signal – it may not be interpreted by an opponent as a definitive statement of what the player will do every hand, but there is no question that repeated bluffs do provide information about your inclination as a player (or state leader), all else being equal. Players who obtain a reputation for bluffing lose the advantage that comes from effective bluffing – that is, winning pots with "weak" cards because people with stronger hands fold. Constant bluffing means that players with weak (but not weaker) hands who would otherwise fold will call

---

14 Matthews 2013; see also Press 2005.

the bluff more often. Obviously, the chances that a weaker hand will prevail against a repeated bluffer is much higher than if you're facing a conservative player who only bets with strong hands, so you should be more inclined to fold if the conservative player raises, and less inclined to fold if the raise is initiated by the repeated bluffer. Dismissing as completely irrelevant information you obtain from repeated bluffs makes no practical sense, in poker *or* international relations. Moreover, it would be dangerous for any opponent to completely discard this reputational information, because it is relevant to deciphering the predilections of folks around the table and the probability that they do or do not have a better hand. In any case, those who subscribe to Matthews's poker strategy have an open invitation to poker night at *my* house.

Matthews continues: "So sure, Obama might have been bluffing when he declared chemical weapons a 'red line.' *But who cares?* Just because that bluff didn't work out doesn't mean that we should keep calling or raising going forward. Sometimes folding just makes sense."[15] Unless, of course, the other side is bluffing with a weaker hand, which is what Matthews completely misses in his assessment of the Syria crisis – he misunderstood how interests, power, and resolve (and a reputation from past cases for not bluffing after a raise) played out in Washington's favor in this case.

There are serious costs to repeatedly bluffing in international relations, because reputations do form. In addition to the significant audience costs that would befall any leader pursuing a strategy of constantly threatening and backing down, a reputation for bluffing would undermine the capacity to mount an effective coercive strategy even in cases where the state's interests and capabilities *are* significant and should have been sufficient to deter or compel – the chances of deterrence failure are greater because the adversary, without perfect information, will be more inclined to assume weaknesses (another bluff, perhaps because of an aversion to casualties) and continue to probe for weaknesses in resolve. In poker, this simply results in an opponent staying in the hand. In international politics, this means a chemical attack that kills 1400 civilians.

Proponents of P-M-H will no doubt argue that there are obvious limits to how often one should bluff, but therein lies the crux of the dilemma, puzzle, problem, question (and the secret to success in poker):

---

15 Matthews 2013, emphasis added.

when and under what conditions is bluffing costly? When are bluffs more or less likely to succeed? And what are the implications of any specific bluff for US foreign policy and security more generally, at what point in time, and in relation to what specific set of issues, challenges, security threats, and international norms? Bad poker analogies often miss too much of what makes international politics so complex and so much more difficult to manage.

To further illustrate the problem with poker analogies, take Ulfelder's effort to apply poker to his analysis of the Syria crisis and related policy advice:[16]

> Now the Obama administration is threatening to strike Assad's forces to punish him for the CW attack. While making this threat, though, the administration is simultaneously signaling that a) the attack will be limited and b) the administration hopes not to have to do more … In poker terms, this approach is like trying to drive your opponent off a pot with a modest bet when you hold a weak hand. Unless your opponent has really weak cards, that kind of bet is usually more effective at enticing that opponent to stay in the hand, not encouraging him to fold. In the Syrian case, the Assad regime has repeatedly signaled that it will play every hand to the end, so this kind of bet *will almost certainly not have the desired effect.* That outcome is even more likely if the opponent has good reason to think your hand is weak. When the Obama administration can't muster much domestic or international support for its punitive strikes and whatever support it can muster is predicated on those strikes being very limited in their scope and intent, then I'd say that's easy to read as a weak hand. It's a bit like waving around a pair of eights and threatening to make a small raise.

The most obvious and serious error in Ulfelder's analysis is his failure to correctly read the strengths and weaknesses of the two hands in this case (actually, three hands if we include Russia). If getting the history (and competing interests and commitments) right is absolutely essential to connecting his poker analogy to his policy advice, this is obviously a significant error. Ulfelder goes on: "To drive a committed rival to fold, you need to really change the expected value of the pot, and this approach *simply doesn't do that to a regime that has shown*

---

itself to be deeply committed to playing every hand to the end" (emphasis added).

Ulfelder failed to view the US position (hand) through the adversary's lens, a mistake shared by many others who misinterpreted the potency of the US threat and misunderstood the pressures, audience costs, and other factors than enhanced the credibility of Obama's threat, as discussed in detail in chapters 4 and 5. In any event, Ulfelder concludes:

> I can see two paths out of the current situation. One is to acknowledge that our tepid raise has failed to drive Assad off this pot and go ahead and fold this hand. The outcome is essentially the same, and we don't incur bigger losses getting there. The other is to change the hand we're playing by committing to do whatever it takes to prevent Assad's forces from using chemical weapons again. In other words, we commit to regime-defeating war if necessary and we signal that stronger commitment to Assad's forces and their backers as clearly as possible.

Regime-defeating war was obviously not required for deterrence success (or a winning hand) in this case. Assad did not have a stronger hand, was not prepared to go to the end, expected the US to strike, and was very concerned about the risks of escalation, in part because both he and Putin had a pretty clear view of how US officials had played these hands in previous cases (raising the stakes through very costly signals). In the end, Assad folded because that was the rational option, all things (and reputations) considered. Fortunately, Obama ignored Matthews's and Ulfelder's poker-infused policy advice, doubled down, and won a pretty large pot – a unanimous UN resolution and the near complete disarmament of Syria's chemical weapons.

Ulfelder's final point reveals another major error in his assessment of the crisis and attendant policy recommendations:

> If I were a ruler considering using chemical weapons at some later date, the lesson I think I'd have learned from Syria so far is that the rest of the world actually isn't willing to pay a steep cost to reinforce this supposed norm for its own sake. In fact, we've developed a tell: if the stakes are high for other reasons, our initial raise will probably be a bluff, and it probably won't be that costly to stay in the hand and see if that's right.

In fact, this is precisely what Obama could not afford to have happen – the US developing a "tell" with respect to its coercive threats and acquiring a reputation for bluffing. Ironically, Assad understood why this would be unacceptable to Obama, which explains why he expected a strike and folded. Ulfelder missed the policy implications of his own poker analogy – the unacceptable audience costs associated with bluffing and the positive coercive effects this had on Assad's assessment of US credibility.[17]

Unintended Consequences of Congressionally Endorsed Bluffing

Finally, many critics downplay or dismiss the costs of bluffing by balancing it against the advantages of controlling a president's capacity to start unilateral wars of choice in the absence of congressional oversight and authorization. As Friedersdorf argued:

> If President Obama is prohibited from intervening [in Syria], other countries may well be reminded that the Constitution gives America's legislature the power to declare war, and marginally discount presidential saber rattling regarding wars of choice that haven't yet been endorsed by Congress ... Obama, and perhaps future presidents, will be less able to credibly threaten unilateral wars of choice. Given how badly such wars have worked out that's no great loss, especially since a credible American threat would still always be a congressional vote away.[18]

This would definitely confine the president's capacity to issue credible threats, but the author never defines what it means to "marginally

---

17 The problem with poker analogies is that they rely heavily on the analyst's interpretation of history, the bargaining positions they assign to each side, their interpretation of the strengths and weaknesses of these bargaining positions, and, perhaps most importantly, their selection of the appropriate poker-game analogy. If Ulfelder replaced his analogy of multiple hands during a night of straight poker with a reference to only one hand in a game of Texas hold 'em, the strategic analysis (and policy advice) would be completely different. In this case, the US was dealt an ace and king of clubs. Assad was dealt two queens. The flop (the first three open community cards everyone shares) included a jack and queen of clubs, and another king. Assad raised (with the Ghouta attack) and the US then re-raised (by reinforcing the deterrent threat). In the end, Assad read the cards, assessed the odds of having a winning hand and folded, even before the last two community cards were dealt (i.e., before Congress even voted).
18 Friedersdorf 2013b.

discount presidential saber rattling" or to engage in "unilateral wars of choice," nor does he take the time to work through some of the unintended consequences of having US interventions guided exclusively by congressional authorization. Friedersdorf simply concludes that "presidents shouldn't be able to credibly threaten wars that the people oppose."[19]

Drum shares the same view regarding the benign effects of a bluff following a congressional "no" vote:[20]

> I really doubt that this vote will be taken as much of a precedent. But if it were, the precedent it sets would be simple: the United States won't undertake military action unless it's so plainly justified that both parties are willing to support it. That would frankly be no bad thing. Unfortunately, once they get in office American presidents of both parties seem to find no end of wars to fight overseas. Reining them in a bit would be commendable.

Yet surely the wisdom of this position relies heavily on a well-functioning US political system in which foreign policies are debated in a clear and balanced way with the national security interests of the state in mind. It is not clear that this approach makes much sense in a divided Congress, where the merits of public policies are secondary to crass domestic political interests and concerns. Judging by the deadlock and pace of legislation in the US Congress during the second Obama administration, it is not clear that the country's national interests are a priority in Washington today – a problem that explains the many unilateral presidential directives Obama has been forced to sign.

Obviously, these political divisions are designed to position the opposition for success in the next election, and passing the president's agenda is not a particularly great way to establish a case for change. But if the priority in Washington today is to avoid passing legislation (or authorizations) that might highlight the wisdom, foresight, and accomplishments of one or the other political party, then very few initiatives will gain any traction, regardless of how pressing they might be. Those in favor of assigning military-deployment authority to avoid the president's unilateralism in Syria are likely to be the first to reject the same

19 Friedersdorf 2013a.
20 Drum 2013a.

suggestion in the next crisis if US credibility is essential to addressing a threat they deem to be important and pressing.

These political/ideological divisions are not only common to practitioners engaged in policy debates; similar biases exist within the academic and scholarly communities when accepting or rejecting competing theories of foreign policy. The implications of these mutually reinforcing divisions in both camps explain the ongoing challenges we face with respect to narrowing the theory-policy gap in international relations, a point to which we turn in the next chapter.

Chapter Eight

Expanding Theory-Policy Gaps in International Relations

We begin the final chapter with a brief summary of our findings, followed by an extended discussion of policy relevance and the larger implications for addressing the theory-policy gap in international relations. Using policy debates during the Syria crisis as a case study, our somewhat provocative conclusion raises serious questions about whether policymakers and academics have the capacity to shed the confirmation biases that inform the foreign policy advice they offer.

With respect to our central findings, the evidence we present clearly shows that reputations are neither consistently present nor entirely absent; they emerge and become more or less relevant through the perceptions of adversaries who have the power to assign or dismiss reputational factors when selecting their crisis management strategies. Despite repeated references to competing "interests" and relative "power" as the sole determinants of crisis behavior, rational deterrence theory predicts that past actions (and inactions) by US officials *do* have an impact on how adversaries perceive Washington's interests and resolve to use power. Understanding the mechanisms through which adversaries interpret US interests and resolve is essential, and reputations are key to understanding the process, related perceptions, specific decisions, and crisis outcomes of coercive encounters. Crises are not entirely identical or completely different – their similarities and differences vary from case to case and, according to the evidence we've compiled, adversaries have repeatedly perceived (and often misperceived) similarities across cases involving the US and other powers. Perceptions of US credibility and resolve are transferable across time both within a protracted crisis and across essentially similar crises, which means the Syria case does convey some relevant information to Iranian officials and to other aspiring chemical weapons and/or WMD states. These findings are confirmed through several case studies of US deterrence encounters in asymmetric conflicts involving the US and smaller powers from 1991 to 2013. Because these cases resemble the 2013 Syria crisis, the findings from these cases were and are particularly important for assessing the strengths and weaknesses of the competing policy options occurring at the time. Finally, such assessments are not only important for understanding and explaining the Syria case, but will be informative in future crises (and associated policy debates) involving the US and smaller intransigent adversaries.

8.1   Theory-Policy Gap(s) and Confirmation Bias(es)

In her strong defense of social science funding from the National Science Foundation (NSF), Senator Elizabeth Warren (D-MA) issued the following argument: "Social science research is a compass for policymakers [that] points us in the right direction."[1] Losing NSF funding for the social sciences, she continued, "will threaten the ability of Congress to make good decisions by cutting off the pipeline of rigorous analysis to identify what policies work and what policies don't work." These thoughts represent the standard view held by those who are concerned about cuts in funding or who lament the growing gap between the academic and policy communities.

The reality, however, is that many policymakers, like Warren, share a misconception of what academics actually provide – in the field of international relations, they assume it's balanced, rigorous, objective research and analysis that usefully informs them about the utility of different foreign policy options. Similarly, international relations scholars share a misconception of what policymakers want – they assume policymakers want balanced, rigorous, objective academic research to inform their foreign policy choices. Those who retain these misconceptions overlook the ideological divisions and related biases that apply to both groups, biases that were apparent in the theory/policy debates over reputations and credibility during the Syria crisis. Premature closure of inquiry regarding the relevance of US credibility and resolve in Syria, based almost exclusively on P-M-H, is a crucial

---

1 Quoted in Mervis 2013; Warren has a particular interest in this debate, being a former academic (legal scholar) of considerable standing herself.

case demonstrating the point. Indeed, the Syria crisis provides an excellent opportunity to explore in more detail the theory-policy gap in international relations.

As a case study, the policy debates at the time reveal deep divides that are rarely discussed in traditional treatments of the subject – it is not simply a question of getting policymakers to listen to academics, or getting academics to more effectively communicate their theories to policymakers – the problems run much deeper. Policymakers (and scholars) often look for "evidence" to support their predetermined policy preferences, and academics (and policymakers) search for and interpret historical evidence to confirm their preferred policy solutions to major crises. Far too much political and intellectual capital has been invested in strengthening these preferences to be able to facilitate a simple transfer between validated international relations theory and sound foreign policy.

Increasingly entrenched political divisions across the US make it very difficult for policy officials to embrace research that happens to conflict with accepted practices and policy positions, regardless of whether the research and findings are derived from strong case studies and well-developed (user-friendly, effectively communicated) applications of sound methodologies. It is simplistic in the extreme to believe that policymakers constitute some easily definable group of individuals committed to finding the "right" policy answers to complex problems in the interests of the state. Rarely does the literature acknowledge the ideologically motivated divisions that permeate the policy world, or the degenerative debates that continue to consume Washington legislators, decision-makers, media, and think tanks. Politicians do not embrace ideas, theories, or policy advice because the research is sound; they typically embrace the advice that reconfirms the utility of policies that distinguish their approach from the other side's. In the current political climate, Weiss and Kittikhoun advise, "the misuse of scientific knowledge for the pursuit of political agendas is ... one reason to assume the role of detached critic who remains above the policy fray."[2]

Another key deficiency with the literature on the theory-policy gap is the inherent bias in its diagnosis and recommended solutions. The gap is typically framed in terms of what scholars need to do to make it easier for decision-makers to see the value-added policy relevance of their

---

2 Weiss and Kittikhoun 2011, 1.

research.[3] Scholars are then asked to consider one or more of the following solutions: (1) ignore general theory in favor of addressing mid-range theories/problems/puzzles/strategies that have a clearer link to the things policymakers are concerned about and can manipulate; (2) clearly communicate the policy relevance of "theoretical" contributions; (3) accommodate the attention span and timeline of a typical policymaker by presenting policy-relevant findings through user-friendly briefing notes (rather than 30-page publications); (4) encourage junior scholars and graduate students to serve in government departments; (5) reshape priorities for tenure and promotion decisions to acknowledge policy work and related publications, and so on. The advice focuses on what academics need to do, but ignores the overarching problem of *confirmation bias* in the academic community.

Scholars who lament the growing gap between the academic and policy communities repeatedly ask the same question – what role can academic theories play in communicating practical, policy-relevant advice, particularly during military-security crises? Unfortunately, the Syria case illustrates the influence of confirmation biases as a major impediment to applying social science research in ways that inform rather than detract from healthy deliberations over US foreign policies. These biases raise several legitimate questions about whether academics can remain sufficiently objective in theory selection and policy advice to maximize the probability of communicating and subsequently implementing the best foreign policies. Cherry-picking only a small selection of scholarship to endorse a less effective strategy in Syria is not likely to narrow the gap between the theory and policy communities in international relations.

Solutions to the theory-policy gap, in other words, tend to depict the scholarly community as a definable group of detached analysts engaged in theory building, social scientific progress, and the cumulation of knowledge. All that is required is for this unbiased group of scholars to clearly communicate to decision-makers the prescriptive value of their scholarship in order to facilitate the implementation of sound foreign (or domestic) policies in the interests of the state. Yet scholars have their own political, ideological, and theoretical biases/agendas, and are rarely receptive to social scientific evidence that challenges their preferred theories. It's important to note that the International Studies

---

3 Jentleson and Ratner 2011; Jentleson 2002; Walt 2005; Tickner and Tsygankov 2008; Nye 2009. See also Nye 2008; Gallucci 2012; Kristof 2014.

Association is expanding not because the field is getting better at selective cumulation (i.e., consensus on the best theories and methods to inform policy), but because of the proliferation of disagreements over competing theoretical and methodological perspectives. Which "valid" theories, based on what objective research, are we supposed to be communicating to policy officials? Both Stephen Walt (a self-described realist) and Joseph Nye (a liberal internationalist) are convinced we can do a better job at communicating our theories to facilitate sound policy, but their theories about international relations are very different, and the policy advice they offer in any crisis will naturally flow from the particular perspectives they embrace.

This explains why established scholars, applying preferred theories, often arrive at competing recommendations on many (if not most) US foreign and domestic policies.[4] Walt,[5] for example, provocatively claimed that had "realists" been in charge of US foreign policy since the end of the Cold War, a whole series of American misadventures would have been avoided (including in the Balkans, Iraq, and Libya) and more appropriate strategies would have prevailed (a greater focus on China, "normal" relations with Israel, etc.). As Adam Elkus correctly points out, however, "international relations realism is such a diverse tradition that putting 'realists' exclusively in charge of US foreign policy would likely produce a cacophony rather than the harmonious symphony [Walt] suggests."[6] The differing implications of, say, offensive versus defensive realism is but one example of the competing policy options that might be gleaned from the realist tradition alone. As "inputs" in the policymaking process,[7] the diversity of IR theories and explanations offers decision-makers a considerable range of potential options, the selection of which is likely to have as much to do with pre-existing preferences and worldviews as it does academic rigor and analytical depth.[8]

---

4 Walt 2012a.
5 Walt 2012b.
6 Elkus 2012.
7 For a discussion of IR theory as an "input" in the policymaking process, and for a seminal treatment of the theory-policy gap more generally, see George 1993.
8 One of the major findings of Keren Yarhi-Milo's (2014) work on decision-makers' perceptions of adversaries was the outsized influence of pre-existing beliefs, biases, and worldviews on assessments of intentions; contradictory information was discounted while supporting information was privileged. Only when confronted with information that made it more cognitively difficult to maintain rather than alter existing perceptions did decision-makers abandon their pre-existing beliefs.

Of course, invoking scholarship in the context of policy debates is one thing; actually implementing those policies is quite another. As Elkus adroitly observes, "[foreign] policymaking is distinguished by domestic political considerations, international policy linkages, and bureaucratic foodfights"; the confluence of all of these factors – and others – creates pressures and problems for policymakers such that a remarkable continuity emerges in US foreign policy, whatever the particular inclinations or avowed "grand strategies" or "doctrines" of the administration of the moment. Walter Russell Mead's critique of Walt echoes Elkus in this regard: "Foreign policy is not driven by ideologues steeped in international theory, but by planners operating within a system of political and institutional constraints."[9] While Mead's ultimate conclusion – that "arcane theory" is essentially irrelevant – overstates the criticism, his core point remains valid: Walt's description of a hypothetical and successful "realist" US foreign policy course over the past two decades drastically oversimplifies the realities of international politics and the attendant policymaking process. The notion that successive administrations could have simply selected "realist" policy options for better international outcomes is precisely the kind of argument that makes policymakers turn a deaf ear to the scholarly community.

8.2 Theory-Policy Gaps and Confirmation Bias: The Case of Post-Iraq Intelligence Reform[10]

Valid causal explanations are essential for evaluating major foreign policy failures and, subsequently, understanding and implementing effective policies moving forward (the ostensible purpose of the many "lessons learned" reports that inevitably emerge following international crises or events). Stephen Walt agrees: a good theory "should be logically consistent and empirically valid, because a logical explanation that is consistent with the available evidence is more likely to provide an accurate guide to the causal connections that shape events."[11] A strong theory also "guides our understanding of the past, and historical interpretations often influence what policy makers do later."[12] Weak

---

9 Mead 2012.
10 Portions of this section are derived from Harvey 2015.
11 Walt 2005, 26–7.
12 Ibid., 30.

theories, on the other hand, can lead to potentially dangerous diagnoses that risk compounding policy errors. As Jentleson and Ratner argue, "It is bad enough for a policy to fail, but if the wrong lessons are drawn that failure can have an additive or even multiplicative effect. Theory deepens understanding of patterns of causality within any particular case by penetrating beyond the situational and particularistic to get at factors with broader applicability be they to be avoided or replicated."[13]

For example, weak explanations of the Iraq War that blame neoconservative ideologues (or a powerful Israeli lobby, for that matter) inevitably lead to premature closure of scientific inquiry. These widely popular accounts are unlikely to acknowledge any value in exploring the scope and nature of intelligence errors prior to the war, or embrace comprehensive intelligence reforms, because, according to these scholars, faulty intelligence had nothing to do with the events that led to war – the WMD threat was essentially fabricated by neocons.

Paul Pillar, a former Bush administration national intelligence officer for the Near East and South Asia, offers the clearest version of the policy advice embedded in this standard account of the war: "WMD was not the principal driver of the Bush administration's decision to invade Iraq," Pillar argues, "and the famously flawed intelligence analysis on the subject had no or almost no influence on the decision."[14] The real problem, according to Pillar, was the politicization of the generally sound WMD intelligence that neoconservatives reframed and exploited. Pillar's explanation leads to a pretty straightforward solution – get rid of the neoconservatives and establish an autonomous (independent) entity that can effectively depoliticize intelligence and serve as a check on government abuse. The new Director of National Intelligence (DNI), established through the 2004 Intelligence Reform and Terrorism Prevention Act of 2004, had the potential to serve this function but, as Pillar argues, the DNI was essentially stripped of the kind of authority and autonomy the position needed to fix the problems.

Of course, if Pillar's diagnosis of the causes of the Iraq War is wrong, then his policy advice is unlikely to solve (and would actually exacerbate) the central problem confronting the American intelligence community. As Mark Lowenthal, a former assistant director of central intelligence for analysis and production, and vice chairman of the National

---

13 Jentleson and Ratner 2011, 8–9. See also Jentleson 2002.
14 Pillar 2011, 15.

Intelligence Council from 2002 to 2005, explains, "Policy makers want and expect close-in intelligence support and intelligence officers want access. This is the dependency that Pillar wants to erase."[15] In rejecting Pillar's solution to a non-existent problem, Brent Durbin reinforces Lowenthal's position: "Analysts need to be both close enough to policymakers to understand their needs, and distant enough to maintain independence. Balancing these competing goals is hard even when the politics are not stacked against the effective use of intelligence."[16] Carl W. Ford is equally skeptical of Pillar's policy advice: "The effectiveness of the [intelligence community] has nothing to do with being 'close' or 'distant,' it is the quality of intelligence that counts. I find the intelligence officers who debate the 'close versus distant' issue often have little idea what policy-makers do, or the type of intelligence they would find most useful."[17]

Ford goes on to summarize the scope of the intelligence failure in Iraq: "No one had much hard evidence; but everyone had strong opinions. In-depth research backing up analysis was missing. Accordingly, policy-makers were free to choose answers, picking those they liked, and ignoring those that conflicted with their cognitive worldview."[18] In other words, the generally accepted (non-exaggerated) intelligence estimates on Iraq's WMD, compiled over decades of UN weapons inspections and documented in numerous US, UK, and UN reports, were flawed, not fabricated, and were more than sufficient to justify a series of rational, coercive moves by the US and UK to compel the Iraqi regime to allow inspectors back into Iraq with a stronger mandate. These reasonable, widely supported decisions set the country on the path to war.

If the problem is not politicization but fundamentally flawed intelligence, then what specific deficiencies would Washington resolve by adopting Pillar's vision of an autonomous DNI or independent congressional intelligence office? Consider the significant financial and opportunity costs incurred by the government if Pillar's explanation and reforms are embraced.[19] The main problem with Pillar's account of

---

15 Lowenthal 2012.
16 Durbin 2012.
17 Ford 2012.
18 Ibid.
19 Also consider the unintended consequences of well-meaning intelligence reforms to address post-9/11 criticisms of stovepiping. The reforms certainly facilitated widespread intelligence sharing across agencies, but they also set the stage for

the Iraq War is its simplicity – his story misses a significant part of the relevant history, much of which *disconfirms* his theory.[20] Pillar's account overlooks important details surrounding key decisions at crucial stages of the crisis, ignores the sequence (and impact) of each of these strategic choices along the path to war, and misunderstands the relationship between the plausibility of widely endorsed intelligence estimates and the rational (generally supported) options selected at each point.

If the causes of this war were considerably more complex than Pillar's account, improving the *quality* of intelligence *is* the key to addressing the crisis. Harvey's case evidence[21] confirms that the intelligence failures were a function of (among other things): (1) the cyclical nature of intelligence failures in a post-9/11 security environment; (2) the absence of Human Intelligence (HUMINT) in Iraq following the departure of inspectors in 1998; (3) the intelligence community's organizational routines and procedures; (4) groupthink, cognitive closure, misperceptions, and the confirmation biases they reinforced; (5) the comparative plausibility of different interpretations of Saddam's actions in relation to the WMD threat; (6) miscalculations on the part of the Iraqi regime (which amplified mutually reinforcing misperceptions); (7) the escalatory logic of coercive diplomacy; and (8) alliance politics. These multiple causal factors (and other enabling conditions) contributed to the sequence of events that set the country on a path to war. If officials in Washington are serious about preventing similar US foreign policy failures in the future, these are the policy-relevant lessons they should embrace and use as a guide for meaningful intelligence reform.

8.3 Theory-Policy Gaps and Confirmation Bias: The Case of Coercive Diplomacy in Syria, 2013

As we document in chapters 1 and 2, the policy advice on Syria derived from P-M-H case studies was not put forward as potentially valuable information the administration might want to consider

---

volumes of classified intelligence and information being leaked by Chelsea (Bradley) Manning and Edward Snowden. Evidently, these are tensions to be managed by the intelligence community rather than problems to be resolved by some rewiring of the organizational wire diagram. The authors would like to thank Andrew Bennett and Colin Elman for this example.

20 See Harvey 2011.

21 Ibid.

when weighing different options to manage a tough foreign policy crisis; the evidence was selected and presented as definitive proof, based on "extensive" research on reputations, that the administration's approach to coercive diplomacy in Syria was seriously flawed, that the strategy was destined to fail, and that retreating would carry no consequences with respect to US interests, credibility, or reputations in this or other cases. However, what Daryl Press actually argues in his book is that a state's reputation is not the *only* factor that matters – the same point rational deterrence theorists have been arguing and illustrating in their scholarship for years. What Press concludes from his findings, however, and what he and others recommended to policymakers during the Syria crisis, is that reputations *do not* matter – as we have shown, this conclusion is inconsistent with the evidence from contemporary US coercive encounters. A more thorough review of the extant scholarship on credibility and reputations would have confirmed that the findings critics repeatedly cited were not definitive enough to warrant their uncritical application to the Syria crisis.

Obviously, decision-makers would be well advised to heed Press's warning: "US enemies may assert that the United States lacks credibility because it backed down in some crisis. But foreign policy analysts should not take these statements at face value."[22] This is true; the uncertainty of international politics demands that no statement (particularly from an enemy) be taken at face value, but it is equally dangerous to embrace forever the conclusion that adversaries *never* assign a reputation to US leaders for being irresolute, or that backing down in past crises imposes no transferable costs to US credibility, or that fighting for credibility is *always* irrational.

Richard Price on Syria

Richard Price's widely circulated commentary in *Foreign Affairs* provides another excellent illustration of an effort to establish theory-policy linkages that led to highly questionable advice on how to strengthen international norms prohibiting the use of chemical weapons.[23] Price presents what he regards as a compelling case against the president's

---

22 Press 2005, 157.
23 Price 2013.

unilateral coercive strategy and in favor of a multilateral approach through the UN. As he explains,

> A failure to attack Syria need not signal a decisive blow to the norm against chemical weapons use, particularly if *moral entrepreneurs* committed to its enforcement *doggedly pursue diplomatic efforts* to ensure that those responsible pay a price ... Absent a perfect storm of moral opportunity, *a long-term commitment* to pressing for Syrian ascension to the Chemical Weapons Convention might best accommodate competing legal and moral imperatives. (emphasis added)

Yet Price is decidedly unclear about what this "dogged pursuit of diplomacy" would look like in practice in light of all available facts surrounding this case. What evidence can Price highlight to provide a plausible argument that these efforts would have worked given the competing political agendas at play? And what measure of success/failure should we use to test the norm-building utility of Price's recommendation favoring a "long-term" commitment to protect Syrian citizens against chemical weapons? Aside from the Obama administration, where exactly are the moral entrepreneurs in this case? Not only were we missing a "perfect storm of moral opportunity" in 2013, there was a conspicuous absence of *any* moral entrepreneurs in this case, because there was (1) no appetite to address the repeated use of chemical weapons (despite over 140,000 casualties in Syria and 1400 deaths from the latest chemical attack); (2) no UK support (parliament voted against joining the US threats/actions); (3) no congressional support or authorization to use force; (4) no public support, given a decade of war in Afghanistan and Iraq; and (5) absolutely no Russian or UNSC consensus on threatening "serious consequences" to protect the ban against chemical weapons.

US coercive diplomacy, which Price dismissed as antithetical to the international norm he was trying to defend, was the very strategy that ultimately served to protect and strengthen the CW norm. It is not clear how Price's policy recommendation would have been better suited to accomplish the same unanimously endorsed UNSC disarmament resolution: "If the UN team's findings point to Assad's culpability, the Security Council should issue a resolution condemning the Syrian use of chemical weapons and strongly encouraging Syria to join the Chemical Weapons Convention. Assad would almost surely refuse, but any opposition group that succeeded him could be persuaded with continued diplomatic carrots and sticks."

Obama decided not to wait for regime change or succession – it was the credible and largely unilateral threat of force that deterred further use of chemical weapons and led to a multilaterally endorsed resolution compelling the Assad regime to dismantle its stockpile of chemical weapons and production facilities. This is arguably the ideal outcome with respect to protecting and strengthening the norm against the use of chemical weapons and "encouraging Syria to join the Chemical Weapons Convention." By stark contrast, Price's strategy (i.e., a long-term commitment to UN diplomacy in the absence of the threat of force) would almost certainly have led to a "decisive blow" to the same chemical weapons norm, increased the probability of future use in Syria, and intensified motivations in other states to proliferate and/or acquire chemical weapons. As Obama stated at the time: "I'm comfortable going forward without the approval of a United Nations Security Council that, so far, has been completely paralysed and unwilling to hold [Syrian president Bashar] Assad accountable."[24]

The president strengthened the "norm-based" credentials of his decision by connecting US policy to the Geneva Protocol, the Chemical Weapons Convention, norms against the indiscriminate killing of civilians, and the associated responsibility to protect civilians against massive atrocities and war crimes.[25] In light of Obama's strategy and its disarmament outcome, the following analysis offered by Price is both puzzling and, as it has turned out, mistaken:

> Whether credibility matters forms the crux of the current debate about US involvement in Syria – *an issue that's almost beside the point if the official US goal is to uphold the international taboo on chemical weapons use.* What's really at stake is whether there is legal precedent for such an attack (no); whether attacking could do more harm than good, including to international law (it might); and whether that taboo would weaken if the United States doesn't attack Syria (perhaps not).[26]

But we now know that credibility was not beside the point – it was essential to upholding the international taboo and to arriving

---

24 Economist 2013.
25 Carpenter 2013.
26 Price 2013, emphasis added.

244 Fighting for Credibility

at an outcome Price and many others never really expected, because they could not imagine the probability that unilateral coercive diplomacy just might work. Instead, Price recommended a multilateral solution:

> Enforcement decisions are made by the UN Security Council, which must determine whether Syria's infraction constitutes a threat to international peace and security. If it does, the Security Council must also specify the appropriate response. Possible measures include rhetorical condemnation; calls for Syria to join the Chemical Weapons Convention (a stricter agreement banning even the possession of chemical weapons); and sanctions, ranging from an arms embargo to economic and diplomatic restrictions.

The fact that Russia's support is required for any UNSC condemnation or enforcement resolution, or that Russian officials consistently and repeatedly denied that the Assad regime was responsible for the attacks (despite overwhelming US and UN evidence to the contrary) was conveniently overlooked by Price. It is still unclear to us how relying on Russian priorities and preferences enhances the international norm or the quality/legitimacy of the multilateral alternative in this case. In the end, Price was right: "The United States (and any nations that join it) *should not have to* take responsibility for international norms; that is a burden that should *ideally* be borne by *all* members of the UN Security Council" (emphasis added). But Responsibility to Protect dictates that, occasionally, states have an obligation to act outside the UN to protect an international norm; this was one of those cases.

Jonathan Mercer on Syria

With the preceding arguments in mind, we thought it would also be useful to dissect the policy recommendation on Syria put forward by Jonathan Mercer in his widely cited *Foreign Affairs* article.[27] In light of repeated references to his work on reputations, assessing the problems with, and errors in, his policy analysis helps to reinforce our observations about theory-policy gaps in international relations.

---

27 Mercer 2013.

When addressing the logic underpinning two putatively rational actors engaged in this crisis, Mercer notes:

> If Assad is a master strategist and game theory devotee, he might engage in three rounds of reasoning. In this case, Assad would believe that Obama is actually more likely to bluff because Obama thinks that Assad thinks that Obama is less likely to bluff. Keeping the logic straight is difficult, but it is also irrelevant: no one knows how many rounds the game will go on, for there is no logical place to stop. *Those who argue that reputation and credibility matter are depending on strategists to be simple-minded, illogical, and blissfully unaware of recursion.* (emphasis added)

That is most definitely *not* the image of adversaries that emerges from the application of rational deterrence theory and research, nor does it come close to encapsulating our analysis of strategic interactions in the Syria crisis or our assessment of Assad's and Putin's decision-making calculus.[28] We argue that reputations and past actions matter because, contrary to assumptions held by proponents of P-M-H, adversaries have imperfect information about US interests, commitments, and willingness to use power (resolve). Our position is that it is wrong to completely dismiss reputations, particularly in light of limitations with respect to generalizability (to Syria) from P-M-H case studies, and equally mistaken to assume that reputations are everything or that transferability and interdependence of credibility across cases are perfect. Ours is a call for balance and a more reasonable interpretation of how and why reputations and past actions matter. There is nothing about RDT that assumes adversaries are simple-minded, illogical, or blissfully unaware of recursion – in fact, we argue the exact opposite. An adversary's assessment of US commitments, resolve, and credibility often relies on past actions in similar cases for perfectly understandable reasons that can be easily picked up by a logical sequence embedded in a well-defined game-theoretic model of rational deterrence in protracted asymmetric crises. Mercer is absolutely correct when he points out that Syrian officials "might think that Obama has no credibility, that he is, in fact, resolute, or that he is driven by other US interests. Whatever conclusion they come to

---

28 The fact that Mercer spends no time considering the effects of Putin's involvement, or the role his interests played in pushing Assad to comply, is a serious deficiency in Mercer's take on the crisis.

will be driven by their own beliefs and interests." But those perceptions are more or less likely to vary in ways predicted by RDT depending on the information the US provides in response to Syria's probes, as these probes are among the only options Syrian officials have, when faced with imperfect information about US interests, to acquire relevant evidence about US commitments and resolve *in this case* (specific reputation). Another potential source, moreover, is information they pick up from US behavior *in similar cases* in the past (general reputation).

Mercer is also correct to point out that "wars should be fought to protect interests and values, not to defend imaginary reputations from simpletons and illogical foes." What he fails to recognize is that wars should also be "threatened" to strengthen deterrence and to protect interests and values by reinforcing real commitments (and reputations) in the eyes of rational and very logical foes.

With all of this in mind, consider Mercer's argument for dismissing the need to reinforce the coercive threat while recommending a new focus on reinforcing the norm against chemical weapons (an argument reminiscent of the position – and faulty logic – adopted by Richard Price):[29] "Instead of worrying about US credibility or the president's reputation, the administration should focus on what can be done to reinforce the longstanding norm against the use of weapons of mass destruction."

Both Mercer and Price share the same mistaken analysis of the problem and solution, a failure to see the link between protecting this particular norm and credibly threatening to fight for the cause. In this case, the best approach to reinforcing a long-standing norm against the use of WMD is to "get rid of the WMD" by issuing a credible threat, *not* by backing off or declaring a bluff. Ironically, the notion that Assad and Putin would somehow capitulate to diplomatic pressure buttressed by some non-existent multilateral consensus in the UN would necessarily assume that US adversaries are, in Mercer's words, *simple-minded* and *illogical* – why else would they suffer the humiliation and loss of security by capitulating to a disarmament agreement in the absence of a retaliatory (costly) threat?

Stephen Walt on Syria

Stephen Walt, another staunch critic of Obama's Syria policy and a proponent of the P-M-H consensus, also recommended backing away

---

29 Mercer 2013.

from the red-line threat, dismissed the notion that fighting for credibility ever makes sense, and overlooked the possibility that effective coercive diplomacy stood the best chance of achieving an outcome he admitted would be in the US's national interest. As a starting point for our assessment of Walt's analysis and policy recommendations in Syria, consider his article from 2000, in which he praises what he considers to be one of the four most significant foreign policy achievements of the Clinton administration: the ratification of the Chemical Weapons Convention prohibiting the development, production, acquisition, stockpiling, transfer, and use of chemical weapons.[30] As he explained then,

> The treaty was signed in the closing days of the Bush administration, and Clinton submitted it for Senate ratification in November 1993. He finally prevailed in April 1997, after a sustained effort to overcome conservative opposition. Russia followed suit soon after, thereby taking on the obligation to destroy the world's largest chemical weapons arsenal by 2007. Given America's conventional military superiority, *eliminating chemical weapons is very much in the US national interest, so the administration deserves credit for this achievement*. (emphasis added)

For someone who has spent a good deal of time making the argument that the US has no interest in the Syria crisis,[31] the outcome in Syria (Assad's accession to the CWC and the dismantling of his chemical weapons arsenal) must have come as quite a pleasant and welcomed surprise. In any case, Walt goes on in his 2000 analysis to offer a strongly "structural realist" overview of the Clinton record:

> Clinton's critics fail to appreciate how changes in the international position of the United States have complicated the making of its foreign policy. The next president will face similar pressures and is likely to adopt similar policies – but is unlikely to achieve significantly better results. Clinton's handling of foreign policy also tells us a great deal about what to expect in the future, regardless of what happens in [the] November [election].

---

30 Walt 2000.
31 The case for isolationism was raised by Jerome Slater in a guest post on Walt's blog. See Slater 2013.

Walt then goes on to outline four goals that dominated the Clinton administration's foreign policy:

First, the administration has sought to dampen security competition and reduce the risk of major war in Europe, East Asia, and the Middle East, largely by remaining militarily engaged in each of these regions. Second, the administration has worked to reduce the threat of weapons of mass destruction (WMD). Third, it has tried to foster a more open and productive world economy, which it correctly sees as an important component of US economic prosperity. Fourth, the administration has tried to build a world order compatible with basic American values by encouraging the growth of democracy and by using military force against major human rights abuses.

As he pointed out then, "these goals are hardly controversial. Indeed, they are virtually identical to the foreign policy priorities of Republican frontrunner George W. Bush." We agree with Walt's overall assessment of the factors that compel US leaders to pursue essentially similar foreign policies, for many of the same structural and domestic political reasons. Yet he seems to have dismissed the importance of these very same imperatives in his comments on Obama's Syria policy – relying instead on the P-M-H conclusion that reputations are irrelevant, fighting for credibility is foolish, and backing away from the red-line threat in favor of "a healthy dose of isolationism" is prudent.[32] Apparently, both his appreciation for the role of structural variables and his distinguished intellectual legacy endorsing a strong commitment to system-based explanations of US foreign policy seem to be reserved for interventions (Kosovo) and administrations he supported. In contrast, his comments on interventions he opposed (Iraq, Libya, Syria) seem to privilege first-image explanations/accounts and a puzzling rejection of structural pressures:[33]

Foreign-policy thinking in Washington is dominated either by neoconservatives (who openly proclaim the need to export "liberty" and never met a war they didn't like) or by "liberal interventionists" who are just as enthusiastic about using military power to solve problems, provided they can engineer some sort of multilateral cover for it. Liberal interventionists sometimes concede that the United States can't solve every problem (at

---

32 Ibid. See also Walt 2013d and 2011a.
33 Walt 2011a.

least not at the same time), but they still think that the United States is the "indispensable" nation and they want us to solve as many of the world's problems as we possibly can.

Walt shared similar sentiments in another post on Libya:[34]

> It's not that the leaders who start these wars can't come up with reasons for what they are doing. Human beings are boundlessly creative, and a powerful state can always devise a rationale for using force. And proponents may even believe it. But the dictionary defines whim as a "sudden or capricious idea, a fancy." A "war of whim" is just that: a war that great powers enter without careful preparation or forethought, without a public debate on its merits or justification, and without thinking through the consequences if one's initial assumptions and hopes are not borne out. Wars of whim aren't likely to bankrupt a nation by themselves or even lead to major strategic reversals. But they are yet another distraction, at a time when world leaders ought to [be] focusing laser-like on a very small number of Very Big Issues (like the economy).

Now consider Walt's critique of the Obama administration's application of coercive diplomacy in Syria. His policy advice is consistently based on a pretty straightforward premise: unless the US is faced with a strategic necessity tied to a clear threat to core national security interests (e.g., a direct threat to American territory, citizens, or key allies), the United States and its allies should resist the temptation to intervene militarily. The "neoconservative," "liberal internationalist," "liberal hawkish," or "liberal imperialist" penchant to intervene in foreign conflicts for humanitarian reasons rarely serves America's long-term strategic interests or core values, Walt repeatedly counsels.[35] But the tendency to attach simplistic labels to complex foreign policy challenges does very little to connect balanced presentations of international relations scholarship to policy-relevant discourse. Moreover, Walt's critique of Obama's Syria policy is particularly puzzling in light of his enthusiastic endorsement of the same policies in 1995 and 1999, when the Clinton administration applied virtually identical deterrent strategies to deal with Slobodan Milošević.[36] As he argued then, US and NATO credibility and reputations were on the line.

---

34 Walt 2011b.
35 Walt 2012a and 2013a.
36 Walt 2000.

Oversimplifications and contradictions aside, the basic assumption underpinning Walt's "realist" policy recommendations is that US presidents have clear choices in these crises: Barack Obama can simply select a foreign policy strategy (Walt's realism) from among several competing alternatives to satisfy a clearly defined set of straightforward objectives. But as a realist, Walt should understand that American foreign and security policies are not determined by a president's political ideology, personal beliefs, or predispositions toward realist, neoconservative, or liberal imperialist predilections. In fact, as Walt himself concludes in other writing, Washington's foreign policies have been pretty patterned and consistent across several very different administrations and leaders, the product of domestic and international pressures over which presidents have very little control.

Candidate Barack Obama, for example, criticized the excesses of the Bush administration's neoconservative foreign policy and homeland security agenda. As president, however, Obama has increased the homeland security budget, significantly expanded the use of drones in the war on terror, and remains committed to prosecuting detainees in Guantanamo Bay through the same military commissions established by Bush, despite crystal-clear promises during the 2008 campaign to close the base immediately upon assuming office.[37] President Obama also has strengthened the Bush administration's National Security Agency surveillance programs, and was instrumental in pushing for a coalition to topple Muammar Gaddafi's regime in Libya. In August–September 2013, when he was poised to launch a unilateral air campaign against the Syrian regime in the absence of a UN Security Council resolution, the president was criticized for being a post-9/11 liberal hawk. Perhaps the clearest illustration of the continuity of US foreign policy can be found in Obama's address at West Point, in which he defends, among other very common foreign policy priorities that reappear in the National Security Strategies of previous administrations, a clear commitment to "unilateralism."

---

37 It is important to note that President Obama reiterated the promise (to close Guantanamo) toward the end of his 2013 State of the Union address – if anything, the fact that he still has a strong preference for shutting it down, but has been unable to do so for six years, reinforces the argument that many other domestic political pressures dictate policy on this matter.

Establishing Continuity in US Foreign Policy

EXCERPTS FROM PRESIDENT OBAMA'S COMMENCEMENT AD-
DRESS AT WEST POINT, 28 MAY 2014 (HTTP://WWW.NYTIMES.
COM/2014/05/29/US/POLITICS/TRANSCRIPT-OF-PRESIDENT-
OBAMAS-COMMENCEMENT-ADDRESS-AT-WEST-POINT.HTML)

(*American exceptionalism: power*) – In fact, by most measures, America has rarely been stronger relative to the rest of the world. Those who argue otherwise – who suggest that America is in decline or has seen its global leadership slip away – are either misreading history or engaged in partisan politics. Think about it. Our military has no peer. The odds of a direct threat against us by any nation are low, and do not come close to the dangers we faced during the Cold War.

(*American exceptionalism: ideas*) – Meanwhile, our economy remains the most dynamic on Earth, our businesses the most innovative. Each year, we grow more energy independent. From Europe to Asia, we are the hub of alliances unrivaled in the history of nations. America continues to attract striving immigrants. The values of our founding inspire leaders in parliaments and new movements in public squares around the globe. And when a typhoon hits the Philippines, or schoolgirls are kidnapped in Nigeria, or masked men occupy a building in Ukraine, it is America that the world looks to for help. So the United States is and remains the one indispensable nation. That has been true for the century past and it will be true for the century to come.

(*Credibility*) – And I would betray my duty to you, and to the country we love, if I sent you into harm's way simply because I saw a problem somewhere in the world that needed to be fixed, or because I was worried about critics who think military intervention is the only way for America to avoid looking weak.

(*Unilateralism*) – First, let me repeat a principle I put forward at the outset of my presidency: The United States will use military force, unilaterally if necessary, when our core interests demand it: when our people are threatened; when our livelihoods are at stake; when the security of our allies is in danger. In these circumstances, we still need to ask tough questions about whether our actions are proportional and effective and just. International opinion matters, but America should never ask permission to protect our people, our homeland or our way of life.

(*Preference for multilateralism: Syria is the exception*) – On the other hand, when issues of global concern do not pose a direct threat to the United States, when such issues are at stake, when crises arise that stir our conscience or push the world in a more dangerous direction but do not directly threaten us, then the threshold for military action must be higher. In such circumstances, we should not go it alone. Instead, we must mobilize allies and partners to take collective action. We have to broaden our tools to include diplomacy and development, sanctions and isolation, appeals to international law, and, if just, necessary and effective, multilateral military action. In such circumstances, we have to work with others because collective action in these circumstances is more likely to succeed, more likely to be sustained, less likely to lead to costly mistakes.

(*Coercive diplomacy in Syria*) – As frustrating as it is, there are no easy answers [to the Syria crisis], no military solution that can eliminate the terrible suffering anytime soon. As President, I made a decision that we should not put American troops into the middle of this increasingly sectarian civil war, and I believe that is the right decision. But that does not mean we shouldn't help the Syrian people stand up against a dictator who bombs and starves his own people. And in helping those who fight for the right of all Syrians to choose their own future, we are also pushing back against the growing number of extremists who find safe haven in the chaos.

(*Multilateralism with unilateral threat*) – Let me make one final point about our efforts against terrorism. The partnerships I've described do not eliminate the need to take direct action when necessary to protect ourselves. When we have actionable intelligence, that's what we do, through capture operations, like the one that brought a terrorist involved in the plot to bomb our embassies in 1998 to face justice, or drone strikes, like those we've carried out in Yemen and Somalia. There are times when those actions are necessary, and we cannot hesitate to protect our people.

(*Justifying unilateralism*) – But as I said last year, in taking direct action, we must uphold standards that reflect our values. That means taking strikes only when we face a continuing, imminent threat, and only where there is no certainty – there is near certainty of no civilian casualties, for our actions should meet a simple test: We must not create more enemies than we take off the battlefield.

(*American exceptionalism: rhetoric and actions*) – I believe in American exceptionalism with every fiber of my being. But what makes us exceptional is not our ability to flout international norms and the rule of law; it is our willingness to affirm them through our actions. And that's why I will continue to push to close Gitmo, because American values and legal traditions do not permit the indefinite detention of people beyond our borders. That's why we're putting in place new restrictions on how America collects and uses intelligence, because we will have fewer partners and be less effective if a perception takes hold that we're conducting surveillance against ordinary citizens. America does not simply stand for stability or the absence of conflict, no matter what the cost; we stand for the more lasting peace that can only come through opportunity and freedom for people everywhere.

(*Democratization*) – Which brings me to the fourth and final element of American leadership: our willingness to act on behalf of human dignity. America's support for democracy and human rights goes beyond idealism; it is a matter of national security. Democracies are our closest friends and are far less likely to go to war. Economies based on free and open markets perform better and become markets for our goods. Respect for human rights is an antidote to instability and the grievances that fuel violence and terror.

Bill Clinton and Al Gore campaigned on promises to focus "like a laser beam" on the failing domestic economy. Yet, once elected, they felt compelled to engage in air campaigns in Bosnia (1995), Iraq (1998), and Kosovo/Serbia (1999), the latter two without a UN mandate, all to strengthen US and NATO credibility. Clinton and Gore were criticized for embracing post–Cold War liberal internationalism.[38] George W. Bush forcefully campaigned against the Clinton-Gore legacy of nation building in Bosnia and Kosovo and promised to focus, instead, on the country's domestic priorities. After the shock of 9/11, of course, President Bush invaded Afghanistan and Iraq, and proceeded to mount two of the most expansive and costly nation-building projects in American history. Bush was mistakenly criticized for blindly adopting a dangerous "neoconservative" foreign policy doctrine, while being praised by others for practicing "democratic realism."[39] Neither of these labels was historically accurate.[40]

---

38 Walt 2000.
39 Krauthammer 2004.
40 Harvey 2011.

The titles assigned to these actions change but the policies are virtually identical. Doctrines and labels, in other words, are meaningless distractions and, worse, superficial explanations for complicated decisions that presidents are often forced to make regardless of initial plans, ideological predispositions, or recommendations by academics, journalists, or foreign policy bloggers. American foreign policies are often driven by unexpected events, unintended consequences, and the momentum of war or coercive diplomacy – factors that lie beyond the control of any president. The notion that priorities can be carefully scripted and managed by embracing Walt's simplified version of realism, or Krauthammer's "democratic realism," or Barry Posen's "restraint," or any other foreign policy doctrine or grand strategy, is a myth. Perpetuating the myth will do very little to narrow the gap between the theory and policy worlds.

Walt's apparent conversion to non-rational, first-image theories of war might also explain his strong preference for idiosyncratic variables when accounting for the Iraq War, which focused almost exclusively on the easily refutable notion that the war was somehow concocted by a small group of very powerful neoconservatives sponsored by an Israeli lobby.[41]

In any case, had critics persuaded officials in the Obama administration to back off, admit the red line was a bluff, and fold, there would be no deterrent barriers at all preventing Syrian officials from continuing to use chemical weapons (in particular, potent CW agents such as sarin gas) against the country's civilian populations or regional foes in the future. Obviously, the right policy in this case was to mount a more effective coercive threat, and it worked. In light of their theory-policy errors, critics should reconsider the utility of the foreign policy theories they claimed to rely on, or at least revisit the evidence they cited in support of the policies they so confidently recommended. Most foreign policy analysts are not in decision-making positions and can easily afford to be mistaken; there are no direct consequences to pushing the wrong policies based on weak arguments. This is perhaps the most significant impediment to narrowing the credibility gap between the academic and policy worlds, particularly during a foreign policy crisis.

---

41 See Harvey 2011 for a comprehensive treatment of the numerous problems with Walt's and many other "neoconist" theories of the Iraq War that pin the blame on leadership and other weak, first-image theories of the war.

Walt's position, informed by P-M-H, was very clear:[42] "If we refrain from using force when vital interests are not involved or when doing so would only make things worse, it says nothing about our willingness to use force when it is truly necessary and when it can achieve clear and well-defined objectives." Walt is right *if* the US is fighting for interests that are not vital. But credibility and reputations are in the eyes of the beholder – if Syrian or Iranian officials read US statements and actions as constituting a clear indication of strong US interest, and if *they* believe that US officials have issued very costly signals because of the implications of backing away from those threats, then backing away *does* send a potentially dangerous signal to Assad, Putin, and Iranian officials regarding US commitments to other interests they claim are vital. Walt's impressions of US interests (which apparently change from administration to administration) are irrelevant here. What matters is how and why *adversaries* interpret US interests and credibility based on signals they interpret from coercive threats. Walt's statement, therefore, should be rephrased accordingly: if we refrain from using force when our adversaries see that vital US interests are involved, or when doing so could achieve a significant victory for those concerned about the use of chemical weapons, this would say a great deal about our willingness to use force to achieve any such objectives in the future.

8.4   From Policy to Theory: The "MIT School" and Syria

In his review of Barry Posen's book *Restraint: A New Foundation for US Grand Strategy*, William Ruger identifies what he calls the "MIT School" of US grand strategy.[43] Dissatisfied with the prevailing consensus that a post–Cold War "unipolar moment" necessitated an assertive foreign policy in order to maintain US global dominance ("liberal hegemony"), the MIT School has argued instead for a return to traditional (i.e., pre–Second World War) American non-interventionism ("restraint"); America's core strategic interests, they contend, can be secured just as (in fact, more) effectively by a pared-down global military footprint and a general disengagement with foreign allies and assets. As Ruger makes clear, Posen's work is unabashedly normative – he is fighting against a perceived policy consensus that he considers *wrong* (not only in

---

42 Walt 2013c.
43 Ruger 2014.

execution but in the underlying principles and goals toward which it is oriented) and outlining an alternative policy that better serves what he considers to be US long-term national and strategic interests: "Posen ... spends the first half of the book explaining in detail what liberal hegemony is and why it so imperils America. In the book's second, meatier half, he lays out his overarching restraint strategy and describes the specific military approach required to support it."[44]

While Posen's work marks the latest and most comprehensive statement of the principles underlying the MIT School viewpoint, an early contribution was the 1997 article "Come Home, America: The Strategy of Restraint in the Face of Temptation"[45] by MIT professor Harvey Sapolsky and two of his then-graduate students, Eugene Gholz and Daryl Press. Again, the orientation of the article is unmistakably normative: "Here we advocate a foreign policy of restraint – the disengagement of America's military forces from the rest of the world."[46] The article is essentially a series of recommendations as to how US foreign policy *should* be conducted moving forward, given what Sapolsky, Gholz, and Press consider to be "America's core national interests." Consider, for example, the following statements and prescriptions:

> For the first time in five decades, America's core national interests are easily within reach. Small wars will likely continue to be frequent, but those wars cannot spread easily to US shores, and their results will not shift the global power balance. Similarly, military threats to America's prosperity are quite low. In fact, the only way the United States could jeopardize its favorable position is to meddle in other nations' affairs, join their wars, and overspend on defense. (pp. 10–11)
>
> America should withdraw the 100,000 soldiers currently stationed in Europe, demobilize most of them, and bring home the equipment currently strewn around Europe ... This would be a clear signal that America would not return US forces to the continent at the drop of a hat. (18)
>
> As in Europe, the United States currently has about 100,000 military personnel stationed in Asia, all of whom should be brought home and demobilized. The United States should end its commitments to Japan and South Korea, cease military cooperation with the Association of Southeast Asian Nations (ASEAN), withdraw from the Australia, New Zealand,

---

44 Ibid.
45 Gholz, Press, and Sapolsky 1997.
46 Ibid., 5.

United States Pact (ANZUS), and terminate the implicit guarantee to Taiwan, giving those nations new incentives to take care of themselves. (20)

Promoting global peace, like encouraging democracy, is a worthy goal for American foreign policy; unfortunately, a military policy to prevent wars, usually called collective security, would be too costly and too ineffective. A force structure that can back up a threat to oppose any aggression would have to be very large. The United States would need to prepare to fight many enemies at once, all around the world. Advocates of this policy might argue that prospective aggressors will soon abandon any expansive intentions, but no one knows how long this would take, how long it would last, and how many wars the United States would have to fight to establish and maintain its credibility. Committing the United States to oppose all aggression would require a force structure significantly bigger than the current one. (42)

Restraint is a robust policy. China can rise and fall; Russia can create and break alliances; Europe could unite or the EU could disintegrate – and still restraint would be best. Until three unlikely conditions are met – the growth of a regional power capable of quickly overwhelming its adversaries, the possibility that an aggressor could consolidate a large fraction of the world's industrial might, and the discovery of a solution to the nuclear problem – the United States need not re-engage. (48)

Americans will have to be sold on some new, ambitious strategy – to prevent war everywhere, to make everyone democratic, or to keep everyone else down. But if Americans simply want to be free, enjoy peace, and concentrate more on the problems closer to home, the choice is clear: it is time to come home, America. (48)

There is much to recommend in the arguments and analysis put forth by Sapolsky, Gholz, and Press (as well as Posen, for that matter). They offer penetrating insight into important debates that have shaped US foreign policy since the end of the Cold War, and present a cogent, articulate, and rhetorically persuasive alternative to more "mainstream" foreign policy orientations. There are also, of course, important counterarguments and criticisms that can be, and have been, leveled at "restraint" proponents.[47] Our objective is not to parse the particulars of this

---

47 For an excellent recent example, see Brooks, Ikenberry, and Wohlforth 2013; their statement in support of American "deep engagement" is in response to an article by Posen in the same issue of *Foreign Affairs* – see Posen 2013.

debate or discuss the relative merits of either side (other than to broadly suggest, as discussed above, that debates over "grand strategy" are not particularly helpful). Instead, our task is to highlight the implicit connection between, and blurred borders demarcating, normative policy positions and ostensibly "objective" social science research as they relate to work on reputations in international politics and broader statements of US grand strategy.

One initial point must be made unequivocally clear – we are in no way arguing that Daryl Press or any other author cited here is in any way disingenuous in the research and analysis they put forth; there is no conscious manipulation of evidence to support pre-existing policy preferences, or deliberately deceptive use of data for political purposes. All scholars (including the present authors) are, in fact, subject to the same biases and related challenges we outline in this chapter, no matter how vigilant we might be in attempting to maintain objectivity or disinterested-observer status. This is, in the end, precisely the point.

As we have repeatedly stated throughout this book, the evidence put forth by Press in his work *Calculating Credibility* accomplishes, inter alia, two things. First, it confirms what many (indeed most) RDT theorists have been finding and arguing for years – that past actions and reputations are not *solely* determinative of deterrence success and/ or failure. Second, based on findings from four historical cases, Press raises questions as to the *relative* importance of past actions in states' calculations of credibility – his archival work suggests that few (if any) references to adversaries' specific past actions were made by state leaders and decision-makers in these particular crisis deliberations. These are interesting findings, based on impressive archival research, but they are hardly definitive, as Press himself seems to acknowledge when he cautions against generalizing from too few cases. Ultimately, however, the scholarly findings contained in his book do not align with the policy recommendations presented at its end. This inconsistency is perfectly embodied in the brief two-page concluding section of the book, entitled "Implications for Future Research and Foreign Policy." For the former, Press correctly points out that his work "should not be taken as the last word" on the relevance of reputations and past actions, and stresses the need for future research given that "the universe of cases that could be studied is large indeed, and the importance of the subject warrants these efforts."[48] A few paragraphs later, however, Press

---

48 Press 2005, 159.

outlines his implications for the execution of US foreign policy by stating flatly: "Countries should not fight wars for the sake of preserving their credibility."[49]

While Press's findings are certainly *suggestive* of these conclusions, they simply do not warrant the degree of certainty with which they are presented. For Press, however, the results of his empirical research largely confirm and support his pre-existing normative preference (as established in the 1997 "Come Home" article) for foreign policy "restraint" – that is, not "meddl[ing] in other nations' affairs" or "fight[ing] to establish and maintain … credibility" – so it is not surprising that he eschews important reasons why practicing restraint can be dangerous in some cases. Though his archival work stands on its own merit, and the theoretical and logical arguments he uses to engage and explain this evidence are reasonable if flawed, the *force* of his policy recommendations reveals confirmation bias – partial evidence is interpreted as definitive, reputations never matter, and credibility is never worth fighting for.

In his assessment of the Syria crisis, the findings of *Calculating Credibility* make the full transition from partial, suggestive empirical findings in a handful of historical cases to definitive and established proof that reputations and past actions have no bearing on the credibility of a coercive threat. In Syria, Press argued, the case for US intervention or punitive strikes "should not rest on a bogus theory about signaling resolve" and instead reflect only the core national interests of the United States; interests that, he and Jennifer Lind argued, were of course nonexistent in Syria, meaning no intervention was warranted. Again, it is no coincidence that this assessment dovetails perfectly with the policy recommendations contained in the broader MIT School of US foreign policy restraint. One would expect, of course, any policy piece or blog post Press might write to reflect this position – such is his right and prerogative – but his analysis of Syria is positioned less as the normative articulation of a policy preference than as an appeal to the established and definitive social scientific evidence regarding reputations in international politics.

While one can hardly blame Press for foregrounding his own work when writing policy commentary, it is striking that so many others similarly emphasized his findings (along with those of Mercer and, to a

---

49 Ibid., 160.

lesser extent, Hopf) in their own assessments of the Syria crisis. Moreover, the force with which they invoked the findings from *Calculating Credibility* mirror the force with which Press himself (over)emphasized its policy implications. They too point to the objective findings of, as Stephen Biddle put it before Congress, "a generation of scholarship" that supposedly debunked the myth that reputations matter in international politics.

Those invoking Press in this manner fall into two categories. First, they, like Press, may be subject to confirmation bias, insofar as the suggestive evidence of *Calculating Credibility* is selected and privileged because it "confirms" a pre-existing preference for American non-intervention. Second – and particularly if they are journalists, politicians, commentators, and so on who might not be familiar with evidentiary standards in the social sciences – they may take the claims of "established" scholarship at face value, deferring to the arguments and evidence of political scientists who have seemingly "settled" the issue. The first category, of course, amplifies and feeds the second – the more established and well-known IR scholars such as Zakaria and Walt push incomplete evidence as decisive and definitive, the more likely it is that others will pick up and run with a similar narrative.

Benjamin Friedman of the Cato Institute was yet another voice pushing the president to abandon red lines in Syria based on the notion that bluffing and past behavior would have no bearing on future credibility.[50] Friedman's critique was two-pronged, arguing that while the initial red-line threat itself was "foolish," Assad's violation of it was still no reason for US action because unpunished red-line crossings hold no consequences in subsequent encounters (making his argument logically inconsistent – as discussed in chapter 7 – for if there are no consequences to being called in a bluff, there is no basis to call the bluff "foolish" in the first place). Friedman makes a series of arguments against the use of air strikes to punish Assad (which would have also precluded the mounting of the coercive threat that eventually lead to the WMD deal). But don't just take his word for it: "Historical studies show that foreigners do not assess US willingness to intervene based on whether they carried out past threats. They focus, instead, on the local balance of military power and the US interests in their case." This is a clear reference to the Current Calculus (power and interest) thesis

---

50 Friedman 2013b.

of Press, so it is fair to assume that the "historical studies" mentioned are also his. Even ignoring the fact that this is a mischaracterization of Press's studies (insofar as they do not show how foreigners assessed US credibility but vice versa, with the partial exception of the appeasement case), no mention is made of the ample work that challenges their findings (see the review of "missing scholarship" in chapter 1, as well as the case evidence presented in chapter 3). Friedman apparently has rejected these works in favor of the arguments and evidence put forth by P-M-H. This is not surprising, given that a review of his commentaries and blog postings for the Cato Institute reveal a persistent and explicit preference for foreign policy "restraint." It is also not surprising that Friedman graduated from Dartmouth College in 2000 (where Daryl Press taught and currently teaches) and is currently a PhD candidate at MIT, with a supervisory committee that includes Harvey Sapolsky and is chaired by Barry Posen.

The cause of foreign policy "restraint" extends far beyond the campus of MIT, of course. Daniel Larison's numerous postings and commentaries for *The American Conservative* were some of the most vociferous and relentless critiques of the "credibility" imperative during the Syria crisis (see chapter 1). Through the course of these critiques, Larison cited at different moments Press, Mercer, and Hopf to ridicule any mention of credibility in the debate over US policy in Syria.[51] This appeal to social scientific "evidence" helped bolster the (for lack of a better word) credibility of his criticism – while Larison was unabashedly normative in his belief that Syrian intervention was foolhardy, he could justify this position as more than simply his personal opinion by referencing the work of P-M-H. It is not surprising, then, that Larison is also a staunch supporter of a broader US foreign policy of "restraint" as outlined by the MIT School. In June of 2014, *The American Conservative* co-hosted (along with George Washington University) a "successful conference promoting a foreign policy of restraint" at which Larison was a participant and Barry Posen a keynote speaker.[52]

Again, our purpose for foregrounding the policy preferences tied to the so-called MIT School of US grand strategy is not to accuse these prominent scholars and commentators of being disingenuous. Rather, by highlighting the blurred nexus between broad normative orientations

---

51 See Larison 2013b, 2013d, and 2013a.
· 52 Larison 2014; for an overview of the conference, see American Conservative staff 2014.

and specific scholarly analysis, our goal is to illuminate a hitherto un-derappreciated but endemic feature of the so-called theory-policy gap. Far from singling out Press, Posen, and others for censure, we discuss them here as but one example of a broader reality with regard to the relationship between theory and policy in international relations. This discussion is apposite, moreover, given its relevance to the Syria crisis discussed in the preceding chapters.

The invocation of P-M-H in the context of the crisis over CW in Syria was, in many ways, ostensibly about *closing* the theory-policy gap. In this view, the cutting-edge scholarship on reputations (and deterrence more broadly) had superseded policymakers' outmoded understand-ing of how credibility could be established and/or maintained in inter-national politics. As Christopher Fettweis explained:

> The IR scholarship on reputation and credibility in international politics has evolved through a couple of clear stages. In the first, early-deterrence theorists like Thomas Schelling argued that actions are *interdependent* [orig. emphasis], that potential adversaries and allies routinely learn fun-damental lessons about the basic disposition of states based upon their behavior in other arenas. In practice, this meant that remaining engaged in otherwise peripheral, pointless ventures (Vietnam, Korea, etc.) made sense as attempts to send messages about US resolve. Four decades of empirical and theoretical work have brought that wisdom into doubt; *today, the dominant view in the academy (if not yet among practitioners)* [em-phasis added] is that actions tend to be *independent* [orig. emphasis], that other states rarely learn the lessons we hope to teach. *The current consen-sus – one that has been supported in recent years by the work of Jonathan Mercer, Ted Hopf, Daryl Press, and many others – is that, despite what practitioners may believe, reputations do not decisively affect the actions of others* [emphasis added].[53]

According to this view, anyone emphasizing this consensus in the context of, for example, policy debates during the Syria crisis was simply bringing policymakers up to date as to the current state of knowledge within the academy ("if not *yet* among practitioners"). As discussed in greater detail in chapters 1 and 2, commentaries on Syria were peppered with references to the objective, established, and

---

53 Fettweis 2012, 1130.

cumulative knowledge of P-M-H; extant academic research – not personal opinion or normative preferences – drove policy recommendations. As we have shown in this book, however, this assessment does not hold up to careful scrutiny. Strong evidence exists to challenge, if not disconfirm, the P-M-H consensus (particularly regarding its specific application to Syria).

Now, we are certain that some of the most vocal critics of Obama's Syria policy, including Stephen Walt and Fareed Zakaria, understand the evidentiary requirements for strong theory and informed policy, or at least appreciate the importance of qualifying any social scientific finding – yet no such caveats were offered when they made their policy recommendations on Syria. Perhaps one of the reasons they were so quick to uncritically embrace the findings from P-M-H was their a priori preference for non-intervention in this case (and more generally) – this particular body of scholarly research was a way to establish the academic credentials of their recommendations. It was very apparent that Walt and Zakaria were opposed to US intervention in Syria for many sound reasons, and they articulated those reasons in their op-eds, blog posts, and television segments. But to the extent that they defended their conclusions about credibility and reputations by relying for evidence on P-M-H, they should have been more circumspect, in terms of both their theory and policy advice.

It is undoubtedly more complicated for Daryl Press and Jonathan Mercer, who, as mentioned above, invoked their own work in discussing Syria. In so doing, the authors are engaging in precisely the type of knowledge mobilization that many call for in attempts to "bridge the gap" between the academy and the policy community. They produced short, jargon-free, accessible, and to-the-point commentary on a pressing international issue, based on their longer, more sophisticated academic research (in addition to citing each other's work). To readers unfamiliar with the broader scholarly literature (and the debates therein), moreover, these appeals are persuasive in exactly the way such bridge-building exercises are intended to be: on the strength of objective and "established" evidence and research.

Herein lies the danger: scholarship that best exemplifies the kind of bridge-building exercises so many cite as *solutions* to the theory-policy gap (clear, short, jargon-free, and definitive summaries of research findings) can actually exacerbate the problem, as evidenced by the Syria case. Tentative, incomplete evidence is packaged as definitive proof for the purposes of policy prescriptions; again, not as purposeful deception, but rather as a largely unavoidable consequence of drawing user-friendly connections between complex international relations theories and incredibly challenging foreign policy debates. At the very least, scholars should be cognizant of the potential for confirmation bias to influence the particular interpretations they privilege when providing advice to policymakers during a military-security crisis.

References

Abrahms, M. 2013. "The Credibility Paradox: Violence as a Double-Edged Sword in International Politics." *International Studies Quarterly* 57 (4): 660–71.

Abrams, E. 2013. "Syria, Iran, and American Credibility." Council on Foreign Relations (blog), 26 April. http://blogs.cfr.org/abrams/2013/04/26/syria-iran-and-american-credibility/.

Alterman, J. 2003. "Coercive Diplomacy against Iraq, 1990–98." In *The United States and Coercive Diplomacy*, ed. R. Art and P. Cronin, 275–303. Washington: United States Institute of Peace Press.

American Conservative staff. 2014. "Toward a New Foreign Policy Consensus." *The American Conservative*, 11 June. http://www.theamericanconservative.com/toward-a-new-foreign-policy-consensus/.

Andrews, W., A. Blake, D. Cameron, and K. Elliot. 2013. "Where Congress Stands on Syria." *Washington Post*, 13 September. http://www.washingtonpost.com/wp-srv/special/politics/where-lawmakers-stand-on-syria/.

Apple, Jr, R.W. 1993. "US and Allied Planes Hit Iraq, Bombing Missile Sites in South in Reply to Hussein's Defiance." *New York Times*, 14 January. ProQuest Historical Newspapers: A1.

Apple, Jr, R.W. 1994. "NATO Again Plans Possible Air Raids on Serbs in Bosnia." *New York Times*, 12 January. ProQuest Historical Newspapers: A1.

Arena, P. 2013. "How Could US Signals of Weakness Bring Russia and Syria to the Table?" *Duck of Minerva*, 14 September. http://duckofminerva.com/2013/09/how-could-us-signals-of-weakness-bring-russia-and-syria-to-the-table.html.

Baczynska, G., and S. Gutterman. 2013. "Russia Says Talks with US on Syria Rocky, Fears Use of Force." *Reuters*, 24 September. http://www.reuters.com/article/us-syria-crisis-russia-usa-idUSBRE98N09N20130924.

Bandow, D. 2013. "Costs of Entering Syria Conflict Too Great." Cato Institute, 9 September. http://www.cato.org/publications/commentary/costs-entering-syria-conflict-too-great.

BBC. 1998a. "Nato Steps towards Kosovo Action." *BBC*, 24 September. http://news.bbc.co.uk/2/hi/europe/179156.stm.

BBC. 1998b. "UN Condemns Kosovo Atrocities." *BBC*, 2 October. http://news.bbc.co.uk/2/hi/europe/184698.stm.

BBC. 1998c. "UK Prepared to Use Force against Iraq." *BBC*, 2 November. http://news.bbc.co.uk/2/hi/uk_news/politics/205356.stm.

BBC. 1998d. "UN Hears Calls for End to Raids." *BBC*, 17 December. http://news.bbc.co.uk/2/hi/events/crisis_in_the_gulf/latest_news/236594.stm.

BBC. 1998e. "Yeltsin Demands End to Strikes: Statement." *BBC*, 17 December. http://news.bbc.co.uk/2/hi/world/monitoring/237086.stm.

BBC. 1999a. "Three-week Deadline over Kosovo." *BBC*, 30 January. http://news.bbc.co.uk/2/hi/europe/265277.stm.

BBC. 1999b. "Milošević: No Foreign Troops." *BBC*, 17 February. http://news.bbc.co.uk/2/hi/europe/281048.stm.

BBC. 1999c. "Clinton Warns Serbs." *BBC*, 19 February. http://news.bbc.co.uk/2/hi/europe/282801.stm.

Becker, E. 1999. "No 'Stonewalling' on Kosovo Peace, Milosevic Is Told." *New York Times*, 20 February. ProQuest Historical Newspapers: A1.

Beehner, L. 2013. "Do Red Lines on WMD Use Matter?" *Political Violence @ a Glance*, 1 May. https://politicalviolenceataglance.org/2013/05/01/do-red-lines-on-wmd-use-matter/.

Beinart, P. 2014. "The US Doesn't Need to Prove Itself in Ukraine." *Atlantic* (Boston, MA), 5 May. http://www.theatlantic.com/international/archive/2014/05/us-credibility-fallacy-ukraine-russia-syria-china/361695/.

Bengio, O. 1992. *Saddam Speaks on the Gulf Crisis: A Collection of Documents.* Jerusalem: Tel-Aviv University.

Biddle, S. 2013. *Congressional Testimony: Assessing the Case for Striking Syria.* Council for Foreign Relations, 10 September. http://www.cfr.org/syria/assessing-case-striking-syria/p31373.

Binder, D. 1993. "US Renews Warning to Serbs on Sarajevo Shelling." *New York Times*, 19 October. ProQuest Historical Newspapers: A8.

Bolton, J. 2013. "Obama Put America in a Red-Line Box on Syria." *Wall Street Journal*, 28 April. http://online.wsj.com/news/articles/SB10001424127887323528404578450561574249892.

Boot, M. 2013. "America's Rapidly Vanishing Credibility." *Commentary Magazine*, 5 May. https://www.commentarymagazine.com/2013/05/05/americas-rapidly-vanishing-credibility-syria-chemical-weapons/.

Borger, J. 2013. "Barack Obama Warns Iran That US Is Still Prepared to Take
Military Action." *The Guardian*, 15 September. http://www.theguardian
.com/world/2013/sep/15/barack-obama-warns-iran-us-military-action.

Borger, J. 2014. "Syria Hands over Final Chemical Weapons for Destruction."
The Guardian, 23 June. http://www.theguardian.com/world/2014/jun/23/
syria-chemical-weapons-final-destruction-un-deadline.

Braumoeller, B.F. 2003. "Causal Complexity and the Study of Politics." *Political
Analysis* 11 (3): 209–33.

Brookings Institution. 2015. "The Search for International Consensus
on Syria and Beyond." Second Annual Justice Stephen Breyer Lecture
on International Law. Panel, 9 April. http://www.brookings.edu/
events/2015/04/09-breyer-lecture-syria-chemical-weapons.

Brooks, S.G., G.J. Ikenberry, and W.C. Wohlforth. 2013. "Lean Forward: In
Defense of American Engagement." *Foreign Affairs* 92 (1): 130–42.

Brown, D. 2013. "Graham: US Must Address Syria Crisis Now." *The Journal
Scene*, 5 September. http://www.journalscene.com/article/20130905/
SJ01/130909789/1059.

Burg, S.L. 2003. "Coercive Diplomacy in the Balkans: The US Use of Force in
Bosnia and Kosovo." In *The United States and Coercive Diplomacy*, ed. R. Art
and P. Cronin, 57–118. Washington: United States Institute of Peace Press.

Burg, S.L., and P. Shoup. 1999. *The War in Bosnia-Herzegovina: Ethnic Conflict
and International Intervention*. New York: M.E. Sharp.

Burns, J.F. 1993. "Dawn Brings a Ray of Hope to a Newly Silent Sarajevo."
New York Times, 4 August. ProQuest Historical Newspapers: A8.

Bush, G.W. 1991. *Exchange with Reporters on Aid to Iraqi Refugees*. Washington,
DC: US Government Printing Office, 11 April. https://www.gpo.gov/
fdsys/pkg/PPP-1991-book1/html/PPP-1991-book1-doc-pg360.htm.

Byman, D. 2013. "Mr. Obama, Don't Draw That Line." *New York Times*, 4 May.
http://www.nytimes.com/2013/05/05/opinion/sunday/dont-draw-that
-red-line.html?_r=0.

Byman, D., and M. Waxman. 1999. "Defeating US Coercion." *Survival: Global
Politics and Strategy* 41 (2): 107–20.

Byman, D., and M. Waxman. 2000. "Kosovo and the Great Air Power Debate."
International Security 24 (4): 5–38.

Byman, D., and M. Waxman. 2002. *The Dynamics of Coercion: American Foreign
Policy and the Limits of Military Might*. New York: Cambridge University Press.

Carpenter, C. 2013. "Why Is the International Community Protecting the Wrong
Norm in Syria?" *Duck of Minerva*, 27 September. http://duckofminerva
.com/2013/09/why-is-the-international-community-protecting-the-wrong
-norm-in-syria.html.

Carter, C.J. 2013. "Obama: Iran More Than a Year Away from Developing Nuclear Weapon." *CNN.com*, 15 March. http://www.cnn.com/2013/03/14/world/meast/israel-obama-iran/.

Carter, R. 1996. "Bridging the Gap II: Evaluating Deterrence." *Mershon International Studies Review* 40 (1): 131–3.

CBS News staff. 1998. "NATO War Planes Take Off." *CBS News*, 14 June. http://www.cbsnews.com/news/nato-war-planes-take-off/.

Chapman, S. 2013. "War in Syria: The Endless Quest for Credibility." *Reason. com*, 5 September. http://reason.com/archives/2013/09/05/war-in-syria -the-endless-quest-for-credi.

Clines, F.X. 1999. "Missiles Rock Kosovo Capital, Belgrade and Other Sites." *New York Times*, 25 March. ProQuest Historical Newspapers: A1.

Clinton Digital Library. 1994. 1994-05-19B, BTF Memorandum re Military Status Report for Sarajevo, Gorazde, and Tuzla. Clinton Presidential Library and Museum, 19 May. http://clinton.presidentiallibraries.us/items/show/12356.

Clinton Digital Library. 1995a. 1995-09-05B, BTF Report re Milosevic, Karadzic, Serbs More United. Clinton Presidential Library and Museum, 5 September. http://clinton.presidentiallibraries.us/items/show/12530.

Clinton Digital Library. 1995b. 1995-09-06, Memo re Mladić Running True to Form. Clinton Presidential Library and Museum, 6 September. http:// clinton.presidentiallibraries.us/items/show/12531.

Clinton Digital Library. 1998. Declassified Documents concerning Russia. Clinton Presidential Library and Museum. http://clinton.presidentiallibraries.us/items/show/16205.

Clinton Digital Library. 1999a. National Security Council, "Declassified Documents concerning Russia." Clinton Presidential Library and Museum. http://clinton.presidentiallibraries.us/items/show/36619.

Clinton Digital Library. 1999b. National Security Council et al., "Declassified Documents concerning PDD-68, International Public Information Policy." Clinton Presidential Library and Museum. http://clinton.presidentiallibraries .us/items/show/36631.

CNN. 1998. "Transcript: President Clinton Explains Iraq Strike." *CNN.com*, 16 December. http://www.cnn.com/ALLPOLITICS/stories/1998/12/16/ transcripts/clinton.html.

CNN. 1999. "West's Plan for Kosovo Talks Get Frigid Reception." *CNN.com*, 27 January. http://www.cnn.com/WORLD/europe/9901/27/kosovo.01/ index.html.

CNN. 2013. "Transcript: Obama Hosts Pelosi, Boehner over Syria." *CNN.com*, 3 September. http://transcripts.cnn.com/TRANSCRIPTS/1309/03/cnr.01.html.

Cohen, R. 1994. "NATO Gives Serbs a 10-Day Deadline to Withdraw Guns." *New York Times*, 10 February. ProQuest Historical Newspapers: A1.

Cohen, R. 1995a. "NATO May Be Called On to Silence Guns in Sarajevo." *New York Times*, 25 May. ProQuest Historical Newspapers: A14.

Cohen, R. 1995b. "Serbs Call and Raise: The Implications of NATO's Air Strikes Hike the Stakes in Bosnia for All Sides in the Conflict." *New York Times*, 27 May. ProQuest Historical Newspapers: 4.

Cohen, R. 1995c. "Honor, Too, Is Put to Flight in Bosnia." *New York Times*, 16 July. ProQuest Historical Newspapers: E1.

Cohen, R. 1998a. "NATO Nears Final Order to Approve Kosovo Strike." *New York Times*, 11 October. ProQuest Historical Newspapers: 8.

Cohen, R. 1998b. "NATO Opens Way to Start Bombing in Serb Province." *New York Times*, 13 October. ProQuest Historical Newspapers: A1.

Cohen, R. 2013. "Red Lines Matter." *New York Times*, 3 September. http://www.nytimes.com/2013/09/04/opinion/global/cohen-red-lines-matter.html?ref=opinion&_r=2&.

Cohen, S. 2014. Interview with Tom Donilon. Fareed Zakaria GPS transcript. *CNN.com*, 9 March. http://transcripts.cnn.com/TRANSCRIPTS/1403/09/fzgps.01.html.

Committee on Homeland Security. 2013. *Crisis in Syria: Implications for Homeland Security*. Hearing before the Committee on Homeland Security, House of Representatives – 1st Session, 113th Congress, no. 113–32, 10 September. https://www.hsdl.org/?view&did=744225.

Conflict Records Research Center. 1990. *Saddam Hussein and the Revolutionary Command Council Discussing the Iraqi Invasion of Kuwait and the Expected US Attack*. CRRC Record no. SH-SHTP-A-001–042, 29 December. http://crrc.dodlive.mil/files/2013/06/SH-SHTP-A-001-042.pdf.

Conflict Records Research Center. 1991a. *Saddam Hussein and Iraqi Officials Discussing a US-led Attack on Faylakah Island and the Condition of the Iraqi Army*. CRRC Record no. SH-SHTP-A-000–666, 24 February. http://crrc.dodlive.mil/files/2013/01/SH-SHTP-A-000-666_TF.pdf.

Conflict Records Research Center. 1991b. *Saddam Hussein Meeting with Advisors Regarding the American Ground Attack during First Gulf War, Garnering Arab and Iraqi Support, and a Letter to Gorbachev*. CRRC Record no. SH-SHTP-A-000–931, 24 February. http://crrc.dodlive.mil/files/2013/01/SH-SHTP-A-000-931_TF.pdf.

Copeland, D.C. 1997. "Do Reputations Matter? What's in a Name? Debating Jonathan Mercer's Reputation and International Politics." *Security Studies* 7 (1): 33–71.

Cordesman, A. 1994. *Iraq's Military Forces: 1988–1993. CSIS Middle East Dynamic Net Assessment, September*. Washington, DC: Center for Strategic and International Studies. https://csis.org/files/media/csis/pubs/iraq88-93.pdf.

Cordesman, A. 2013a. *President Obama and Syria: The "Waiting for Godot"* *Strategy*. Washington, DC: Center for Strategic and International Studies, 1 September. https://www.csis.org/publication/president-obama-and-syria -waiting-godot-strategy.

Cordesman, A. 2013b. *US Strategy in Syria: Having Lost Sight of the Objective ...* Washington, DC: Center for Strategic and International Studies, 12 September. https://csis.org/publication/us-strategy-syria-having-lost-sight-objective.

Corker, B. 2014. "Obama Is an Unreliable Ally." *Washington Post*, 5 August. https://www.washingtonpost.com/opinions/bob-corker-obama-is-an -unreliable-ally/2014/08/05/83f99670-1c92-11e4-ae54-0cfe1f974f8a_story .html.

Crescenzi, M.J.C. 2007. "Reputation and Interstate Conflict." *American Journal of Political Science* 51 (2): 382–96.

Crosette, B. 1994. "Iraqi Denounces Sanctions." *New York Times*, 8 October. ProQuest Historical Newspapers: 6.

Crosette, B. 1998a. "Iraq Threatens to Stop Work of a UN Inspection Team." *New York Times*, 13 January. ProQuest Historical Newspapers: A4.

Crosette, B. 1998b. "Iraqis Break Off All Cooperation with Inspectors." *New York Times*, 6 August. ProQuest Historical Newspapers: A1.

Crosette, B. 1998c. "Iraq Says It Won't Let UN Resume Spot Arms Checks." *New York Times*, 29 September. ProQuest Historical Newspapers: A11.

Crosette, B. 1998d. "In New Challenge to the UN, Iraq Halts Arms Monitoring." *New York Times*, 1 November. ProQuest Historical Newspapers: A1.

Crosette, B. 1998e. "UN Orders Inspectors and Relief Staff out of Iraq." *New York Times*, 12 November. ProQuest Historical Newspapers: A14.

Crosette, B. 1998f. "Arms Teams to Conduct Spot Checks in Iraq." *New York Times*, 8 December. ProQuest Historical Newspapers: A10.

Daalder, I.H., and M.E. O'Hanlon. 2000. *Winning Ugly: NATO's War to Save Kosovo*. Washington, DC: Brookings Institution Press.

Dafoe, A., J. Renshon, and P. Huth. 2014. "Reputation and Status as Motives for War." *Annual Review of Political Science* 17: 371–93.

Danilovic, V. 2002. *When the Stakes Are High: Deterrence and Conflict among Major Powers*. Ann Arbor: University of Michigan Press.

Davis, J. 2000. *Threats and Promises: The Pursuit of International Influence*. Baltimore: Johns Hopkins University Press.

De Luce, D. 2015. "Hagel: The White House Tried to 'Destroy' Me." *Foreign Policy*, 18 December. http://foreignpolicy.com/2015/12/18/hagel-the -white-house-tried-to-destroy-me/.

Deulfer, C. 2004. *Comprehensive Report of the Special Advisor to the Director of Central Intelligence on Iraq's WMD*. US Central Intelligence Agency,

30 September. https://www.cia.gov/library/reports/general-reports-1/iraq
_wmd_2004/index.html.

Devroy, A., and R.J. Smith. 1993. "Clinton Reexamines a Foreign Policy under
Siege." *Washington Post*, 17 October. https://www.washingtonpost.com/
archive/politics/1993/10/17/clinton-reexamines-a-foreign-policy-under
-siege/794fbbd6-349c-44d4-94b2-65868bd53587/.

Dilanian, K., and D.S. Cloud. 2013. "US Saw Yearlong Rise in Chemical
Weapons Use by Syria." *Los Angeles Times*, 6 September. http://www
.latimes.com/world/middleeast/la-fg-syria-intel-20130907,0,2289261
.story#ixzz2mKOqBKH5.

Doder, D., and L. Branson. 1999. *Milosevic: Portrait of a Tyrant*. New York: The
Free Press.

Douthat, R. 2013. "Gambling with the Presidency." *New York Times*, 7 September.
http://www.nytimes.com/2013/09/08/opinion/sunday/douthat-gambling
-with-the-presidency.html?ref=rossdouthat&_r=1&.

Dowd, M. 1991. "Bush Stands Firm on Military Policy in Iraqi Civil War." *New
York Times*, 14 April. ProQuest Historical Newspapers: 1.

Downs, G.W., and M.A. Jones. 2002. "Reputation, Compliance, and International
Law." *Journal of Legal Studies* 31 (1): S95–114.

Drezner, D. 2013a. "Swing and a Miss: The Sabermetric Spat about
Whether It's Important for a President to Appear 'Credible.'" *Foreign
Policy*, 16 September. http://foreignpolicy.com/2013/09/16/swing-and
-a-miss/.

Drezner, D. 2013b. "Who 'Won' Syria?" *Foreign Policy*, 17 September. http://
foreignpolicy.com/2013/09/17/who-won-syria/.

Drezner, D. 2013c. "Syria, Iran, and the Credibility Fairy." *Foreign Policy*, 19
September. http://foreignpolicy.com/2013/09/19/syria-iran-and-the
-credibility-fairy/.

Drum, K. 2013a. "Let's Please Stop Pretending That Obama Is Reluctant to
Take Military Action." *Mother Jones*, 9 September. http://www.motherjones
.com/kevin-drum/2013/09/obama-syria-congress-dionne.

Drum, K. 2013b. "Domestic Credibility Is More Fragile than International
Credibility." *Mother Jones*, 10 October. http://www.motherjones.com/
kevin-drum/2013/10/domestic-credibility-more-fragile-international
-credibility.

Durbin, B. 2012. *Roundtable 3-15 on Intelligence and US Foreign Policy: Iraq, 9/11,
and Misguided Reform*. International Security Studies Forum, 4 June. https://
issforum.org/roundtables/3-15-intelligence-us-foreign-policy.

Easley, J. 2013. "Obama's Thoughtful Diplomatic Triumph on Syria Leaves His
Critics Speechless." *Politicus USA*, 14 September. http://www.politicususa

.com/2013/09/14/obamas-thoughtful-diplomatic-truimph-syria-leaves
-critics-speechless.html.

Economist. 2013. "Syria and International Norms: The Greater Harm." Blog, 16
September. http://www.economist.com/blogs/democracyinamerica/2013/09/
syria-and-international-norms.

Elkus, A. 2012. "Walt and Unreal Realism." *Rethinking Security* (Tumblr), 1 May.
http://rethinkingsecurity.tumblr.com/post/22207054985/walt-and-unreal
-realism.

Engel, P. 2016. "Former US Defense Secretary: Obama Hurt US Credibility
When He Backed Down from His Red Line on Syria." *Business Insider*,
26 January. http://www.businessinsider.com/robert-gates-syria-red-line
-obama-2016-1.

Entous, A., N. Malas, and R. Abushakra. 2013. "As Syrian Chemical Attack Loomed,
Missteps Doomed Civilians." *Wall Street Journal*, 22 November. http://www.wsj
.com/articles/SB10001424052702303914304579194203188283242.

Erlanger, S. 1998a. "NATO May Act against Serbs in Two Weeks." *New York
Times*, 2 October. ProQuest Historical Newspapers: A1.

Erlanger, S. 1998b. "Sees a Quick Test: President Says Hussein Retreated in
Face of a Threat of Force." *New York Times*, 16 November. ProQuest Historical
Newspapers: A1.

Etzioni, A. 2013. "The Risk of Blurring the Red Lines: Going Back on
Declarations Inclines Others to Test US Resolve." *National Interest*,
26 April. http://nationalinterest.org/commentary/the-risk-blurring-the
-red-lines-8402.

Facts on File Yearbook. 1998. "NATO Lifts Air Strike Threat against Yugoslavia."
Facts on File News Service 58 (3021), 29 October: 764.

Fallows, J. 2013. "Syria: Some Arguments for Intervention, and a Response."
Atlantic (Boston, MA), 31 August. http://www.theatlantic.com/
international/archive/2013/08/syria-some-arguments-for-intervention
-and-a-response/279241/.

Farley, R. 2013a. "Adversaries Determine Credibility." *The Diplomat* (blog),
18 September. http://thediplomat.com/flashpoints-blog/2013/09/18/
adversaries-determine-credibility/.

Farley, R. 2013b. "Don't Mistake US Hesitancy over Syria for Weakness." *Global
Times*, 21 October. http://www.globaltimes.cn/content/819271.shtml#.
UmZtvhYaxUQ.

Fearon, J. 1994. "Signaling versus the Balance of Power and Interest: An
Empirical Test of a Crisis Bargaining Model." *Journal of Conflict Resolution* 38
(2): 236–69.

Fearon, J. 1997. "Signaling Foreign Policy Interests: Tying Hands versus Sinking Costs." *Journal of Conflict Resolution* 41 (1): 68–90.

Fearon, J. 2013a. "Threading Needles in Syria." *The Monkey Cage*, 29 August. http://themonkeycage.org/2013/08/29/threading-needles-in-syria/.

Fearon, J. 2013b. "'Credibility' Is Not Everything but It's Not Nothing Either." *The Monkey Cage*, 7 September. http://themonkeycage.org/2013/09/07/credibility-is-not-everything-but-its-not-nothing-either/.

Feaver, P. 2013. "A 'Credible' Threat Likely Did Not Catalyze the Russian-Syrian Gambit." *Foreign Policy*, 11 September. http://foreignpolicy.com/2013/09/11/a-credible-threat-likely-did-not-catalyze-the-russian-syrian-gambit/.

Federation of American Scientists. 1998. *UNSCOM Chairman Butler's Report to UN Secretary General.* UNSCOM Reports to the Security Council, 15 December. http://fas.org/news/un/iraq/s/butla216.htm.

Fettweis, C. 2012. "Book Review. The Shadow of the Past: Reputation and Military Alliances before the First World War, by Gregory D. Miller." *Perspectives on Politics* 10 (4): 1130–1.

Fettweis, C. 2014. "Wrong Beliefs about the Ukraine Crisis: No. 1, That the Stakes Are High for US." *Foreign Policy*, 30 April. http://foreignpolicy.com/2014/04/30/wrong-beliefs-about-the-ukraine-crisis-no-1-that-the-stakes-are-high-for-u-s/.

Fisher, M. 2013a. "The Red Line Fallacy: What Everyone Gets Wrong about Why the US Would Strike Syria." *Washington Post* (blog), 28 August. http://www.washingtonpost.com/blogs/worldviews/wp/2013/08/28/the-red-line-fallacy-what-everyone-gets-wrong-about-why-the-u-s-would-strike-syria/.

Fisher, M. 2013b. "The 11 Questions Congress Faces on Syria." *Washington Post* (blog), 3 September. http://www.washingtonpost.com/blogs/worldviews/wp/2013/09/03/the-11-questions-every-member-of-congress-faces-on-syria.

Fisher, M. 2013c. "Yes, Iran Is Watching Obama's Handling of Syria Closely. Why That's Great News." *Washington Post* (blog), 19 September. http://www.washingtonpost.com/blogs/worldviews/wp/2013/09/19/yes-iran-is-watching-obamas-handling-of-syria-closely-why-thats-great-news/.

Fisher, M. 2013d. "Good News from Syria (really): Chemical Weapons Being Dismantled on Schedule." *Washington Post* (blog), 18 October. http://www.washingtonpost.com/blogs/worldviews/wp/2013/10/18/good-news-from-syria-really-chemical-weapons-are-being-dismantled-on-schedule/.

Ford, C.W. 2012. *Roundtable 3-15 on Intelligence and US Foreign Policy: Iraq, 9/11, and Misguided Reform.* International Security Studies Forum, 4 June. https://issforum.org/roundtables/3-15-intelligence-us-foreign-policy.

Fortna, P. 2013. "Why the CW Inspection Plan Doesn't Have to Be Perfect, or Even Close, to Succeed." *Political Violence @ a Glance*, 13 September. http:// politicalviolenceataglance.org/2013/09/13/why-the-cw-inspection-plan -doesnt-have-to-be-perfect-or-even-close-to-succeed.

Freedman, L., and E. Karsh. 1993. *The Gulf Conflict, 1990–1991: Diplomacy and War in the New World Order*. Princeton, NJ: Princeton University Press.

Freilich, C. 2013. "Syria Deal: As Good as It Gets?" *National Interest*, 14 September. http://nationalinterest.org/commentary/syria-deal-good-it -gets-9064.

Friedersdorf, C. 2013a. "Presidents Shouldn't Be Able to Credibly Threaten Wars That the People Oppose." *Atlantic* (Boston, MA), 6 September. http:// www.theatlantic.com/politics/archive/2013/09/presidents-shouldnt-be -able-to-credibly-threaten-wars-that-the-people-oppose/279410/.

Friedersdorf, C. 2013b. "A Vote against Syria Won't Destroy the President's Credibility." *Atlantic* (Boston, MA), 10 September. http://www.theatlantic .com/politics/archive/2013/09/a-vote-against-syria-wont-destroy-the -presidents-credibility/279498/.

Friedman, B. 2013a. *Credibility over "Red Lines" No Reason for War*. Cato Institute, 26 August. http://www.cato.org/publications/commentary/ credibility-over-red-lines-no-reason-war.

Friedman, B. 2013b. "Credibility over 'Red Lines' No Reason for War." *Orange County Register*, 27 August. http://www.ocregister.com/articles/credibility -522870-war-military.html.

Friedman, B. 2014. "The Credibility Debate in US Foreign Policy." *National Interest*, 11 August. http://nationalinterest.org/feature/the-credibility -debate-us-foreign-policy-11049.

Friedman, G. 2013. "Strategy, Ideology and the Close of the Syrian Crisis." *Stratfor Global Intelligence*, 17 September. http://www.stratfor.com/weekly/ strategy-ideology-and-close-syrian-crisis.

Fukuyama, F. 1995. "Book Review. Peripheral Visions: Deterrence Theory and American Foreign Policy in the Third World, 1965–1990, by Ted Hopf." *Foreign Affairs* 74 (3): 167.

Gall, C. 1999. "After 2d Day with Milosevic, Envoy Reports No Progress." *New York Times*, 11 March. ProQuest Historical Newspapers: A6.

Gallucci, R.L. 2012. "How Scholars Can Improve International Relations." *Chronicle of Higher Education*, 26 November. http://chronicle.com/article/ How-Scholars-Can-Improve/135898/.

Gelpi, C., P.D. Feaver, and J. Reifler. 2009. *Paying the Human Costs of War: American Public Opinion and Casualties in Military Conflicts*. Princeton: Princeton University Press.

Gelpi, C., and J. Mueller. 2006. "(Response) The Cost of War: How Many Casualties Will Americans Tolerate?" *Foreign Affairs* 85 (1): 139–44.

George, A. 1993. *Bridging the Gap: Theory and Practice in Foreign Policy.* Washington, DC: United States Institute of Peace Press.

George, A., and R. Smoke. 1974. *Deterrence in American Foreign Policy: Theory and Practice.* New York: Columbia University Press.

Gholz, E., D.G. Press, and H.M. Sapolsky. 1997. "Come Home, America: The Strategy of Restraint in the Face of Temptation." *International Security* 21 (4): 5–48.

Gibler, D.M. 2008. "The Costs of Reneging: Reputation and Alliance Formation." *Journal of Conflict Resolution* 52 (3): 426–54.

Goddard, S. 2013. "Syria and the Problems of Compellence." *Duck of Minerva,* 30 August. http://www.whiteoliphaunt.com/duckofminerva/2013/08/syria -and-the-problems-of-compellence.html.

Goertz, G. 1995. *Contexts of International Politics.* Cambridge: Cambridge University Press.

Goldberg, J. 2014. "Netanyahu Says Obama Got Syria Right." *Bloomberg View,* 22 May. http://www.bloombergview.com/articles/2014-05-22/netanyahu -says-obama-got-syria-right.

Goldberg, J. 2016. "The Obama Doctrine." *The Atlantic,* April, 317 (3): 70–90. http://www.theatlantic.com/magazine/archive/2016/04/the-obama -doctrine/471525/.

Goldstein, J.S., and J.C. Pevehouse. 1997. "Reciprocity, Bullying, and International Cooperation: Time-series Analysis of the Bosnia Conflict." *American Political Science Review* 91 (3): 515–29.

Goodman, J. 2013. "What's at Stake with Syria? Reputation, Credibility, and Future Deterrence." *The Smoke-Filled Room* (blog), 6 September. https:// thesmokefilledroomblog.wordpress.com/2013/09/06/whats-at-stake-with -syria-reputation-credibility-and-future-deterrence/.

Gordon, M.R. 1992. "US Shoots Down an Iraqi Warplane in No-Flight Zone." *New York Times,* 28 December. ProQuest Historical Newspapers: A1.

Gordon, M.R. 1993a. "Iraq Is Reported to Move Missiles into Areas Patrolled by US Jets." *New York Times,* 5 January. ProQuest Historical Newspapers: A1.

Gordon, M.R. 1993b. "Iraq Given Friday Deadline on Missiles." *New York Times,* 6 January. ProQuest Historical Newspapers: A8.

Gordon, M.R. 1993c. "Iraq Apparently Rebuffs Allies on Missiles Deployed in South." *New York Times,* 8 January. ProQuest Historical Newspapers: A1.

Gordon, M.R. 1993d. "US Says Baghdad Removed Missiles." *New York Times,* 10 January. ProQuest Historical Newspapers: 1.

Gordon, M.R. 1993e. "Bush Said to Plan Air Strike on Iraq over Its Defiance." *New York Times*, 13 January. ProQuest Historical Newspapers: A1.

Gordon, M.R. 1993f. "Hitting Hussein with a Stick, Keeping a Sledgehammer Ready." *New York Times*, 14 January. ProQuest Historical Newspapers: A8.

Gordon, M.R. 1993g. "Clinton Backs Step." *New York Times*, 18 January. ProQuest Historical Newspapers: A1.

Gordon, M.R. 1993h. "Raids in 2 Regions." *New York Times*, 19 January. ProQuest Historical Newspaper: A1.

Gordon, M.R. 1993i. "Iraq Says It Won't Attack Planes and Agrees to UN Flight Terms." *New York Times*, 20 January. ProQuest Historical Newspapers: A1.

Gordon, M.R. 1994a. "US Pilots Fire after 2 Warnings to Leave Area Are Ignored: NATO Downs 4 Planes Used by Serbs." *New York Times*, 1 March. ProQuest Historical Newspapers: A1.

Gordon, M.R. 1994b. "The Bluff That Failed: Serbs around Gorazde Are Undeterred by NATO's Policy of Limited Air Strikes." *New York Times*, 19 April. ProQuest Historical Newspapers: A1.

Gordon, M.R. 1994c. "US Sends Force as Iraqi Soldiers Threaten Kuwait." *New York Times*, 8 October. ProQuest Historical Newspapers: 1.

Gordon, M.R. 1994d. "Pentagon Moving a Force of 4,000 to Guard Kuwait." *New York Times*, 9 October. ProQuest Historical Newspapers: 1.

Gordon, M.R. 1994e. "No-Troop Zone Is Considered for Future." *New York Times*, 12 October. ProQuest Historical Newspapers: A1.

Gordon, M.R. 1994f. "US Plans to Keep Planes and Tanks in the Gulf Area." *New York Times*, 14 October. ProQuest Historical Newspapers: A1.

Gordon, M.R. 1998. "Milosevic Pledges Steps to Hold Off Attack from NATO." *New York Times*, 17 June. ProQuest Historical Newspapers: A1.

Gradstein, L. 2013. "Israel under Pressure to Give Up Chemical, Nuclear Weapons." *Jerusalem Post*, 18 September. http://www.jpost.com/Middle-East/Israel-Under-Pressure-To-Give-Up-Chemical-Nuclear-Weapons-326452.

Griswold, A. 2015. "*Morning Joe* Guest: US Credibility Took 'Major Hit' after Obama's Syria Red Line." *Mediaite*, 29 September. http://www.mediaite.com/tv/morning-joe-guest-u-s-credibility-took-major-hit-after-obamas-syria-red-line/.

Guisinger, A., and A. Smith. 2002. "Honest Threats: The Interaction of Reputation and Political Institutions in International Crises." *Journal of Conflict Resolution* 46 (2): 175–200.

Haas, L.J. 2014. "US Credibility Already in Tatters over Syria." *International Business Times*, 4 September. http://www.ibtimes.com/fighting-words/us-credibility-already-tatters-over-syria-1402571.

Hagel, C. 2013. *Statement on Syria before the Senate Foreign Relations Committee as Delivered by Secretary of Defense Chuck Hagel*. US Department of Defense. Washington DC, 3 September. http://archive.defense.gov/Speeches/Speech.aspx?SpeechID=1802.

Haggerty, B. 2013. *Debating US Interests in Syria's Civil War*. MIT Center for International Studies, 16 September. http://web.mit.edu/cis/editorspick _audit_091613_syria.html.

Halper, D. 2013. "Boehner: 'I'm going to support the President's call for action' in Syria." *Weekly Standard*, 3 September. http://www.weeklystandard.com/blogs/boehner-im-going-support-presidents-call-action-syria_752675.html.

Harvey, F. 1997. "Deterrence and Ethnic Conflict: The Case of Bosnia-Herzegovina, 1993–1994." *Security Studies* 6 (3): 180–210.

Harvey, F. 1998. "Rigor Mortis or Rigor, More Tests: Necessity, Sufficiency, and Deterrence Logic." *International Studies Quarterly* 42 (4): 675–707.

Harvey, F. 1999. "Practicing Coercion: Revisiting Success and Failures Using Boolean Logic and Comparative Methods." *Journal of Conflict Resolution* 43 (6): 840–71.

Harvey, F. 2006. "Getting NATO's Success in Kosovo Right: The Theory and Logic of Counter-Coercion." *Conflict Management and Peace Science* 23 (2): 139–58.

Harvey, F. 2011. *Explaining the Iraq War: Counterfactual Theory, Logic and Evidence*. London, New York: Cambridge University Press.

Harvey, F. 2015. "'What if' History Matters: Comparative Counterfactual Analysis and Policy Relevance." *Security Studies* 24 (3): 413–24.

Harvey, F., and P. James. 2009. "Deterrence and Compellence in Iraq, 1991–2003: Lessons for a Complex Paradigm." In *Complex Deterrence: Strategy in the Global Age*, ed. T.V. Paul, P. Morgan, and J. Wirtz, 222–56. Chicago: University of Chicago Press.

Harvey, F., and A. Wilner. 2012. "Counter-Coercion, the Power of Failure and the Practical Limits of Deterring Terrorism." In *Deterring Terrorism: Theory and Practice*, ed. A. Wenger and A. Wilner, 95–116. Palo Alto, CA: Stanford University Press.

Haselkorn, A. 1999. *The Continuing Storm: Iraq, Poisonous Weapons, and Deterrence*. New Haven, CT: Yale University Press.

Hedges, C. 1995a. "UN Warns Serbs of Bombing if They Attack Dutch Unit." *New York Times*, 10 July. ProQuest Historical Newspapers: A1.

Hedges, C. 1995b. "Bosnian Serbs Open Drive on a 2d UN 'Safe Area.'" *New York Times*, 14 July. ProQuest Historical Newspapers: A8.

Hedges, C. 1995c. "Serbs Keeping Up a Heavy Barrage on 3 'Safe Areas.'" *New York Times*, 23 July. ProQuest Historical Newspapers: 1.

Holbrooke, R. 1998. *To End a War*. New York: Random House.

Hopf, T. 1994. *Peripheral Visions: Deterrence Theory and American Foreign Policy in the Third World, 1965–1990*. Ann Arbor: University of Michigan Press.

Horst, A. 2004. "Foreign Perceptions of American Casualty Sensitivity: Is Your Reputation Worth Fighting For?" Unpublished manuscript, Massachusetts Institute of Technology.

Hosmer, S.T. 2001. *The Conflict over Kosovo: Why Milosevic Decided to Settle When He Did*. Santa Monica: RAND Corporation.

Huth, P.K. 1997. "Reputations and Deterrence: A Theoretical and Empirical Assessment." *Security Studies* 7 (1): 72–99.

Huth, P.K., and B. Russett. 1984. "What Makes Deterrence Work? Cases from 1900 to 1980." *World Politics* 36 (4): 496–526.

Huth, P.K., and B. Russett. 1988. "Deterrence Failure and Crisis Escalation." *International Studies Quarterly* 32 (1): 29–45.

Ibrahim, Y.M. 1991. "Iraq Rejects European Plan for Kurdish Haven in North." *New York Times*, 10 April. ProQuest Historical Newspapers: A12.

Ibrahim, Y.M. 1993. "Iraqi Aide Defends Removal of Equipment in Border Zone." *New York Times*, 12 January. ProQuest Historical Newspapers: A2.

Ibrahim, Y.M. 1994. "Iraq Signals Acceptance of UN Move." *New York Times*, 17 October. ProQuest Historical Newspapers: A10.

Ibrahim, Y.M. 1998. "UN Measure Skirts Outright Threat of Force against Milosevic." *New York Times*, 25 October. ProQuest Historical Newspapers: 6.

Jakobsen, J. 2013. "America's Prestige and the War against Syria." *Popular Social Science*, 30 August. http://www.popularsocialscience.com/2013/08/30/americas-prestige-and-the-war-against-syria/.

Jakobsen, P.V. 2000. "Reinterpreting Western Use of Coercion in Bosnia-Herzegovina: Assurances and Carrots Were Crucial." *Journal of Strategic Studies* 23 (2): 1–22.

Jehl, D. 1993. "Serbs Must Withdraw Promptly or Face Air Strikes, US Insists." *New York Times*, 11 August. ProQuest Historical Newspapers: A1.

Jehl, D. 1994. "Clinton's Line in the Sand." *New York Times*, 10 October. ProQuest Historical Newspapers: A1.

Jehl, D. 1998. "Arms Inspectors Get Cool Reception in Iraq." *New York Times*, 18 November. ProQuest Historical Newspapers: A14.

Jentleson, B.W. 2002. "The Need for Praxis: Bringing Policy Relevance Back In." *International Security* 26 (4): 169–83.

Jentleson, B.W., and E. Ratner. 2011. "Bridging the Beltway–Ivory Tower Gap." *International Studies Review* 13 (1): 6–11.

Jervis, R. 1976. *Perception and Misperception in International Politics*. Princeton: Princeton University Press.

Jervis, R. 1979. "Deterrence Theory Revisited." *World Politics* 31 (2): 289–324.

Jervis, R., R.N. Lebow, and J.G. Stein. 1985. *Psychology and Deterrence.*
Baltimore: Johns Hopkins University Press.

Judis, J.B. 2013. "It's Time to Intervene in Syria." *New Republic,* 30 April. http://
www.newrepublic.com/article/113068/syria-intervention-why-obama
-should-authorize-force.

Keesing's Record of World Events. 1998. June, 44 (6): 42356. http://keesings
.com/article/23082.

Kessler, G. 2013. "President Obama and the 'Red Line' on Syria's Chemical
Weapons." *Washington Post* (blog), 6 September. http://www.washingtonpost
.com/blogs/fact-checker/wp/2013/09/06/president-obama-and-the-red
-line-on-syrias-chemical-weapons/.

Kifner, J. 1994. "An Envoy Finds 'No Need' for Air Strikes." *New York Times,*
21 February. ProQuest Historical Newspapers: A1.

Kinzer, S. 1998. "Iraq Rebuffs France on Plan for Compromise on UN Weapons
Inspections." *New York Times,* 22 December. ProQuest Historical Newspapers:
A18.

Klein, E. 2013a. "The Five Best Arguments for Striking Syria – and the Best
Rebuttals." *Washington Post* (Wonkblog), 10 September. http://www
.washingtonpost.com/blogs/wonkblog/wp/2013/09/10/the-five-best
-arguments-for-striking-syria-and-the-best-rebuttals/.

Klein, E. 2013b. "The White House May Really Be about to Win on Syria."
Washington Post (Wonkblog), 10 September. http://www.washingtonpost.
com/blogs/wonkblog/wp/2013/09/10/the-white-house-may-really-be
-about-to-win-on-syria/.

Knopf, J.W. 2013. "Use with Caution: The Value and Limits of Deterrence
against Asymmetric Threats." *World Politics Review,* 11 June. http://www
.worldpoliticsreview.com/articles/13006/use-with-caution-the-value-and
-limits-of-deterrence-against-asymmetric-threats.

Krauss, C. 1991. "US Will Airdrop Food and Clothes to Kurds in Iraq." *New York
Times,* 6 April. ProQuest Historical Newspapers: 1.

Krauthammer, C. 2004. "Democratic Realism." *Free Republic,* 12 February.
http://www.freerepublic.com/focus/f-news/1078705/posts.

Krauthammer, C. 2013. "Pink Line over Damascus: Obama Has Backed Himself
into a Corner." *National Review Online,* 9 May. http://www.nationalreview
.com/article/347895/pink-line-over-damascus-charles-krauthammer.

Kristof, N. 2014. "Professors, We Need You!" *New York Times,* 15 February. http://
www.nytimes.com/2014/02/16/opinion/sunday/kristof-professors-we
-need-you.html.

Kydd, A. 2000. "Trust, Reassurance, and Cooperation." *International Organization*
54 (2): 325–57.

Lake, D. 2009. "The Limits of Coercive Airpower: NATO's 'Victory' in Kosovo Revisited." *International Security* 34 (1): 83–112.

Larison, D. 2013a. "The 'Credibility' Argument for Syrian Intervention Is Nonsense." *The American Conservative*, 29 April. http://www.theamericanconservative.com/larison/the-credibility-argument-for-syrian-intervention-is-nonsense/.

Larison, D. 2013b. "The Desperation of the Syria Hawks' 'Credibility' Argument." *The American Conservative*, 6 May. http://www.theamericanconservative.com/larison/the-desperation-of-the-syria-hawks-credibility-argument/.

Larison, D. 2013c. "No War for Credibility (II)." *The American Conservative*, 10 May. http://www.theamericanconservative.com/larison/no-war-for-credibility-ii/.

Larison, D. 2013d. "The Cult of 'Credibility.'" *The American Conservative*, 13 May. http://www.theamericanconservative.com/larison/the-cult-of-credibility/.

Larison, D. 2014. "The American Conservative: Realism and Reform." *The American Conservative*, 12 September. http://www.theamericanconservative.com/larison/the-american-conservative-realism-and-reform/.

Lebow, R.N. 1981. *Between Peace and War: The Nature of International Crises.* Baltimore: Johns Hopkins University Press.

Lebow, R.N. 1995. "Book Review. Peripheral Visions: Deterrence Theory and American Foreign Policy in the Third World, 1965–1990, by Ted Hopf." *Political Science Quarterly* 110 (2): 320–1.

Lebow, R.N. 2001. "Deterrence and Reassurance: Lessons from the Cold War." *Global Dialogue* 3 (4): 119–32.

Lebow, R.N., and J.G. Stein. 1989. "Rational Deterrence Theory: I Think, Therefore I Deter." *World Politics* 41 (2): 208–24.

Lebow, R.N., and J.G. Stein. 1990. "Deterrence: The Elusive Dependent Variable." *World Politics* 42 (3): 336–69.

Levy, J.S. 1997. "Prospect Theory, Rational Choice, and International Relations." *International Studies Quarterly* 41 (1): 87–112.

Levy, J.S. 2008. "Deterrence and Coercive Diplomacy: The Contributions of Alexander George." *Political Psychology* 29 (4): 537–52.

Levy, J.S. 2012. "Coercive Threats, Audience Costs, and Case Studies." *Security Studies* 21 (3): 383–90.

Lewis, A. 1999. "In Credibility Gulch." *New York Times*, 20 March. ProQuest Historical Newspapers: A15.

Lewis, P. 1994. "UN Warns Serbs on Gorazde: Move Could Lead to Air Strikes." *New York Times*, 10 April. ProQuest Historical Newspapers: A1.

Lieberman, E. 1994. "The Rational Deterrence Debate: Is the Dependent Variable Elusive?" *Security Studies* 3 (3): 384–427.

Lieberman, E. 1995a. *Deterrence Theory: Success or Failure in Arab-Israeli Wars?* McNair Paper 45, October. Washington: National Defense University Press.

Lieberman, E. 1995b. "What Makes Deterrence Work? Lessons from the Egyptian-Israeli Rivalry." *Security Studies* 4 (4): 851–910.

Lieberman, J., and J. Kyl. 2013. "Inaction on Syria Threatens US Security." *Wall Street Journal*, 5 September. http://online.wsj.com/news/articles/SB100014 24127887324432404579053661192848056.

Lowenthal, M. 2012. *Roundtable 3-15 on Intelligence and US Foreign Policy: Iraq, 9/11, and Misguided Reform.* International Security Studies Forum, 4 June. https://issforum.org/roundtables/3-15-intelligence-us-foreign -policy.

Loyola, M. 2013. "Syria and US Credibility." *National Review Online*, 8 September. http://nationalreview.com/corner/357889/syria-and-us-credibility -mario-loyola.

Mahoney, J. 2012. "The Logic of Process Tracing Tests in the Social Sciences." *Sociological Methods & Research* 41 (4): 570–97.

Manzi, J. 2013. "A Dissent on Syria." *National Review Online*, 5 September. http://www.nationalreview.com/corner/357680/dissent-syria-jim-manzi.

Matthews, D. 2013. "Why Obama Shouldn't Care about Backing Down on Syria." *Washington Post* (Wonkblog), 12 September. http://www.washingtonpost .com/blogs/wonkblog/wp/2013/09/12/why-obama-shouldnt-care-about -backing-down-on-syria/.

McCain, J., and L. Graham. 2014. "McCain and Graham: Obama Is Failing the Middle East, and US Interests There." *Washington Post*, 25 October. http:// www.washingtonpost.com/opinions/mccain-and-graham-obama -is-failing-the-middle-east-and-us-interests-there/2013/10/25/47e8f016 -3d83-11e3-a94f-b58017bfee6c_story.html.

McManus, R. 2013. "Threats and Credibility: How Obama's Decision to Seek Congressional Authorization for Syria May Have Been a Game Changer." *The Monkey Cage*, 11 September. http://themonkeycage.org/2013/09/threats -and-credibility-how-obamas-decision-to-seek-congressional-authorization -for-syria-may-have-been-a-game-changer/.

Mead, W.R. 2012. "'Realists' in Foreign Policy?" *American Interest*, 2 May. http:// www.the-american-interest.com/2012/05/02/realists-in-foreign-policy/.

Mead, W.R. 2013. "If Obama Doesn't Bomb Syria Now, He's Toast." *American Interest*, 5 September. http://www.the-american-interest.com/ blog/2013/09/05/if-obama-doesnt-bomb-syria-now-hes-toast/.

Menon, R. 2013a. "Don't Use US Credibility as a Reason to Attack Syria." *Los Angeles Times*, 5 September. http://articles.latimes.com/2013/sep/05/opinion/la-oe-menon-syria-vote-credibility-20130905.

Menon, R. 2013b. "Obama's Weak Syria Case." *National Interest*, 6 September. http://nationalinterest.org/commentary/obamas-weak-syria-case-9004.

Mercer, J. 1996. *Reputation and International Politics*. Ithaca, NY: Cornell University Press.

Mercer, J. 2010. "Emotional Beliefs." *International Organization* 64 (1): 1–31.

Mercer, J. 2013. "Bad Reputation: The Folly of Going to War for 'Credibility.'" *Foreign Affairs*, 28 August. http://www.foreignaffairs.com/articles/136577/jonathan-mercer/bad-reputation.

Mervis, J. 2013. "Senator Warren Says Fighting for Science Is a Top Priority." *Science*, 5 November. http://news.sciencemag.org/people-events/2013/11/senator-warren-says-fighting-science-top-priority.

Milbank, D. 2013. "The GOP Wants to Have It Both Ways on Syria." *Washington Post*, 3 September. http://www.washingtonpost.com/opinions/dana-milbank-the-gop-wants-to-have-it-both-ways-on-syria/2013/09/03/a1755e36-14d3-11e3-880b-7503237cc69d_story.html.

Miller, A.D. 2013a. "The Limits of Military Force in Syria." *Newsday*, 28 August. http://www.newsday.com/opinion/oped/miller-the-limits-of-military-force-in-syria-1.5974912.

Miller, A.D. 2013b. "Can Obama Afford Not to Bomb Syria?" *Foreign Policy*, 9 September. http://foreignpolicy.com/2013/09/09/can-obama-afford-not-to-bomb-syria/.

Miller, G.D. 2012. *The Shadow of the Past: Reputation and Military Alliances before the First World War*. Cornell Studies in Security Affairs. Ithaca, London: Cornell University Press.

Miller, J. 1998. "American Inspector on Iraq Quits, Accusing UN and US of Cave-In." *New York Times*, 27 August. ProQuest Historical Newspapers: A1.

Miller, S.A. 2014. "The Knives Are Out: Panetta Eviscerates Obama's 'Red Line' Blunder on Syria." *Washington Times*, 7 October. http://www.washingtontimes.com/news/2014/oct/7/panetta-decries-obama-red-line-blunder-syria/.

Miller, Z.J. 2013. "McCain: Blocking Syria Strike Would Be 'Catastrophic.'" *Time*, 2 September. http://swampland.time.com/2013/09/02/mccain-blocking-syria-strike-would-be-catastrophic/.

Mitton, J. 2015. "Selling Schelling Short: Reputations and American Coercive Diplomacy after Syria." *Contemporary Security Policy* 36 (3): 408–31.

Morgan, P.M. 1983. *Deterrence: A Conceptual Analysis*. New York: SAGE.

Morgan, P.M. 1997. "Getting Respect Gets No Respect." *Mershon International Studies Review* 41 (1): 117–19.

Morgan, P.M. 2003. *Deterrence Now*. Cambridge: Cambridge University Press.

MSNBC staff. 2013. Obama: "It's fair to say that I haven't decided" (Interview). *MSNBC News*, 9 September. http://www.msnbc.com/msnbc/watch-obama-its-fair-say-i-haven.

Mueller, J. 2005. "The Iraq Syndrome." *Foreign Affairs* 84 (6): 44–55.

Myers, S.L. 1996a. "Pentagon Sees a New Threat by Iraq Forces." *New York Times*, 31 August. ProQuest Historical Newspapers: 1.

Myers, S.L. 1996b. "UN Halts Deal for Iraq Oil Sales as US Pledges Action on Attack." *New York Times*, 2 September. ProQuest Historical Newspapers: 1.

Myers, S.L. 1996c. "US Attacks Military Targets in Iraq." *New York Times*, 3 September. ProQuest Historical Newspapers: A1.

Myers, S.L. 1998. "US and Britain End Raids on Iraq, Calling Mission a Success." *New York Times*, 20 December. ProQuest Historical Newspapers: 1.

Myers, S.L. 1999. "NATO Plan Calls for Widening Strikes on Air Defenses and Heavy Weapons." *New York Times*, 20 March. ProQuest Historical Newspapers: A6.

Myers, S.L., and S. Erlanger. 1998a. "US Is Stepping Up Military Threats against the Serbs." *New York Times*, 7 October. ProQuest Historical Newspapers: A1.

Myers, S.L., and S. Erlanger. 1998b. "US to Back NATO Military Action against Serbs in Kosovo." *New York Times*, 8 October. ProQuest Historical Newspapers: A16.

New York Times. 1992. "Excerpts from Bush's Talk: Iraqi Air Zone Is Off-Limits." 27 August. ProQuest Historical Newspapers: A14.

New York Times. 1994. "World Leaders Express Shock and Outrage at Blast." 6 February. ProQuest Historical Newspapers: 12.

New York Times. 1995. "America's Plan for Bosnian Peace." Opinion, 18 August. ProQuest Historical Newspapers: A24.

New York Times. 1996. "Iraq Tests the Limits." Opinion, 2 September. ProQuest Historical Newspapers: 20.

New York Times. 1998a. "The Iraq Agreement." Opinion, 23 February. ProQuest Historical Newspapers: A18.

New York Times. 1998b. "Touring Iraq's Presidential Sites." Opinion, 30 March. ProQuest Historical Newspapers: A16.

New York Times. 1998c. "Holbrooke Warns Serbs' Leader on Kosovo." 24 June. ProQuest Historical Newspapers: A8.

New York Times. 2002a. "After Talks, Iraq Rejects Arms Inspections." 6 July. ProQuest Historical Newspapers: A5.

New York Times. 2002b. "Experts Arrive in Baghdad to Prepare Logistics."
19 November. ProQuest Historical Newspapers: A20.

Nye, J. 2008. *Conversations with History: Theory and Practice in International
Relations*. Berkeley: Institute of International Studies. http://conversations.
berkeley.edu/content/joseph-s-nye.

Nye, J. 2009. "Scholars on the Sidelines." *Washington Post*, 13 April. http://
www.washingtonpost.com/wp-dyn/content/article/2009/04/12/
AR2009041202260.html.

Organisation for the Prohibition of Chemical Weapons. 2014. *Third Report
of the OPCW Fact-Finding Mission in Syria*. Technical Secretariat, 18
December. http://photos.state.gov/libraries/netherlands/328666/pdfs/
THIRDREPORTOFTHEOPCWFACTFINDINGMISSIONINSYRIA.pdf.

Organisation for the Prohibition of Chemical Weapons. 2015. *Syrian Chemical
Destruction Data*. 27 July. https://www.opcw.org/special-sections/syria/
destruction-statistics/.

Orme, J.D. 1992. *Deterrence, Reputation and Cold-War Cycles*. London: Macmillan.

Pach, J. 2013. "Adversaries Determine Credibility." *The Diplomat*, 18 September.
http://thediplomat.com/2013/09/adversaries-determine-credibility/.

Paul, T.V., P.M. Morgan, and J.J. Wirtz. 2009. *Complex Deterrence: Strategy in the
Global Age*. Chicago: University of Chicago Press.

Pavel, B., and A. Ward. 2013. "Obama's Syria Decision and US Global
Credibility." *Atlantic Council* (blog), 31 August. http://www.atlanticcouncil
.org/blogs/new-atlanticist/obama-s-syria-decision-and-u-s-global
-credibility.

Pelley, S. 2008. "Interrogator Shares Saddam's Confessions." *60 Minutes Online*, CBS
News, 27 January. http://www.cbsnews.com/stories/2008/01/24/60minutes/
main3749494.shtml.

Perlez, J. 1998. "Serbian Pullback: US Special Envoy Says Election Is Promised
in Disputed Region." *New York Times*, 14 October. ProQuest Historical
Newspapers: A1.

Perlez, J. 1999a. "US Weighs Its Reaction to Massacre in Kosovo." *New York
Times*, 17 January. ProQuest Historical Newspapers: 6.

Perlez, J. 1999b. "NATO's Kosovo Bid Is Rebuffed by Serbs." *New York Times*,
20 January. ProQuest Historical Newspapers: A1.

Perlez, J. 1999c. "US to Push NATO to Issue Ultimatum to Serb Leader."
New York Times, 21 January. ProQuest Historical Newspapers: A3.

Perlez, J. 1999d. "Kosovo Situation Worsens as Serbs Press Offensive." *New York
Times*, 21 March. ProQuest Historical Newspapers: 2.

Perlez, J. 1999e. "Milosevic to Get One 'Last Chance' to Avoid Bombing."
New York Times, 22 March. ProQuest Historical Newspapers: A1.

Peterson, T.M. 2013. "Sending a Message: The Reputation Effect of US
Sanction Threat Behavior." *International Studies Quarterly* 57 (4): 672–82.

Pillar, P. 2011. *Intelligence and US Foreign Policy: Iraq, 9/11, and Misguided
Reform*. New York: Columbia University Press.

Posen, B. 2013. "Pull Back: The Case for a Less Activist Foreign Policy." *Foreign
Affairs* 92 (1): 116–29.

Press, D. 2005. *Calculating Credibility: How Leaders Assess Military Threats*. Ithaca,
NY: Cornell University Press.

Press, D., and J. Lind. 2013. "Red Lines and Red Herrings." *Foreign Policy*,
6 May. http://foreignpolicy.com/2013/05/06/red-lines-and-red-herrings/.

Preston, J., and T.S. Purdum. 2002. "UN Inspectors Can Return Unconditionally,
Iraq Says." *New York Times*, 17 September. ProQuest Historical Newspapers: A1.

Price, R. 2013. "No Strike, No Problem: The Right Way to Nurture a Norm."
Foreign Affairs, 5 September. http://www.foreignaffairs.com/articles/139903/
richard-price/no-strike-no-problem.

Purdum, T.S., and J. Preston. 2002. "Powell Says UN Ought to Hold Up Iraq
Inspections." *New York Times*, 2 October. ProQuest Historical Newspapers: A1.

Qazi, S.H. 2013. "America's Credibility Is Not at Stake in Syria." *The World Post*,
12 September. http://m.huffpost.com/us/entry/3895111.

Quester, G. 1995. "Book Review. Peripheral Visions: Deterrence Theory and
American Foreign Policy in the Third World, 1965–1990, by Ted Hopf."
American Political Science Review 89 (3): 805.

Richter, G. 2013. "Rep. Grimm: Changed Mind on Syria Because US Credibility
Already Lost." *Newsmax*, 5 September. http://www.newsmax.com/
NewsmaxTv/grimm-syria-credibility-lost/2013/09/05/id/524091/.

Ross, D. 2013. "Blocking Action on Syria Makes an Attack on Iran More Likely."
Washington Post, 9 September. http://www.washingtonpost.com/opinions/
blocking-action-on-syria-makes-an-attack-on-iran-more-likely/2013/09/09/
dd655466-1963-11e3-8685-5021e0c41964_story.html.

Ruger, W. 2014. "A Realist's Guide to Grand Strategy." *The American Conservative*,
26 August. http://www.theamericanconservative.com/articles/a-realists
-guide-to-grand-strategy/.

Sartori, A.E. 2005. *Deterrence by Diplomacy*. Princeton, NJ: Princeton University Press.

Schaub, G. 1996. *Management through Coercion*. Paper presented at the 37th
Annual ISA Convention, 16–20 April, San Diego, CA.

Schelling, T.C. 1960. *The Strategy of Conflict*. Cambridge: Harvard University Press.

Schelling, T.C. 1966. *Arms and Influence*. New Haven, London: Yale University
Press.

Schmidt, W.E. 1992. "Iraq Says It Is Ready to Fight Allies over Air Zone." *New
York Times*, 27 August. ProQuest Historical Newspapers: A14.

Schmitt, E. 1993. "Allied Strike: Swift and Unchallenged." *New York Times*, 14 January. ProQuest Historical Newspapers: A8.

Schmitt, G.J. 2013. "Is Syria Like Bosnia?" *American Enterprise Institute*, 17 September. http://www.aei.org/article/foreign-and-defense-policy/regional/middle-east-and-north-africa/is-syria-like-bosnia/.

Sciolino, E. 1991a. "US Warns against Attack by Iraq on Kurdish Refugees." *New York Times*, 11 April. ProQuest Historical Newspapers: A1.

Sciolino, E. 1991b. "US Troops to Build Camps in North Iraq to Aid Kurds; Bush Sees 'Temporary' Role." *New York Times*, 17 April. ProQuest Historical Newspapers: A1.

Sciolino, E. 1991c. "Iraq and UN to Carve Out Routes in Plan to Speed Refugees' Return." *New York Times*, 19 April. ProQuest Historical Newspapers: A1.

Sciolino, E. 1994a. "US Said to Plan Bosnia Ultimatum Urging Air Strikes." *New York Times*, 9 February. ProQuest Historical Newspapers: A1.

Sciolino, E. 1994b. "US Offers Plan to Avoid Threat from Iraq Again." *New York Times*, 13 October. ProQuest Historical Newspapers: A1.

Seib, G.F. 2013. "Syria Credibility Gap: Where's the Risk?" *Wall Street Journal*, 9 September. http://m.us.wsj.com/articles/SB10001424127887323864604579064963818091016?mobile=y.

Sell, L. 2002. *Slobodan Milosevic and the Destruction of Yugoslavia*. Durham: Duke University Press.

Shanker, T., and M.R. Gordon. 2013. "Officials Make Case for Strike before Senate Panel." *New York Times*, 3 September. http://www.nytimes.com/2013/09/04/world/middleeast/officials-make-case-for-strike-before-senate-panel.html.

Shannon, V. 2013. "Broadening the Reputation Debate over Syria." *E-International Relations*, 28 September. http://www.e-ir.info/2013/09/28/broadening-the-reputation-debate-over-syria/.

Shenon, P. 1996. "Iraq Orders Halt to Missile Strikes on American Jets." *New York Times*, 14 September. ProQuest Historical Newspapers: 1.

Shenon, P., and S.L. Myers. 1998. "US Says It Was Just Hours away from Starting Attack against Iraq." *New York Times*, 15 November. ProQuest Historical Newspapers: 1.

Shields, M., and D. Brooks. 2013. "Shields and Brooks on Syria as 'Test Case' for Obama's Credibility." *PBS Newshour*, 6 September. http://www.pbs.org/newshour/bb/politics-july-dec13-shieldsbrooks_09-06/.

Shimshoni, J. 1988. *Israel and Conventional Deterrence: Border Warfare from 1953–1970*. Ithaca: Cornell University Press.

Simons, A. 2013. "Syria: Whose Credibility? It's Not America's, but Obama's, That's on the Line." *National Interest*, 6 September. http://nationalinterest.org/commentary/syria-whose-credibility-9000.

Sitaraman, G. 2014. "Credibility and War Powers." *Harvard Law Review* 127 (3): 123–36.

Slater, J. 2013. "Syria, Credibility, and 'Armchair Isolationism.'" *Foreign Policy*, 5 September. http://foreignpolicy.com/2013/09/05/syria-credibility-and -armchair-isolationism/.

Slaughter, A.-M. 2014. "Stopping Russia Starts in Syria." *Project Syndicate*, 23 April. http://www.project-syndicate.org/commentary/anne-marie-slaughter-on -how-us-intervention-in-the-syrian-civil-war-would-alter-vladimir-putin-s -calculus-in-ukraine.

Snyder, G., and P. Deising. 1977. *Conflict among Nations: Bargaining, Decision Making, and System Structure in International Crises.* Princeton: Princeton University Press.

Specter, M. 1994. "Moscow Withdraws Its Objections to NATO Strikes near Gorazde." *New York Times*, 24 April. ProQuest Historical Newspapers: 14.

Stein, J.G. 1991. "Deterrence and Reassurance." In *Behavior, Society, and Nuclear War*, vol. 2. ed. P. Tetlock, J.L. Husbands, R. Jervis, P.C. Stern, and C. Tilly, 8–72. New York: Oxford University Press.

Stein, J.G. 1992. "Deterrence and Compellence in the Gulf, 1990–91: A Failed or Impossible Task?" *International Security* 17 (2): 147–79.

Stein, J.G. 2013. "Threat Perception in International Relations." In *The Oxford Handbook of Political Psychology*, 2nd ed., ed. L. Huddy, D.O. Sears, and J.S. Levy, 364–94. Oxford: Oxford University Press.

Stephens, B., I. Bremmer, J. Harman, G. Rose, and J. Micklethwait. 2016. "Obama in Syria." *The Charlie Rose Show*, 21 April. https://charlierose.com/videos/27058.

Stewart, P. 2013. "US Credibility on Iran at Stake in Syria Decision: Hagel Says." *Reuters*, 3 September. http://www.reuters.com/article/2013/09/03/us -syria-crisis-usa-hagel-idUSBRE9820YY20130903.

Stigler, A.L. 2002/3. "A Clear Victory for Air Power: NATO's Empty Threat to Invade Kosovo." *International Security* 27 (3): 124–57.

Stokes, D. 2013. "Syria and Obama's 'Credibility Spiral.'" *RUSI Analysis*, Royal United Services Institute, September 10. https://rusi.org/commentary/ syria-and-obamas-credibility-spiral.

Sudetic, C. 1991. "US-Iraqi Standoff Hinders Kurd Relief at Camp." *New York Times*, 24 April. ProQuest Historical Newspapers: A10.

Sudetic, C. 1994a. "Serbs Take Key Area above Bosnia Town." *New York Times*, 10 April. ProQuest Historical Newspapers: 10.

Sudetic, C. 1994b. "US Planes Bomb Serbian Position for a Second Day." *New York Times*, 12 April. ProQuest Historical Newspapers: A1, A10.

Takeyh, R. 2013. "Red Lines, Allies and Enemies." *New York Times*, 18 September. http://www.nytimes.com/2013/09/18/opinion/global/red-lines-allies -and-enemies.html?r=0.

Tang, S. 2005. "Reputation, Cult of Reputation, and International Conflict." *Security Studies* 14 (1): 34–62.

Telegraph staff. 2013. "The Full Text of the French UN Resolution on Syria." *Telegraph*, 11 September. http://www.telegraph.co.uk/news/worldnews/middleeast/syria/10301732/The-full-text-of-the-French-UN-resolution-on-Syria.html.

Tickner, J.A., and A. Tsygankov. 2008. "Risks and Opportunities of Crossing the Academy/Policy Divide." *International Studies Review* 10 (1): 155–77.

Tillman, T. 2013. "A 'War for Credibility'? Experts Voice Syria Concerns on 'MHP.'" *MSNBC*, 4 September. http://www.msnbc.com/melissa-harris-perry/war-credibility-experts-voice-syria.

Tingley, D.H., and B.F. Walter. 2011. "The Effect of Repeated Play on Reputation Building: An Experimental Approach." *International Organization* 65 (2): 343–65.

Tomz, M. 2012. *Reputation and International Cooperation: Sovereign Debt across Three Centuries*. Princeton: Princeton University Press.

Trachtenberg, M. 2012. "Audience Costs: An Historical Analysis." *Security Studies* 21 (1): 3–42.

Ulfelder, J. 2013. "President Obama, You're the Fish in This Morbid Game of Poker." *Dart-Throwing Chimp* (blog), 7 September. http://dartthrowingchimp.wordpress.com/2013/09/07/president-obama-youre-the-fish-in-this-morbid-game-of-poker.

United Nations Security Council. 1991. *S/RES/0688, Resolution 688 (1991)*. United Nations, 5 April. http://fas.org/news/un/iraq/sres/sres0688.htm

United Nations Security Council. 1994a. *Statement by the President of the Security Council, S/PRST/1994/58*. United Nations, 8 October. http://www.un.org/en/ga/search/view_doc.asp?symbol=S/PRST/1994/58.

United Nations Security Council. 1994b. *S/RES/949, Resolution 949 (1994)*. United Nations, 15 October. http://fas.org/news/un/iraq/sres/sres0949.htm.

United Nations Security Council. 1998a. *S/RES/1154, Resolution 1154 (1998)*. United Nations, 2 March. http://www.un.org/Depts/unscom/Keyresolutions/sres98-1154.htm.

United Nations Security Council. 1998b. *S/RES/1199, Resolution 1199 (1998)*. United Nations, 23 September. http://unscr.com/en/resolutions/doc/1199.

United Nations Security Council. 1998c. *S/RES/1205, Resolution 1205 (1998)*. United Nations, 5 November. http://www.un.org/Depts/unscom/Keyresolutions/sres98-1205.htm.

United Nations Security Council. 2002. *S/RES/1441, Resolution 1441 (2002)*. United Nations, 8 November. http://www.un.org/Depts/unmovic/documents/1441.pdf.

United Nations Security Council. 2013a. *S/RES/2118, Resolution 2118(2013)*. United Nations, 27 September. http://www.securitycouncilreport.org/atf/cf/%7B65BFCF9B-6D27-4E9C-8CD3-CF6E4FF96FF9%7D/s_res_2118 .pdf.

United Nations Security Council. 2013b. *Security Council Requires Scheduled Destruction of Syria's Chemical Weapons, Unanimously Adopting Resolution 2118 (2013)*. United Nations, 27 September. http://www.un.org/News/Press/docs/2013/sc11135.doc.htm.

United States Congress. 2013. "Authorization for Use of Military Force Resolution Text." *Wall Street Journal*, 3 September. http://blogs.wsj.com/washwire/2013/09/03/full-text-senate-foreign-relations-committee-resolution -on-syria/.

United States Department of State. 1995. *1995-09-04b – State Department Cable, Ambassador Holbrooke to Secretary of State*. Bosnia, Intelligence, and the Clinton Presidency Central Intelligence Agency FOIA Archives. http://www.foia.cia.gov/sites/default/files/1995-09-04B.pdf.

United States Department of State. 2013a. *Statement on Syria – Remarks by John Kerry, Secretary of State, Treaty Room*. Washington, DC, 30 August. http://www.state.gov/secretary/remarks/2013/08/213668.htm.

United States Department of State. 2013b. *Framework for Elimination of Syrian Chemical Weapons*. 14 September. http://www.state.gov/r/pa/prs/ps/2013/09/214247 .htm.

Van Evera, S. 1997. *Guide to Methods for Students of Political Science*. Ithaca: Cornell University Press.

Vasquez, J. 1997. "The Realist Paradigm and Degenerative versus Progressive Research Programs: An Appraisal of Neotraditional Research on Waltz's Balancing Proposition." *American Political Science Review* 91 (4): 899–912.

Volsky, I., J. Legum, and R. Leber. 2013. "Will Congress Support Military Action in Syria?" A ThinkProgress Whip Count [updated]. *Think Progress*, September 9. http://thinkprogress.org/politics/2013/09/02/2561371/congress-support -military-action-syria-thinkprogress-whip-count/.

Von Clausewitz, C. 2008. *On War*. Trans. M. Howard and P. Paret. New York: Oxford University Press.

Waldie, P. 2013. "'We're not talking about war': Kerry Outlines 'unbelievably small' Strike on Syria." *Globe and Mail*, 9 September. http://www .theglobeandmail.com/news/world/were-not-talking-about-war-kerry -outlines-unbelievably-small-strike-on-syria/article14184543/.

Walt, S. 2000. "Two Cheers for Clinton's Foreign Policy." *Foreign Affairs* 79 (2). http://m.foreignaffairs.com/articles/55848/stephen-m-walt/two-cheers -for-clintons-foreign-policy.

Walt, S. 2005. "The Relationship between Theory and Policy in International Relations." *Annual Review of Political Science* 8: 23–48.

Walt, S. 2011a. "Is America Addicted to War? The Top 5 Reasons Why We Keep Getting into Foolish Fights." *Foreign Policy*, 4 April. http://foreignpolicy.com/2011/04/04/is-america-addicted-to-war/.

Walt, S. 2011b. "Whatever Happened to the War in Libya?" *Foreign Policy*, 11 July. http://foreignpolicy.com/2011/07/11/whatever-happened-to-the-war-in-libya/.

Walt, S. 2012a. "Top 10 Lessons of the Iraq War." *Foreign Policy*, 20 March. http://foreignpolicy.com/2012/03/20/top-10-lessons-of-the-iraq-war-2/.

Walt, S. 2012b. "What If Realists Were in Charge of US Foreign Policy?" *Foreign Policy*, 30 April. http://foreignpolicy.com/2012/04/30/what-if-realists-were-in-charge-of-u-s-foreign-policy/.

Walt, S. 2013a. "Top 10 Warning Signs of 'Liberal Imperialism.'" *Foreign Policy*, 20 May. http://foreignpolicy.com/2013/05/20/top-10-warning-signs-of-liberal-imperialism/.

Walt, S. 2013b. "We're Going to War Because We Just Can't Stop Ourselves." *Foreign Policy*, 27 August. http://foreignpolicy.com/2013/08/27/were-going-to-war-because-we-just-cant-stop-ourselves/.

Walt, S. 2013c. "An Open Letter to My Congressman about Syria." *Foreign Policy*, 6 September. http://foreignpolicy.com/2013/09/06/an-open-letter-to-my-congressman-about-syria/.

Walt, S. (@stephenWalt). 2013d. "Latest Hawk variation: Syrian chem use is a moral outrage that demands a very limited response that poses no risk of escalation or quagmire." 6 September, 12:30 p.m. Tweet.

Walter, B.F. 2006. "Building Reputation: Why Governments Fight Some Separatists but Not Others." *American Journal of Political Science* 50 (2): 313–30.

Washington Post staff. 2013. "Full Transcript: Kerry, Hagel and Dempsey Testify at Senate Foreign Relations Committee Hearing on Syria." *Washington Post*, 3 September. www.washingtonpost.com/politics/2013/09/03/35ae1048-14ca-11e3-b182-1b3bb2eb474c_story.html.

Weiner, T. 1996. "Iraq Pulling Out, but Leaving Spies Behind, US Says." *New York Times*, 6 September. ProQuest Historical Newspapers: A1.

Weisiger, A., and K. Yarhi-Milo. 2015. "Revisiting Reputation: How Past Actions Matter in International Politics." *International Organization* 69 (2): 473–95.

Weiss, T.G., and A. Kittikhoun. 2011. "Theory vs. Practice: A Symposium." *International Studies Review* 13 (1): 1–5.

Weller, M. 1999. "The Rambouillet Conference on Kosovo." *International Affairs* 75 (2): 211–51.

Western, J. 2013a. "What's Wrong with Red Lines?" *Duck of Minerva*, 7 May. http://www.whiteoliphaunt.com/duckofminerva/2013/05/whats-wrong -with-red-lines.html.

Western, J. 2013b. "Not All Interventions Are the Same." *Duck of Minerva*, 27 August. http://www.whiteoliphaunt.com/duckofminerva/2013/08/ not-all-interventions-are-the-same.html.

White House. n.d. *Chemical Weapons Attack in Syria: News and Updates.* http:// www.whitehouse.gov/issues/foreign-policy/syria.

White House. 2013a. *Remarks by the President to the White House Press Corps.* Office of the Press Secretary, 20 August. http://www .whitehouse.gov/the-press-office/2012/08/20/remarks-president -white-house-press-corps.

White House. 2013b. *Remarks by the President before Meeting with Members of Congress on the Situation in Syria.* Office of the Press Secretary, 3 September. http://www.whitehouse.gov/the-press-office/2013/09/03/remarks -president-meeting-members-congress-situation-syria.

White House. 2013c. *Remarks by the President in Address to the Nation on Syria.* Office of the Press Secretary, 10 September. http://www.whitehouse.gov/ the-press-office/2013/09/10/remarks-president-address-nation-syria.

White House. 2013d. *Statement by the President on US-Russian Agreement on Framework for Elimination of Syrian Chemical Weapons.* Office of the Press Secretary, 14 September. http://www.whitehouse.gov/the-press -office/2013/09/14/statement-president-us-russian-agreement-framework -elimination-syrian-ch.

Whitney, C.R. 1993. "NATO to Join US in Planning Air Strikes against Serbs' Forces." *New York Times*, 3 August. ProQuest Historical Newspapers: A1.

Whitney, C.R. 1994. "Deadline Set for Gorazde Pullback – Warning Includes Four Other Areas." *New York Times*, 23 April. ProQuest Historical Newspapers: 1.

Whitney, C.R. 1995a. "Diplomatic Moves Pressed by Paris." *New York Times*, 28 May. ProQuest Historical Newspapers: 1.

Whitney, C.R. 1995b. "Allies Extending Shield to Protect All Bosnia Havens." *New York Times*, 2 August. ProQuest Historical Newspapers: A1.

Whitney, C.R. 1996. "From Allies, US Hears Mild Applause or Silence." *New York Times*, 4 September. ProQuest Historical Newspapers: A10.

Whitney, C.R. 1998. "2 NATO Generals to Warn Milosevic of Air Raids." *New York Times*, 24 October. ProQuest Historical Newspapers: A4.

Whitney, C.R. 1999a. "Talks on Kosovo Wind Up as Only the Albanians Sign." *New York Times*, 19 March. ProQuest Historical Newspapers: A9.

Whitney, C.R. 1999b. "UN Council Acts: NATO Troops Now Plan to Begin Moving into Kosovo." *New York Times*, 11 June. ProQuest Historical Newspapers: A1.

Wilner, A. 2015. *Deterring Rational Fanatics*. Philadelphia: University of Pennsylvania Press.

Wirtz, J.J. 2012. *Deterring the Weak: Problems and Prospects*. Proliferation Papers, Institut Français des Relations Internationales. http://ultimaratio-blog.org/wp-content/uploads/pp43wirtz.pdf.

Woods, K., J. Lacey, and W. Murray. 2006. "Saddam's Delusions: The View from the Inside." *Foreign Affairs* 85 (3): 2–26.

Yarhi-Milo, K. 2013. "In the Eye of the Beholder: How Leaders and Intelligence Communities Assess the Intentions of Adversaries." *International Security* 38 (1): 7–51.

Yarhi-Milo, K. 2014. *Knowing the Adversary: Leaders, Intelligence, and Assessment of Intentions in International Relations*. Princeton: Princeton University Press.

Zagare, F.C. 1990. "Rationality and Deterrence." *World Politics* 42 (2): 238–60.

Zagare, F.C. 2004. "Reconciling Rationality with Deterrence: A Re-examination of the Logical Foundations of Deterrence Theory." *Journal of Theoretical Politics* 16 (2): 107–41.

Zagare, F.C., and D.M. Kilgour. 2000. *Perfect Deterrence*. Cambridge Studies in International Relations. Cambridge: Cambridge University Press.

Zakaria, F. 2013. "US Credibility Is Not on the Line in Syria." *Washington Post*, 8 May. https://www.washingtonpost.com/opinions/fareed-zakaria-us-credibility-is-not-on-the-line-in-syria/2013/05/08/0c38db80-b7fa-11e2-b94c-b684dda07add_story.html.

Zakaria, F. 2014. "Enough with the Tough Guy Debate." Global Public Square (blog), *CNN.com*, 7 March. http://globalpublicsquare.blogs.cnn.com/2014/03/07/enough-with-the-tough-guy-debate/.

Index

Afghanistan, 13, 33, 52, 152, 159, 161, 164, 169, 172, 183, 188
Aidid, Mohamed Farrah, 44. *See also* Somalia
air strikes, 52, 102; in Bosnia-Herzegovina, 67, 95, 108–19; in Iraq, 45, 138, 141, 143–7; in Kosovo, 121–5, 127, 129–31, 133–4; in Libya, 52; threat vis-à-vis Iran, 199, 206–7; threat of in Syria, 5–6, 9, 20–2, 26–7, 92, 153, 158–67, 169–71, 175–6, 179, 181–3, 185–90, 191, 193–4, 198–9, 202n19, 204–5, 210, 212–16, 220, 223, 227–9, 259–60
Al-Assad, Bashar, 5–13, 20–8, 46, 84, 87, 100n61, 106–8, 150–80, 182, 185–90, 193–6, 198, 202n19, 205, 210, 213–16, 220–3, 227–9, 242–7, 255, 260
Albania, 120–8, 132, 172
Albright, Madeleine, 95, 116, 122, 125, 127, 134
al-Qaeda, 97n57, 159
Annan, Kofi, 122, 142
asymmetric crises: in Bosnia-Herzegovina, 108–20; in Iraq, 135–48; in Kosovo, 120–35; in

Syria, 5–28, 149–80; between the US and smaller powers, 5, 23, 28–9, 33–4, 49, 70, 76, 83, 99n60, 105, 108, 162–3, 188, 219, 233, 245
audience costs, 32, 38, 166, 171, 181–90, 200, 203, 224, 226, 228–9. *See also* costly signals
authorization for the use of military force (AUMF), 229–30; in Iraq, 33; in Syria, 21, 149n1, 163, 166, 171–2, 181–6, 189, 207, 242

balance: of interests, 16, 19, 42, 44, 48, 78–80, 84–5, 87, 157, 162, 167, 207, 218, 232, 260; of power, 16n36, 19, 33, 42–5, 48, 58, 75, 78–80, 84–5, 87, 157, 162, 167, 194, 207, 218, 232, 251, 256, 260
Berlin crises (1958–61), 34, 41, 43–4. *See also* Press, Daryl
Biddle, Stephen, 18, 55, 159–61, 163, 165, 220–2, 260
bluffing, in international politics, 4, 12, 14, 16, 20–1, 31–2, 43, 46, 49, 57, 78, 85, 91, 98, 102, 114, 128, 151, 158, 163, 170, 186, 194, 196, 200, 212–13, 216–31, 245–6, 254, 260

Bosnia-Herzegovina: Annexation
Crisis (1908–9), 34; war in, 23,
28, 33, 44, 52, 67, 83n28, 95, 105,
108–20, 129, 131, 134–5, 137, 148,
166, 169, 171–2, 188, 215, 253
Boutros-Ghali, Boutros, 111
Bush, George H.W., 136–8, 144, 146, 247
Bush, George W., 62, 186, 189, 238,
248, 250, 253
Butler, Richard, 143. *See also* United
Nations Special Commission
on Iraq

Canada, 103
casualty aversion, 33, 45, 68, 88n38,
95–7, 131–3, 146–7, 169, 172, 179,
208, 221, 226
chemical weapons: chlorine, 23,
24n59, 26n67, 153–4; norms against,
21, 161, 171, 175, 185, 195, 203, 208,
233, 241–4, 246–7, 255; in Syria,
4–14, 16n36, 21–6, 28, 46, 53, 61, 84,
87, 98, 101, 106n1, 149–61, 163–5,
167–77, 179, 182–3, 185, 187, 190,
192–6, 198–9, 201–2, 205, 208,
213–14, 220–4, 226–8, 242–4, 247,
254, 262
Chemical Weapons Convention
(CWC), 22–4, 153, 242–4, 247
China, 61, 93, 132, 141, 144, 178, 192,
196, 236, 257
chlorine gas. *See* chemical weapons
Clinton, Bill, 95, 109n11, 111, 121n49,
123, 125, 127, 130, 134, 139–41,
144–5, 247–9, 253
coercive diplomacy, 3–6, 8, 14n29,
16, 21–4, 27–9, 31–3, 36–7, 46, 49,
60–1, 67, 69, 71n1, 72–82, 85, 87, 93,
95, 98, 103–6, 108–10, 112, 117–19,
128–9, 131–3, 145, 147, 149, 152–3,

155–6, 158, 160, 168, 170, 172,
174–5, 180, 192, 199–202, 212, 215,
220–1, 226, 228–9, 232, 239–42, 244,
246–7, 249, 252, 254–5, 259–60
coercive threats. *See* coercive diplomacy
Cold War, 16, 34, 106, 168, 180, 251;
post–, 5, 34, 236, 253, 255, 257
compellence. *See* coercive diplomacy;
deterrence
confirmation bias, 28–9, 69, 97n56,
217, 231–50, 253–64
Congress, US, 5, 7, 9, 21–2, 26–7, 33, 53–4,
97n57, 149n1, 156, 159, 161, 166–7,
171–2, 174, 181–90, 195, 198, 205, 214,
220, 229–31, 233, 239, 242, 260
congressional authorization.
See Congress
costly signals, 73, 74n8, 80, 82, 109,
113, 166–7, 171, 178, 228, 255.
See also audience costs
counter-coercion, 75, 96, 100, 132–3, 179
credibility: calculating, 13, 17, 20,
29, 41, 48, 53, 58, 60, 72, 82–4, 89,
91n45, 93, 103, 106, 113, 134, 148,
161, 166, 179, 186, 189, 191, 197–8,
208–9, 223, 225, 258; complex,
28, 33, 48, 100n61, 195–6, 202–10,
218, 223; paradox, 28n68, 175–7,
189, 210–11, 215; spiral, 163–5.
See also rational deterrence theory;
reputation; resolve
Cuban Missile Crisis (CMC), 34, 41,
43–4, 179
Current Calculus (CC) theory, 41–2,
44, 53, 65, 83–4, 157, 260. *See also*
P-M-H; Press, Daryl

Dempsey, Martin, 189
deterrence, 4, 11, 16–17, 24, 26, 29,
31–3, 35–6, 40, 42, 44–5, 48–9, 56–8,

61, 66–9, 72–4, 76–82, 88n38, 90–2,
95, 97, 99–101, 104–5, 107, 112, 162,
168–71, 175–6, 187–8, 192, 195,
197–8, 204, 213, 216, 219, 224, 226,
233, 241, 246, 258, 262; vis-à-vis
Iran, 6, 161, 195, 203–4; vis-à-vis
Iraq, 135, 138–41, 145, 147; on the
longitudinal nature of, 66–7, 73,
107, 118, 168, 214; vis-à-vis North
Korea, 6, 195; vis-à-vis Serbia,
108–9, 111, 114–15, 117–19, 128,
134–5, 249; vis-à-vis the Soviet
Union, 39–40; vis-à-vis Syria, 6–7,
10–11, 13, 14n29, 17, 20, 22–4, 26,
98, 149–52, 156, 163–4, 167, 169–70,
173, 176, 178, 181–3, 187, 193–4,
199, 202–3, 213–14, 220, 222, 224,
228, 229n17, 243, 245, 254; Syria
vis-à-vis Israel, 24, 155, 160, 213,
223. See also coercive diplomacy;
rational deterrence theory
domestic politics: and casualty
aversion 96, 97n57; of great
powers, 75; Serbian, 131, 133;
shocks, 65; Syrian, 160; US, 33,
58, 93, 97n57, 110, 158, 160–1, 166,
169, 179, 181–90, 198, 200, 203–4,
214, 224, 227, 230, 236–7, 248, 250,
253. See also casualty aversion;
Congress

enduring rivalries, 57–8, 66, 76, 97,
135, 147. See also protracted crisis
escalation, 21, 37, 57, 67, 108, 118, 149,
163–7, 169–71, 175, 178, 187, 189,
205, 207, 213–14, 216, 220–1, 224,
228. See also mission creep

falsifiability, 44, 84, 88n38
Fearon, James, 74n8, 78–82, 166, 177–8

Federal Republic of Yugoslavia
(FRY), 120–33
France, 109, 113, 115, 120, 126,
137–8, 141

Gaddafi, Moammar, 61, 164, 166, 250.
See also Libya
Gates, Robert, 25
Ghouta, chemical attacks, 3–6, 26,
84, 149–51, 156–7, 161, 166, 168,
170, 172, 174, 185, 193, 221, 223–4,
229n17. See also chemical weapons
Goražde, 111–14
grand strategy, US, 254–5, 258, 261
Guantanamo Bay, 224, 250

Hagel, Chuck, 7, 26n66, 151, 171,
191, 193
Haiti, 54, 131
Holbrooke, Richard, 115–16, 122–4,
127, 130–1
honesty, 57, 59, 216n6. See also
bluffing; credibility; reputation
Hopf, Ted, 4, 15–16, 28, 30, 32, 34–6,
38–41, 53, 69, 180, 218–19, 260–2.
See also P-M-H
House Committee on Homeland
Security, 18, 55, 159–60, 163,
220, 260
Human Intelligence (HUMINT), 240
Hussein, Saddam, 32–3, 45, 52, 61–2,
68, 83n28, 88n38, 93–4, 96, 102,
130–1, 137, 139–40, 143–7, 151, 166,
176, 179, 208, 216, 240. See also Iraq

incomplete information, 52, 60, 85,
148. See also uncertainty
intelligence reform, post-Iraq, 237–40
International Atomic Energy Agency
(IAEA), 142–3

international norms, 21, 152, 171, 175,
182, 203, 208, 227, 241–4, 253
international relations theory,
28–9, 44n32, 50, 59, 65, 68, 234–5,
236n7, 237–8, 247, 250, 253–4,
262–3; constructivist, 68; liberal
internationalist, 236, 249, 253;
realist, 68, 183, 236–7, 247, 249–50,
253–4. *See also* rational deterrence
theory; theory-policy gap
International Studies Association
(ISA), 236
Iran, 6–11, 17, 28n68, 94, 103, 151–2,
155–6, 161, 168, 191–211, 218–19,
232, 255
Iraq: 1991 (Gulf) war, 52, 91, 135–6;
2003 war, 13, 17n36, 45, 52, 62, 91,
93, 135, 144–6, 152, 159, 161, 163–4,
169, 172–4, 176, 183, 188–9, 195,
208–9, 215, 238–40, 242, 248, 253–4;
coercive diplomacy vis-à-vis, 23,
28, 33, 45, 52, 61–2, 67, 105, 129,
131, 133, 135–48, 169, 180, 188, 215,
236, 240, 253. *See also* Hussein,
Saddam
ISIS, 184
Israel, 6–7, 23–4, 66–7, 154–6, 160, 168,
174, 192, 199–201, 203, 206–7, 213,
236, 238, 254

Joint Comprehensive Plan of Action
(JCPOA) 205, 211. *See also* Iran
Jordan, 7, 156, 168, 171, 203

Kerry, John, 8, 20, 22, 26, 154, 167,
171–6, 193, 198
Kim Jung-il, 62
Kim Jung-un, 196, 202
Kosovo, 22–3, 28, 32–3, 52, 61, 83n28,
88n38, 91, 95, 105, 120–35; Kosovo

Liberation Army (UCK), 124–7
Kurds, 136, 140, 151
Kuwait 45, 138–41, 146. *See also* Iraq:
1991 (Gulf) war

Libya, 33, 52, 54, 163–4, 169, 172, 188,
215–16, 236, 248–50

Markale massacre, 110, 115–16, 166
Mercer, Jonathan, 4, 15–16, 18, 21, 28,
30, 32–6, 38, 40, 46–51, 53, 57–8,
64–6, 69, 76, 78, 89, 91, 98, 100, 157,
180, 191, 193, 198, 200–1, 218–19,
221–3, 259, 261–3; on Syria, 244–6.
See also P-M-H
Middle East, 16, 39, 159, 178, 199, 201,
204, 206, 213, 215, 248
Milošević, Slobodan, 44, 52, 61, 68,
83n28, 95–6, 102, 115–16, 120–35,
166, 176, 179, 249. *See also* Federal
Republic of Yugoslavia (FRY); Serbia
mission creep, 21, 87, 161, 163–5, 181,
187, 220
MIT school, of US foreign policy,
255–64
Mladić, Ratko, 109, 111, 114–20. *See also*
Bosnia-Herzegovina

National Science Foundation
(NSF), 233
NATO, 12, 22, 52, 61, 67, 95, 171–2, 176,
249, 253; in Bosnia-Herzegovina
108–20, 166; in Kosovo, 120–35
Netanyahu, Benjamin, 154, 207
no-fly-zone (NFZ): in Bosnia-
Herzegovina, 110; in Iraq, 136–9,
141; in Libya, 164; as part of a
strategic sequence, 169
North Atlantic Council (NAC),
123

North Korea, 6–8, 62, 103, 151, 168, 191–211, 218

Obama, Barack, 4–6, 9–10, 12–15, 17, 20–8, 30, 46, 49, 53–4, 57, 67–8, 92, 98, 106–8, 149–58, 161–3, 166–75, 177, 179, 181, 183–7, 190–1, 193–4, 197–201, 204–5, 210, 212–16, 218, 220–1, 223, 226–30, 242–3, 245–6, 248–50, 254, 263; on US foreign policy, 251–3

Obama administration. *See* Obama, Barack

Operation Deliberate Force (ODF), 115–17, 169. *See also* Bosnia-Herzegovina

Operation Desert Fox (ODF), 32, 45, 52, 94–5, 129–31, 144–5, 169, 253. *See also* Iraq: coercive diplomacy vis-à-vis

Operation Horseshoe, 52, 132

Operation Iraqi Freedom. *See* Iraq: 2003 war

Organisation for the Prevention of Chemical Weapons (OPCW), 24, 154n11

Organization for Security and Cooperation in Europe (OSCE), 123

Panetta, Leon, 25

Past Actions (PA) theory, 35, 37n18, 41–3, 53, 75, 77, 88, 90. *See also* P-M-H; Press, Daryl

perceptions, 15n33, 37n18, 38–9, 42n28, 43, 45, 52, 68, 73, 81–5, 86n35, 91, 93–6, 98–100, 102–3, 105, 107, 115, 117, 129, 131–2, 134–5, 146–8, 151, 157, 160, 162, 168, 179–80, 187, 196–7, 201–2, 204–5, 209–10, 219–20, 232, 236n8, 240,

246; misperceptions, 15n33, 66, 72, 82, 93–5, 99, 102–3, 107, 145–7, 219, 220n11, 236n8, 240, 246

P-M-H: consensus, 4–5, 16n36, 17–20, 23, 30–4, 36, 38, 45, 48, 50, 52–6, 59, 61, 63, 66, 68–72, 75–7, 79–80, 82, 89, 92, 95–6, 101, 104–8, 113, 118, 120, 134, 148, 150, 157–68, 179, 191, 193, 197, 202, 205–8, 212, 216–22, 224, 226, 233, 240, 245–6, 248, 255, 261–3. *See also* Hopf, Ted; Mercer, Jonathan; Press, Daryl

Posen, Barry, 254–7, 261–2. *See also* MIT school

premature closure of inquiry, 30–2, 45, 50–4, 219, 233, 238

Press, Daryl, 4, 15–16, 18–19, 21–2, 28, 30, 32–6, 38–47, 50–1, 53, 55, 57, 59, 64–6, 69, 75–8, 82–4, 87–91, 98, 100n61, 157, 168n40, 179, 191–3, 196, 198, 200–1, 217–19, 221, 225, 241, 256–63. *See also* P-M-H

Price, Richard, 241–4, 246

probing, 67, 73–4, 80–2, 86, 93, 97, 148, 168, 197, 223, 226; in Bosnia-Herzegovina, 108–13, 166; in Iraq, 137, 140; in Syria, 12, 24n59, 149, 161, 167, 170–2, 202n19, 205, 223–4, 246

protracted crisis, 24n59, 44, 57–8, 73–4, 76, 82, 97, 104–8, 112, 168–75, 219, 232, 245

psychological theory, 16n34, 48, 68, 100. *See also* Mercer, Jonathan

public opinion: vis-à-vis casualties, 176, 179, 184; vis-à-vis response to Syrian CW crisis, 13, 68, 97n57, 149, 152, 159, 161, 166, 169, 172, 184, 188, 201, 242. *See also* casualty aversion

Putin, Vladimir, 13, 22–3, 27, 92, 108,
150, 156, 160, 162–3, 166–7, 171,
176–9, 185–90, 198, 200, 202n19,
213–16, 220, 228, 245–6, 255
Pyongyang. *See* North Korea

Rambouillet conference, 126–9, 133–5
rational deterrence theory (RDT),
5, 28–32, 35, 38–40, 48, 53, 67–8,
71–108, 112–13, 118, 120, 135,
147, 150, 152, 156–7, 167, 170, 178,
181–90, 213–14, 232, 241, 245–6, 258;
criticisms of, 35, 40, 53, 75, 79–82,
96, 104, 157–62, 245, 258; necessity
and sufficiency, 76–9; prerequisites
of, 67, 72–82, 95, 97n56, 99, 103–4,
108n5, 110, 112, 114, 117–19, 135,
149, 156–7, 173, 197–8, 202n19, 215.
See also deterrence; reputation
red lines: in coercive diplomacy,
200–1, 204, 207, 212, 218, 221–2,
260; in Syria, 4–6, 10–13, 15, 19–21,
25–7, 46, 49, 53, 57, 67–8, 84, 101,
107, 149–52, 154, 156, 158, 161–2,
166, 168–71, 173–5, 177, 187, 192–3,
195–6, 201, 204, 214–15, 217–18,
220–2, 224, 226, 247–8, 254, 260
reputation: in the eye of the beholder,
15, 28, 72, 91, 99–104, 178–9,
185–90, 196, 201, 202n19, 207, 209,
219, 255; general, 58, 68, 72, 74, 76,
96–9, 104–17, 129, 131–4, 145–6,
148, 150, 157, 169–70, 178, 218–19,
246; and imperfect information,
82–8; and miscalculations, 93–6;
specific, 58, 67–8, 72, 74, 76, 96–9,
104–17, 113, 119, 129, 133–4, 146–8,
150, 157, 169–70, 178, 219, 246,
258; transferability, 3, 13–15,
17n36, 18n39, 20, 28–9, 36, 58–9,

61–4, 66, 69, 72, 85, 88–93, 98–104,
151–2, 179, 188, 191–212, 216–19,
222–3, 232, 234, 241, 245; of the
US, 6–7, 10–14, 15n33, 17–18, 20,
23, 27, 32–4, 37, 45, 48–9, 52, 54,
56–7, 61–2, 66, 68–9, 71–2, 76, 85,
89–148, 150–2, 157–8, 160, 162–9,
176, 178–80, 187–9, 191–3, 196, 198,
200–1, 202n19, 208–11, 217–26,
228–9, 232–3, 241, 245–6, 248–9,
255, 258–9. *See also* credibility;
resolve
resolve, 3–5, 8, 10, 13, 14–16, 18–21,
23, 28, 32–5, 38–9, 41, 45, 47–53,
57, 61–4, 67, 71–81, 83, 85–6, 89–90,
91n45, 92–7, 99–104, 108–14, 116–19,
121, 124, 133, 135, 138–40, 145–7,
149, 151, 157, 161, 163, 166–72,
175, 178, 182, 185, 187, 190–1, 197,
199–201, 203–5, 207, 210, 214,
216n6, 217, 219, 223, 226, 232–3,
245–6, 259, 262; of Barack Obama,
200, 214; of Bashar al-Assad, 160; as
a component of rational deterrence
theory, 72–81, 85, 91n45, 93, 95, 97,
100–1, 104, 118–19, 135, 149n1, 157,
190, 197, 201, 204, 245; protecting,
4, 8, 10, 13, 14, 18–19, 21, 33, 35, 38,
63, 67, 74, 85, 95, 97, 101, 103, 108,
110–13, 116, 118–19, 139, 163, 166,
171, 182, 185, 223, 259, 262; of the
Soviet Union, 41; of the US, 5, 8,
10, 13, 14–16, 19–21, 23, 28, 32–4,
38–9, 45, 49, 52, 61–2, 67, 71, 75, 83,
86, 88n38, 89–92, 94, 96–7, 101–2,
108–14, 116–19, 121, 124, 133, 135,
138–40, 145–7, 149, 151, 161, 163,
166–72, 175, 178, 182, 185, 187, 190–1,
197, 199, 201, 203–5, 207, 210,
214, 223, 226, 232–3, 245–6, 259,

262. *See also* credibility; rational deterrence theory; reputation
Responsibility to Protect, 203, 243–4. *See also* international norms
Russia, 247, 257; vis-à-vis Bosnia-Herzegovina, 112–13, 117; vis-à-vis Iraq, 137, 140–2, 144; vis-à-vis Kosovo, 120–2, 124, 131–3; vis-à-vis Syria, 5, 22, 27, 61, 153, 155–7, 166–7, 176–7, 178, 187, 193–4, 198, 202, 209, 213, 215, 227, 242, 244; vis-à-vis Ukraine, 18n39

sanctions: against the Federal Republic of Yugoslavia (FRY), 120; against Iran, 210; against Iraq, 139, 142; against Syria, 213, 244; threat of, 62, 65, 252
Sarajevo, 108–10, 112–17, 166. *See also* Bosnia-Herzegovina
Saudi Arabia, 25, 140, 171
Schelling, Thomas, 35–6, 40, 44, 71n1, 103, 164n28, 176, 198, 262
Serbia, 67, 109, 108–25, 127–8, 253
social science research, 11, 14n30, 69; evidentiary requirements, 38, 46, 49, 77, 260, 263; funding, 233; and policy, 233–5, 258
Somalia, 44, 54, 61, 88n38, 131, 137, 252
Soviet Union: American assessments of, 34, 41, 43–4, 102–3, 179; assessments of US credibility, 16, 34, 38–40
Srebrenica, massacre, 114, 171
Supreme Allied Commander Europe (SACEUR), 122–5
Syria: chemical weapons (CW) crisis, 3–31, 33–4, 38, 45–6, 49–50, 52–3, 55–8, 61, 66–9, 84, 87, 91–3,

97–8, 100–8, 148, 232–5, 240–50, 252, 254–5, 259–63; alternative explanations of, 212–31; vis-à-vis American domestic politics, 181–90; deterrence failure and success in, 149–80; relevance to other international relationships, 191–211

Tehran. *See* Iran
theory-policy gap, 29, 32, 50, 69, 231–64
tipping point: in Bosnia-Herzegovina, 110, 113, 166; vis-à-vis Iran, 205; in Syria, 149, 161, 167–75, 216, 224

Ukraine, 14, 17n36, 18n39, 30, 69, 92, 200, 209, 251
uncertainty, in international relations, 52–3, 65, 85, 97, 104, 241. *See also* incomplete information
United Arab Emirates (UAE), 140, 171
United Kingdom (UK), 32–4, 43, 52, 93, 109, 115, 120–1, 130, 137–8, 141–5, 159, 239, 242
United Nations: in Bosnia-Herzegovina, 108–18, 120, 166; Chapter VII, 172; disarmament resolution in Syria (UNSCR 2118), 5, 22, 24, 149, 153–5, 176, 187, 203, 228, 242; inspectors, 22, 130, 143–4, 216, 239 (*see also* United Nations Special Commission on Iraq); in Iraq, 136–44; in Kosovo, 120, 122, 131; multilateralism, 204, 242–4, 246, 250, 253; Rapid Reaction Force, 115–17; Security Council, 54, 97n57, 122–3, 138, 141, 145, 159, 172, 178, 204, 211, 213, 242–4; UNSCR 668 (on Iraq), 136–7; UNSCR 949 (on Iraq), 140;

UNSCR 1154 (on Iraq), 142; UNSCR
1199 (on Kosovo), 121; UNSCR
1205 (on Iraq), 143; UNSCR 1441
(on Iraq), 33, 94, 144–5
United Nations Monitoring,
Verification and Inspection
Commission (UNMOVIC), 144
United Nations Special Commission
on Iraq (UNSCOM), 141–4

Vietnam, 16, 38–40, 45, 53, 61, 88n38,
131, 146, 262

Walt, Stephen, 15, 18, 21, 69, 157–8,
191, 236–7, 246–50, 253–5, 260, 263
Warren, Elizabeth, 233
weapons of mass destruction
(WMD), 7–8, 11, 23–4, 28, 33, 84,
90, 93, 130, 144, 153–4, 156–7, 167,
181, 188, 196, 205, 208, 213, 222,
233, 238–40, 246, 248, 260. *See also*
chemical weapons

Zakaria, Fareed, 18–19, 21, 54, 69, 92,
157, 191, 195, 260, 263